HOW TO DRAW MANGA:
Macromedia Flash Techniques, Illustrating Bishoujo Characters
Edited by Aki Ito

This book was first designed and published in 2003 by Graphic-sha Publishing Co., Ltd.
This English edition was published in 2004 by Graphic-sha Publishing Co., Ltd.
1-14-17 Kudan-kita, Chiyoda-ku, Tokyo 102-0073 Japan

Artwork: Nobayashi, Sanbaisoku, Yusa Mimori,
Teru, Gaten Boya
Cover Drawing: Nobayashi
Original Desing & Layout: Toyonori Motoyoshi
English Title Logo Design: Hideyuki Amemura
English Edition Layout: Yuuki Saito (Pallet)
English Translation Management: Língua fránca, Inc. (an3y-skmt@asahi-net.or.jp)
Japanese Edition Editor: Masahiko Satake (Graphic-sha Publishing Co., Ltd.)
Foreign Language Edition Creative Director: Kumiko Sakamoto (Graphic-sha Publishing Co., Ltd.)

First printing: February 2004

ISBN: 4-7661-1408-6
UPC: 8-24869-00039
Printed and bound in China by Everbest Printing Co., Ltd.

HOW TO DRAW MANGA

Macromedia FLASH Techniques

Illustrating Bishoujo Characters

Aki Ito

CONTENTS

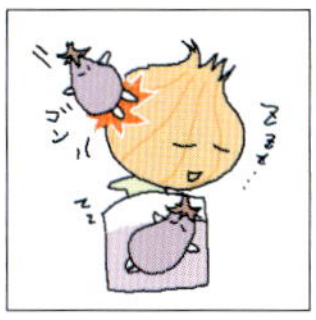

Teru

Essentials

Starting with moving from the rough sketch to the line drawing, techniques on creating and using gradations are discussed. More advanced three-color gradations are also covered to broaden the reader's range of technical Flash possibilities.

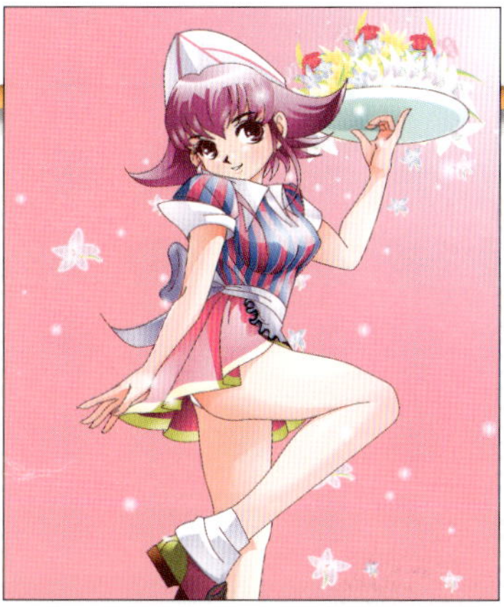

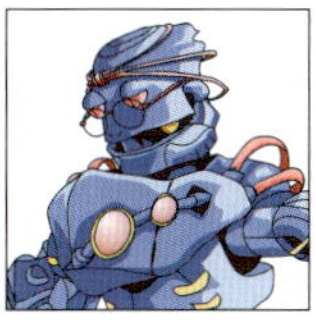

Gaten Boya

Essentials

Discussion includes methods on starting Flash projects from the eyes as well as an introduction on Grouping and on using the Toolbar more efficiently. Further, the illustrator's secrets on creating a unique pen-and-ink style are revealed.

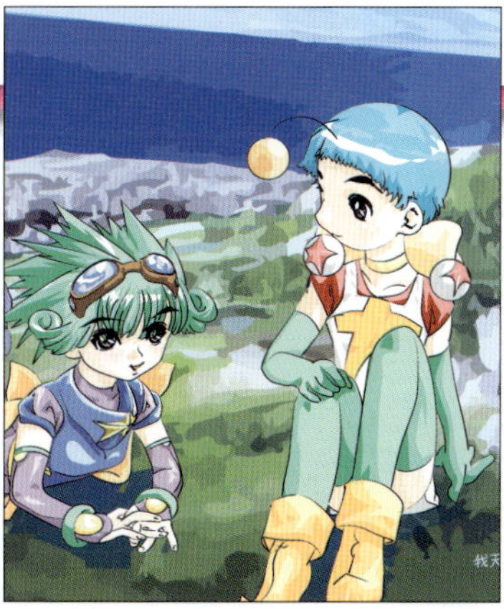

Supplement
How to Make Your Characters Cuter

Ten Asazuma

Essentials

The fundamentals of drawing cute girls, sketching, the peculiarities of Bishoujo graphics, and some thoughts on coloring

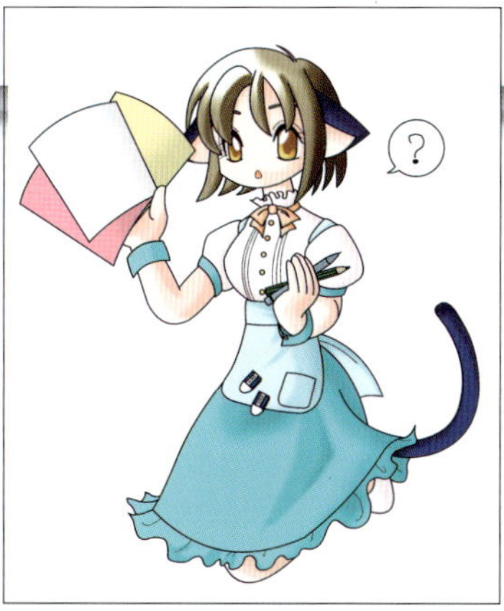

Flash Rocks!

Images you create using Flash are drawn and rendered using vectors. Instead of retaining data for each and every pixel, Flash remembers things like the size and length of a given image--more on this later. Even though Flash is a vector-based drawing tool, you can draw pictures with it just as with any other painting software, so even a beginner can quickly begin drawing. First, let's take a look at three points you should keep in mind for drawing cute girls.

Point 1 You Can Tweak Your Lines after You've Drawn Them

In Flash, lines appear exactly as you trace them using your mouse or tablet. From the moment you begin, you'll be able to draw lines more or less exactly as you like. Even if you don't draw them well, you'll be able to alter them a bit at a time with just a click and drag of the mouse. Your drawings aren't carved in stone; you can make a rough sketch and then go back later to remove the lines you don't need. Then, you can take your time and adjust what's left until you're happy with the results.

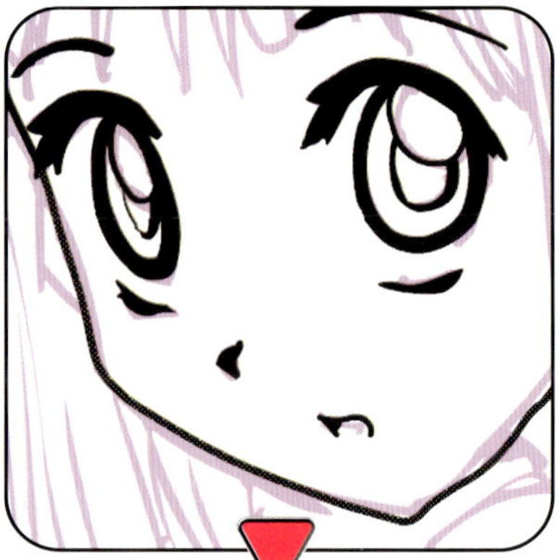

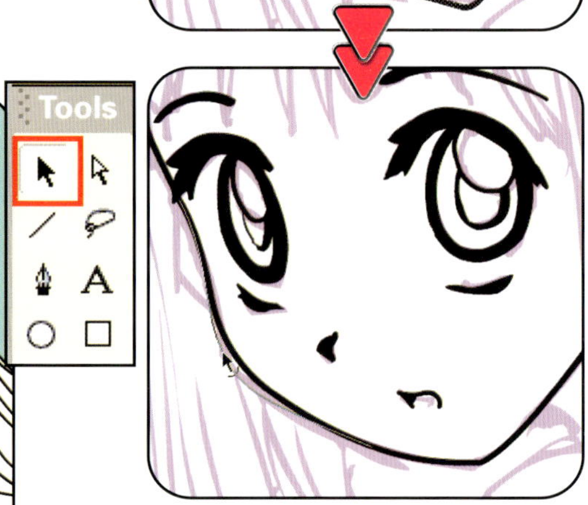

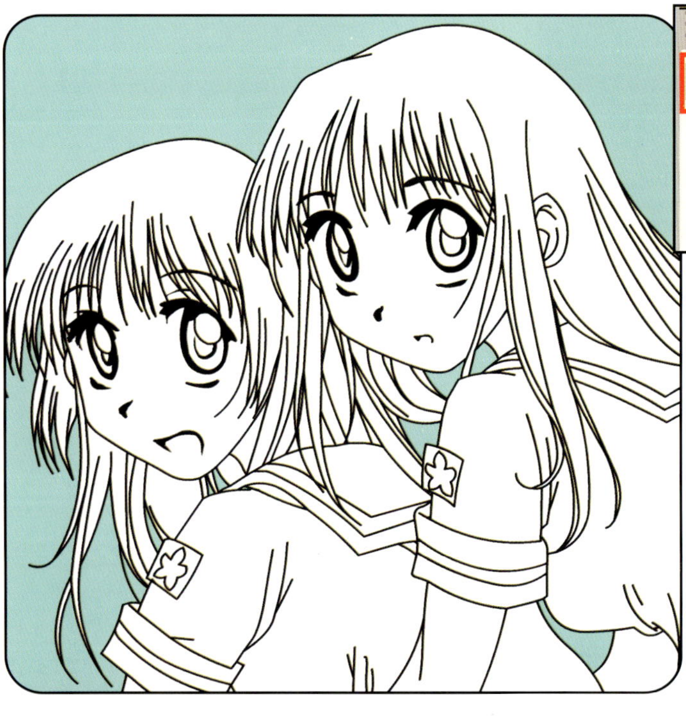

You can use the Arrow Tool to band, lengthen, or otherwise adjust the lines you draw in Flash to your hearts content. You can even use the Smooth modifier to automatically smoothen a jagged line.

Point 2 Use Gradational Fills to Get a Finish Just Like Painting Software

People tend to think you can only paint solid colors in Flash, but by using gradational fills you can create drawings with just as much depth as any other painting tool.

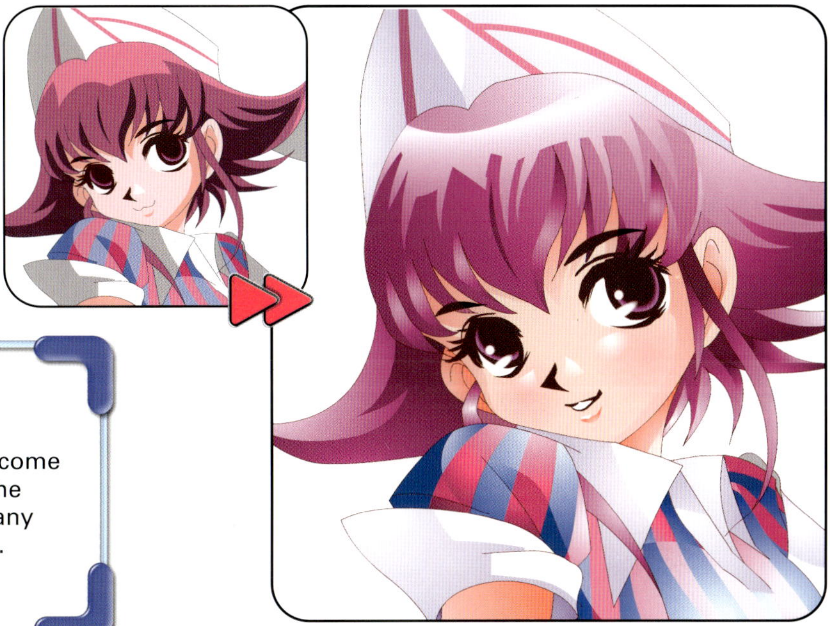

Once you've applied to gradational fills, you can come back later and fine-tune the angle, position, or make any number of other changes.

Point 3 Infinitesimal Size, Infinite Scalability

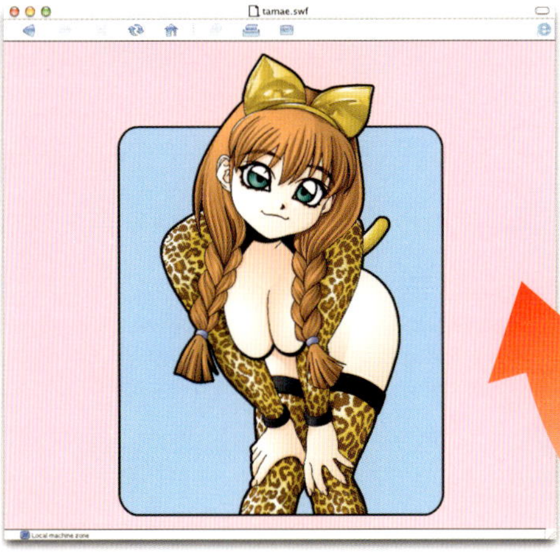

In Photoshop and other painting tools, when you zoom in on an image the quality goes down proportionately. However, since Flash's vector drawings store their information as a pattern, they are drawn and redrawn according to whatever size they are displayed at. As a result, even when you zoom in on them they stay smooth.

Because vector based graphics have a very small file size, they are perfect for publishing on the Internet.

This only takes up 64 KB!

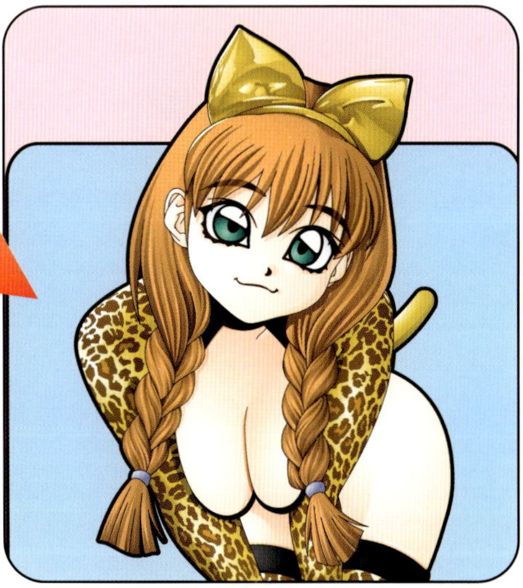

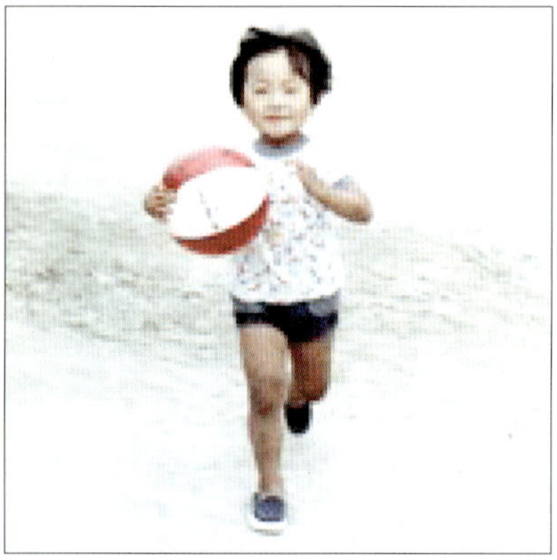

Tamotsu Nobayashi

Birth year
1968

Residence
Osaka

Tools
I use a slotloading iMac and nothing else. I've kept it just as I bought it, although I've thought about upgrading the memory from 64M from time to time. I use no extra peripherals whatsoever!

Software
Flash 4, Photoshop 3.0

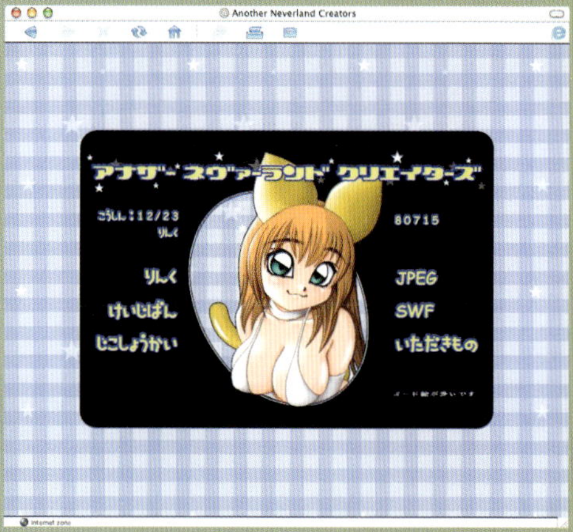

Another Neverland Creators
http://www.uri.sakura.ne.jp/~anc/

People Who Have Given Form to My Sense of Taste and Imagination (titles omitted)

David Bowie
King Crimson
Brian Eno
The Cure
Bauhaus
Kobo Abe
Takeshi Yoro
William S. Burroughs
Albert Camus
Kurt Vonnegut
Osamu Tezuka
Hideo Azuma
Dick Bruna
Trevor Brown
H.R. Giger

Favorite Movies/Anime

Anything by Terry Gilliam
Anything by George Roy Hill
"Hellraiser" directed by Clive Barker
"Videodrome" directed by David Cronenberg
"Bladerunner" directed by Ridley Scott
"Nosferatu" directed by Werner Herzog
"Deer Hunter" directed by Michael Cimino
"Possession" directed by Andrzej Zulawski
"Lupin the Third" by TMS Entertainment, Ltd.
"Dokonjo Gaeru" by TMS Entertainment, Ltd.
"Marco" by Nippon Animation
"ESPer Mami" by SHIN-EI Animation Co.,Ltd.
"Ribbon no Kishi" by Osamu Tezuka
"Fushigi na Merumo" by Osamu Tezuka
"Katri, Girl of the Meadows" by Nippon Animation
"Anne of Green Gables" by Nippon Animation
"Fun Family Moomin" by Telescreen
"Ideon" by Sunrise, Inc.
"Armored Trooper VOTOMS UDO" by Sunrise, Inc.
"Urusei Yatsura Movie 2: Beautiful Dreamer" directed by Mamoru Oshii
"Tenshi no Tamago" directed by Mamoru Oshii
"Lupin the Third: Castle of Cogliostro" directed by Hayao Miyazaki
"Laputa: Castle in the Sky" directed by Hayao Miyazaki
"Hi no Tori: Houou Hen" directed by Rintaro
"Yuniko" by Toshio Hirata

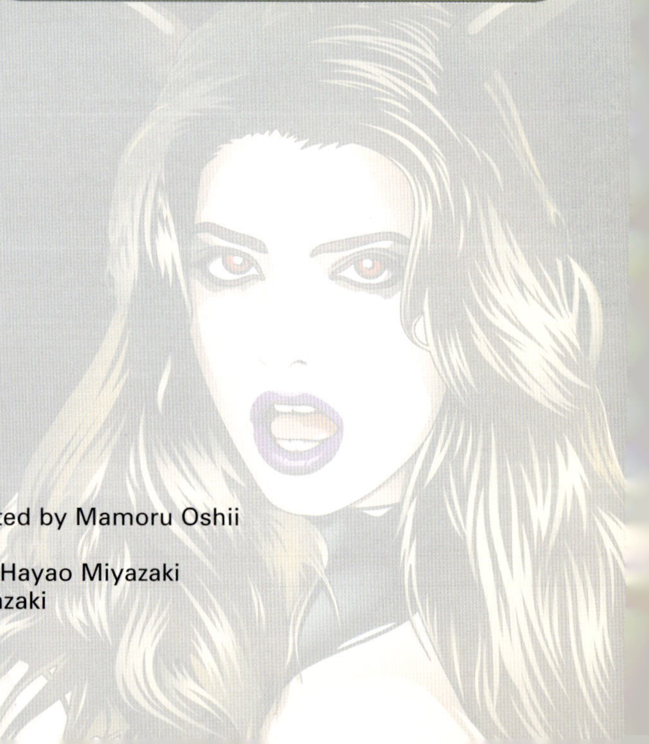

Making a Rough Sketch

Graying out your lines in advance for easier tracing later is key.

For me, the rough sketch stage is for getting my drawings' pose and composition exactly how I want it to make tracing it easier. We will get to drawing fine details like costume patterns in Flash soon, but not just yet. Flash handles graphic data by drawing your illustration from a set of instructions, so I arbitrarily set my vertical size according to my monitor: about 700 pixels. The horizontal size of my rough draft can vary according to the situation, but this time I've set it to 500 pixels. Once I complete my rough sketch I will gray it out and save it as a PICT file.

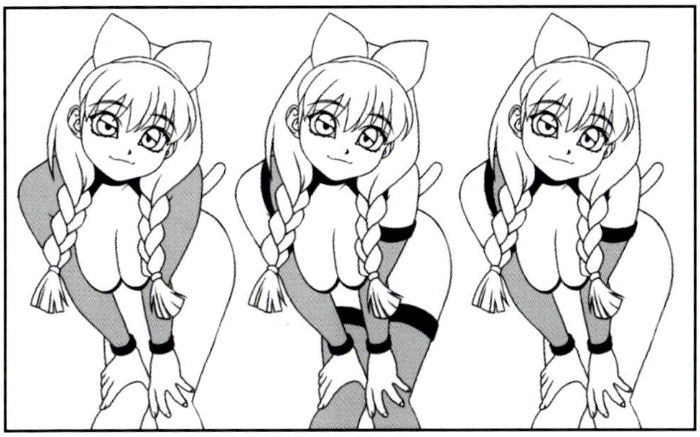

▲ The character on the left has a basic costume on, but I've tried drawing a couple different versions. I've decided on the basic costume top and on the lower body of the middle one.

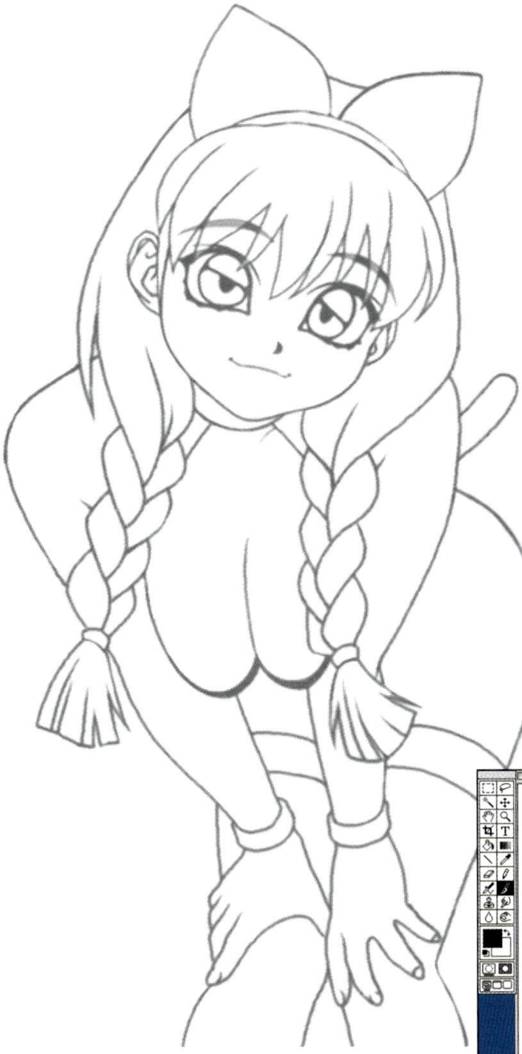

◀ This is the grayed out rough sketch after saving it to disk. This image is just for tracing, so saving it at a low resolution is fine.

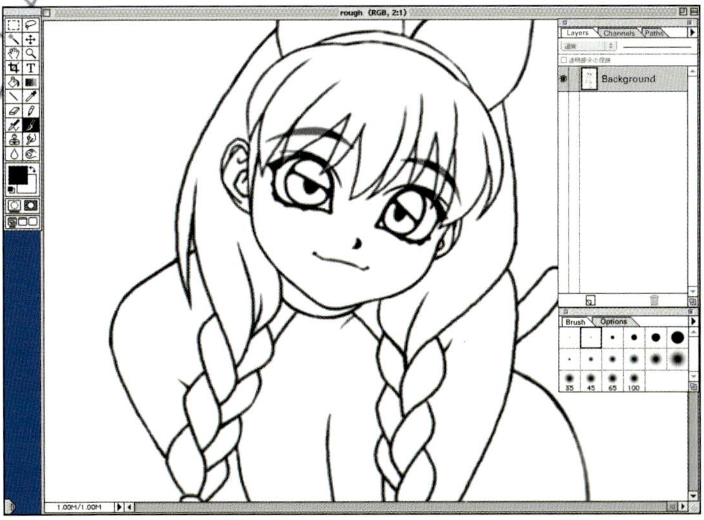

▲ I'm making my rough sketch in Photoshop. When I'm done, I'll gray it out and save it as a PICT file or some other Flash-friendly format.

Point

Other than PICT files, Flash can read BMP, TIFF, PNG, and JPEG file formats. So long as Flash can read your rough sketch file, it doesn't matter what file format you use.

Loading Your Rough Sketch into Flash

Adjust the work area to fit your rough sketch, and set up your tracing.

Choose Import under the File menu (File → Import) to load your rough sketch into Layer 1 on the Timeline.

Use the Movie Properties window to adjust the size of the work area to your sketch. You're ready to start your trace.

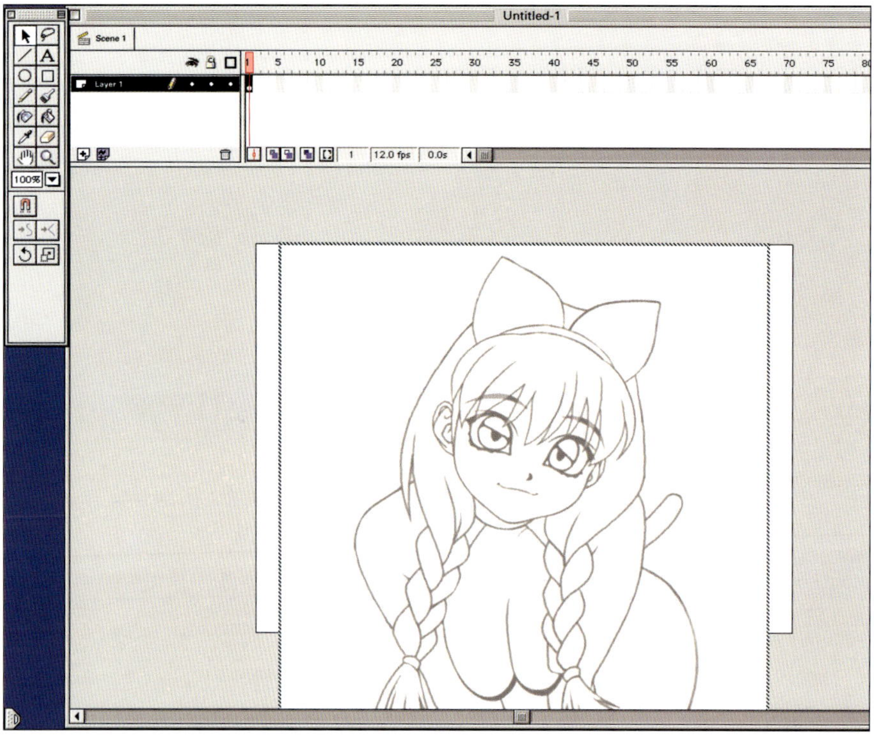

This is what your sketch should look like after you load it up. Notice how it juts out over the edge of the Stage, Flash's white work area.

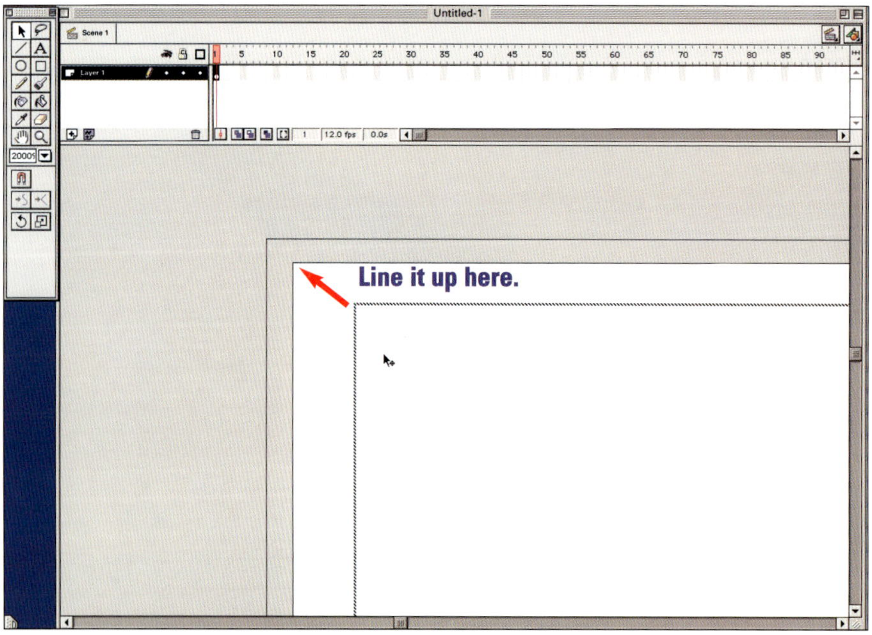

Drag the upper left corner of your sketch to the upper left corner of the Stage (the white work area) until they are perfectly aligned. Make sure your sketch doesn't stick out here.

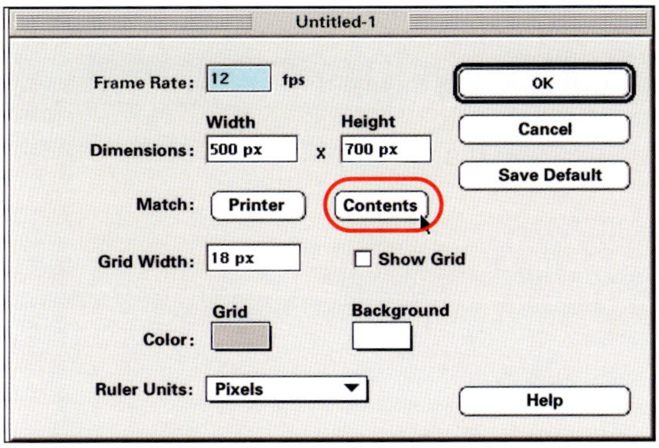

▲ Choose Modify → Movie and the Movie Properties window will pop up. Click on the Contents button in the Match field to match the Stage to your sketch. Be careful here. If your sketch is sticking out over the top edge of the Stage, then it won't resize properly.

Point

In Flash MX, choose Modify → Document and click the Contents button in the Document Properties window. Also note that you can select your background color in this window, which will come in handy if this program is in your toolbox.

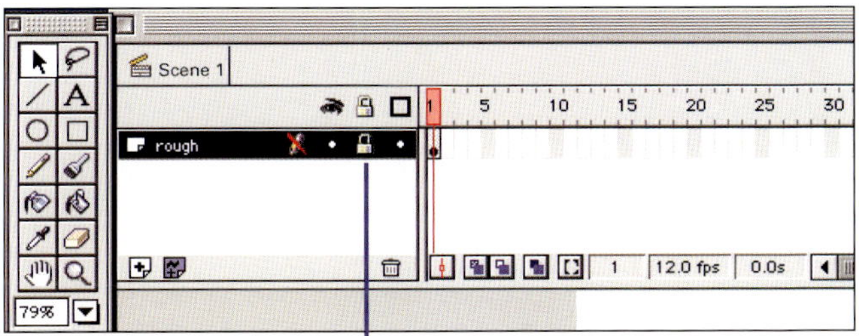

Lock it by clicking here.

◀ You should get into the habit of locking layers you won't be altering. This way you can avoid mistakes like coloring the wrong layer, working in one layer but thinking it's actually another, etc.

Click on the black dot under the lock symbol, and it will turn into a lock icon, letting you know that layer is locked down. Click on the lock icon to unlock the layer.

▼ You are now ready to start tracing.

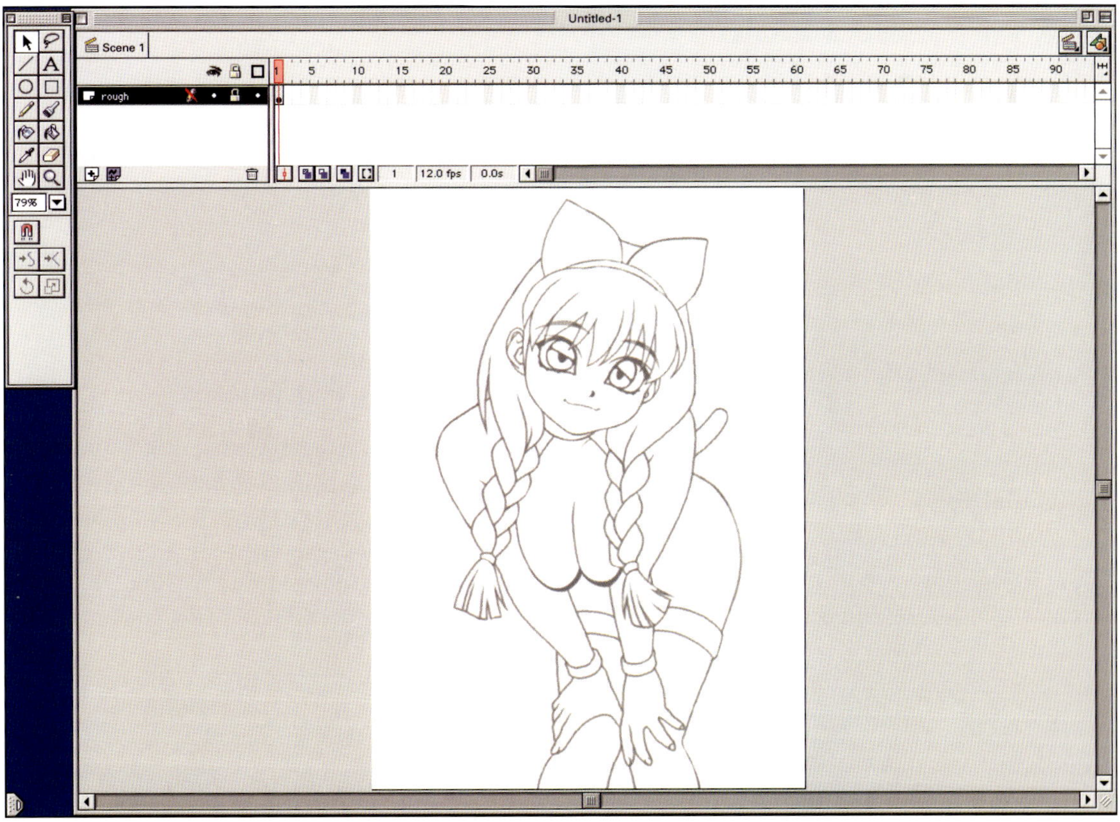

Flash Techniques for Fading Out Your Rough Sketch

As we explained earlier, preparing your rough sketch in grayed out lighter colors in advance makes it easier to trace later on, but even if you've drawn yours in stark black you can fade it out using the following technique. You can also use this technique when tracing photographs.

Step 1

Click on your sketch; choose Insert → Convert to Symbol, and a Symbol Properties window will pop up. Check the Graphic button and click "OK."

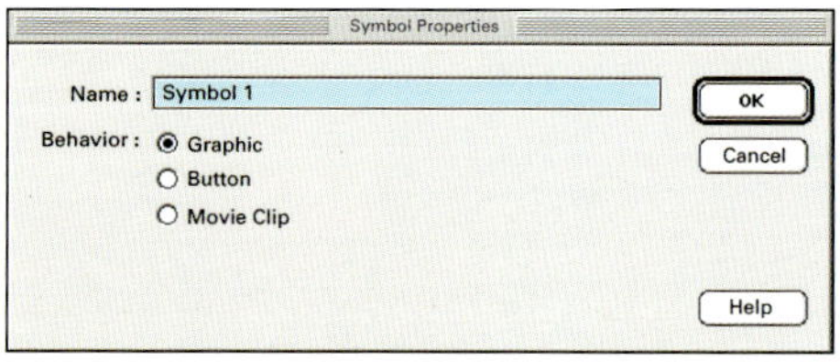

Double click on your sketch and an Instance Properties window will appear. Click the Color Effect tab and choose Alpha in the Color Effect pull-down menu. By lowering the alpha value you can increase the image transparency as much as you like. Increasing the Brightness value will achieve the same effect. When you're done making changes click "OK."

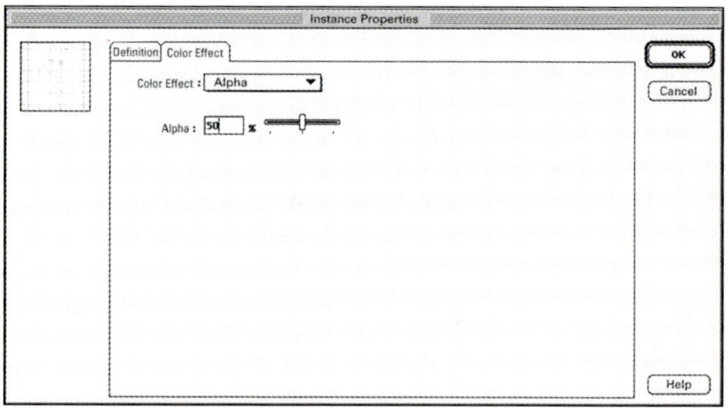

In Flash MX, you change the Alpha value by choosing Alpha in the Color pull-down menu of the Property Inspector. ▶

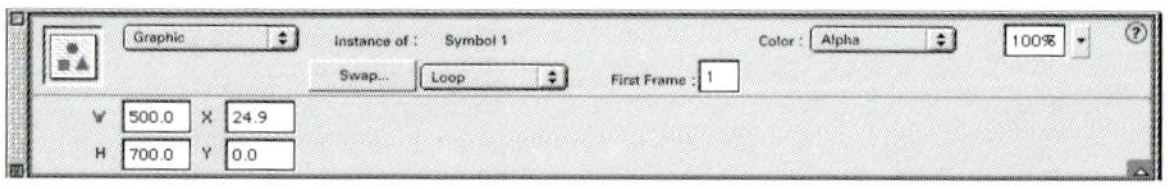

Point

Symbols are objects that share the same properties and can be used as many times as you like within a given project. Graphics, buttons, and movie clips are the three kinds of symbols, and each symbol you place onto the Stage is called an Instance of that symbol. You can greatly reduce both production time and file size when making animations by turning your graphics into symbols. However, this feature won't come up much in books like this one that don't deal with animation.

Step 2

Choose Window → Colors, choose white on the palette in the Solid tab, and click New. Lower the alpha value as you like and click the Change button. Somewhere around 50% is best.

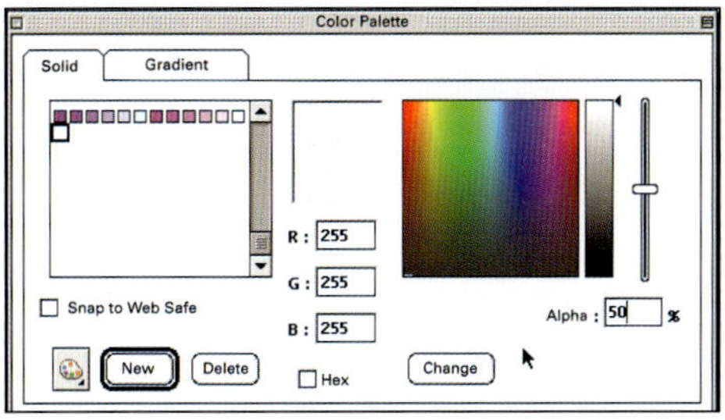

In this next phase, we'll make your black lines appear gray by creating a new, semi-transparent layer on top of your sketch.

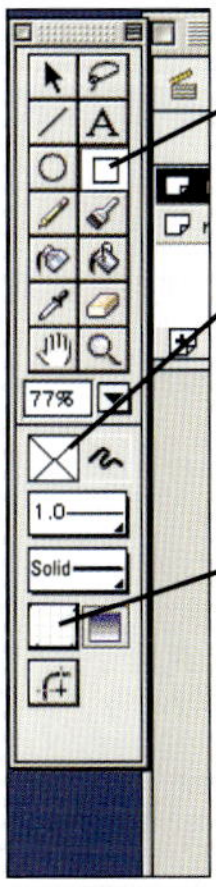

First, choose the Rectangle Tool in your Toolbox.

Then, click on the Line Color button, and choose the empty color swatch from your palette so you don't leave any lines.

Next, click on the Paint Color button and select the alpha-lowered white color you created earlier.

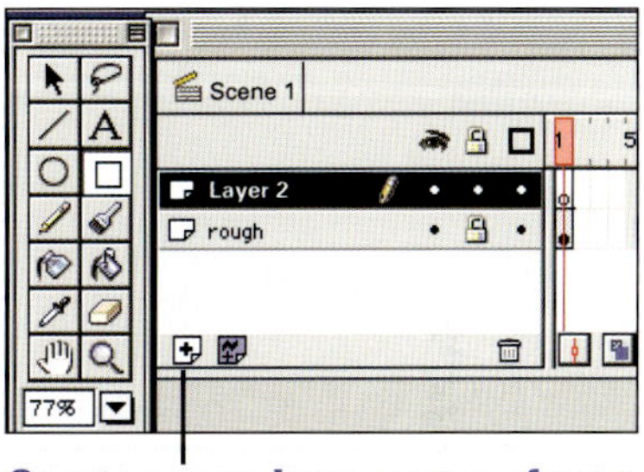

Create a new layer on top of your rough sketch.

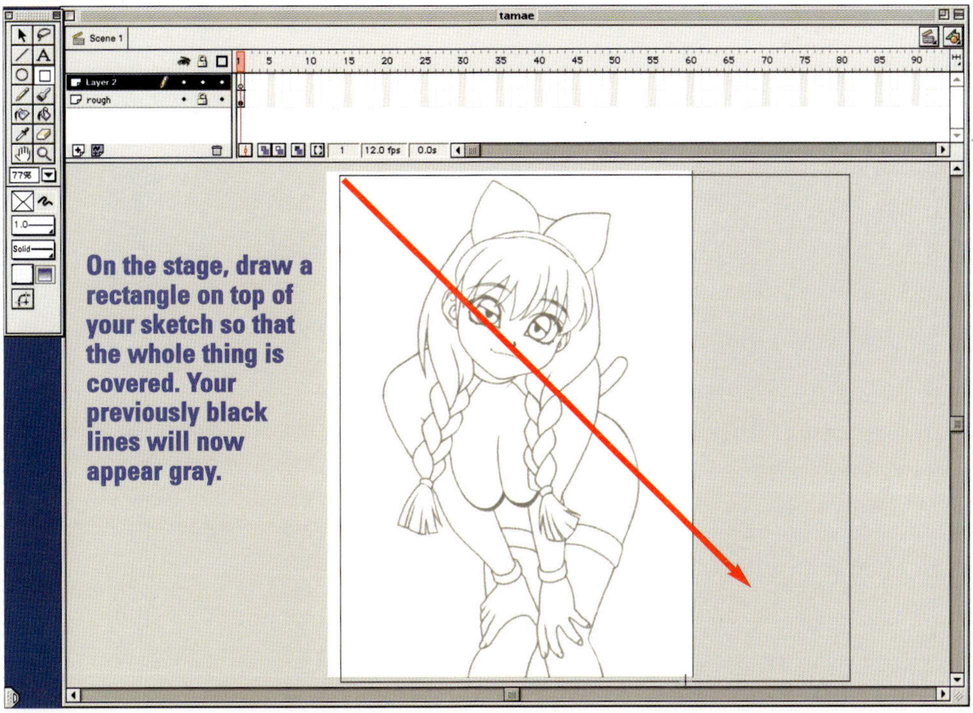

On the stage, draw a rectangle on top of your sketch so that the whole thing is covered. Your previously black lines will now appear gray.

Tracing the Rough Sketch

Use bold strokes: you can go back later and make as many changes as you see fit. The Smooth function is a good example. Its ability to soften bumpy lines will make it your new best friend.

Trace your sketch in the new layer you've just created. Even if you don't trace it perfectly, you can come back later and edit it. Don't worry too much about trying to get it perfect. You can get rid of any lines you don't need by clicking on them and hitting the Delete key, or you can select several lines at once by holding down the Shift key while you click on them and hit the Delete key to wipe them out in one swipe. Finally, if you use the Smooth function, you can clean up your trace a bit.

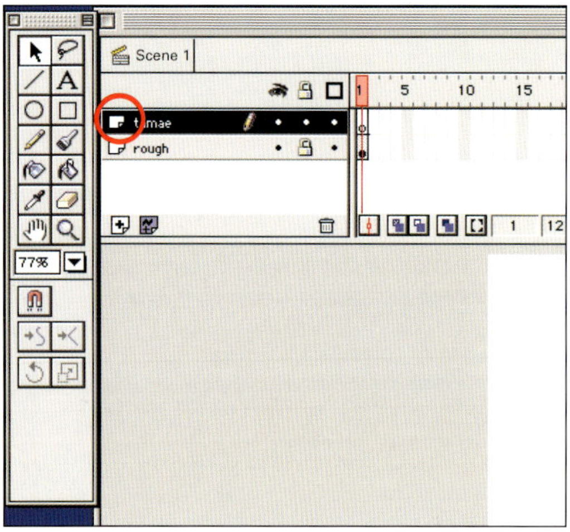

▲ Trace your sketch in the new layer you've just created. Double click on the layer name to assign it a new name.

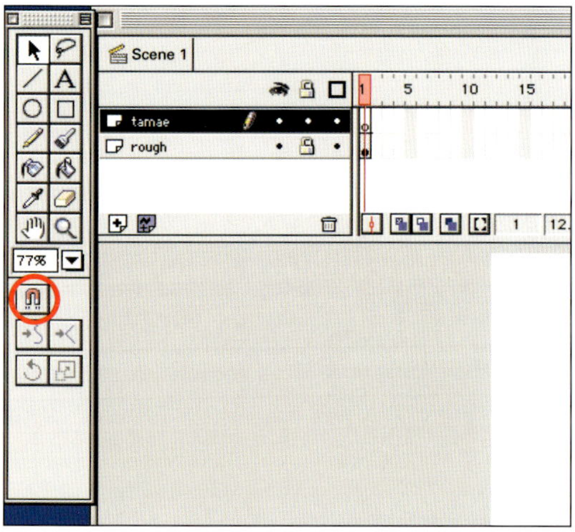

▲ If the Snap to Objects button is in the on position, lines will stick together automatically if they are sufficiently close to each other. When you're drawing a picture, this function can cause problems, so you should turn it off.

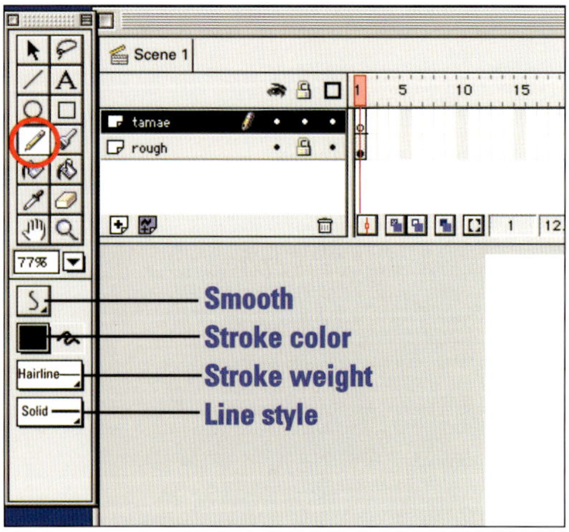

▲ Select the Pencil Tool in the toolbar, select the Smooth option, and set your line thickness to hairline. Make your line black, and set the type to Solid. In Flash MX, choose the line thickness and type in the Property Inspector.

Point

The Pencil Tool has the following three options:

Straighten
Changes what you draw to a straight line, a gentle curve, or a simple geometric shape.

Smooth
Makes a bumpy or jagged line smoother.

Ink
What you draw is pretty much what you get. The further down you go on this list, the larger your file will become every time you save it. Altering lines you draw in Ink mode can be very tedious, so Smooth should be just right.

How to Remove Unwanted Lines

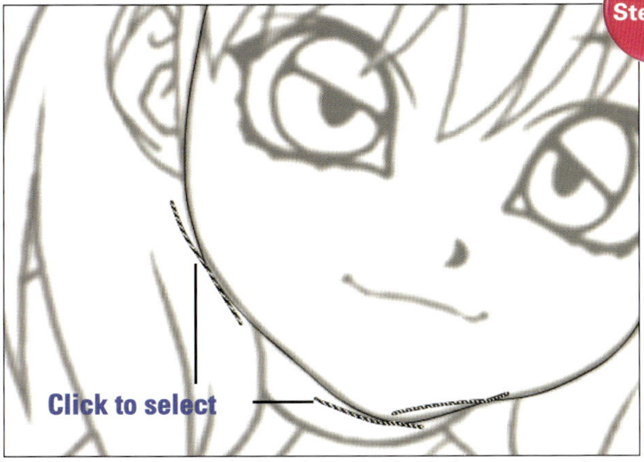

▲ You can go back and edit it later easily, so draw your tracing in bold strokes. Erase unwanted lines by clicking on them and hitting the Delete key.

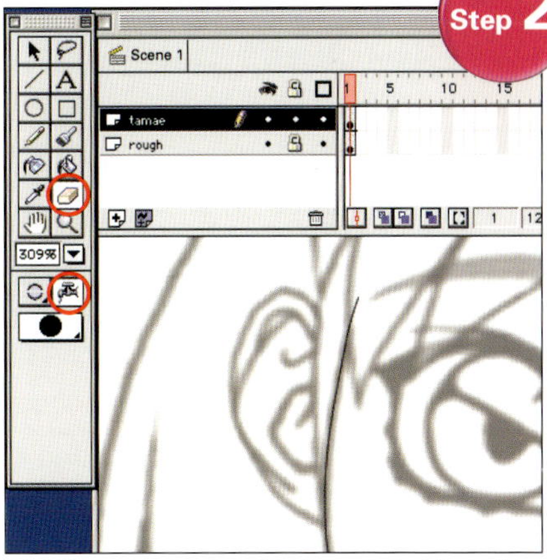

▲ You can also get rid of unwanted lines by clicking on them with the Faucet modifier in the Eraser toolbar.

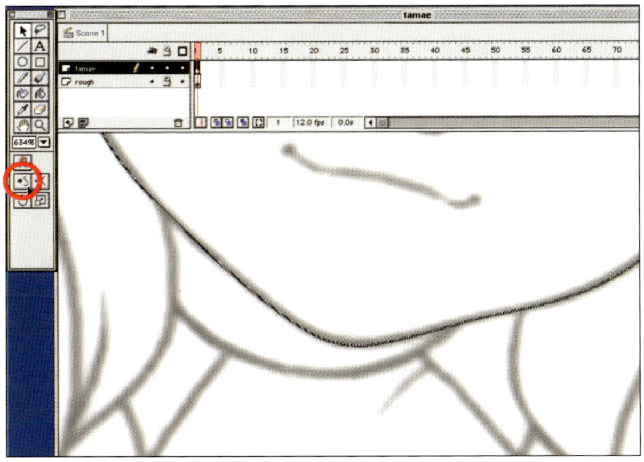

▲ Use the Smooth modifier under the Arrow Tool. Every time you click this button, it changes the selected bumpy line into a smoother one, but use caution. If you overdo it, you'll warp the line beyond recognition.

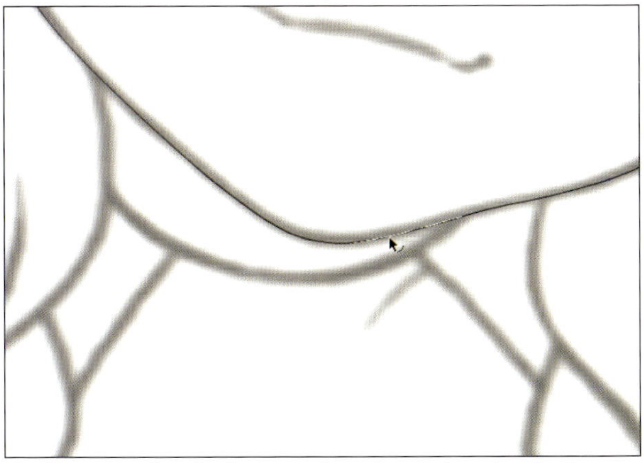

▲ You can pull and adjust your lines directly by using the Arrow Tool. When you're done, you can use the Smooth modifier again as needed.

Smoothing

Point
In Flash, when you cross two lines, each line cuts the other off at the point of intersection. This makes it easier delete the unneeded portions and draw a single smooth line without necessarily doing it in one stroke.

Pull and Adjust Your Lines

Point
Draw, Remove, Pull and Adjust, and Smoothing are all the techniques you need to complete the trace of your rough sketch.

Tracing the Rough Sketch, Continued

With the trace partially finished, it's a good idea to save those lines that need no further adjustments as a group.

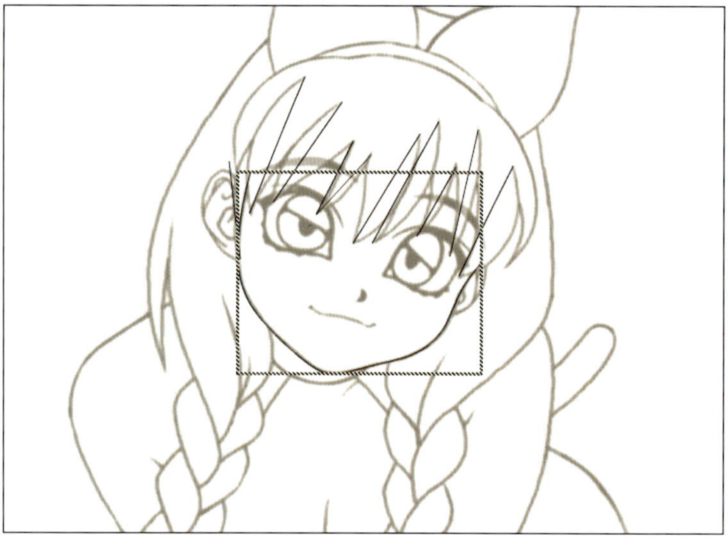

▲ You can select all the completed lines in your trace and protect them by choosing Modify → Group. Here, I'm grouping the outline of the face. To ungroup something, select the things you've grouped together and choose Modify → Ungroup. Now you're free to adjust the previously grouped items.

Point

You'll use the Group and Ungroup functions quite a bit, so it would be a good idea to remember the following keyboard shortcuts:

Group
Command + G (Mac)
Ctrl + G (Windows)

Ungroup
Command + Shift + G
Ctrl + Shift + G (Windows)

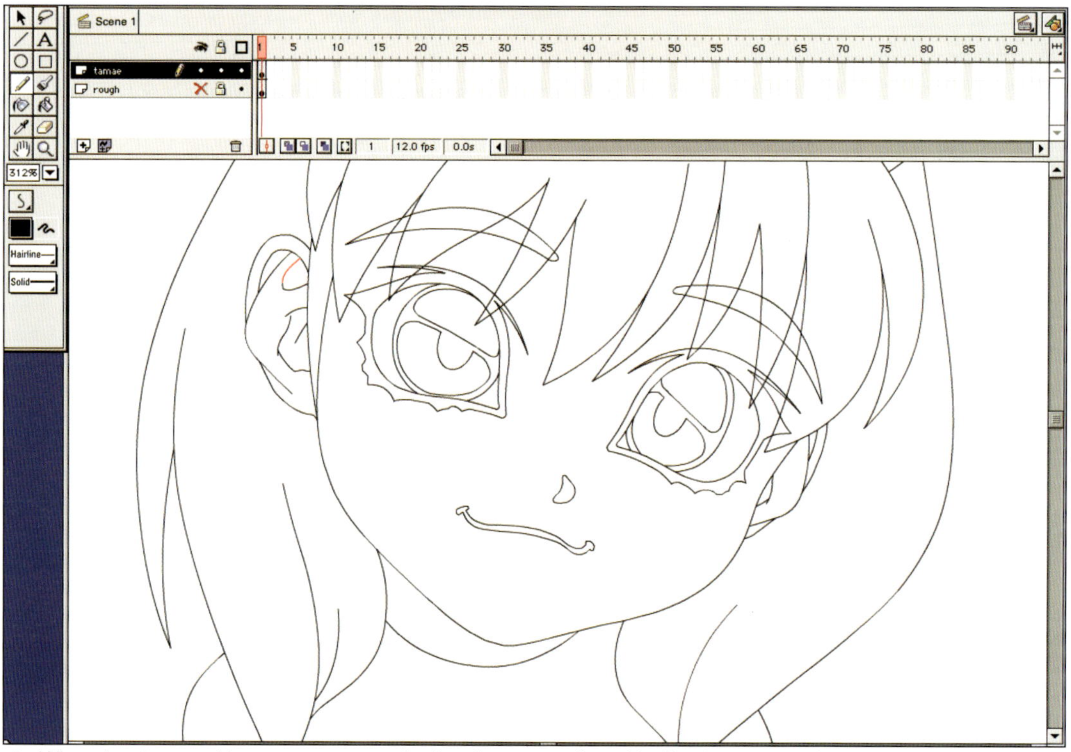

▲ When there's something you want to emphasize, draw an outline of it, like the corners of the mouth pictured here. Now fill it in over the original, staying within your outline. When you're done, go back and erase the outline, and voila! You can also use the Brush Tool for emphasis when you draw a figure, and then adjust it using the Arrow Tool. Of course, if you're using a tablet then none of this is necessary.

I'm drawing the leopard print with the Pencil Tool in Ink mode, and I won't be Smoothing it this time. By doing this I'm increasing my file size, but it's important to do all this by hand and not use any kind of pattern. Mission Rough Sketch: Complete.

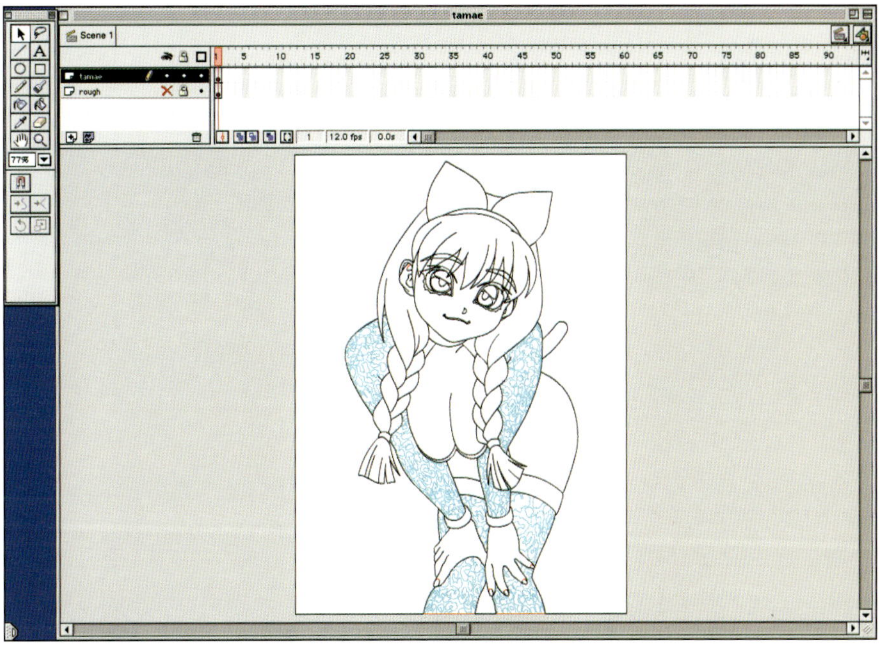

Point

Using the Pencil Tool in Ink mode reproduces on-screen what you draw precisely as you draw it, so it's perfect for small, detailed areas. It also requires a large amount of data storage, so when you save your image your file size will be that much bigger. If you Smooth what you draw you can decrease the amount of data, but doing so will subdue your work and sacrifice its subtle nuance.

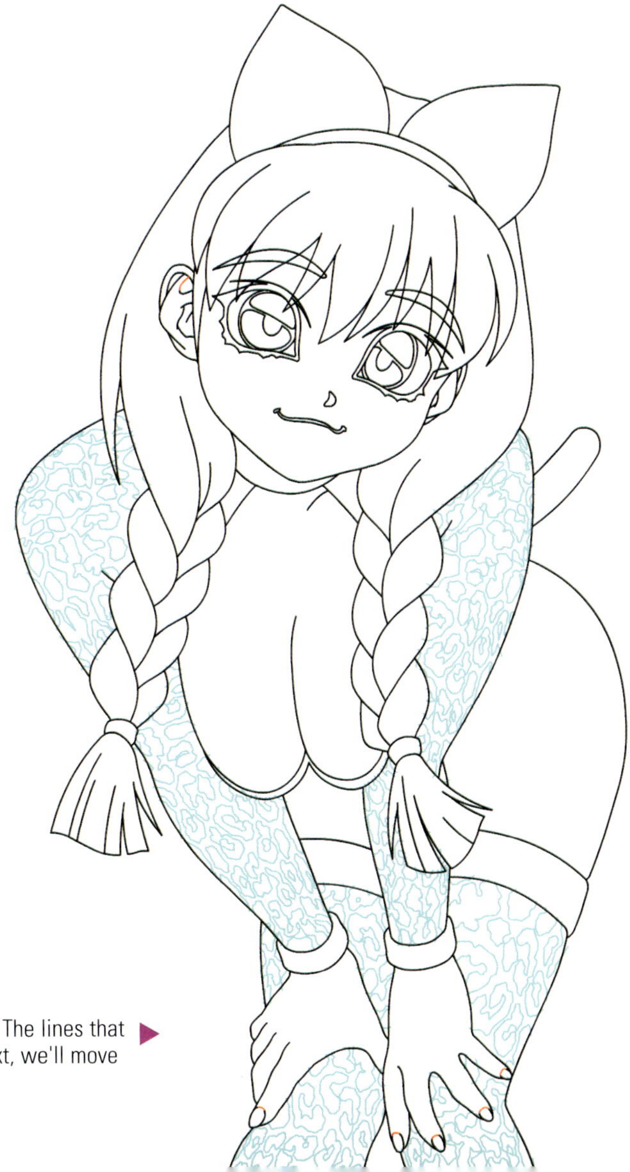

The trace of your sketch is now complete. The lines that remain will become your "main lines." Next, we'll move onto coloring.

Coloring

Drawing fill lines and coloring with gradations are all the basics you need.

Once your main lines are complete you could just start coloring right away, but instead let's mark off some areas and fill them and with the Paint Bucket Tool as we go. It's easiest if you draw your fill lines in a different color than your main lines so you can see them more clearly. Later, it'll be easier to erase them as well. We'll be making use of gradations and color palettes at this stage. In Flash, even after you're done coloring you can change the shape, orientation, and other characteristics of gradational fills. Adjust the fill as you go until you're happy with it, and when you're done get rid of the fill lines.

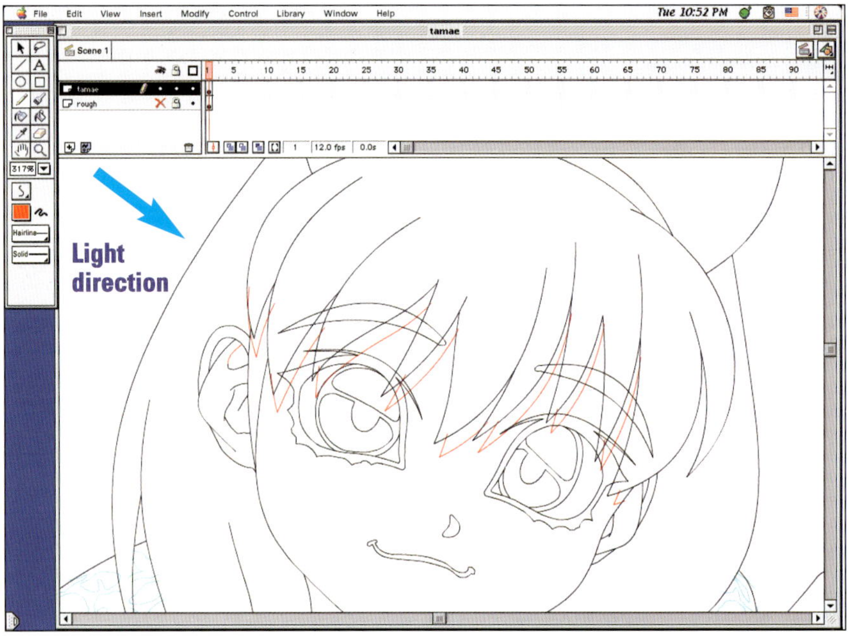

◀ Make your fill lines a different color than your main lines. By double clicking on them, you can select an entire group of same-colored lines. Try drawing the fill lines as you group main lines. Here, the light source is in the upper left and in front of the character, so I'm drawing the shadows from her bangs like so.

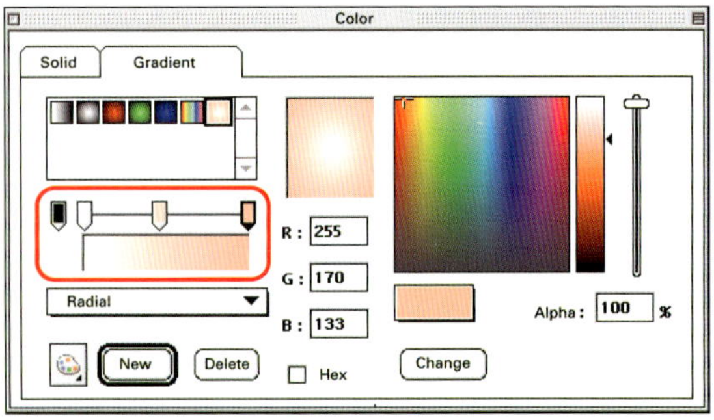

▲ We're making a gradation to color the areas we've marked off with our fill lines. You can still create effects like cell animation without using gradations, however.

Point

In FLASH MX, create gradations by using the Color Mixer. A gradation basically functions as a smooth transformation between two colors, but you can also make more complex gradations by dragging additional color markers in between the first two. Pictured here are the results of adding a third marker to a gradation between white and flesh tones. Sliding the marker along the gradation adjusts the tone.

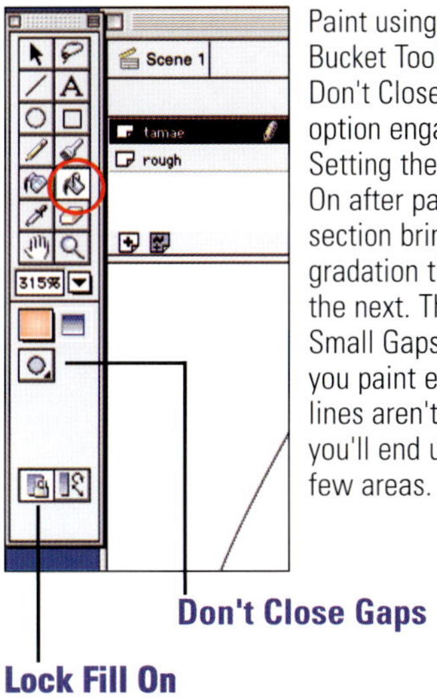

Paint using the Paint Bucket Tool, with the Don't Close Gaps option engaged. Setting the Lock Fill to On after painting one section brings the gradation through to the next. The Close Small Gaps option lets you paint even if your lines aren't closed, but you'll end up missing a few areas.

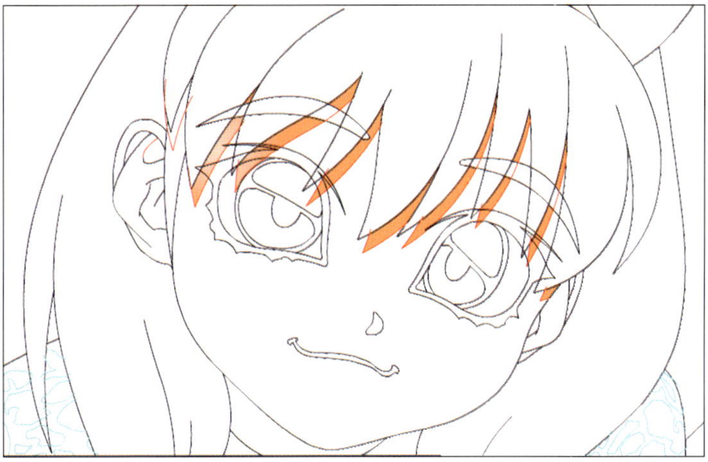

Point

In Flash, you can use the Close Gaps button to paint over areas marked off by lines even if there are gaps in those lines. The settings range from Close Small Gaps to Close Large Gaps. However, you can end up missing a lot of areas, so here we've set it to Don't Close Gaps, and we start painting only when we're sure all our lines are closed. The "Lock Fill On" function connects the same gradation to areas that are separated from each other, producing a scaled effect. If you paint with it off, each area will end up with its own gradation.

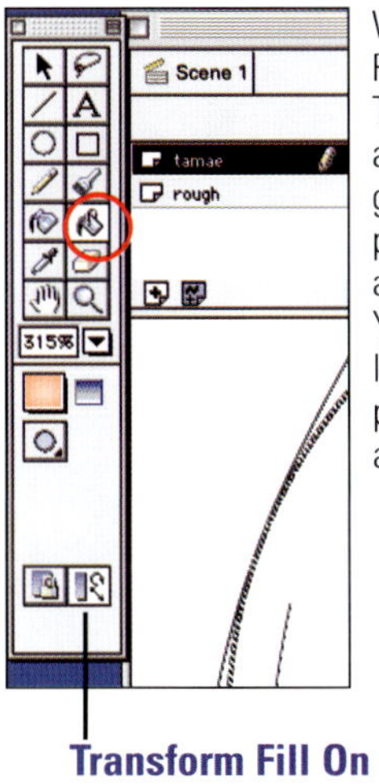

When you turn on the Paint Bucket's Transform Fill option and alter your gradation, a center point and a handle will appear.
You can change the location of the center point or move a handle as you wish.

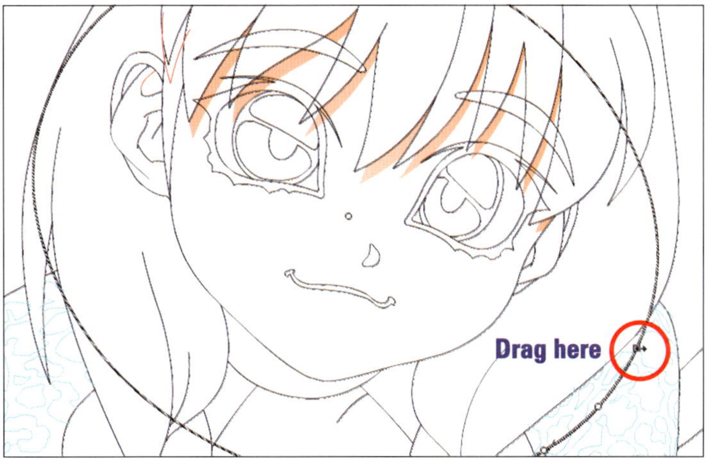

Point

Apply the Transform Fill Tool on a gradational fill you've used, and you can change its orientation and dimensions. As you draw nearer to completing your project, you can do this has much as you need to while looking at other areas you've finished. For the shadows on these bangs, I've made the gradient a little darker toward the hairline, where it's harder for the light to reach.

Coloring, Continued

For a neat finish, use gradients and break down your coloring into 3 or 4 stages.

It'd be fair to say we've pretty much already covered all the basic coloring techniques and tools you'll use for drawing with Flash. Now we'll start stacking fills and gradations to finish off our project.

In this section, we'll pull out a few fill lines and explain the finer points of coloring our creation.

Point

Balancing colors and gradations can be fairly difficult for beginners. It would be a good idea to start by coloring in rough strokes, and then go back and take care of the smaller details one by one. Pay attention to the "feel" of your colors as you add to your creation. I think painting in three or four stages and then later adding expression with gradients should about do it.

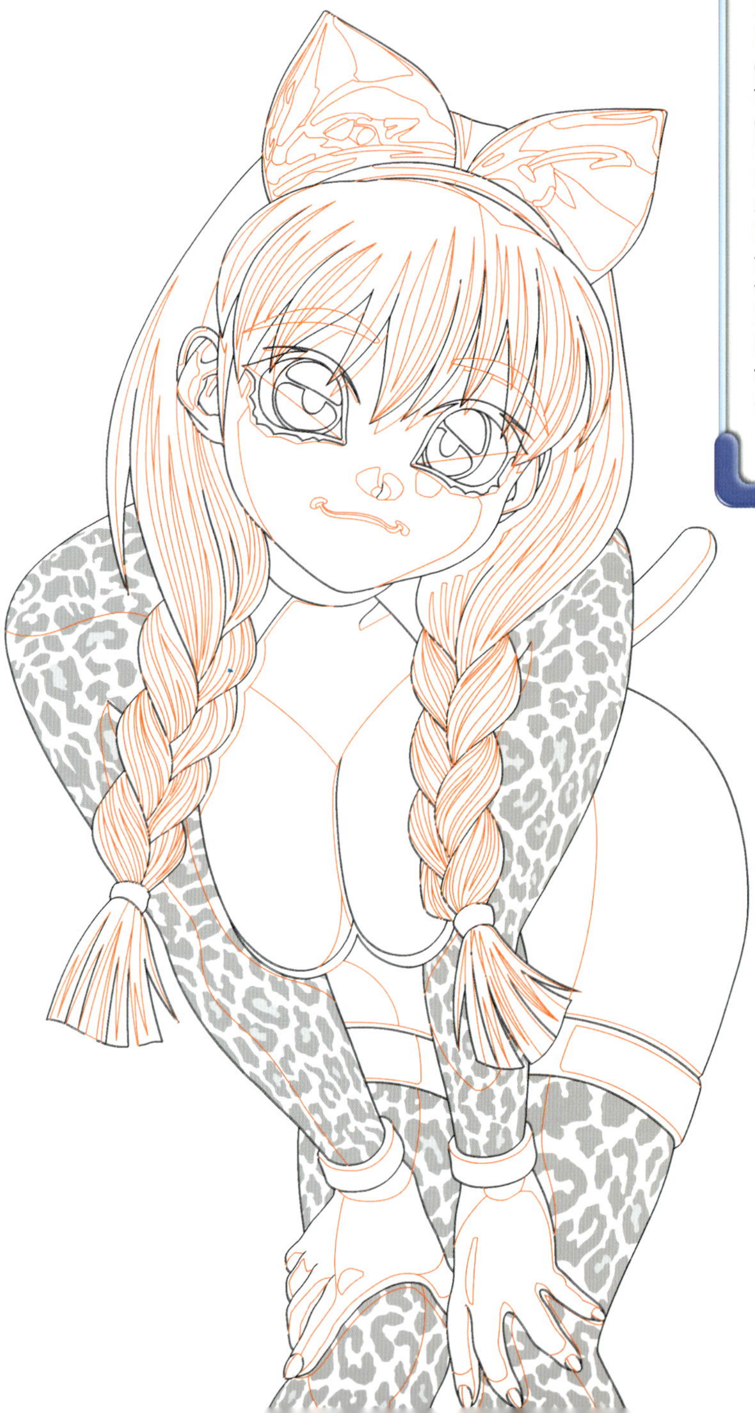

This is what my illustration looks like with all of my fill lines exposed. I'm not going to color everything all at once, but rather color each section and then apply a gradation to it, one at a time. It is the result of this repetitive process that makes a good color scheme. I went especially slowly with the hair, changing and altering it a little bit at a time for a flowing effect. A monotonous, uniform flow would just be dull and uninteresting.

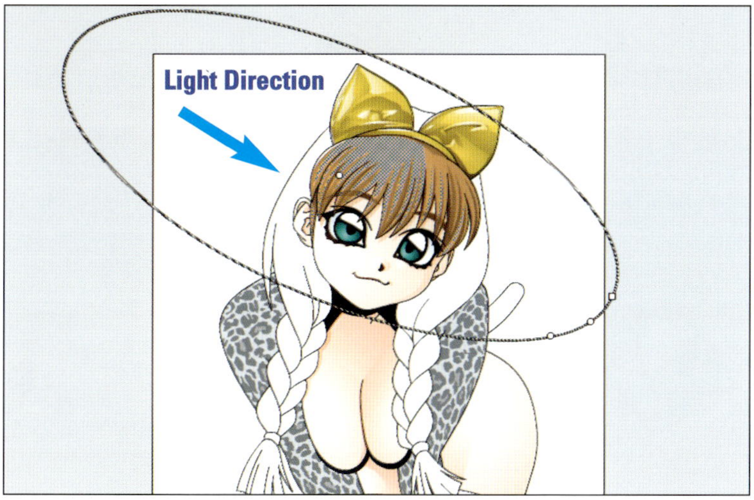

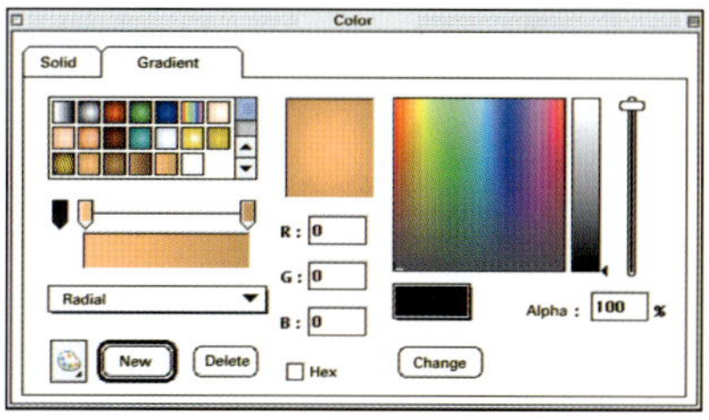

Start by separating the hair into large, bright and dark sections. Except for the highlights, the section marked here in blue is the brightest part of the hair.

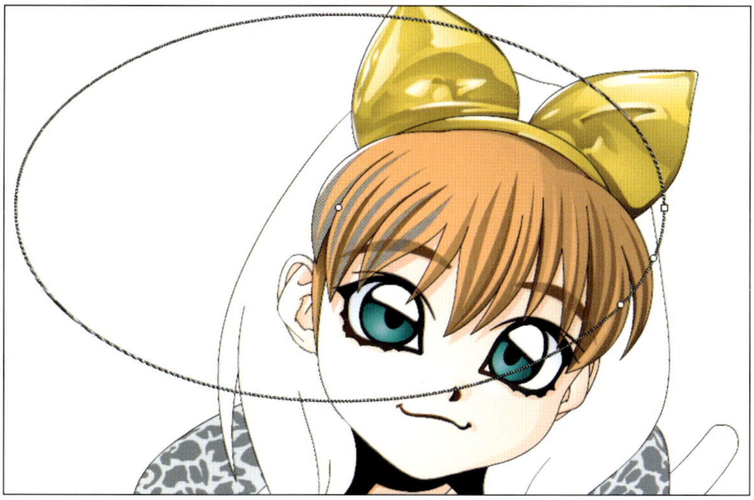

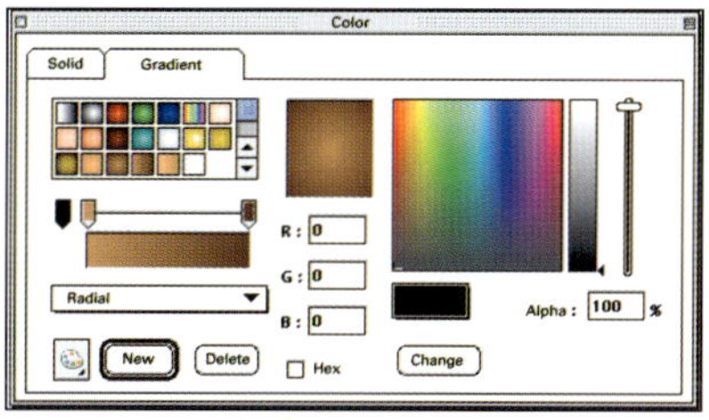

Next, we'll color in some finer details. Start by drawing fill lines with the flow and shape of the shadows cast by the hair, and then applying a somewhat darker gradation.

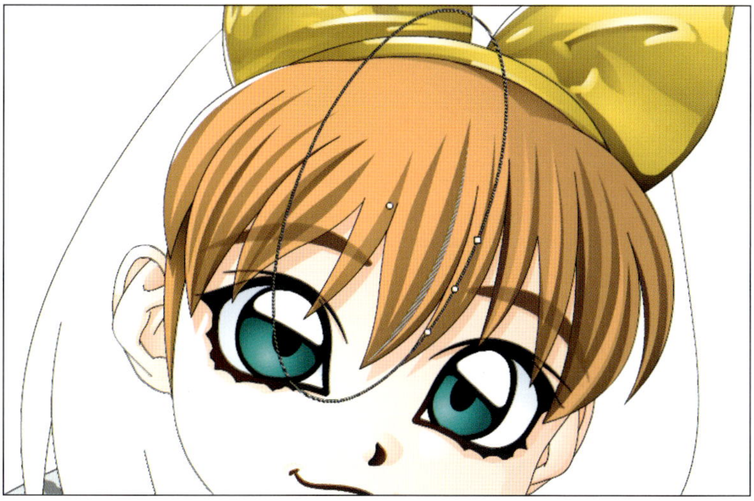

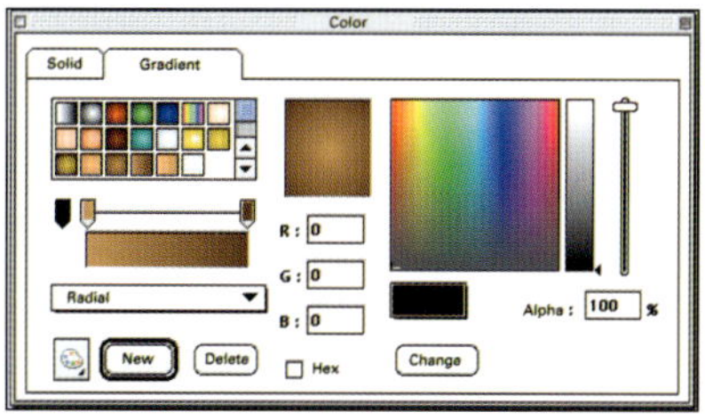

Here, I'm applying a darker gradation. I've used the gradation in the same way as I did earlier, but this time I've used a darker part of it. Since I'm adding subtle color variations a bit at a time, I won't really use the Lock Fill modifier. Just add them separately, one at a time.

Painting, Continued

Skillfully blend two gradations to bring out the cleavage.

Now we'll get into how to connect two gradational areas and blur the lines between them. This effect gives off a vibe totally different from simple cell shading, and lends new powers of expression and versatility to your Flash projects.

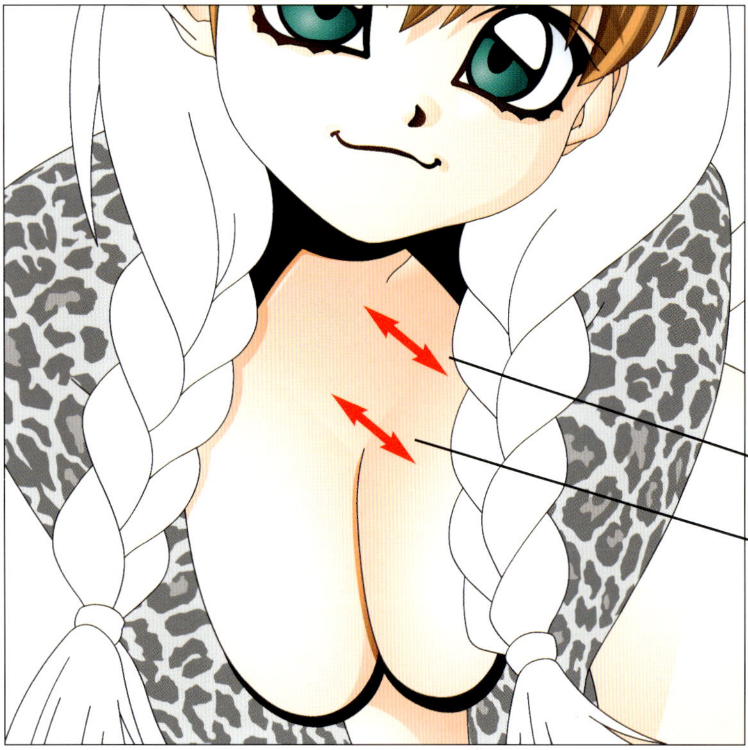

Point

For sections where you want to de-emphasize the borders between your gradations, adjust the colors in each one to be like the other. In this way, you can gradually make the borders seem to disappear.

The gradations are smoothly blended here.

The gradations are abruptly joined here.

Skillfully adjusting the gradations in the smooth and abrupt sections and brings out the cleavage naturally.

What's the big secret?

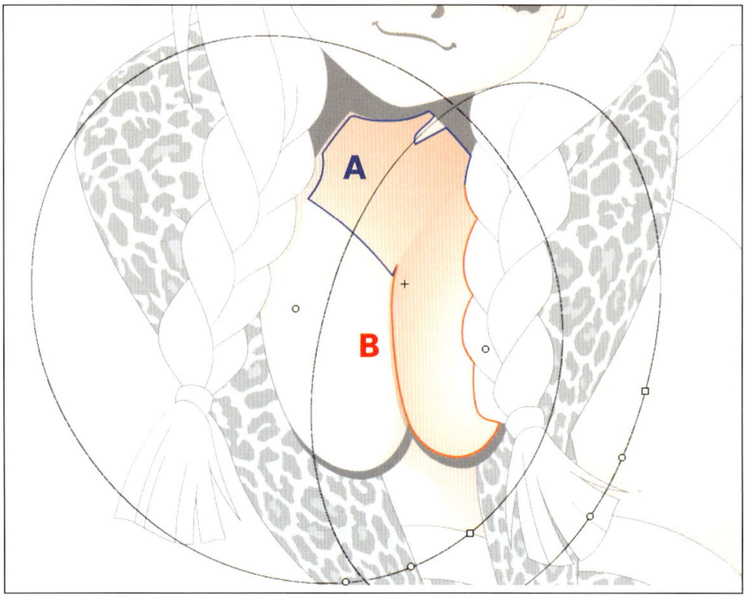

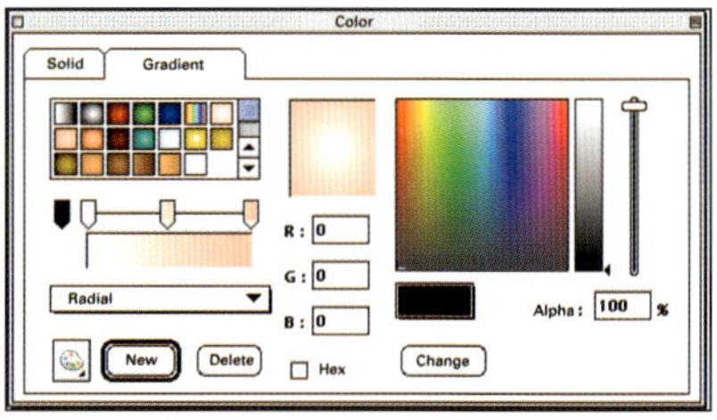

Fix the border between area A, outlined in blue, and area B, outlined in red, so that it becomes less noticeable to further away you get from the cleavage. So you can more easily see the relation between the two areas, we've shown you both gradational bounding circles here. (This is a composite image.)

How to Make See-Through Bangs

Reveal the eyes and eyebrows by putting them in a separate layer and making the hair semitransparent with a custom "See-Through Gray."

In this section we'll introduce a technique for making your coloring semitransparent. Colors have an Alpha value, and that value is normally set at 100%. By making that value smaller the color becomes more and more transparent. Use this technique to allow what's underneath your coloring to show through. Here, I'm going to make the bangs seem semitransparent. But what I'm actually going to do is put the eyes and eyebrows in a separate layer, mark off the parts that are covered by the bangs, and paint them over with a 50% alpha black fill. Then I'll take that layer and put it on top of the bangs.

Point
To easily separate the eyes and eyebrows into their own layer, select them and choose Edit → Cut. In a new layer, choose in the Edit → Paste in Place.

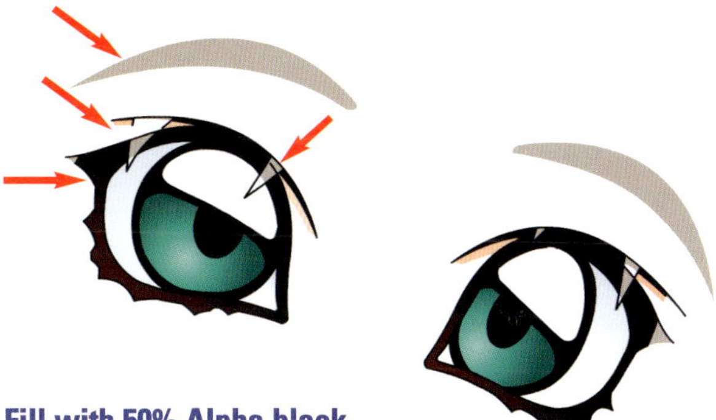

◀ Separate only the eyes and the eyebrows into their own layer, fill in the areas covered by the bangs with 50% alpha black, and then return it to your drawing. Shown here is what just the layer should look like when you're done.

Fill with 50% Alpha black.

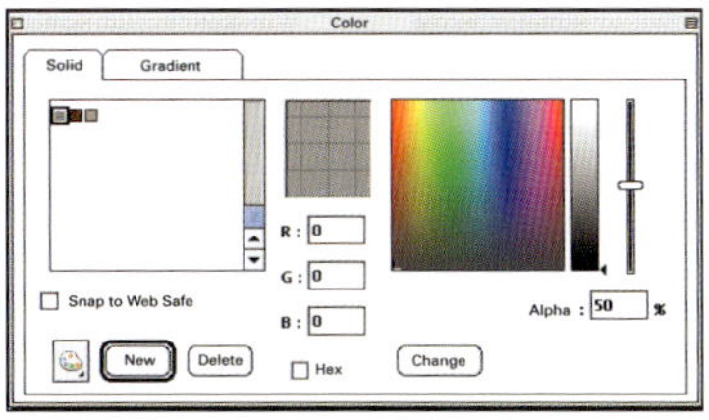

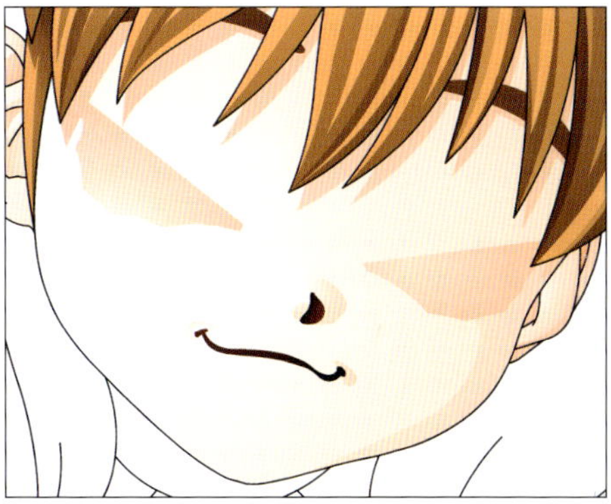

▲ This is what the drawing looks like underneath the eyes and eyebrows layer. I haven't done anything special at this point.

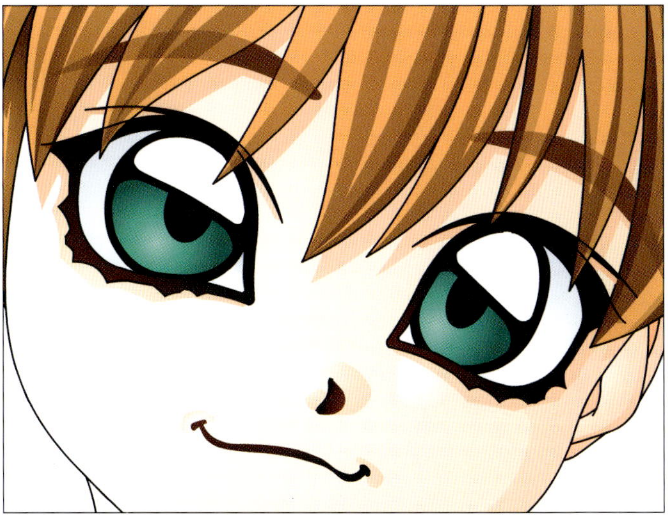

▲ With the layers stacked, the eyes and eyebrows show "through" the bangs.

Point
Adding a slightly blue-gray gradation to the areas above the white of the eye is a technique often used in Anime. It's strange, but it makes the eyes seem more three-dimensional. Adding a slightly brighter gradation to the iris and pupil produces a feeling of transparency.

Painting a Realistic Leopard Skin

Use Lock Fill on the spots within a given fill line boundary to unify them into the same gradation.

Coloring the leopard skin is done using the same basic gradational techniques we've already discussed. First, with your light direction in mind, apply a gradation to the sections delineated by your fill lines. At this point, it's probably a good idea to think of the background color as being separate from the spots. Use the Lock fill modifier on all the spots in a given fill line boundary and then apply your gradation.

Clothing background color only

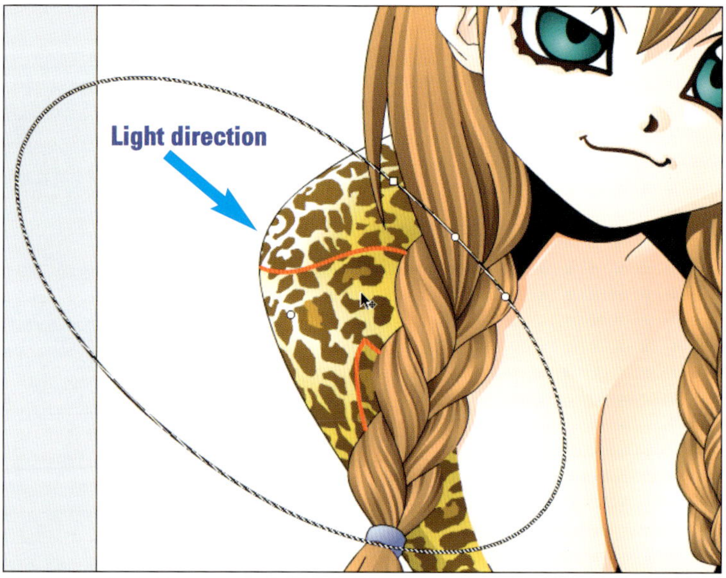

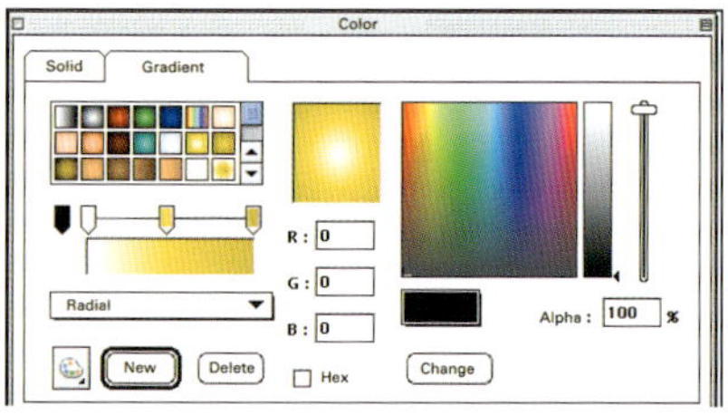

▲ Follow the fill lines and apply a gradation to the leopard skin's background. Choose the orientation of your gradation so that the side facing the light and any protrusions (such as the shoulder) appears brighter.

Point
The clothes' background and spots are different in color, but they're all in the same surface so their direction has to be the same.

Clothing pattern only

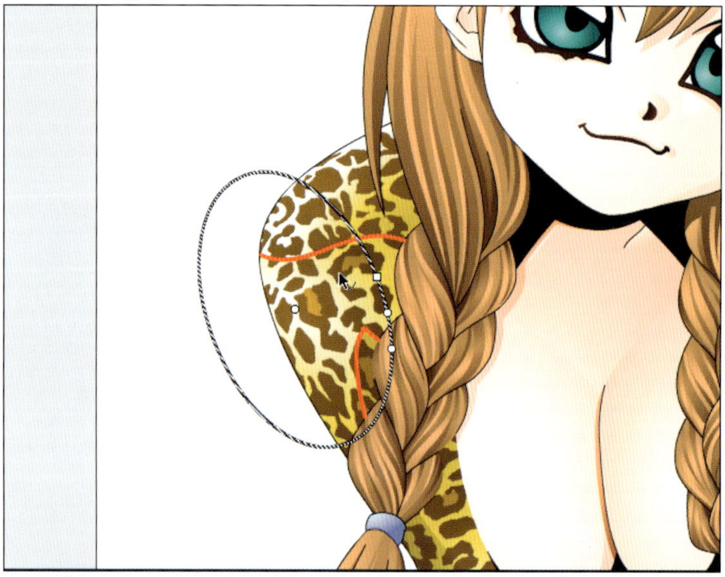

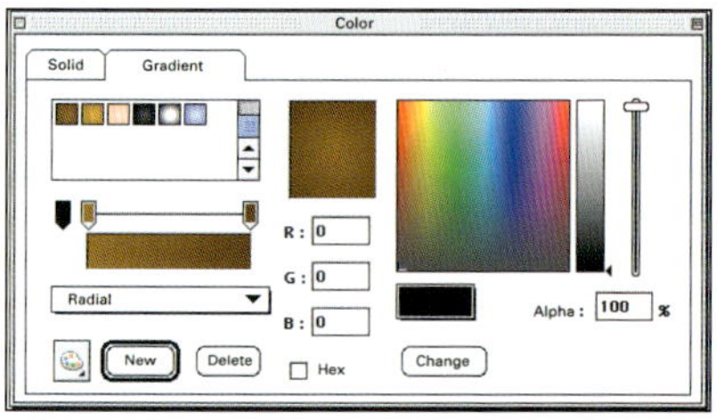

▲ Use the Lock fill modifier on all the spots in a given fill line boundary and then apply your gradation to them all. Remember, you can always adjust the size or angle of your gradient later.

Techniques for Drawing Fill Lines across Groups

When you draw a line across an area that you've grouped together, it gets buried beneath the group, and fill lines won't be displayed if they are colored. Instead, draw your lines in a new layer. Once you've done that, just copy and then paste them into the old layer: choose Edit → Paste in Place. This way, you can get your fill lines to show up nicely without wrecking your drawing.

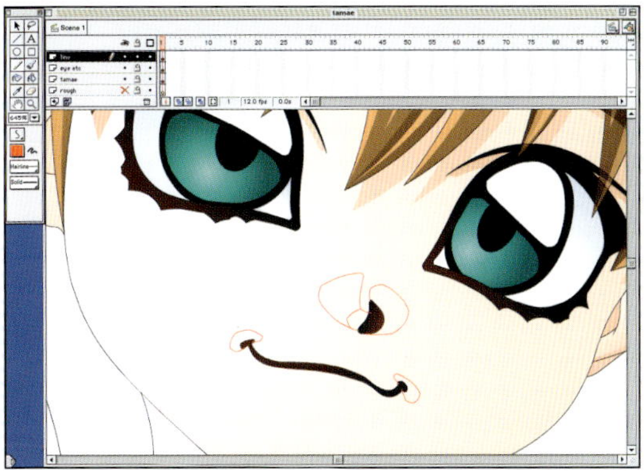

▲ Since you can't draw fill lines on top of grouped objects (they get buried beneath the group), draw them in a new layer and then paste them back into the old one.

Character Completion

You can color the remaining areas using basically the same ideas.

Use the gradation techniques we've discussed so far to handle the rest of the character.

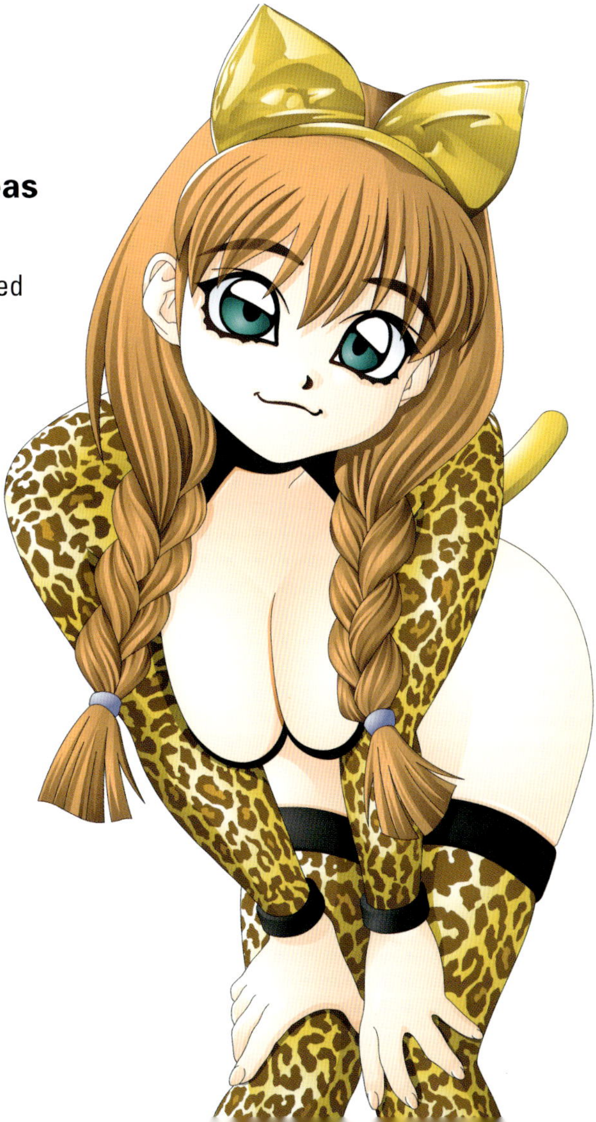

Draw the Background Using Basic Shapes

Make your characters stand out by using simple backgrounds and frames.

Create a new background layer at the very bottom of the stack. We've used the Rectangle Tool to turn the Stage blue from top to bottom, and then again to draw a smaller pink rectangle; we've used the Round Rectangle modifier to set the corner radius to 30 points.

Projects split into multiple layers can become cumbersome at the layout stage, so unify your backgrounds into a single layer. After we cover how to make your characters stand out with a thick outline, we'll finish off your project after a few words on balance and arrangement.

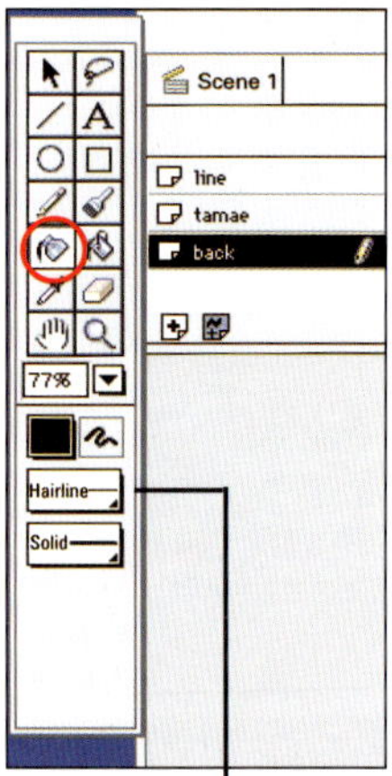

Choose Custom in this menu to enter line thickness in points.

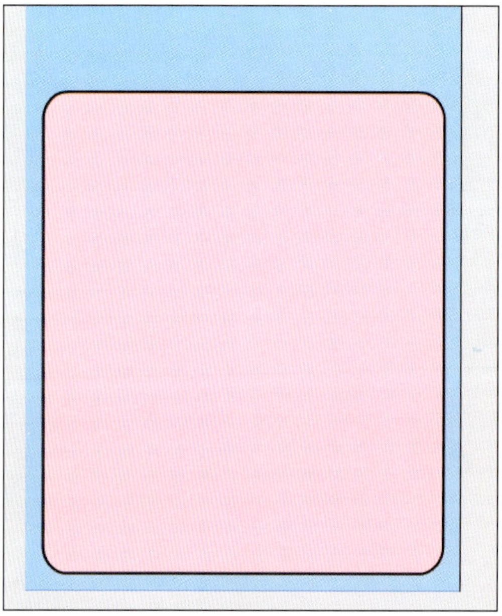

I've hidden the character layers here and used the Ink Bottle to color our rounded rectangle pink. The rectangle's border thickness is set to 3 points. Next, double click the border and choose Modify → Curves → Lines to Fills. In Flash MX, choose Modify → Shapes.

Point

Converting a line to a fill makes it possible to add to it an additional frame, a gradation, or any of a number of other variations that aren't available to ordinary lines.

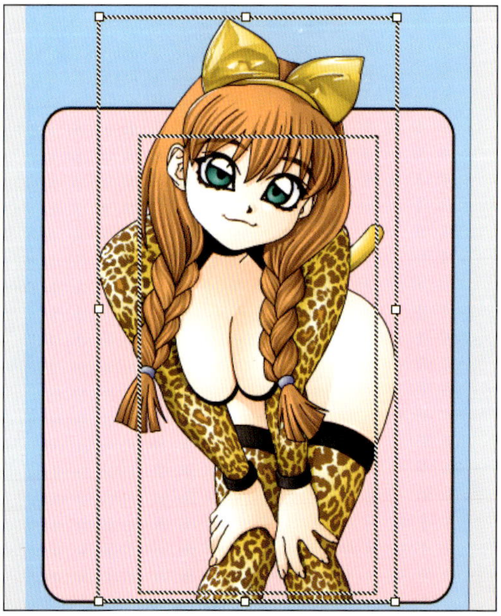

Show the character layer and enlarge or shrink it to fit in with the background.

Unifying a Multilayered Image without Losing Vertical Integrity

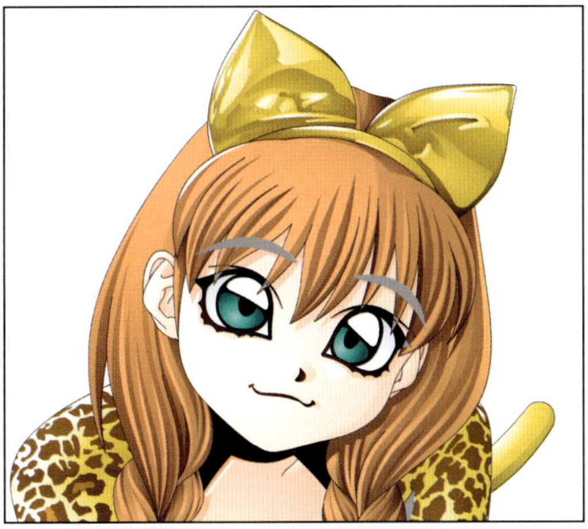

▲ When the vertical integrity between two images is lost, transparent fills, like the eyebrows pictured here, lose their see-through effect, rendering them unusable.

In Flash, there is no "Flatten Image," or "Flatten Visible Layers" function as in Photoshop. So, unifying a multilayered image means going layer by layer, using Edit → Cut on one layer and then using the Paste in Place command (in the same menu) on the next. Normally, this would destroy the vertical integrity of your project and turn the whole thing into one big image. If you have used Alpha-altered transparent fills, this can cause problems by making the colors beneath them change or disappear. To prevent this, you should make each layer its own Group in advance. That way, even if you unify your images into a single layer, each individual image remains separate and you can preserve vertical integrity.
To manage the vertical integrity afterwards, choose Modify → Arrange.

How to Make an Outline for Your Character

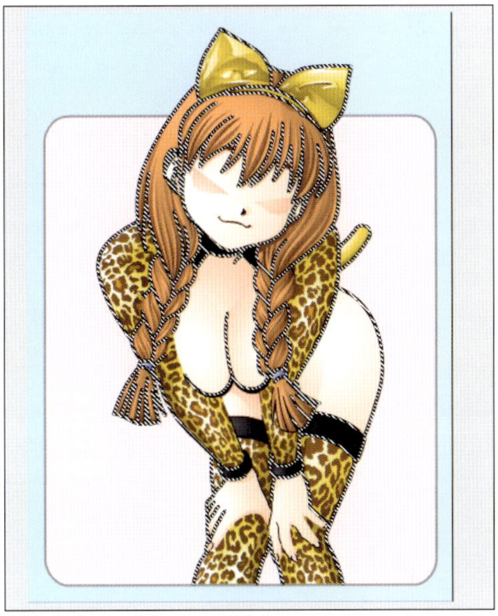

▲ Double click on your character lines and copy them-choose Edit → Copy.

Point

When you double click on something that has been grouped, Flash enters Edit Group mode—a "Group" icon appears in the timeline, as pictured here. At this point you can edit the group as you like in its "grouped" state. When you're done, click on "Scene."

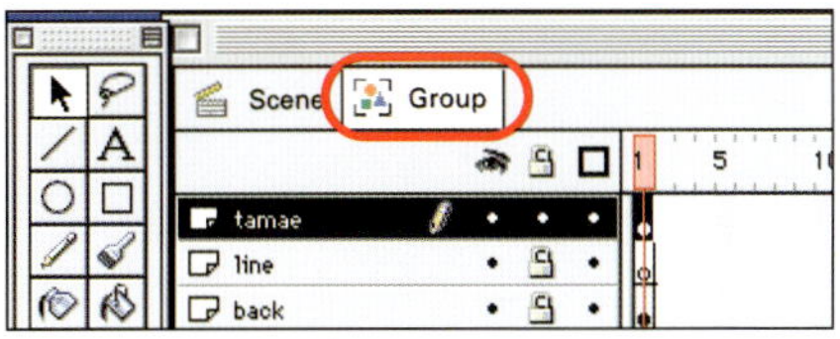

If you are in Group Edit mode, get out of it, and then create a new layer between your character and the background. Hide any other layers, and choose Edit → Paste in Place in the new layer. ▶

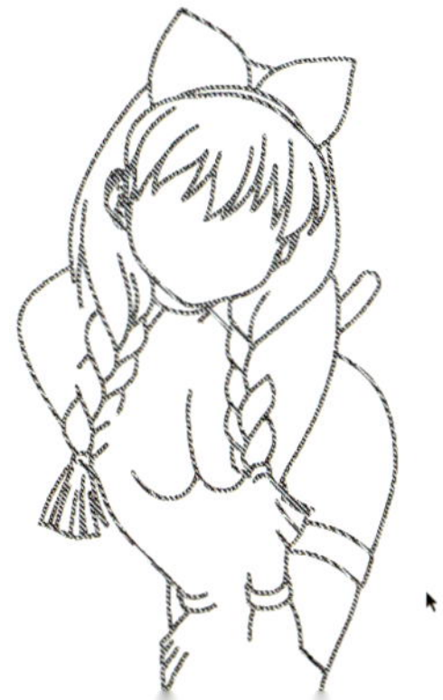

How to Make an Outline for Your Character, Continued

Leaving only the outer borderlines, erase all the character lines on the interior and paint it over in black. When you're done, erase the borderlines, too. The result is a black fill, or "shadow," that matches your character precisely.

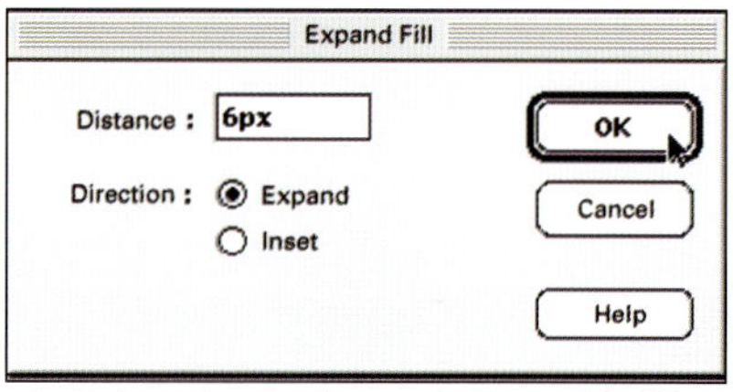

Select the shadow and choose Modify → Curves → Expand Shape. Expand the shadow outward 6 pixels.

Show all the layers, and you're able to attach a nice, thick outline around the edges of your character. I didn't really like the background color scheme, so I swapped the pink and blue. The character is now complete.

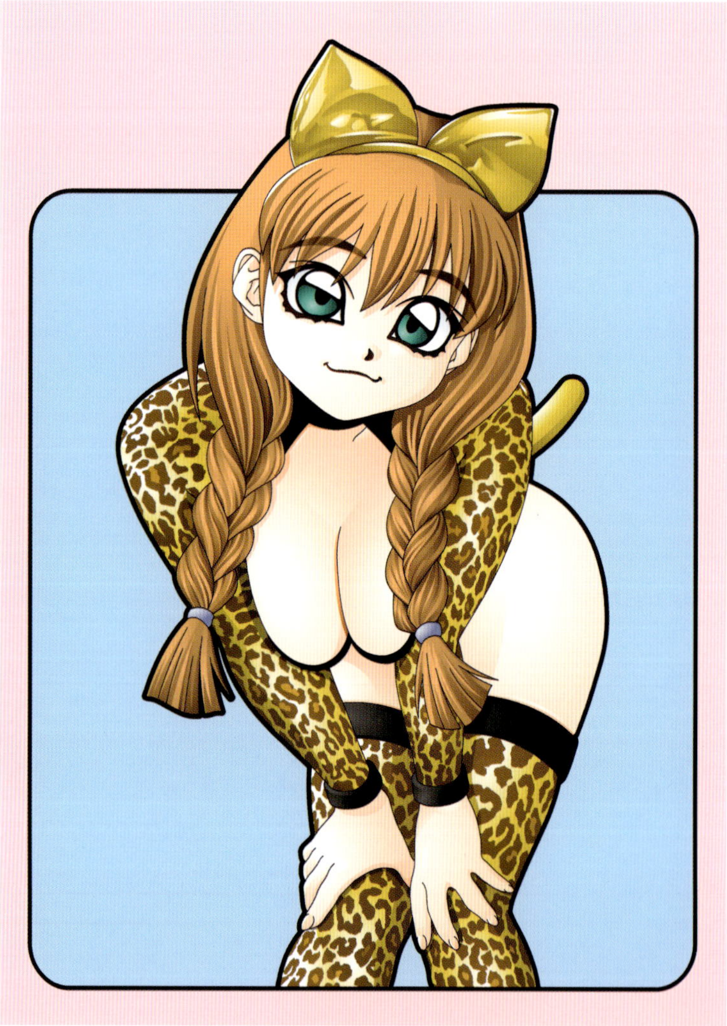

Point

The project is now complete, but we need cover publishing in order to show it off on the Web. Move on to the next section for an explanation.

Publishing

Automatically creating SWF and HTML files for showing your creation off on the Web

Flash creations are basically made for display on the Web. Save your work in a "SWF" file format designed for playback and create an HTML file to display it. The Publish function does all this for us automatically. Choosing File → Publish and using it with the default settings is usually not a problem. The files Publish creates are stored in the same location as your FLA files.

Here I'll explain a few Publish settings you should know about for showing off your Flash graphics.

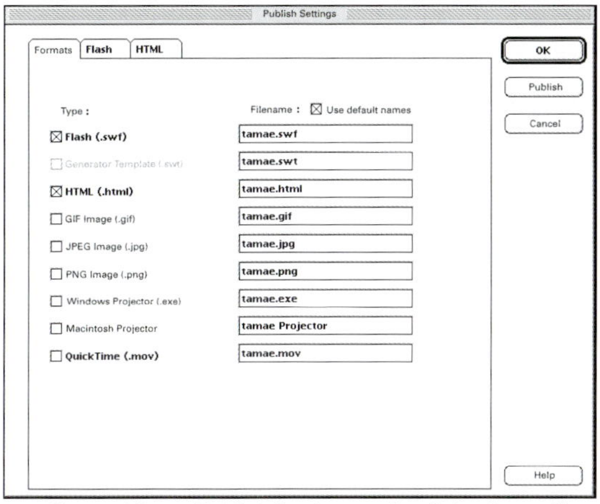

▲ Choose File → Publish Settings and a dialog box will appear. In the Format tab, make sure the Flash and HTML types are checked. You can change your file names here; you can also choose to save your work as a GIF or JPEG image, or as a QuickTime movie.

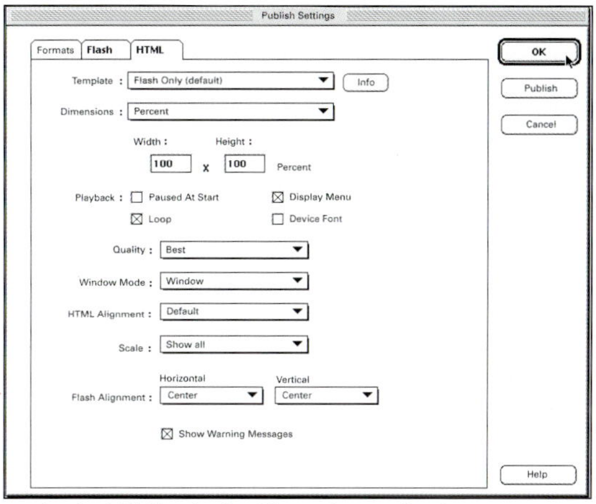

▲ In the HTML tab, the Dimension setting is set to Percent, and the Width and Height are both set to 100%. These settings ensure that your creation will shrink or enlarge so that it is shown in its entirety, regardless of the size of the browser window. If you want to show your creation off at a specific size, set the Dimension to Match Movie or Pixels and specify the Width and Height in pixels. Set Quality to Best—if your creations are shown on a less powerful computer, any animated sequences will be slower, but for inanimate creations like ours the Best setting doesn't pose a problem.

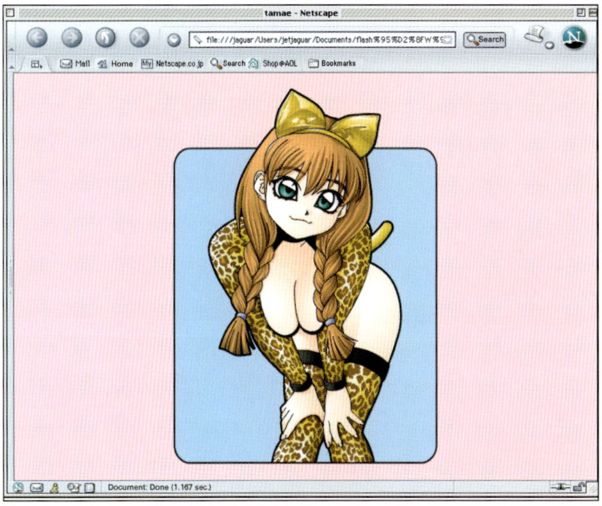

▲ Publishing creates an HTML file and an SWF file in the same location your FLA files are stored. Double clicking the HTML file will read it into your browser and display your creation. When you're ready show it off on the Internet, upload the HTML and SWF files to your server.

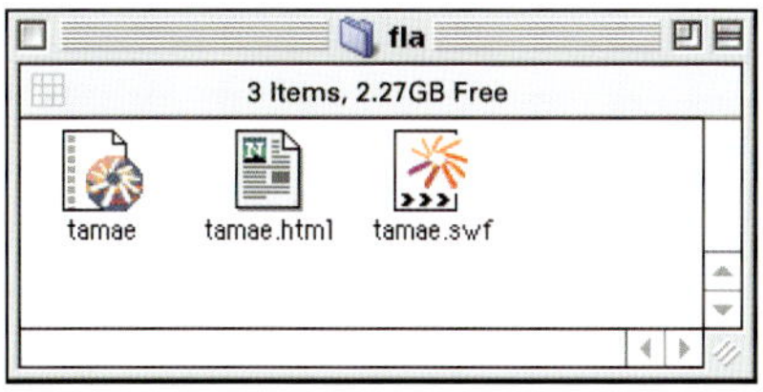

Gallery

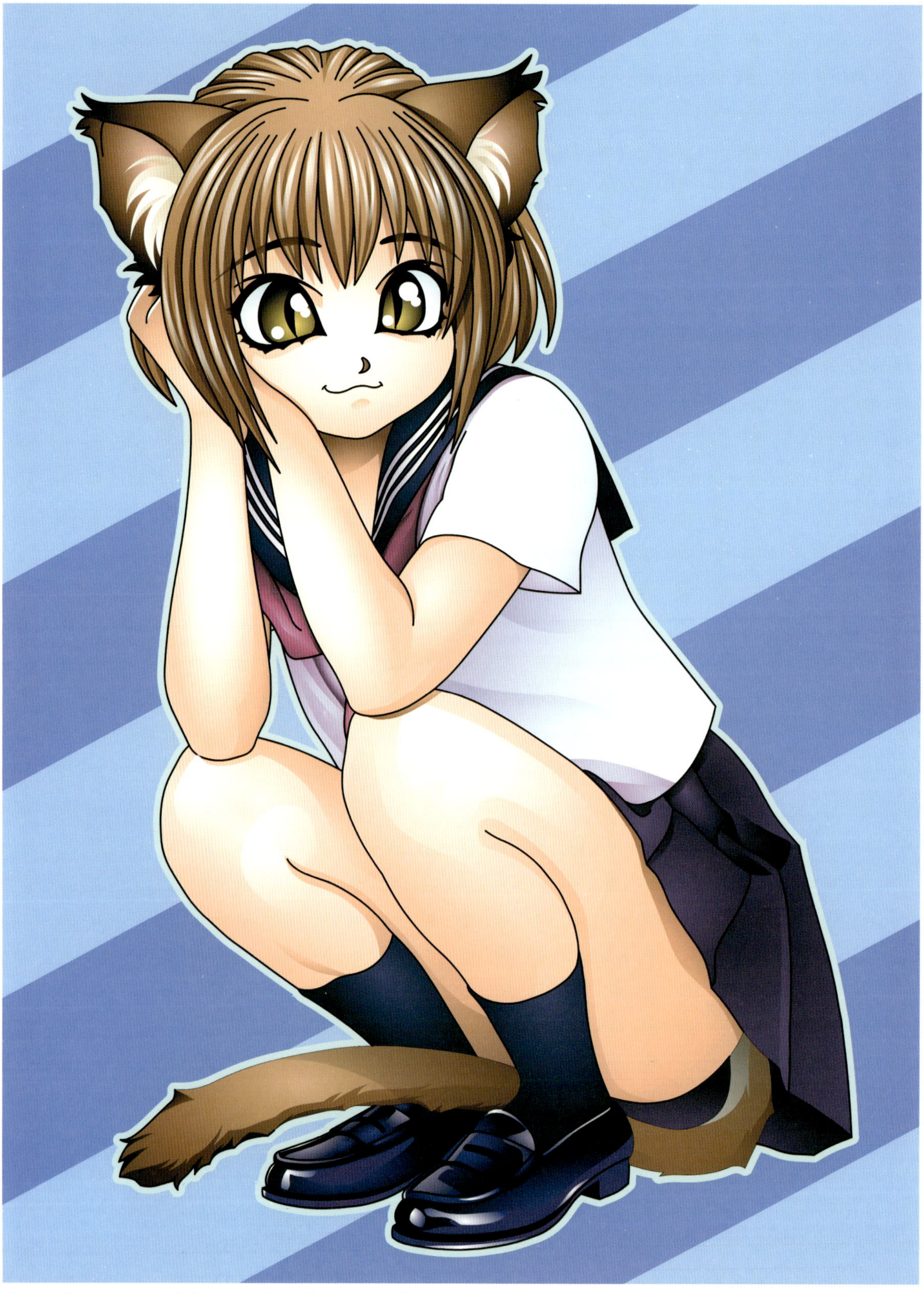

I usually try to avoid the sort of outfits you might see someone wearing around the neighborhood, but in this case I felt like making an exception. The background pattern is from the cover of "Urusei Yatsura," Volume 12.

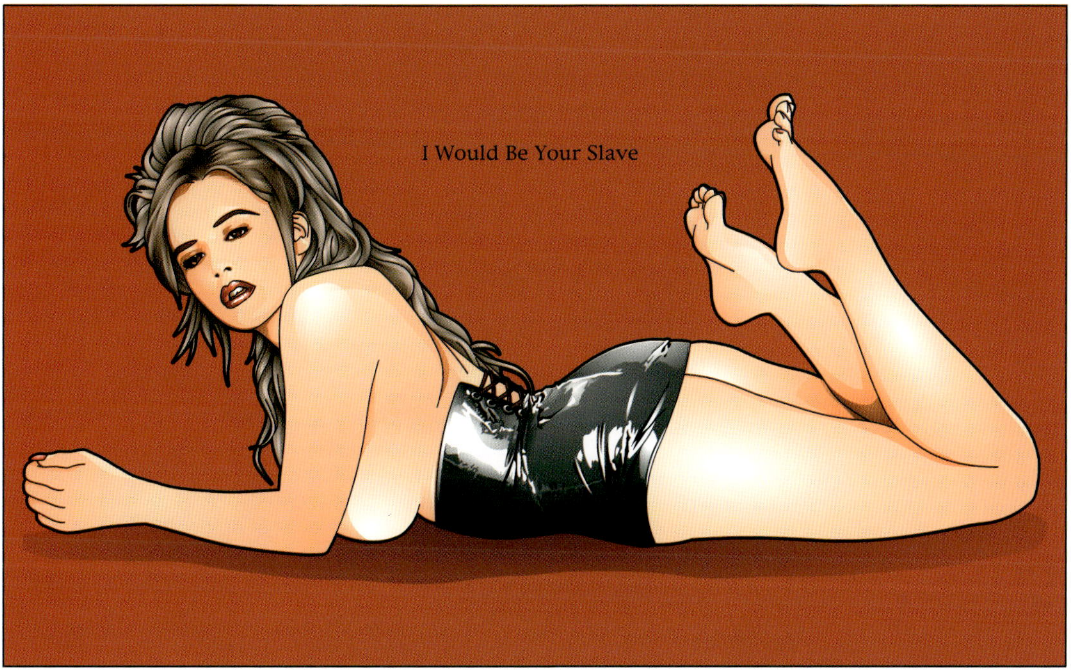

When I draw "normal" people, this kind of costume comes up a lot. "I Would Be Your Slave" is a David Bowie song title, but I don't know whether or not this character is interested.

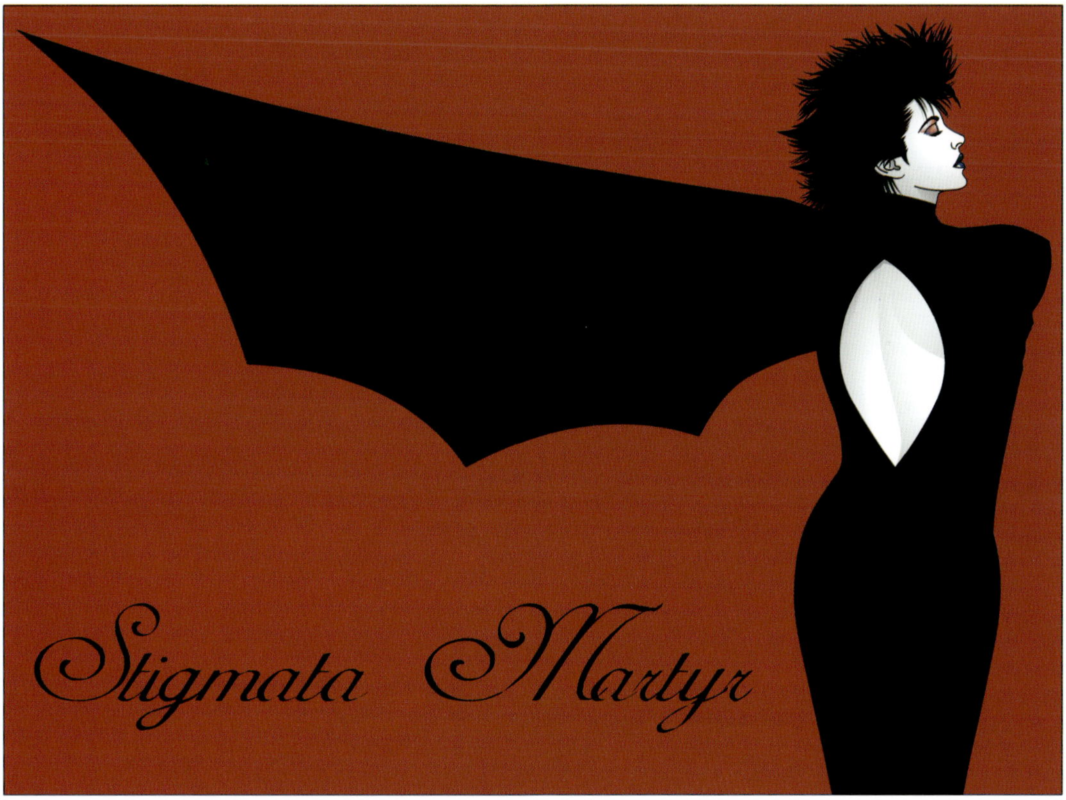

On the actual website, her body is facing forward, very busty, but right after the website came out, I thought, "Hmm. Maybe the back'd be better." So I took this chance to turn her around. Once a piece is put up on a site, if I start to fix it just because I feel like it I'll never stop, so I usually refrain.

"Stigmata Martyr" is a song by the band Bauhaus I was listening to when I drew this. Whenever I add Western language to my work, it's usually because I'm listening to that kind of music.

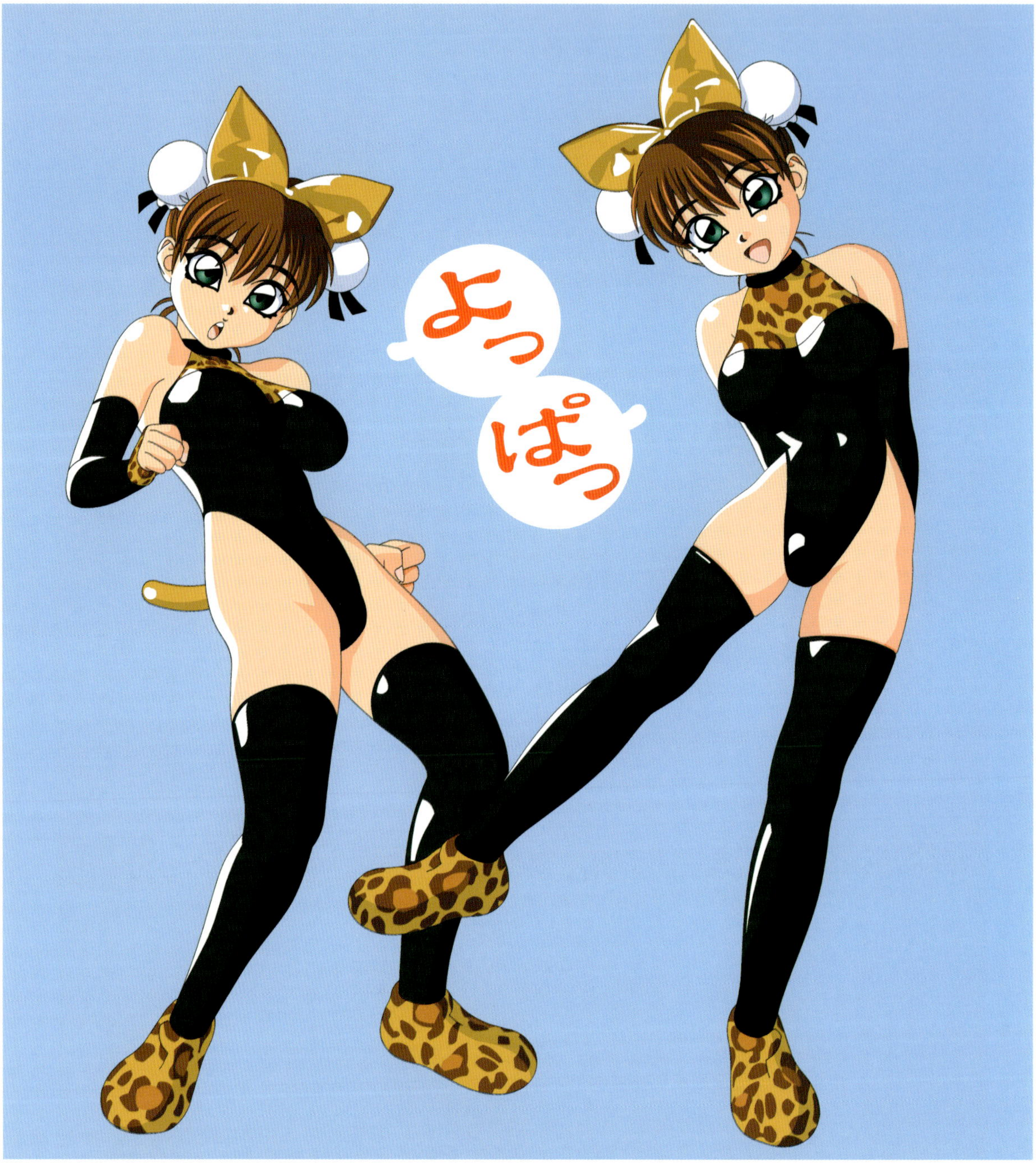

This is the only real Flash-esque piece on my site. When the mouse cursor tries to float over their bodies, these two ceaselessly avoid it. I have a certain desire to do more of this type of thing, but I haven't really come up with much.

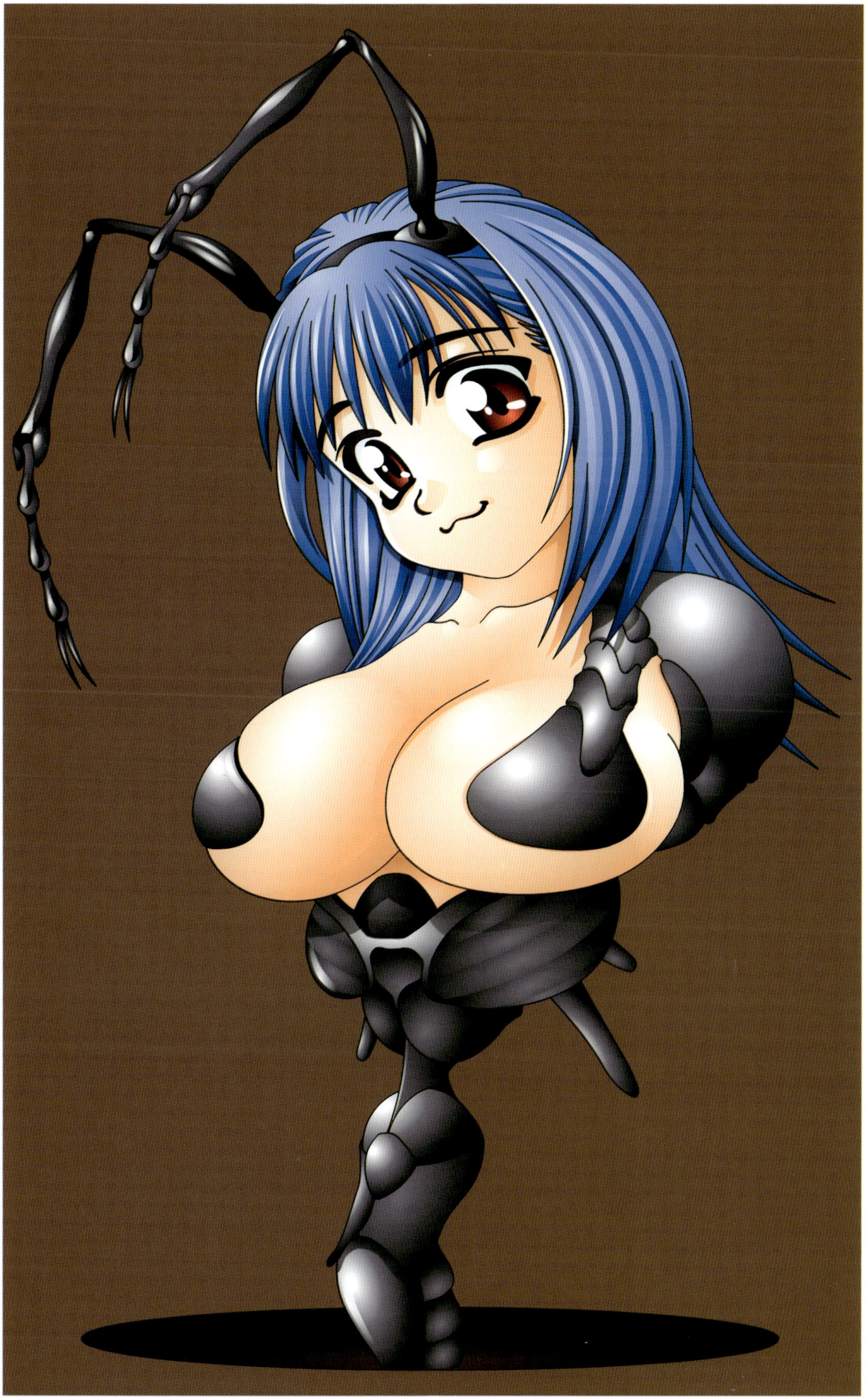

I felt like drawing something with antlike antennae and legs sticking out of it, and this cutie is the result. I thought maybe she'd start creeping around, but it's just a still image.

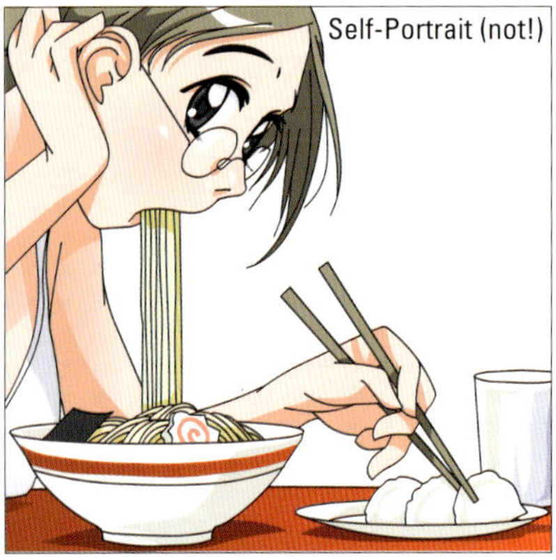
Self-Portrait (not!)

Computer
Custom-built PC compatible
Celeron 1.2GHz
Windows XP Home Edition

Memory
512MB

Hard Disk
40GB

Monitor/Tablet
Wacom Cintiq C-1500X
The color display on 32-bit LCD monitors leaves something to be desired, so I use it in conjunction with a regular monitor (a Mitsubishi 17"), both at 1024 x 768 resolution.

Software
Macromedia Flash 4
Macromedia Flash MX
Adobe Photoshop 6.0

Flash MX is a bit cumbersome when used on a machine with a slower processor. So, I usually use version 4, and just write action script in MX.

Sanbaisoku

Penname Origin
I chose it out of my desire to someday be able to draw faster!

Date of Birth
Let's keep that a secret for now.

Residence
Hokkaido

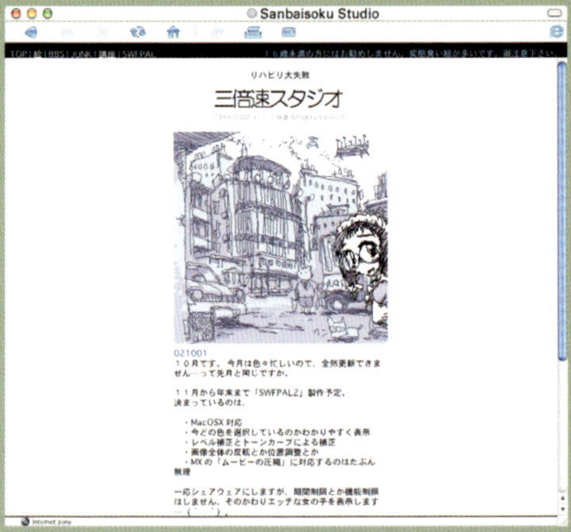

Sanbaisoku Studio
http://www.momiji.sakura.ne.jp/~3x/

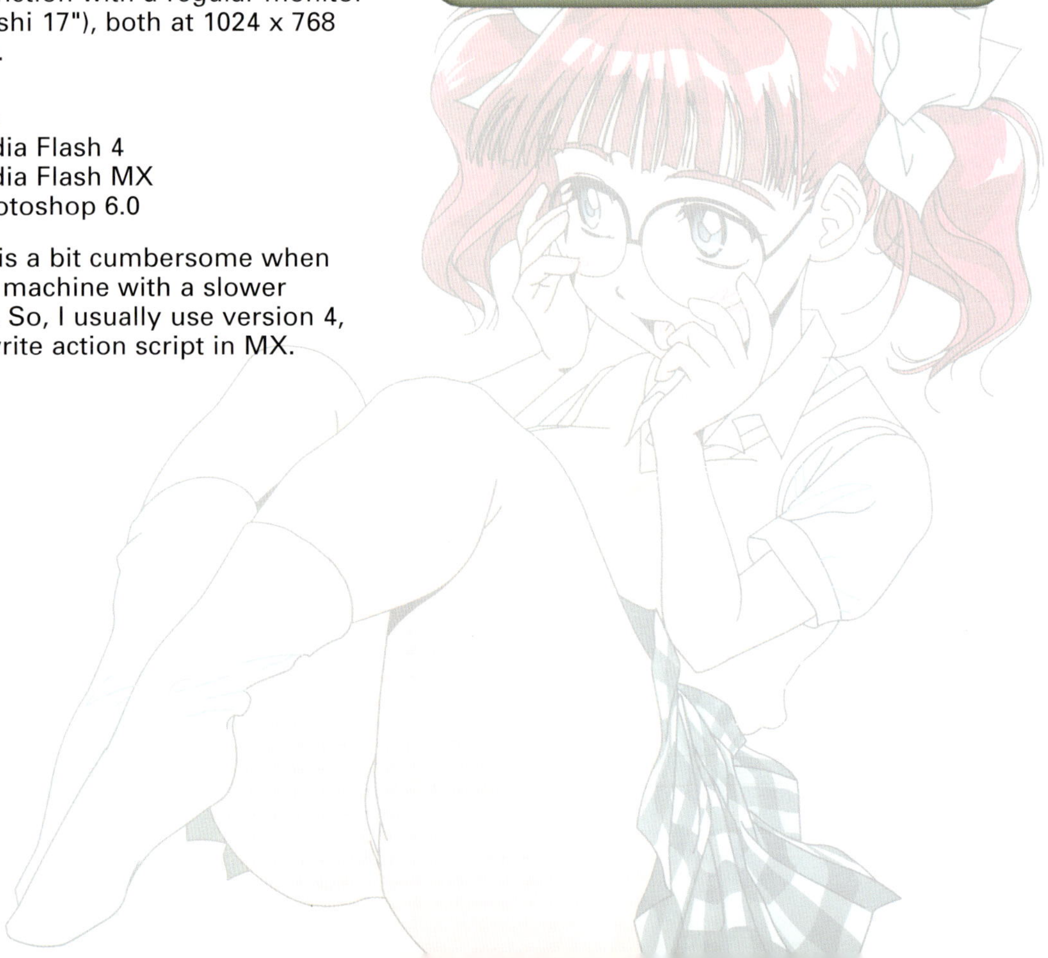

The Rough Sketch

Try looking at the mirror image of your sketch.

Draw your sketches in Flash with the Brush Tool and turn on the Pressure modifier. Of course, you can draw with a real pencil and paper, too, but once you get used to it, drawing directly in Flash is definitely easier. You can save the time it would take you to scan and import your drawings, you don't have to worry about the size or shape of your paper, and you can easily change the pose or the composition of your characters. It's also much easier to adjust facial expressions or body features in Flash than on paper.

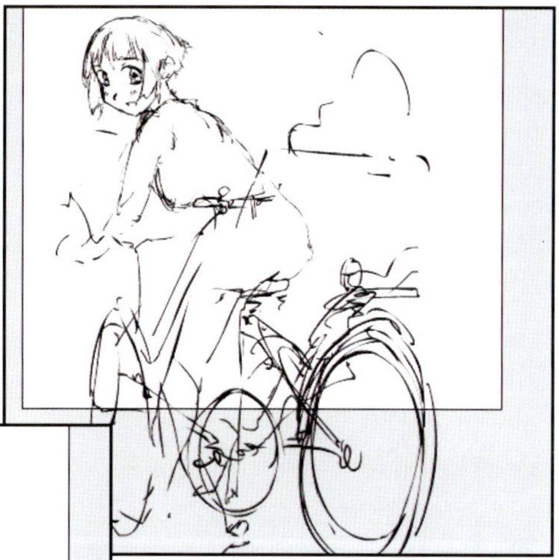

▲ From the midst of all this doodling, I've chosen to draw a girl riding a bike.

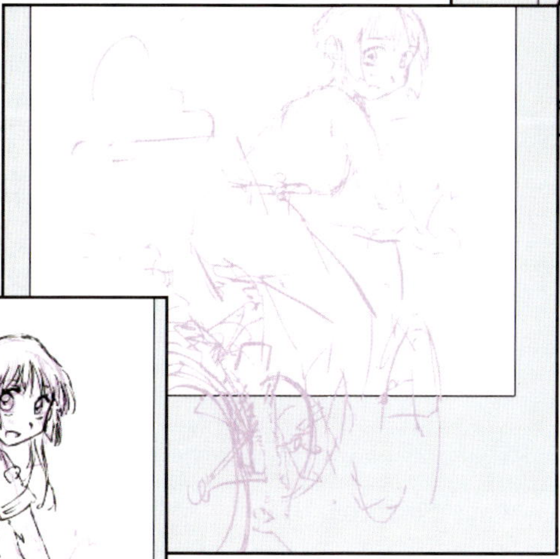

◀ By reversing the image, it's easier to figure out what you want to draw. Here, I've made the head a little bigger and adjusted the pose of her arms and the bicycle. Finally, I selected the whole sketch and washed it out with the Paint Bucket Tool.

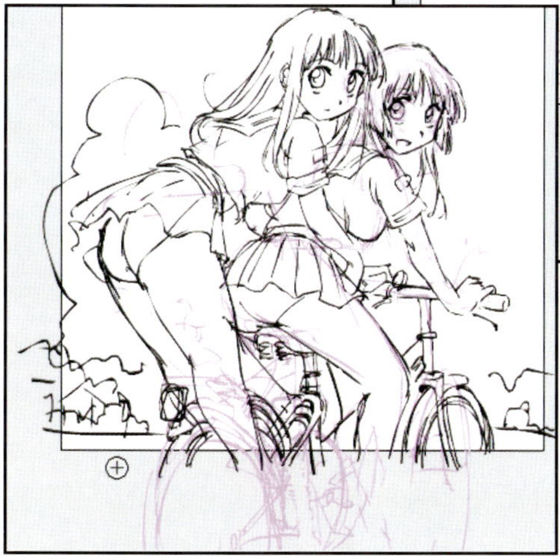

▲ Lock (prevent further changes) your sketch layer and create a new one on top of it. Add the details of your drawing to this new layer. This girl here looked lonely so I sketched in a friend for her. Get all the main features, such as the hair or clothing, more or less in place at this point so you don't get confused when you start tracing.

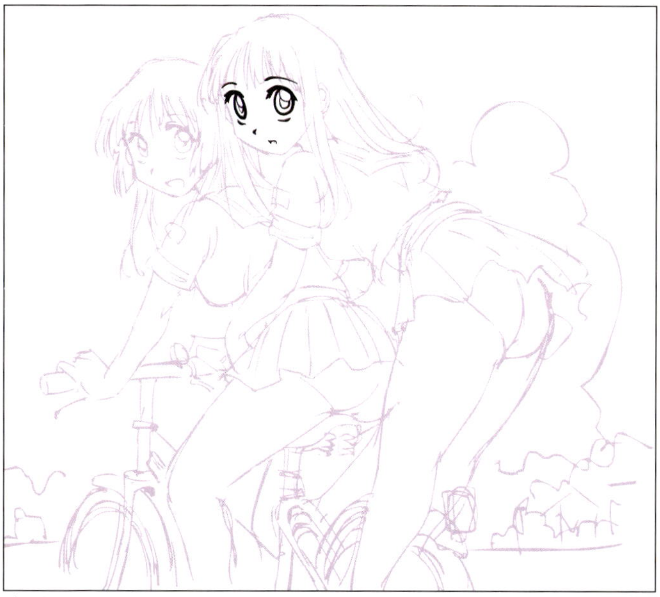

▲ Repeat what we've covered so far to complete your rough sketch. After this we're going to move on to tracing, so use the Paint Bucket to wash everything out in a lighter color. At this point we can get rid of our initial doodle.

Point

Pictures that look out of balance when you reverse them horizontally are usually sketched incorrectly. Flip your sketch around often at this stage and be sure to correct anything that seems out of place.

Basic Tracing Techniques

To put a quick, sharp finish on your line drawings, use the Pencil Tool.

Use the Pencil Tool to ink over your work—with this tool, anyone can draw crisp, clean lines just like a professional artist. Not being able to change the stroke pressure is unfortunate, but for drawing pictures with little difference in strength between strokes, such as cell animation, the Pencil really is the tool of choice. The feel of drawing with this tool in Flash can change quite a bit depending on the Aspect Ratio and how fast you draw. Zoom out on your sketch and it will seem like no matter how carefully you trace your sketch, all you get is a bunch of dirty—looking lines-so many worms crawling across your screen. On the other hand, if you zoom in and work too swiftly, you'll lose a lot of detail and end up with cold, mechanical lines.

It takes practice to be able to draw lines exactly as you imagine them, but once you get accustomed to it you should be able to do more work and get it done faster than you could with Painter or Photoshop.

Here, I'll cover the techniques you should know for using the Pencil Tool.

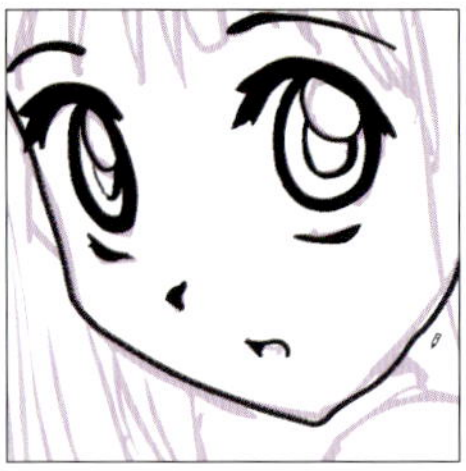

▲ Look at the outline of the face, from cheek to chin. At this stage, it doesn't matter if your lines are crooked.

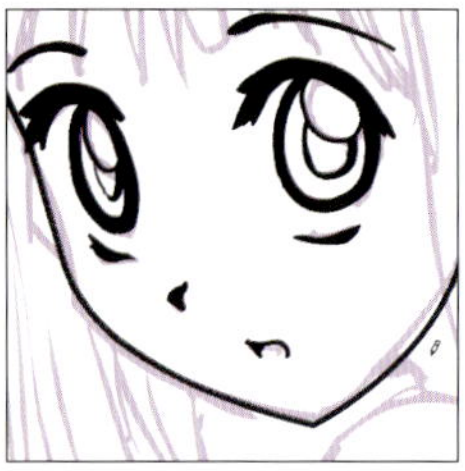

▲ Press and hold Ctrl and click on a line to select it. Choose Modify → Curves → Smooth and apply it 2 or 3 times. This will lessen the number of unnecessary anchor points used to define the line and make it easier to manipulate.

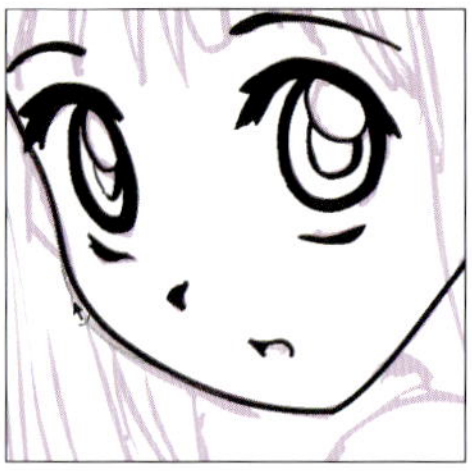

▲ Press Ctrl + Shift and hit the "A" key (or click on some white space) to deselect the line, and you'll then be able to fine tune it by holding down the Ctrl key and dragging the line with the mouse. Try to get into the habit of using this technique to adjust your lines on the fly.

Point
While you're drawing, you should rest on hand on the Undo shortcut keys (Ctrl + Z, by default). Since you'll be able to Undo whenever you like, draw your lines boldly.

How thick should the lines be?

I draw with the default Stage size (550 x 400) and a line thickness around 0.5 to 0.7 points. If you're drawing on a larger Stage, your lines will look weak at that thickness, so you might want to increase that a bit. In theory, if you keep the same Stage size-to-thickness ratio, you should be able to draw the same way on any stage. So, a good target ratio might be a line thickness equal to approximately 1/100th of the Stage width. Of course, that can change according to the characteristics and subject matter of your work, so that's not necessarily a strict rule.

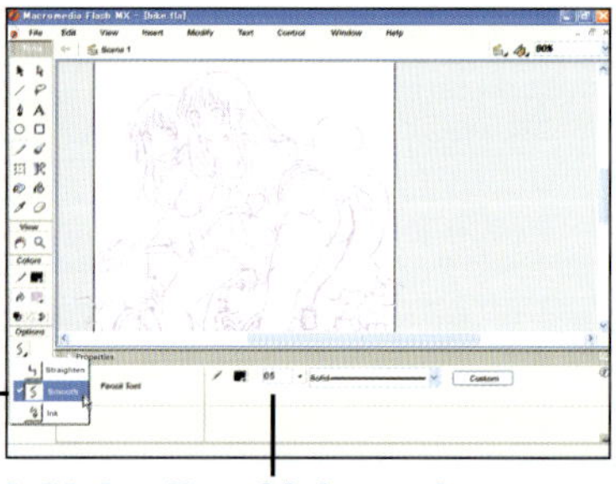

I think a line thickness between 0.5 and 0.75 points is just right for the default Stage size (550 x 400).

Keep your Pencil Tool set to Smooth

Crossing Lines and Erasing the Excess

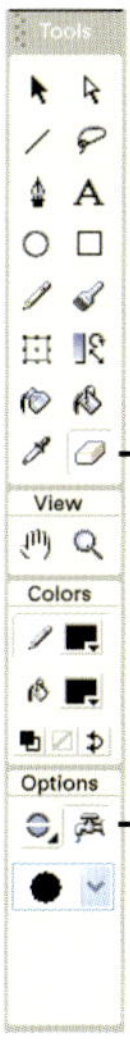

Use the Eraser Tool's Faucet modifier option.

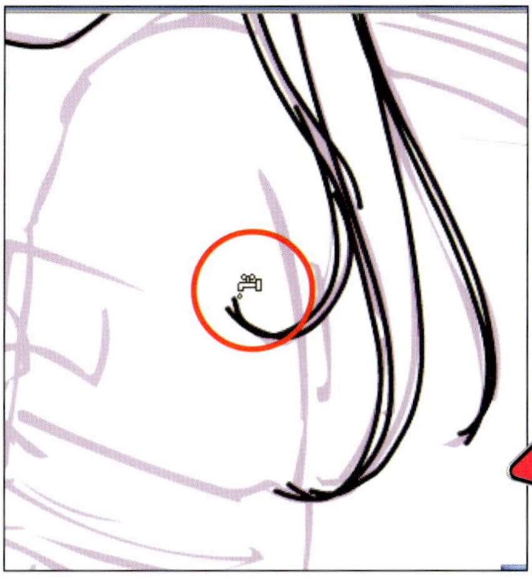

▲ Thinking ahead to coloring, carefully clean up any line intersections. To do this, purposely draw a little bit more than you need sticking out of the intersection and use the Eraser Tool to snip off the extra bits afterwards.

Point
Useful shortcuts:
E key: change to the Eraser Tool.
Y key: change to the Pencil Tool.

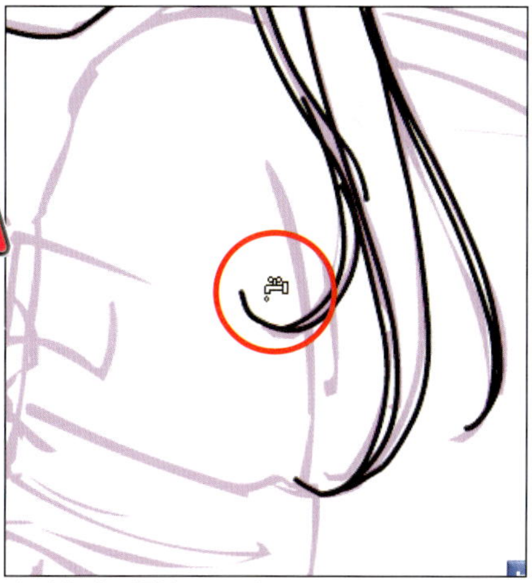

▲ Hit the "E" key to change to the Eraser Tool and click on any protruding lines you don't want. When you're finished, hit the "Y" key to go back to the Pencil Tool.

Connect your lines and eliminate any gaps.

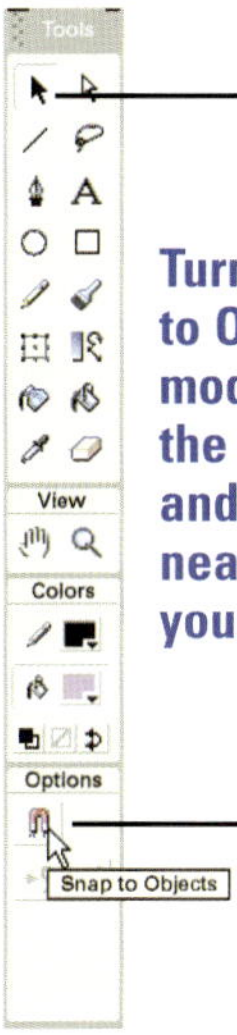

Turn the Snap to Objects modifier on for the Arrow Tool and you can neatly connect your lines.

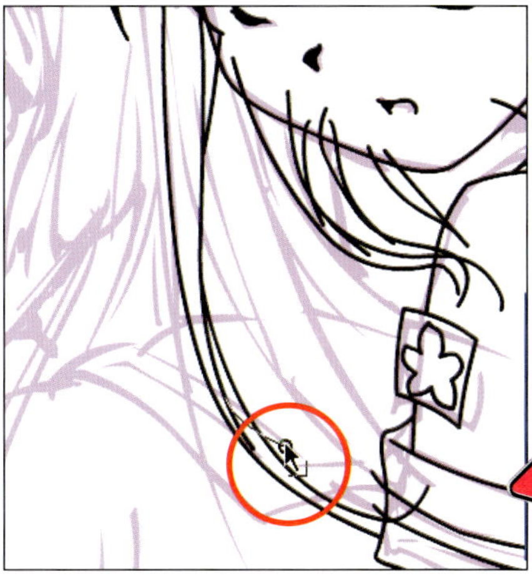

▲ Hold down Ctrl and use the mouse to pull your lines together.

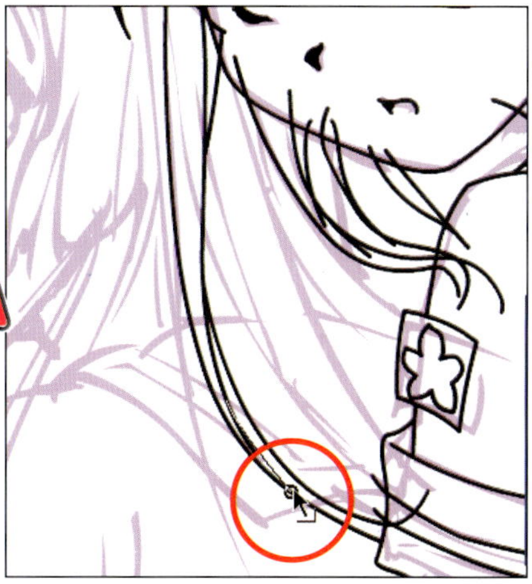

▲ Here, I'm connecting my lines. Anytime you want to do this you can turn on the Snap to Objects modifier, but don't forget to turn it off when you're done. Everything will stick to everything else if you don't!

Point
When your lines don't properly connect, you can use the Arrow Tool to pull them together. At any time, you can use the Arrow Tool while you're drawing by pressing the Ctrl key.

Pulling Out a Corner in the Middle of a Line

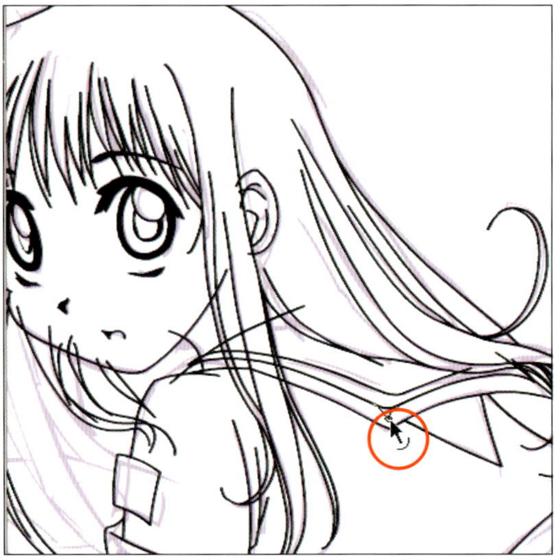

▲ Press and hold Ctrl + Alt and use the mouse to pull the section you want into a corner.

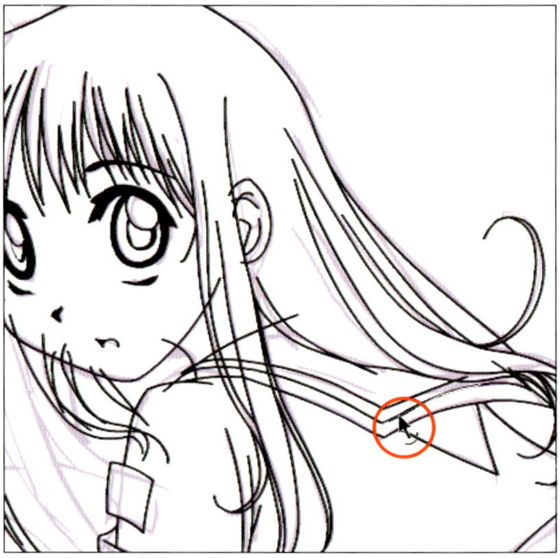

▲ I've made this previously rounded bit here into a corner.

Point
Hold down the Ctrl and Alt keys and use the mouse to pull a line out into a corner.

Convenient keyboard shortcuts

Create and keep keyboard shortcuts for all the commands you use often. Once you get used to them, you can work more comfortably since you don't have to needlessly move your hands all the time. For me, the default shortcut for the Snap to Objects modifier (Ctrl + Shift + /) is hard to use, so I redefined it so I can turn it on and off just by pressing the "/" key. My Smooth shortcut is "Ctrl + F," and since I use the Flip Horizontal command a lot, I made that one "Ctrl + Spacebar." However, that's the default command for the Magnifier Tool, so you'll probably want to designate a different shortcut for that, too.

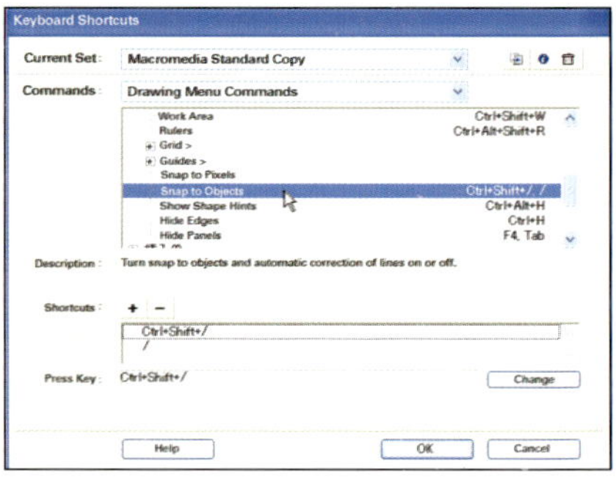

▲ This is the dialog where you can enter and change your keyboard shortcuts. In Windows, this is in the Edit menu. Under Mac OS X, choose Keyboard Shortcuts in the Flash menu.

Point
My Snap to Objects shortcut is the "/" key. Setting my Smooth command to Ctrl + F turned out to be useful.

Use the Brush Tool for a Hand-Drawn Feel

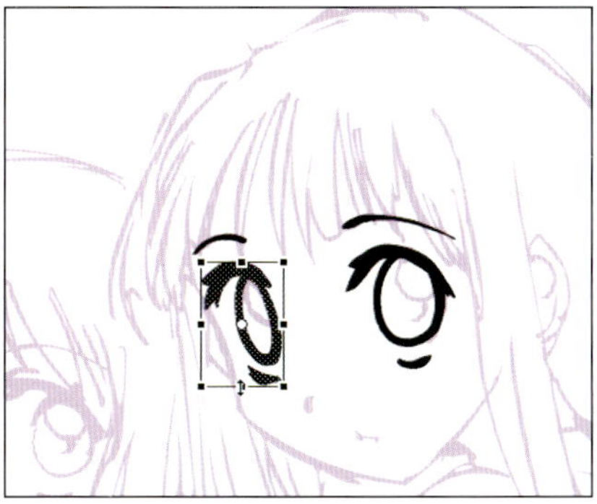

▲ Even if you notice something wrong, you won't be able to adjust the facial composition later using the Brush Tool. Pay special attention to the size and direction of the right and left eyes.

I also make use of the Brush Tool for inking over parts of the face, like the eyes and eyebrows. I don't think using the Pencil Tool adequately captures the expression of the rough sketch.

The thickness of Flash's Brush Tool is fixed not to the stage but to the window size, so even if you change the Aspect Ratio the relative size of the brush stays the same. In other words, zooming in will shrink your brush, and vice versa. When you choose the Brush Tool for inking over your project, try not to stop halfway through and use the Magnifier Tool. Try to draw at one fixed Aspect Ratio as much as possible.

Make life easier by using lots of layers for the ink over.

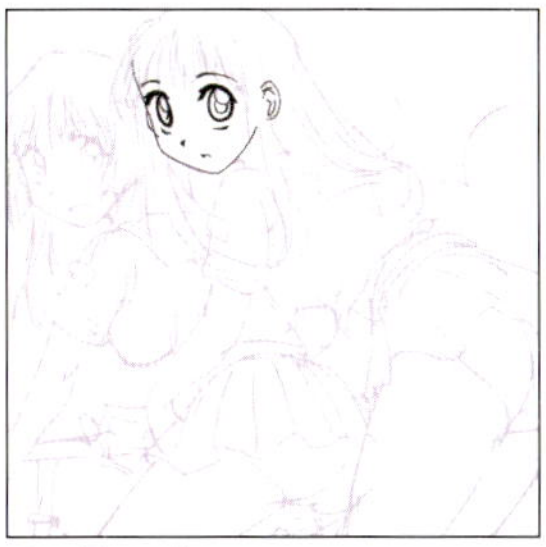

▲ Face layer

Point

At this stage, we're ready to trim down our file size with Modify → Curves → Optimize. This modifier is really meant to be used only after you've completed a project, but its side-effects can cause lines to disappear and colors to change, and often people totally forget to use it all. So let's do it now.

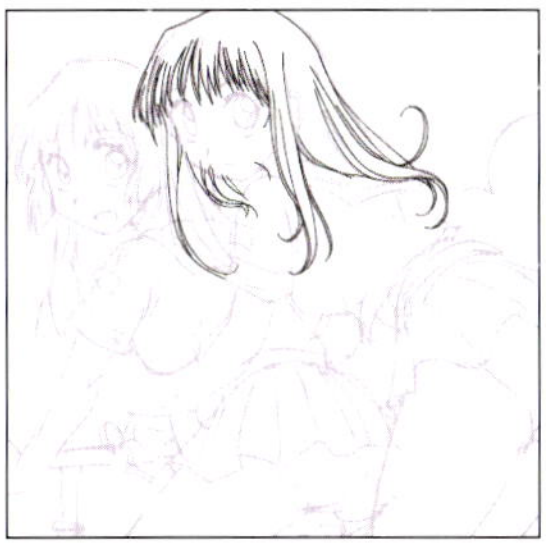

▲ Hair layer

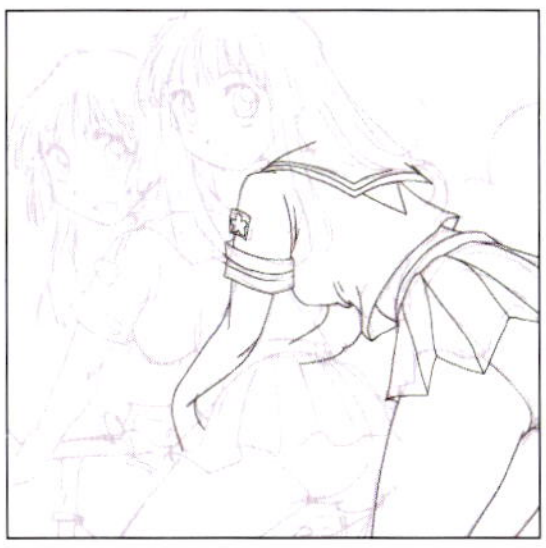

▲ Body layer

Use as many layers as you like. Doing the inking in separate layers makes it a lot easier to adjust the line drawing later since individual lines won't stick together. At this point the rough sketch trace is complete. (To differentiate between layers and for the sake of convenience, each has been shown here in a different color. In the actual drawing all lines are black.) ▶

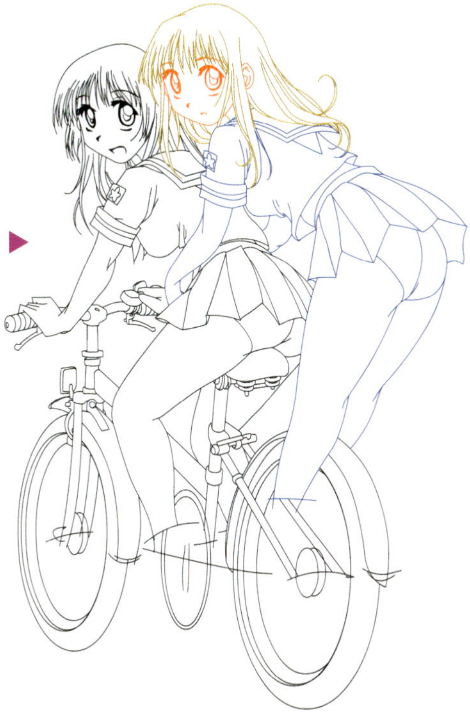

Coloring

Save time by sampling your colors from other images

Use the Paint Bucket Tool to color in your illustration. You can create your own colors in the Color Mixer, but finding just the right one isn't always easy. Instead of spending a lot of time finding it by trial and error, it's better to find a color you like in another picture or photograph and use the Eyedropper Tool to sample it.

Click on the color you want to use.

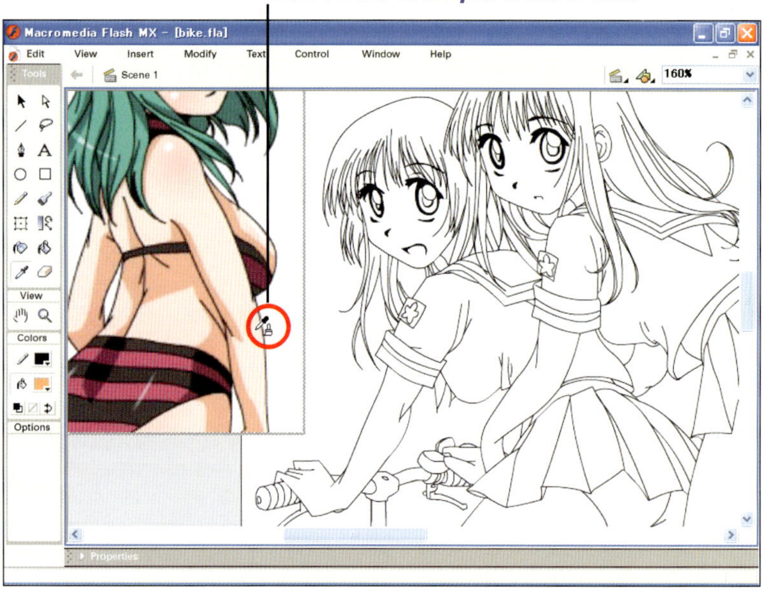

▲ To import an image with the colors you want to sample, choose File → Import. Set the image window someplace where it won't get in your way, and use the Eyedropper Tool to sample it.

Point

Special cases aside, Eyedropper Tool (click the Eyedropper icon or hit the "I" key) can copy the attributes of another gradation, texture, or line, but it can't copy anything from a locked layer or a color from another application.

If you click here, your cursor will turn into an eyedropper and you will be able to sample anything on your screen, even other applications.

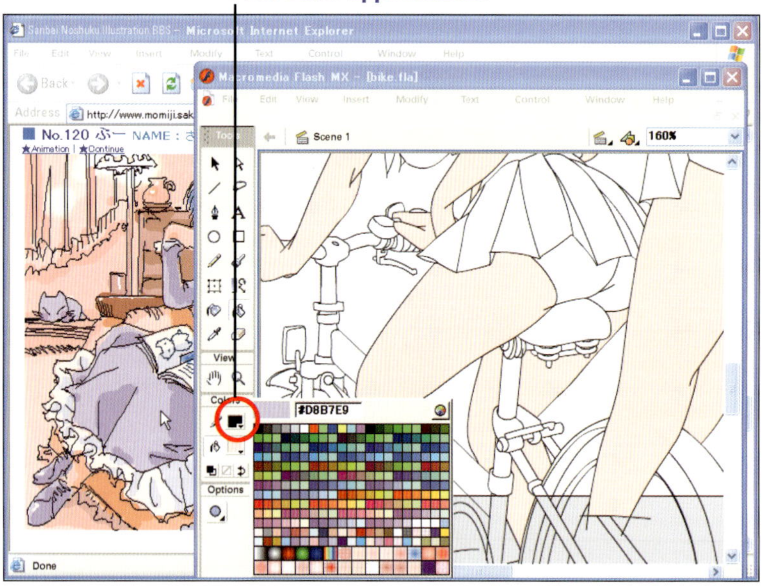

▲ To sample a color from another application, such as a web browser, click on the color swatch in the Ink Bottle Tool or the Paint Bucket Tool Swatches panel—your cursor will change to an eyedropper—and click on any color on your screen that you want to sample.

Point

The Eyedropper Tool from the Swatches panel can sample any color from any source on your screen, but it can't copy any line or fill attributes. This tool is useful when you want to match a fill color to a line color or when you want to sample only a color from the middle of a gradation.

Discovering Unpainted Areas

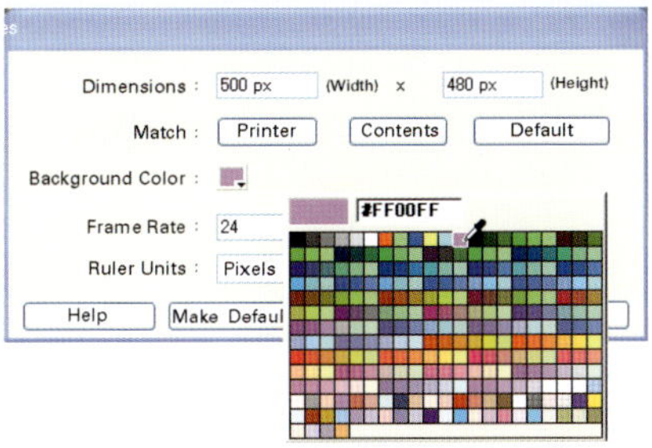

▲ Choose Modify → Document and click on the Background Color swatch. Change the color to something that will stand out.

Artists frequently forget to paint over white areas in their work, so be careful. If you leave a part of your character unpainted, it can have unintended results, like the background colors showing through the character in strange ways. Use this effect to check your character.

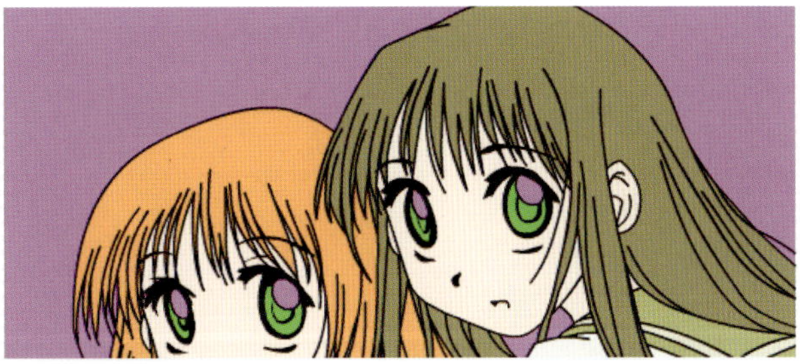

▲ Unpainted sections take on the new background color and become easier to find. Here, the pupils have been left unpainted.

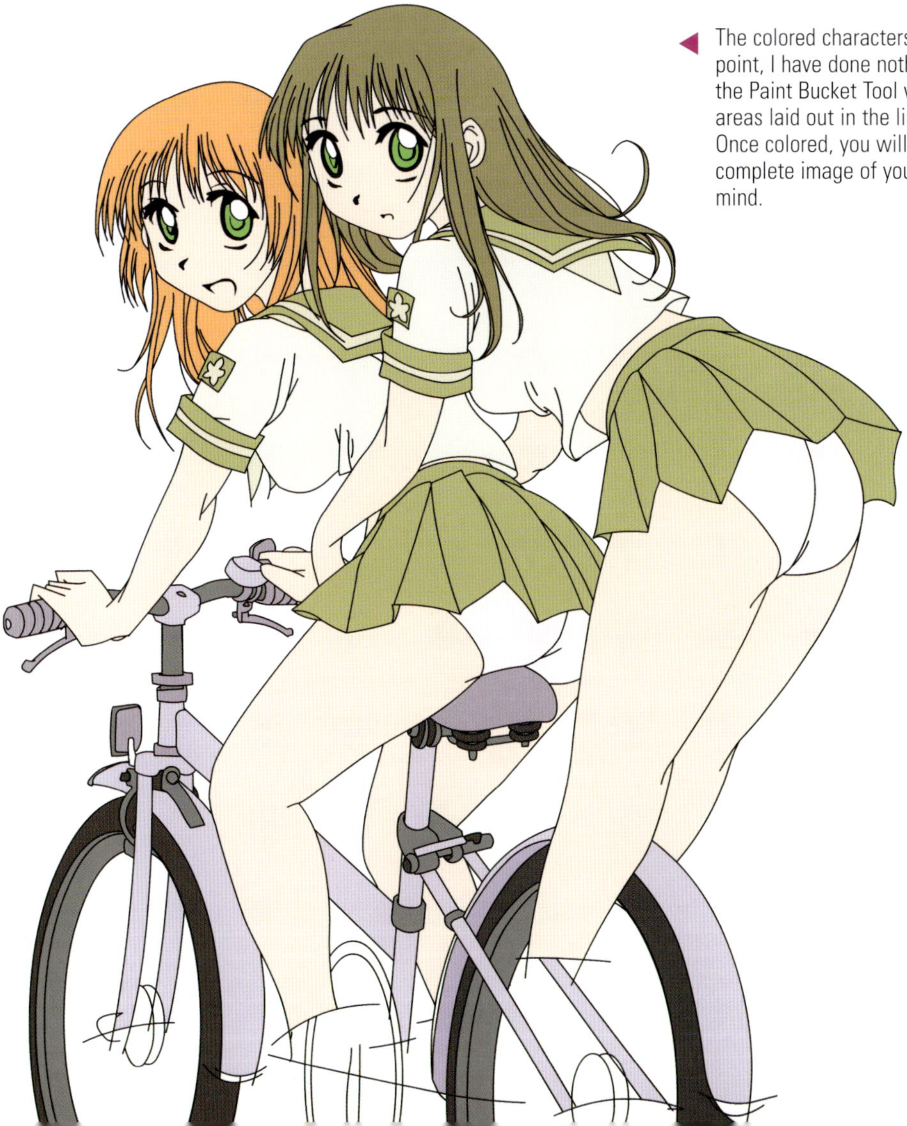

◀ The colored characters: Up to this point, I have done nothing but use the Paint Bucket Tool within the areas laid out in the line drawing. Once colored, you will have a more complete image of your piece in mind.

Painting Cell Animation-style Fills

Shading unlit areas is strictly essential.

Next, we draw some fill lines. Shading unlit areas is essential, but we don't need to be too concerned with the particulars of the light source or its direction. If the results have depth and look good, that's sufficient. Fill lines around obviously uneven body areas like the elbows and knees are especially important, so try out a few different arrangements and choose the ones that look best.

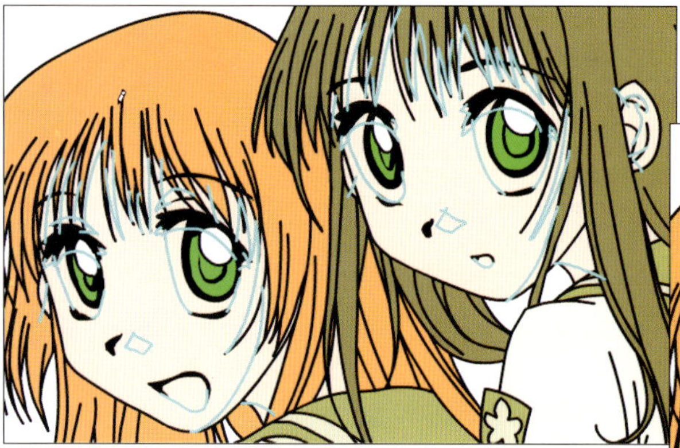

▲ Here's what the faces look like with the fill lines in place.

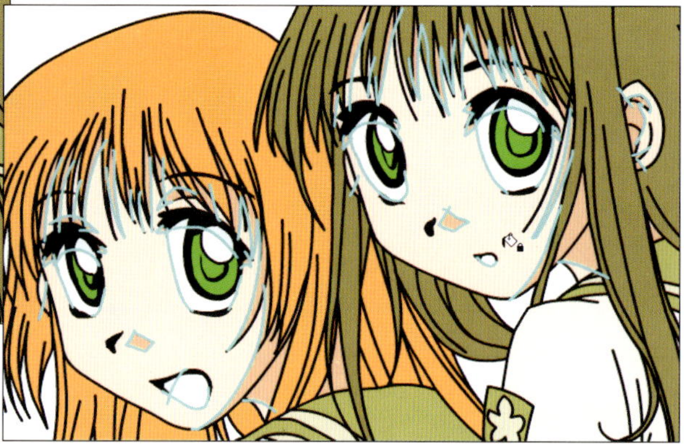

▲ Here they are after painting in the fills. Since you don't need them anymore, erase all the fill lines.

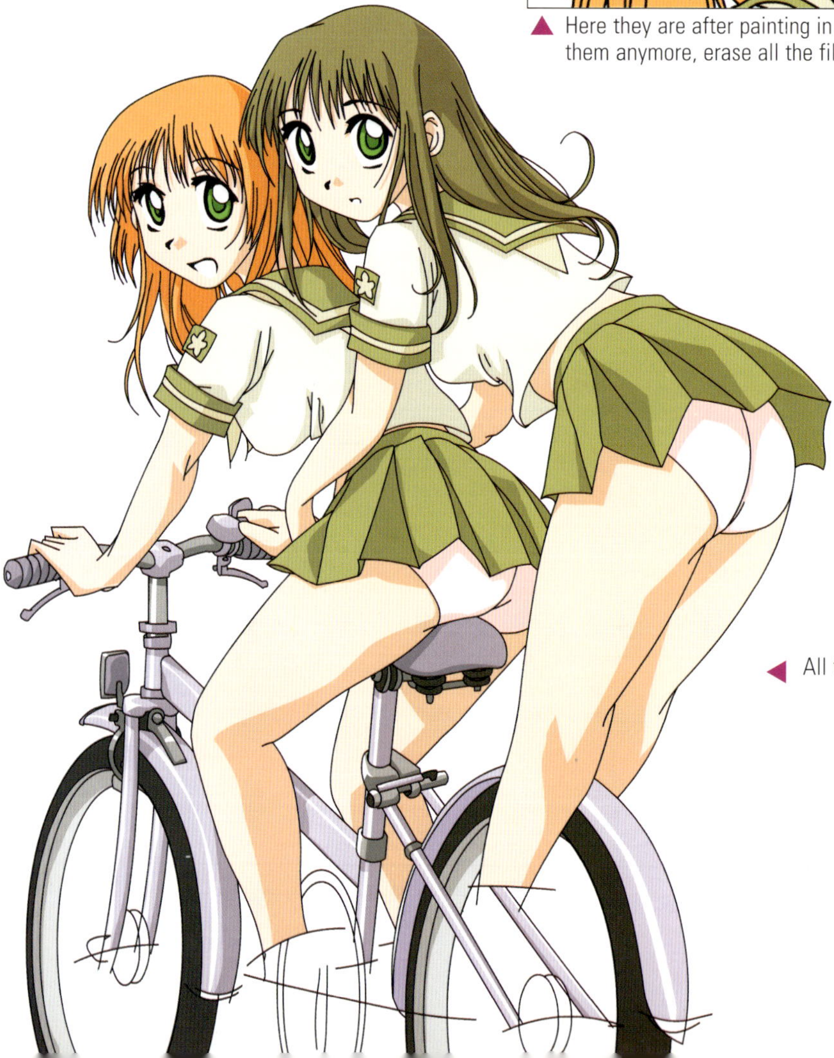

◀ All the fills are now complete.

Erasing fill lines efficiently

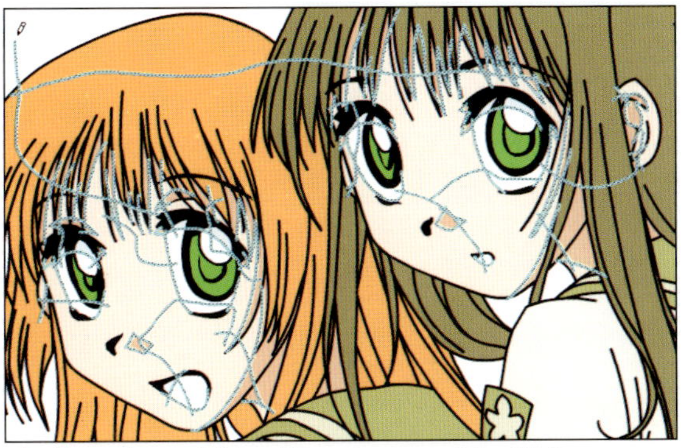

▲ If you draw additional lines to connect the fill lines, then you can select them all with one double-click.

When you're through painting your fills, erase the now unnecessary fill lines. You can erase them one at a time if you want, but that takes a lot of time and effort. If you unify your fill lines by drawing them in the same color, then you can select all the same-colored lines by double-clicking on them. After that you need only hit the Delete key to erase them in one swoop. Repeat this process and erase all the fill lines.

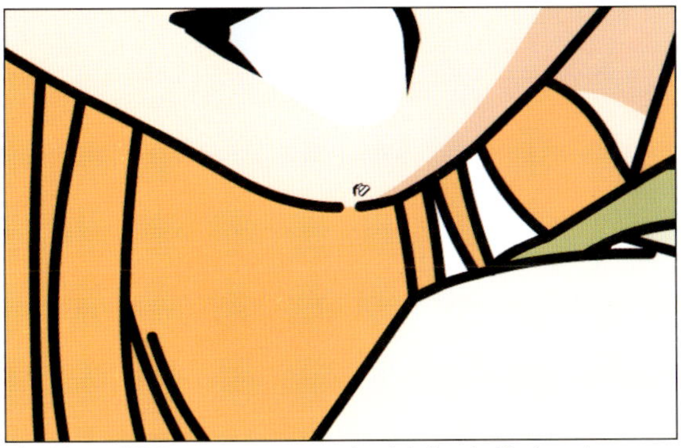

▲ If any fill lines get cut, use the Ink Bottle Tool and click on the broken area.

Here, a bit of the black borderline has accidentally been erased along with the blue fill lines. When this happens you mustn't forget to go back and repair the damage. Hit the "I" key to change over to the Eyedropper Tool, and sample a bit of nearby borderline. The cursor will change to the Ink Bottle Tool automatically; you can use it to reconnect the two broken lines by clicking between them.

Point
You can use this method if the broken section is part of a fill line.

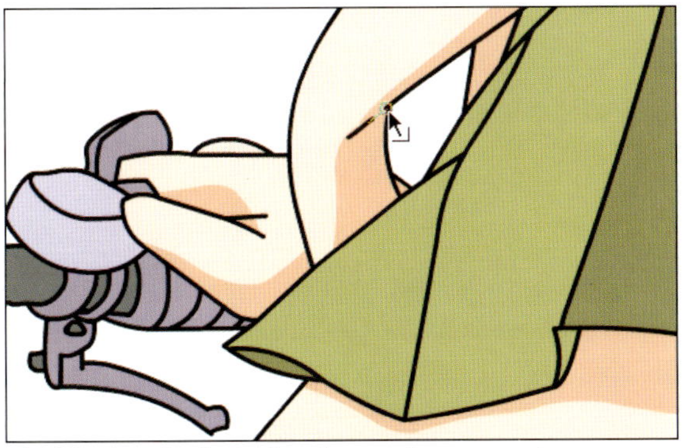

▲ If both ends of a broken line are the same color, you can't use this method to repair them. However, you can reconnect them by pressing Ctrl and dragging the ends together.

Point
Unless they are fill lines, if both ends of a broken line are the same color, you cannot use the Ink Bottle Tool to repair them.

Expressing Subtle Shadows and Accenting Shades

Use gradients sparingly.

Artwork filled in a cell animation-style feels flat, so we're going to apply some gradations to give ours a sense of substance. However, this doesn't mean it's alright to apply them all over everything. Instead, use them sparingly to greater effect.

The darkened area cast by one object onto another by blocking a source of light is a "shadow," and is best left as is. A "shade" is a darkened area that is not directly exposed to a light source-this is where we should apply a gradation.

Point
In situations where we have both shades and shadows, we leave the shadows alone and gradate the shades.

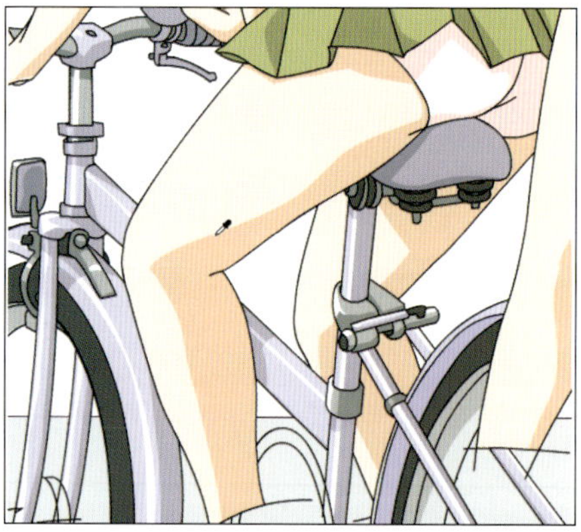

▲ Here, the darkened area of the thigh has two parts: one is blocked from the light source by the bicycle seat (a shadow), and one is simply on the side opposite the light source (a shade).

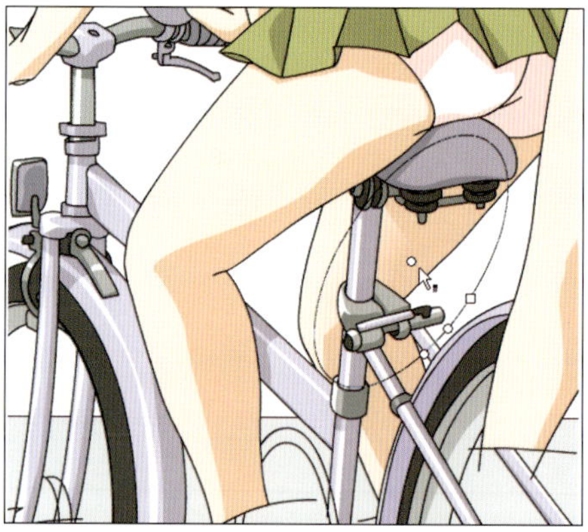

▲ Apply a gradation to the shaded area.

Creating gradations

Once your fills are done, making gradations with which to shade them is easy. Use the following method with the Color Mixer to create them.

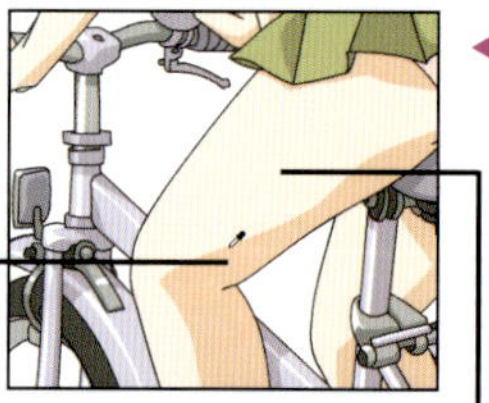

◀ Sample a color from your image with the Eyedropper Tool.

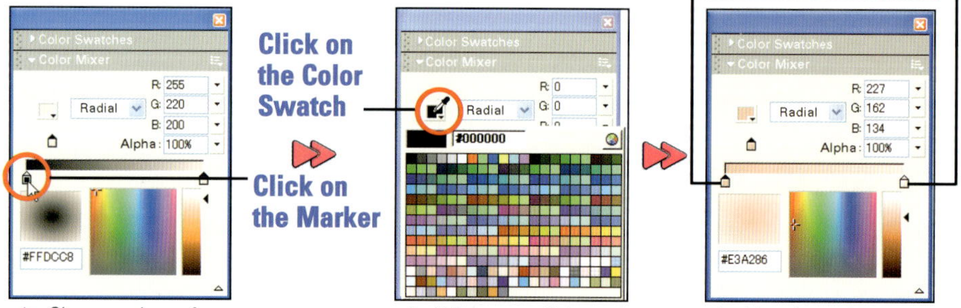

▲ Choose a base for your new gradation from the preloaded Color Space shown here, and click on the marker you want to change.

▲ When you click on the Color Swatch your cursor will turn into the Eyedropper Tool.

▲ Use the same process to sample both the lighter color and the darker color from your image as shown here. You have now created a gradation between the two colors.

Put a Little Red on the Cheeks for a Lively, Fresh Expression

Apply a light red gradation around the right and left cheekbones.

Reddening the cheeks is also done with a gradation.

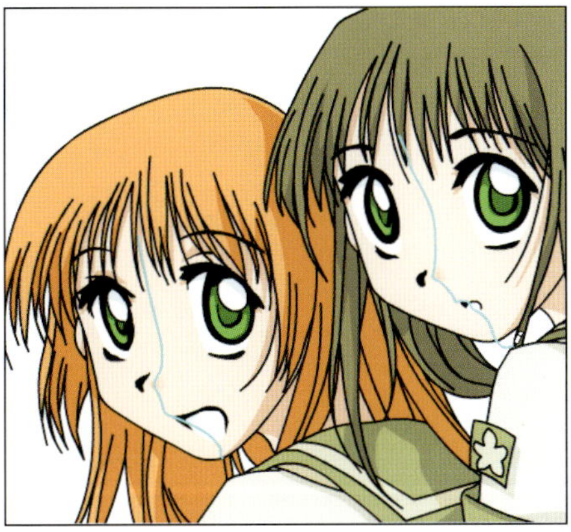

▲ To redden the cheeks with a gradation, first divide the faces in half with fill lines.

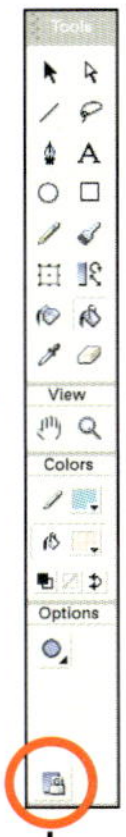

Lock Fill Off

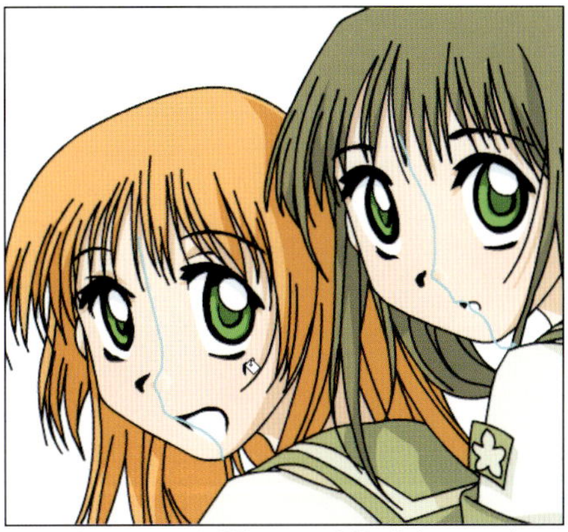

▲ With the Lock Fill set to Off, click on each right and left cheek.

Transform Fill Tool

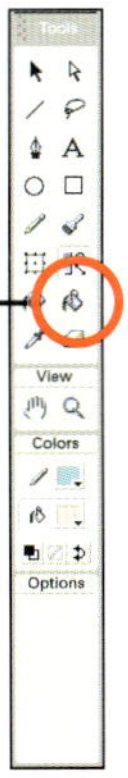

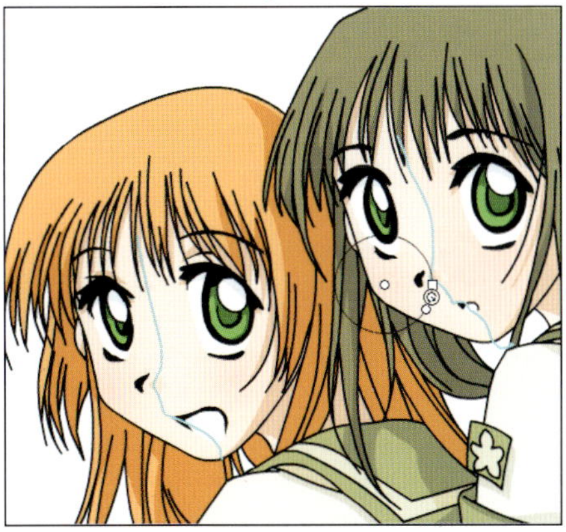

▲ Use the Transform Fill Tool to adjust the shape of the gradation and conceal its borders. Try to make the cheeks blush red a bit.

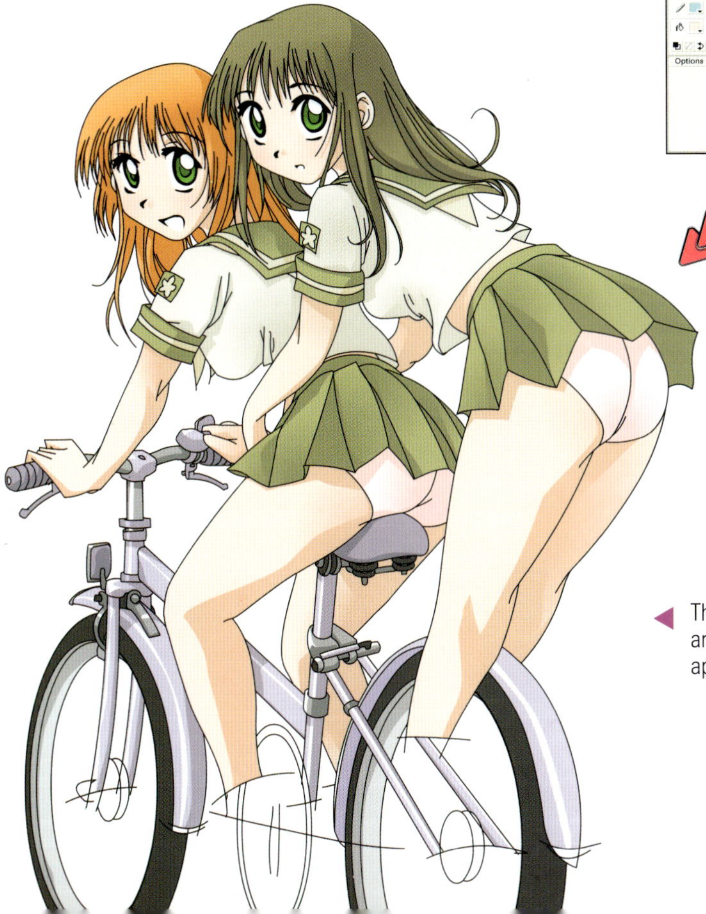

◀ The gradations are now fully applied.

Point

If you leave the Lock Fill modifier in the On position, then all the separate gradations will be connected to one another. You will lose all separation of the right and left cheeks, so remember to turn the Lock Fill off.

Highlighting

Stack a new layer on top for the highlights.

Create a new layer on top of your image to hold your highlights and use the Brush Tool to draw them. The highlights themselves are radial gradations that are white in the center and fade to transparency around the edges. We can use these to easily add natural highlighting to our image.

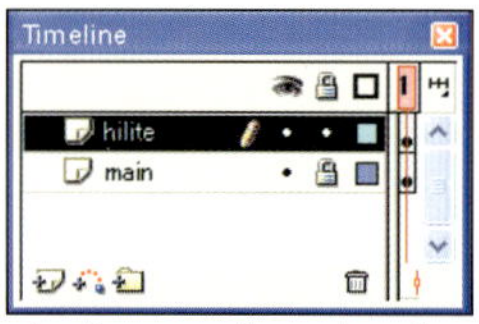

▲ Create a layer just for your highlights on top of the layer you've used so far to hold your character.

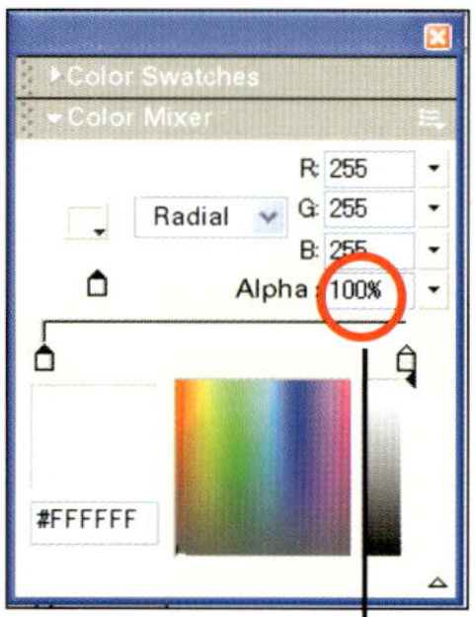

Lowering the Alpha value makes a gradation more transparent.

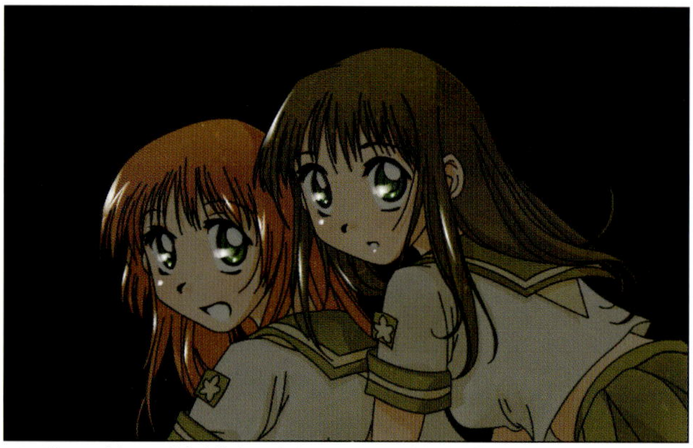

▲ Here, I have highlighted the eyes and hair. So you can easily see the highlights, I've slightly darkened the lower layer.

I've added highlights to the legs and the bike as well using the same methods. This looks much more three dimensional. ▶

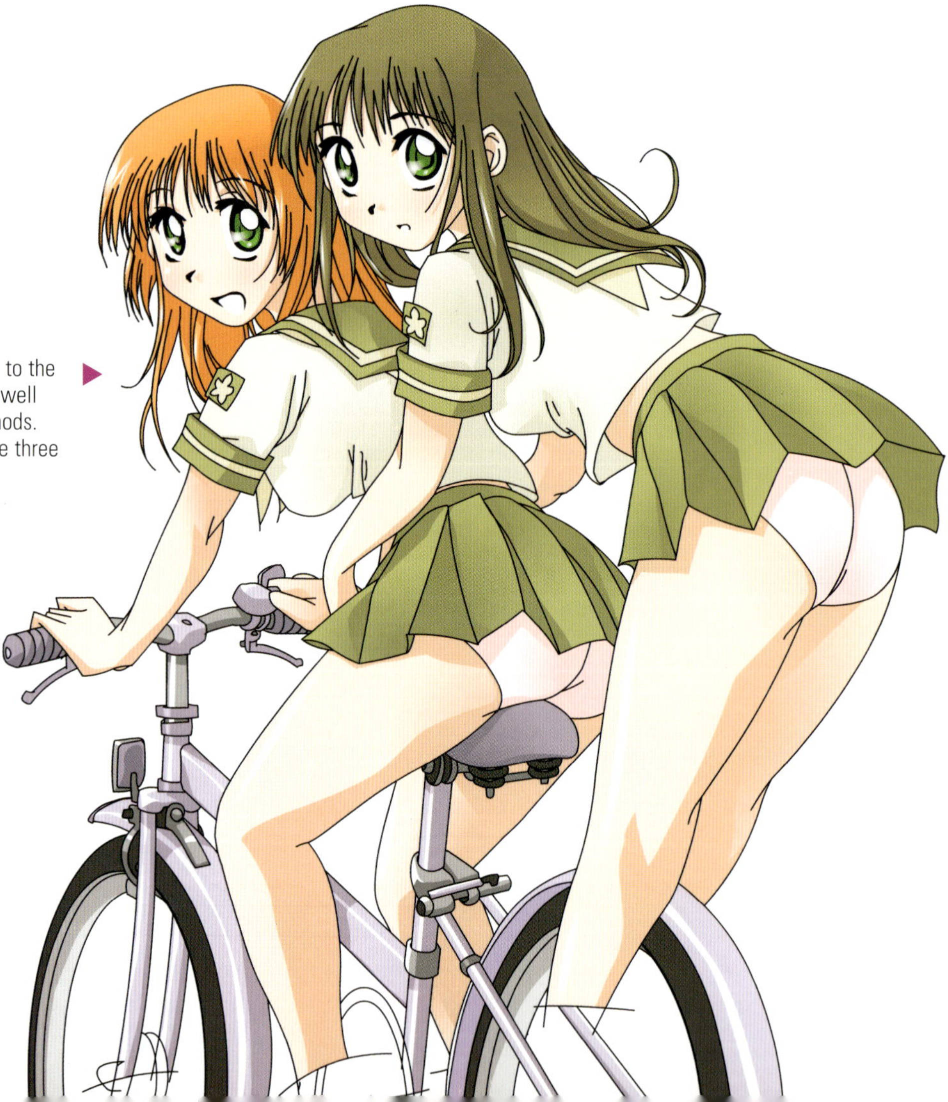

Composing the Foreground and Background

How to use a pre-made Photoshop image

I have drawn the background, sky, and foreground grass in Photoshop and imported them. Since Flash renders images using vector data, its files tend to be very small. Even someone in a slower network environment can quickly display something done in Flash, which is an advantage. However, these images here are all bit maps (e.g. non-vector data), so if we use too many of them the file size will increase considerably. We want to limit that as much as possible, so use bit maps sparingly.

▲ This is the JPEG background image I've saved. You want a picture that won't pixelate too badly when it's blown up, so choose something hazy.

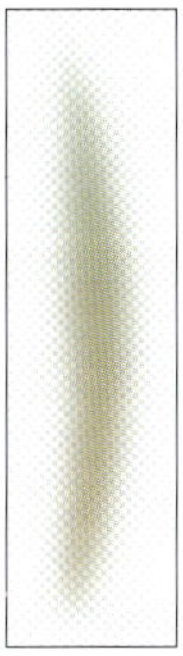

▲ I'd like to arrange the grass in the foreground in a slightly haphazard pattern, allowing the characters to show through the gaps. So, I'll save the grass as a PNG image, since that format can store Alpha values.

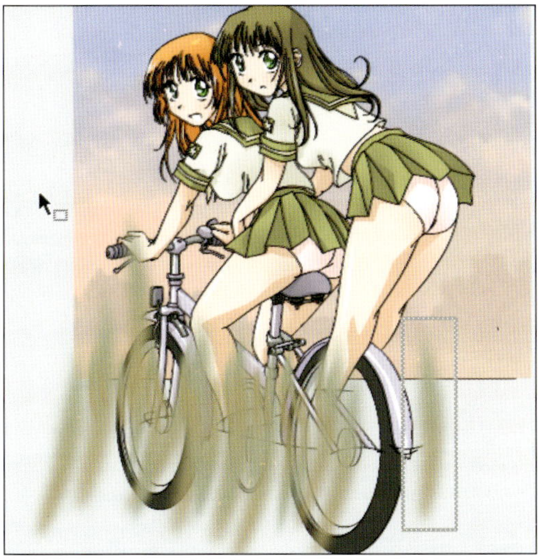

▲ Create new layers below and above your character layer, and insert the background and foreground into each, respectively. I'm trying to create increased variety in the grass by using Scale and Rotate.

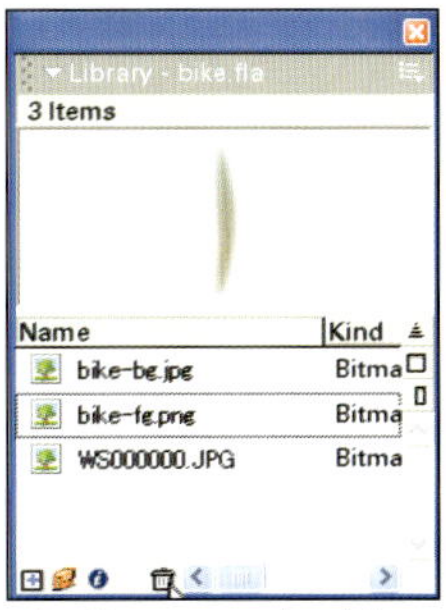

▲ Be sure to load images you want to use again in the future into the Library.

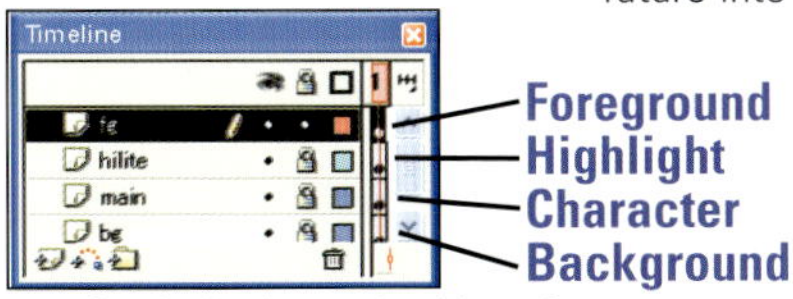

▲ Stack the layers in this order.

Point
By saving images you intend to import at JPEG's, you can reduce their file size. By copying and reusing the same, smaller image inside Flash to make a larger picture, you can keep your overall file size from getting too big.

Point
Compared to JPG's, PNG images have a larger file size, and they store translucency values poorly at low resolutions. So to keep my project's file size under control, I've decided to draw just one slightly oversized "blade" of grass to copy and use repeatedly inside Flash.

Point
Import your background and foreground images using File → Open as Library. You can keep overall file sizes under control by reusing images loaded into your library. Just by using the Scale and Rotate modifiers, you can create a surprising array of variations on a single image.

Composing the Foreground and Background, Continued

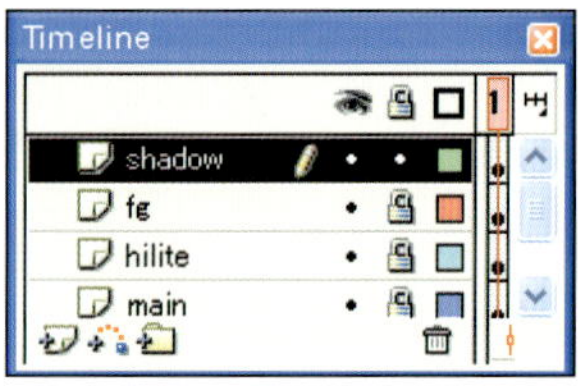

▲ Add a new "Effects" layer to the top of the stack.

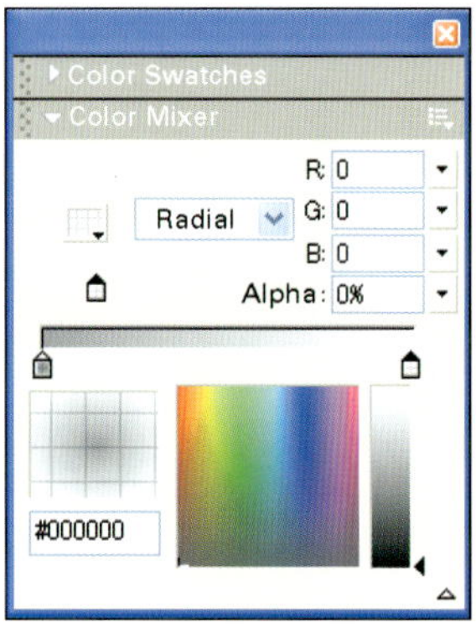

▲ Create a new gradation between semi-transparent black and completely clear.

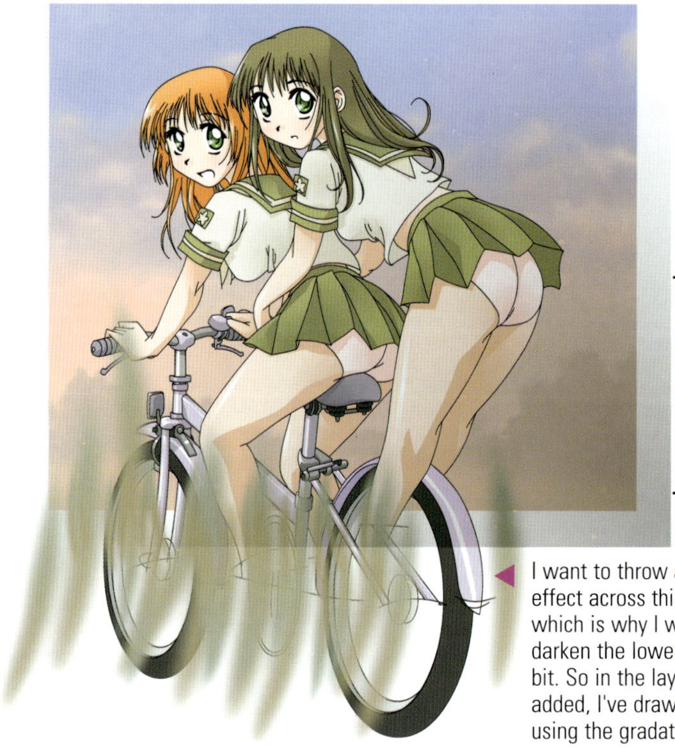

This area gets darker.

◀ I want to throw a shadow effect across this whole image, which is why I wanted to darken the lower right corner a bit. So in the layer I've just added, I've drawn a square using the gradation to the left.

Cutting out your work

Depending on the length and breadth (or the "aspect ratio") of the browser window used to view your drawing, parts of it that hang off the edge of the Stage may be visible. Conceal those parts with a Mask.

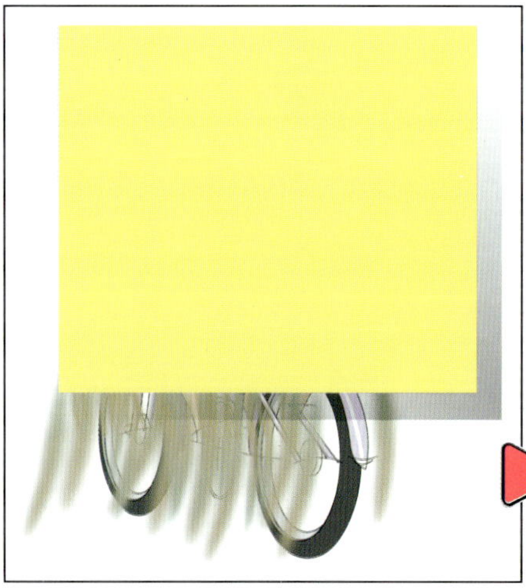

▲ Insert yet another new layer at the top of the stack and in it draw a rectangle the same size as your drawing in an appropriate color.

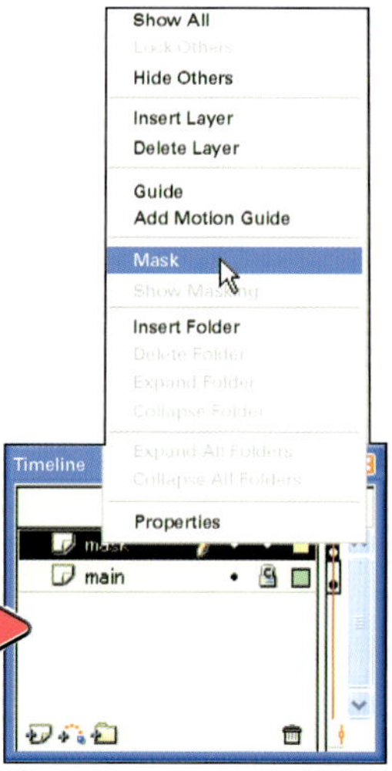

▲ Change the new layer to a Mask as shown here.

Point
The Mask layer's effects are present only when the layer is locked.

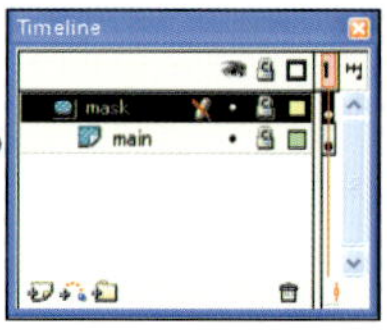

▲ Lock the layer, and anything beyond the edge of the mask will not be displayed.

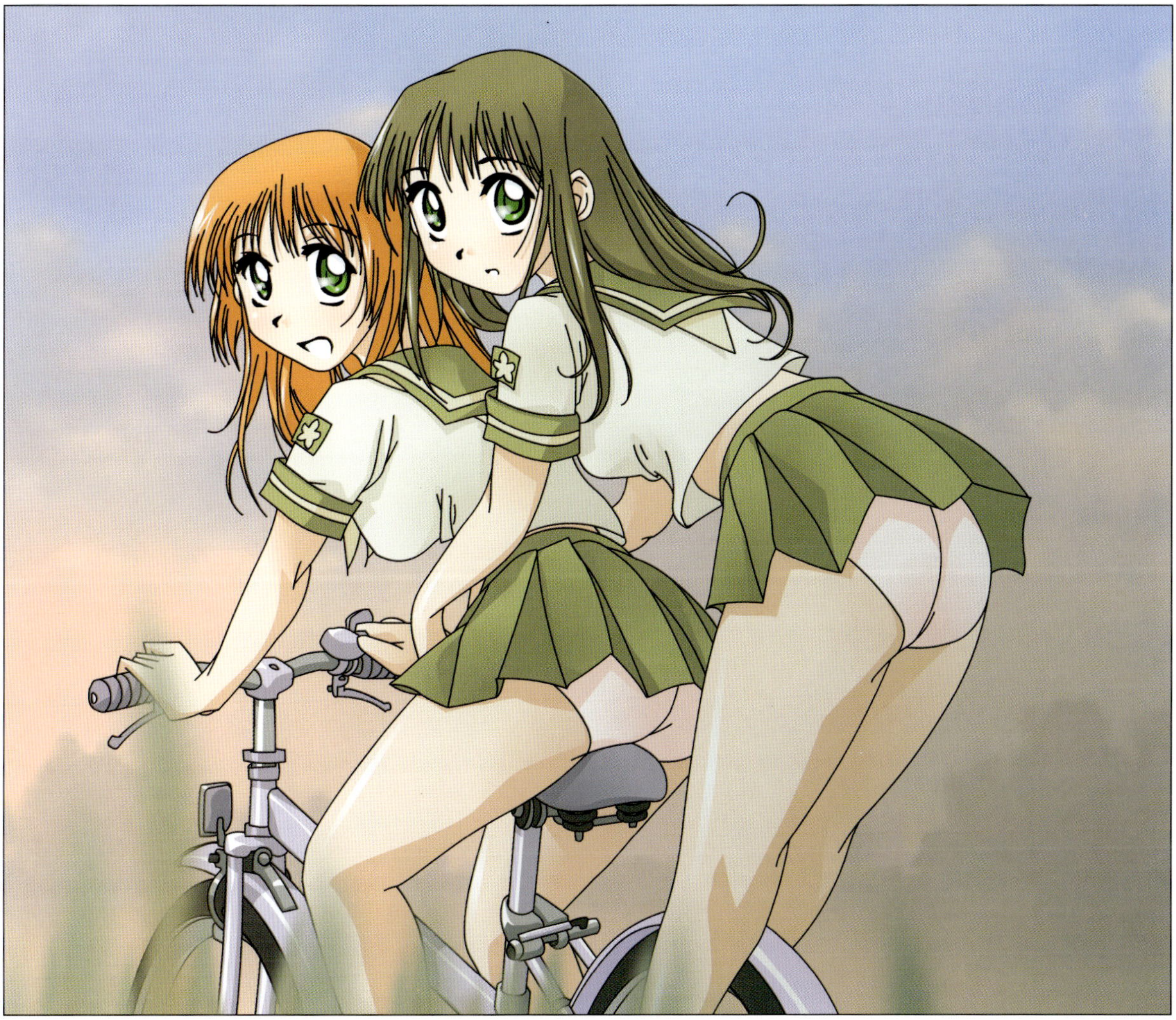

▲ At this point, our Flash work is done-the picture is completed.

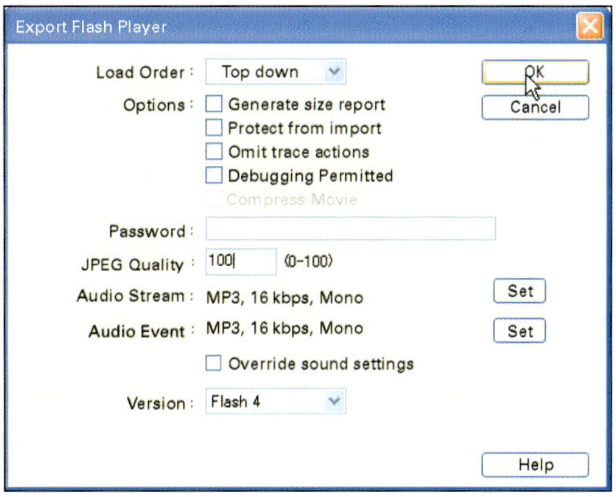

▲ Save your work as a Flash Movie (an SWF file) with File → Export Movie, and choose Top Down as your Load Order. This is necessary because if you display the bottom layer first, the areas off-stage that are supposed to be hidden by the Mask will be visible.

Post-Completion Color Adjustment

Blanket color changes are difficult in Flash itself—use my freeware instead.

From here on in I'll be using a freeware tool I wrote, "SWFPAL," to further adjust the colors in my picture. SWFPAL is a tool that can read SWF files and change their associated color palettes. With this tool you can make the bothersome task of making blanket changes to all your colors in Flash easier. Since SWFPAL changes the palette colors, you can use it on Flash movies, too.
SWFPAL freeware is available for download from my home page,
http://www.momiji.sakura.ne.jp/~3x/index-e.html

I will be putting out a version for the Macintosh as soon as possible.

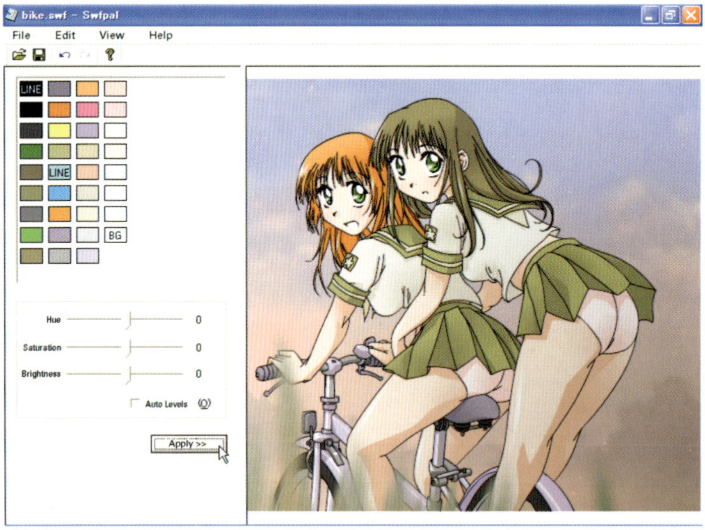

▲ When you load a Flash movie (an SWF file), the colors used are displayed in a table at the upper left, and a preview image is displayed on the right.

Point
Line colors are indicated by "LINE" and background colors are indicated by "BG." Colors with no markings are normal fills. If the Preview doesn't seem to be displaying properly, try hitting the Refresh key at the bottom left.

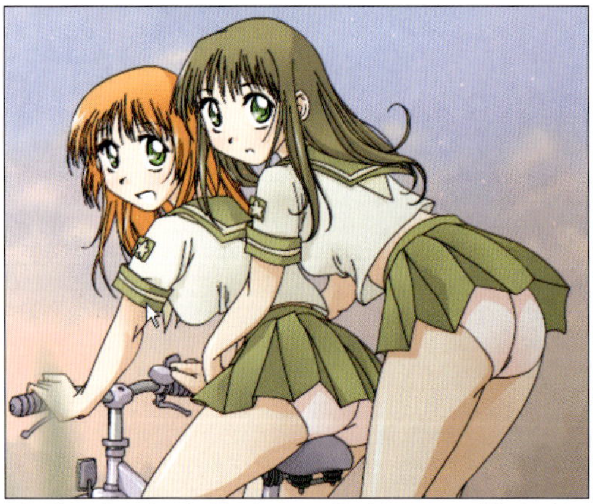

▲ Use the simple Eyedropper Tool (press and hold Alt and click on the preview image) to select the color you want to change. However, with semi-transparent layers or special color effects, it's easy to accidentally sample the wrong color this way. If that happens, take a good look at the color table in the upper left and find your color there.

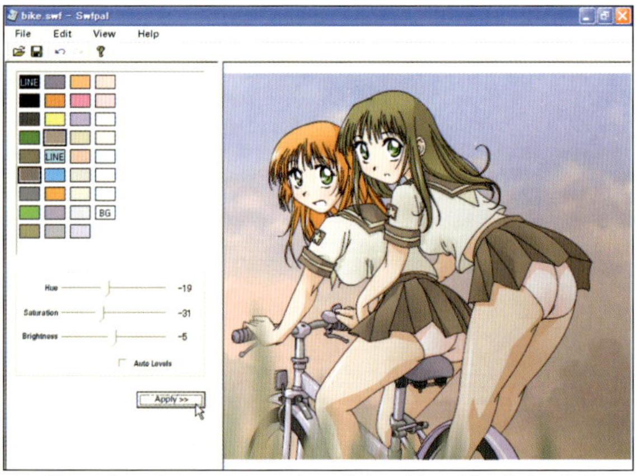

▲ Here, I've changed the color of the skirts. The Color Balance interface is basically the same as the Color Picker tool in Photoshop. Use the three sliders at the lower left, "Hue," "Saturation," and "Brightness" to adjust your colors. Pressing the Refresh button gives you a preview on the right side of the screen that shows the effects of the changes you make.

Point
It is not possible to adjust images loaded as JPEG's or PNG's with SWFPAL.

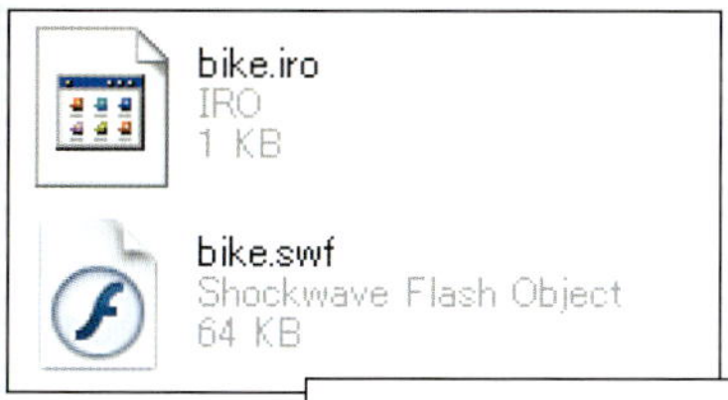


```
[SWFPAL SCRIPT]
@fill #b9bcfb -> #4f4248
@fill #04751e -> #047121
@fill #c28ca7 -> #5c6659
@fill #445b66 -> #435864
.
.
@fill #ffffff -> #fefefe
@fill #4e8ee7 -> #8ca9c1
[END]
```

Retouching your Work in Flash

Using SWFPAL will probably make you want to go back and do some detailing, like taking care of small, unpainted areas. If you do, be sure to create and save the new color table by choosing File → Color Table → Save.

When you're done editing your SWF file in Flash and return to SWFPAL, if you choose File → Color Table → Open and import your new color table, you can save yourself the time of editing it all over again.

◀ Color tables are written to disk with an ".iro" file extension. The contents are a simple text file indicating which colors have been changed into what.

Completion!

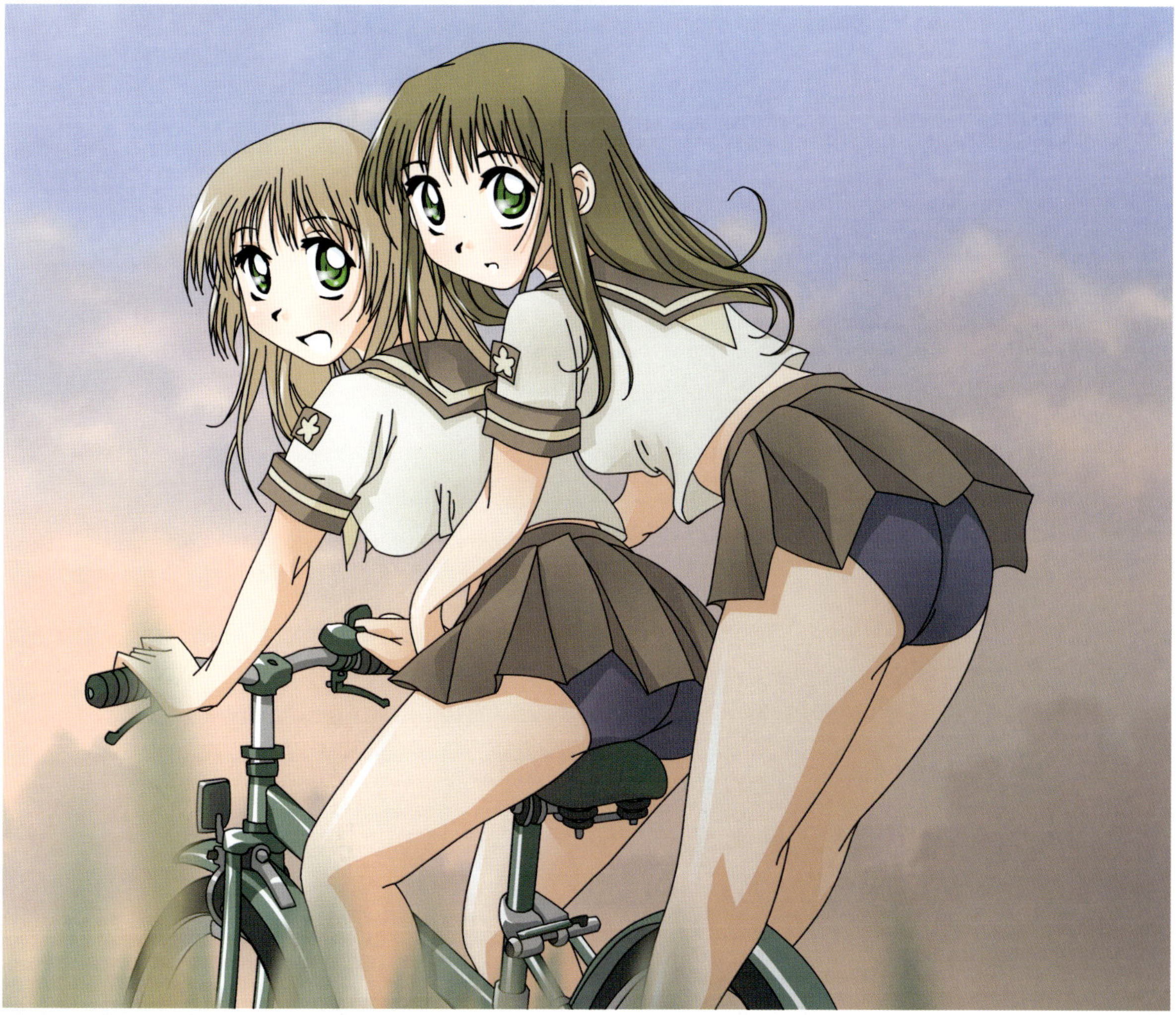

▲ I turned their underwear into bloomers, adjusted the color of their hair and the bike to match the background, and lowered the saturation level. Now it's done.

Putting your Creation on the Web

Using browser frames is an easy way to present your work.

There are basically two ways to put your creation on the Web: using the "<a>" tag and using the "<embed>" tag. The easiest way is creating a link to your work using the <a> tag. When someone clicks on it, your creation will be displayed, taking up the entire browser window. Browsers can directly display SWF files, so if all you want to do is show off your work, that's enough—your creation will automatically grow or shrink to fit the browser window.

Next, we will apply this functionality and explain how to use frames to show off your work along with text, icons, or other media.

Point

The <a> tag has the advantage of allowing a user to download your work by right-clicking on the link. If you use the <embed> tag to embed a Flash movie in HTML, most people won't know how to download it and you'll be inundated with e-mail saying, "Tell me how to download this stuff!" If you choose the <embed> tag to display your work, you would be both wise and kind to have an <a> tag in there reading, "Downloads here!"

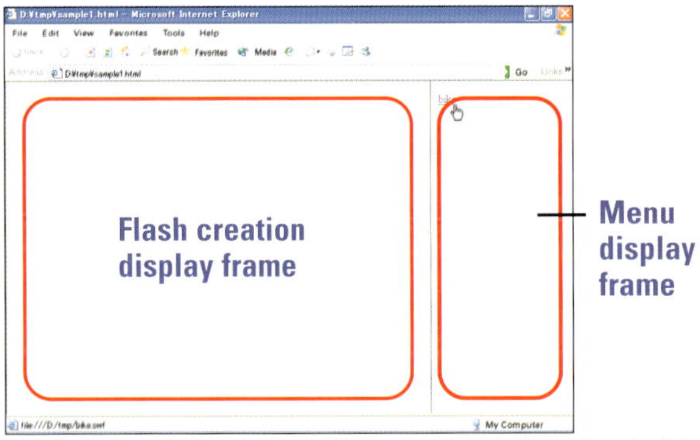

▲ Split the window into two frames: a "menu frame" and a "display frame." Specify the width of the menu frame only. When I load the sample1.html file, it will be framed as above, and the right frame will be loaded with the "menu.html" file.

```
frameset cols="*,200">
<frame src="" name="left">
<frame src="menu.html" name="right">
</frameset>
```

▲ HTML example: sample1.html

```
<a href="bike.swf" target="left">bike</a>
```

▲ HTML example: menu.html
Here, the name of the project is "bike.swf," and the title is "bike."

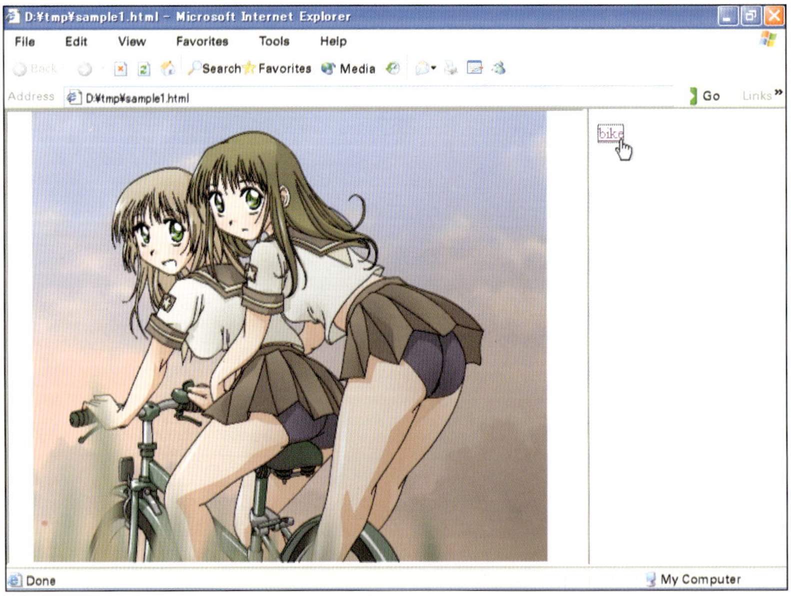

◀ Clicking on the title of my piece in the menu frame, "bike," brings it up in the display frame on the left.

Three Case Studies of Using the <embed> Tag

● Specifying the display size of your work

Use the <embed> tag when you want to have more control over the way your work is displayed or when you want to combine your work with some other media, such as text. In the HTML file that File → Publish automatically produces, <embed> and <object> tags are nested inside complex structures, but for the pieces like the ones we're making in this book, using just the <embed> tag is sufficient.

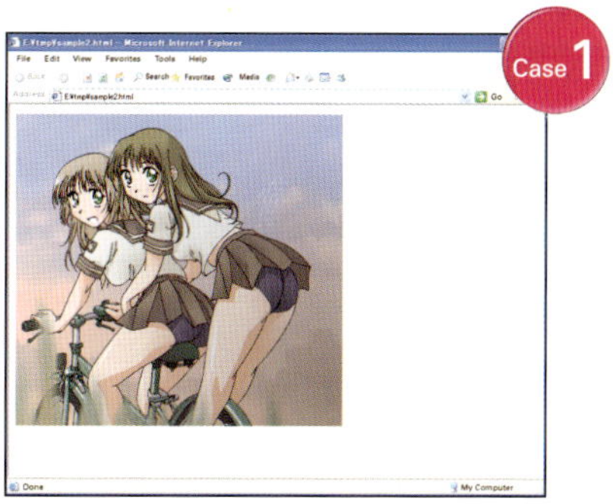

▲ Here, the image is displayed at the specified width and height. When you display your work with text, write <embed> tags into the HTML source where you want it to be displayed.

```
<embed src=bike.swf            ← Flash movie file name
width=500                      ← Display width
height=480                     ← Display height
type=application/x-shockwave-flash   ← We don't need this, either, but we'll leave it in
></embed>                              just in case (everything else below is omitted).
```

▲ **Case 1:** An example of the simplest <embed> tag usage.

● Displaying your work without leaving any white space in the window

Since we are able to freely enlarge or shrink the pictures we draw in Flash to match our viewers' environment, let's get creative with our tag usage and try to find the most effective way to display our work at maximum size. We should be able to take a picture and leave completely different impressions on our viewers by changing its size.

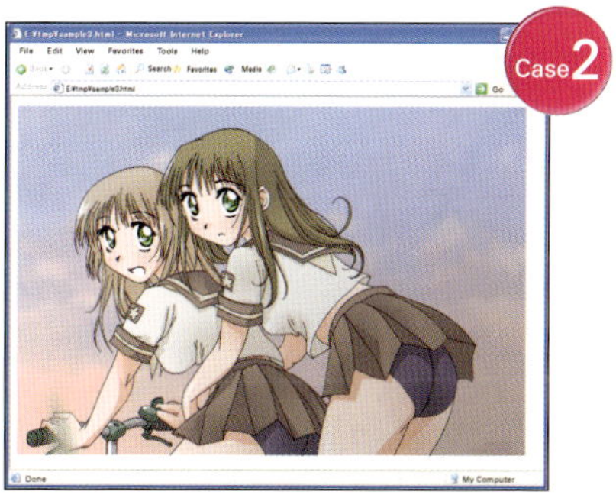

▲ Images are enlarged (or shrunk) such that they leave no white space when displayed. There are no scroll bars, either, so anything beyond the edge of the window won't be displayed.

```
<embed src=bike.swf                 ← Flash movie file name
width=100% height=99%               ← Specify width and height as a percentage
scale=noborder salign=t></embed>
```

▲ **Case 2:** An example of displaying without leaving any white space in the window. With the specification "scale=noborder," you are directing the browser to enlarge your piece such that it leaves no white space. You can specify the alignment of your piece with the "salign" attribute. Setting salign to "t" aligns it with the top of the screen, "b" with the bottom, before enlargement.

● Matching your work to the width of the browser and enlarging or shrinking the display to fit

By adding in some JavaScript, we can detect a browser's width and enlarge or shrink the display of our work to fit. If your piece is particularly long, then the viewer can use the scroll bar to look at the whole thing.

```
<head>
<script language="JavaScript">
<!--
// Find out the browser's width
function getClientWidth() {
  if (navigator.appName.charAt(0) == "M") {
    return document.body.clientWidth;
  } else {
    return window.innerWidth;
  }
}
// Match the width to the browser and display the SWF file
function showSWF(name, w0, h0) {
  w = getClientWidth() - 30; // Add a little extra width
  h = h0 * (w / w0);         // Compute the height

  document.write("<embed src=", name);
  document.write(" width=", w, " height=", h);
  document.write(" type=application/x-shockwave-
flash></embed>");
}
//-->
</script>
</head>
<body>
<script language="JavaScript">
  showSWF("bike.swf", 500, 480);
</script>
```

▲ **Case 3:** An example of using JavaScript to match the width of a piece to the browser window and then blowing it up.

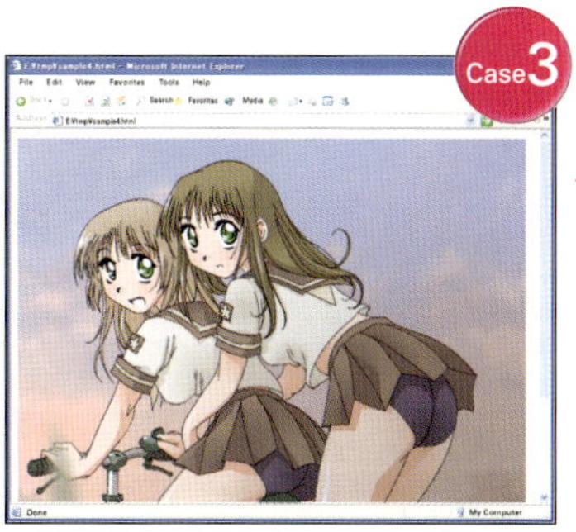

◀ If your piece goes beyond the bottom window, you can scroll up and down it with the scrollbar.

Gallery

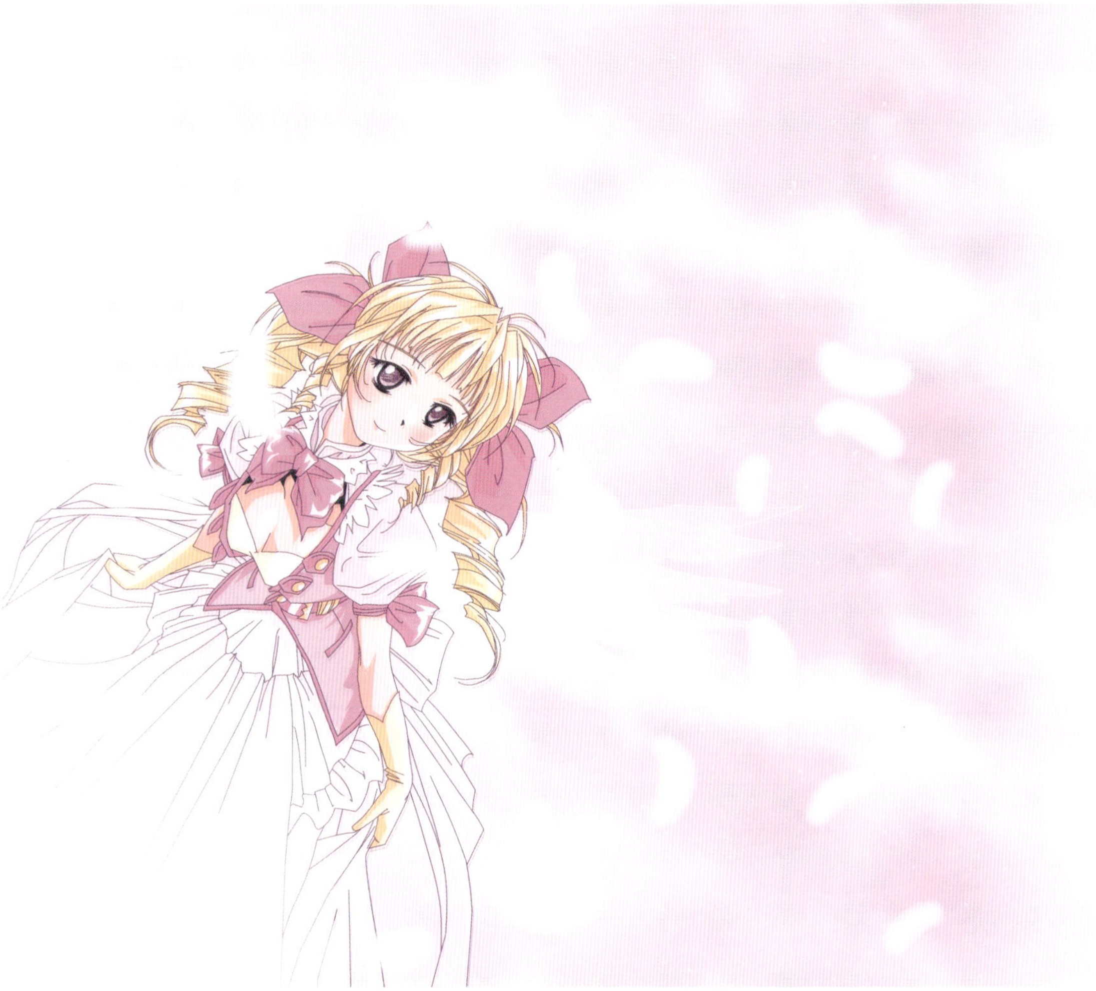

Umm, this one's double exposed, but that's no mistake. On a computer screen, I think this piece is really nice—it has a cell animation-like translucent feel to it. But I was really worried that maybe it wouldn't turn out well in print, hence the double exposure. Also, by expanding or contracting the white space to the right, I can be sure that the layout of this piece won't fall apart, even if it's displayed at a different aspect ratio.

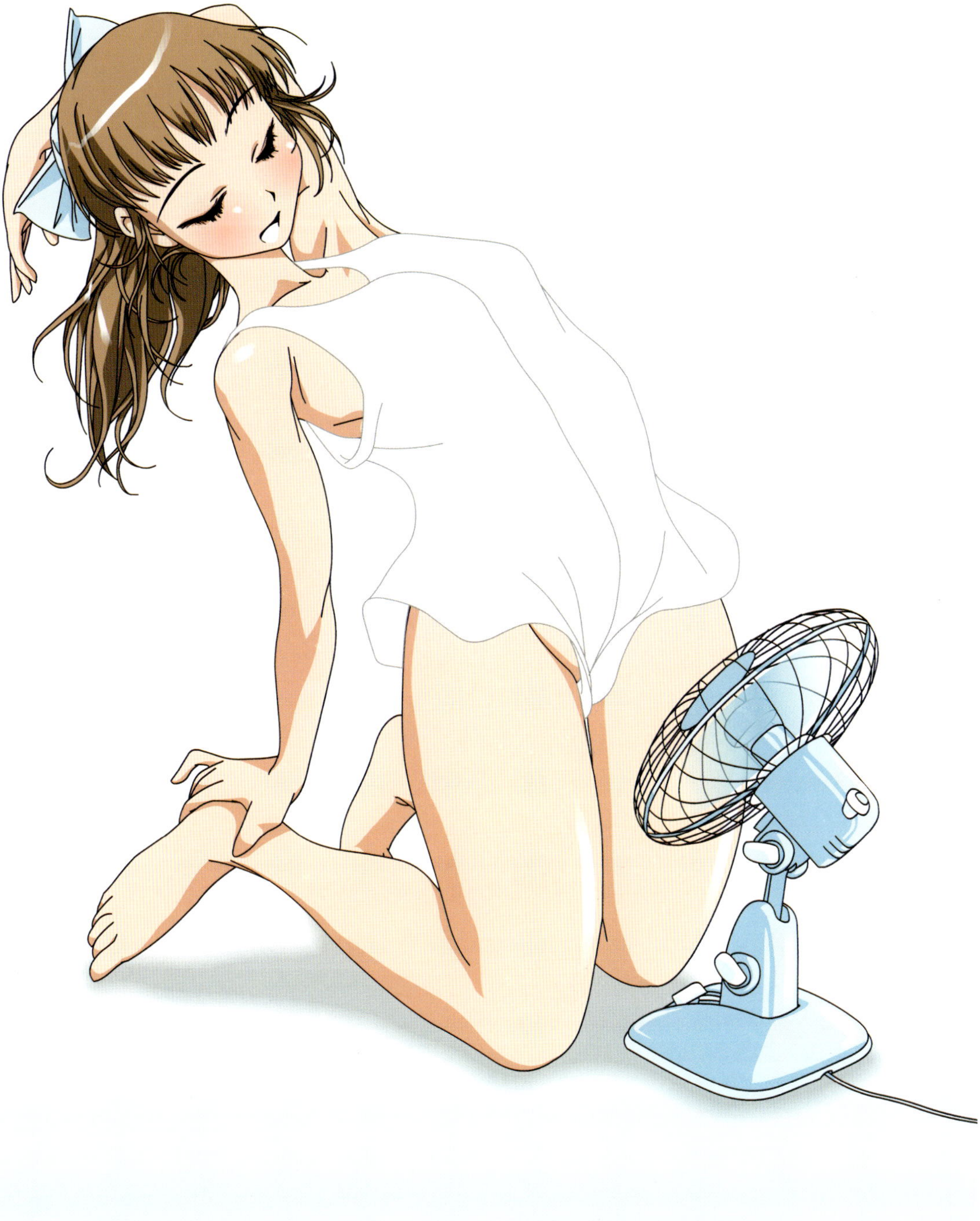

This is a summer greeting card from 2001. "God, I just want to cool down..." is the idea behind this one, so at first I drew a nude girl in front of the fan. But then I thought she looked like she'd catch cold if her stomach got too chilly, so I ended up putting some clothes on her.

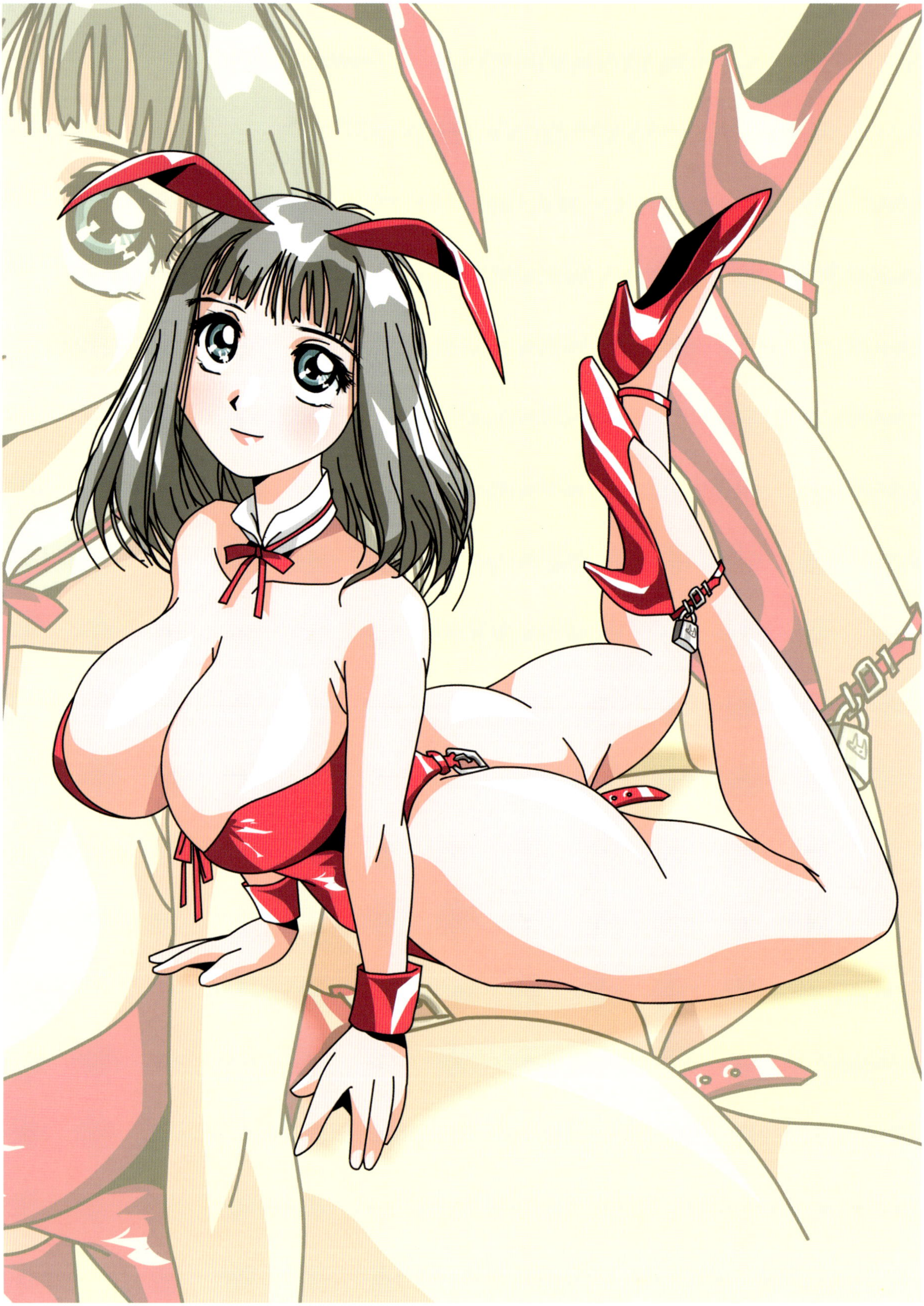

I love bunny girls—I'm constantly drawing them. Whenever I do a layout with a human character at its center, I imagine the browser's aspect ratio can be however big it wants to be. But then somehow, I end up with a picture where the character's pose is almost nonsensically bent into a boxlike shape. Looks a little uncomfortable, doesn't it?

An Onimusume [Demon Maiden]. I drew this one in two hours flat. One of Flash's strengths is being able to turn out complete pieces quickly. It's perfect for me since I can never stick with anything very long. If you're someone who gets frustrated often by an inability to finish anything, then I highly recommend you give Flash a whirl.

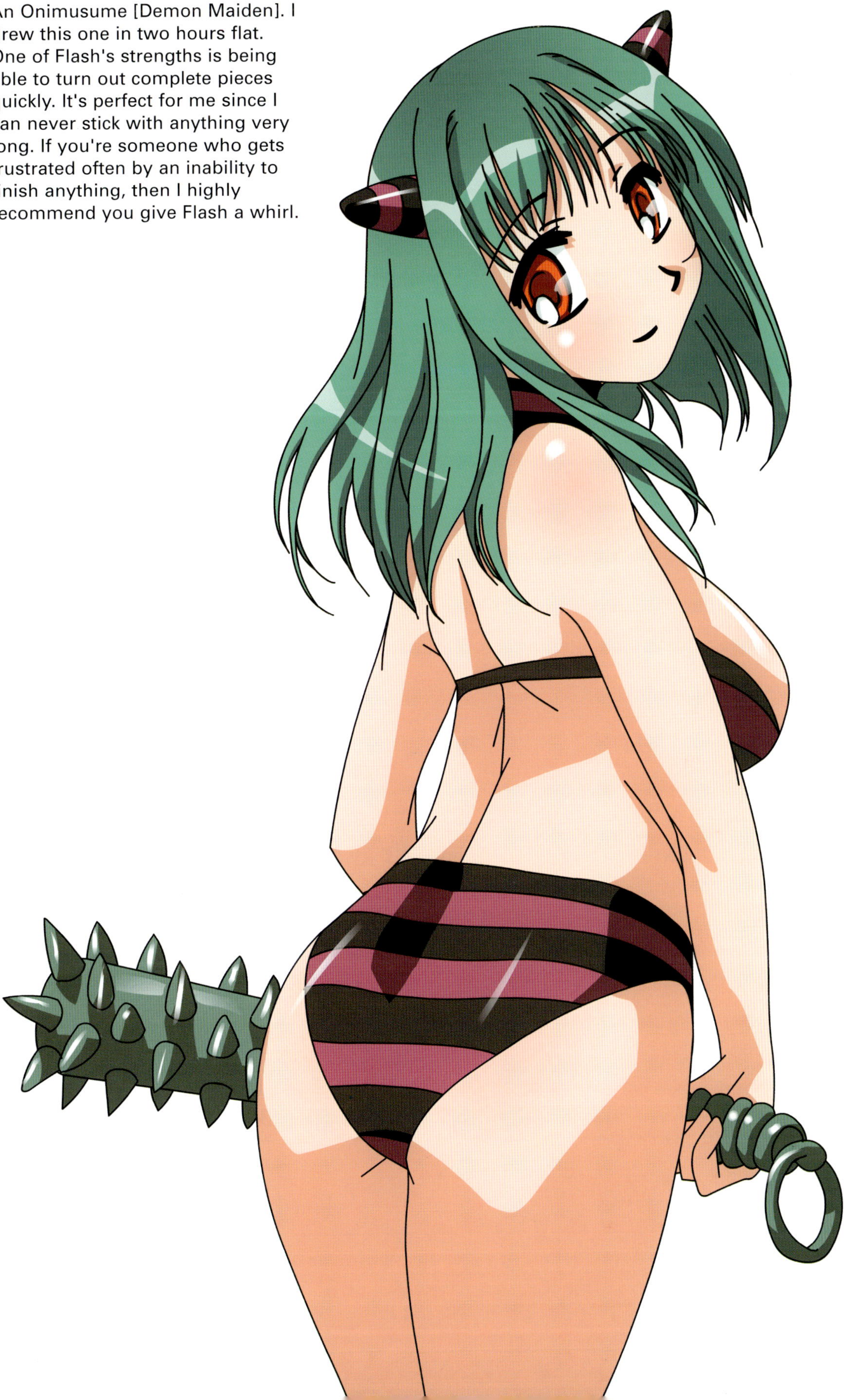

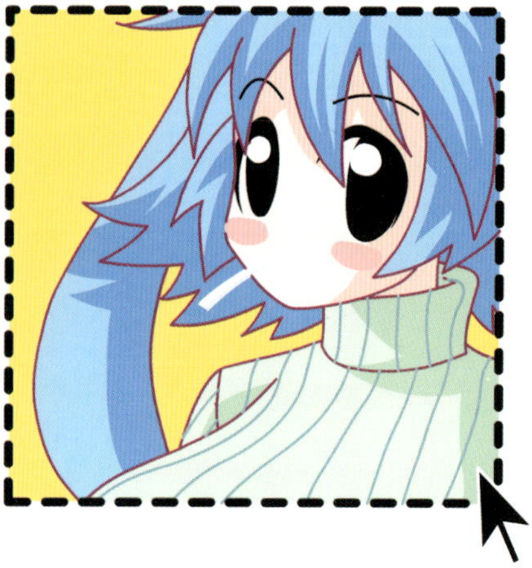

Penname
Mimori Yusa

I was born (in 1973) and raised in Osaka, and I'm still there—I haven't gone anywhere at all.

I'm a Virgo born in the Year of the Ox, so I tend to be a dreamer, constantly moving at my own pace.

Reason for getting into Flash
Stumbling across a website called Teru's World first got me interested. When I saw the graphics the site's operator, Teru, had created with Flash, I was stunned and smitten with the beauty of Flash. I still am. These days, Teru has become my mentor, and he helps me a great deal. Without him, I probably never would have gotten into Flash. Perhaps I still truly haven't.

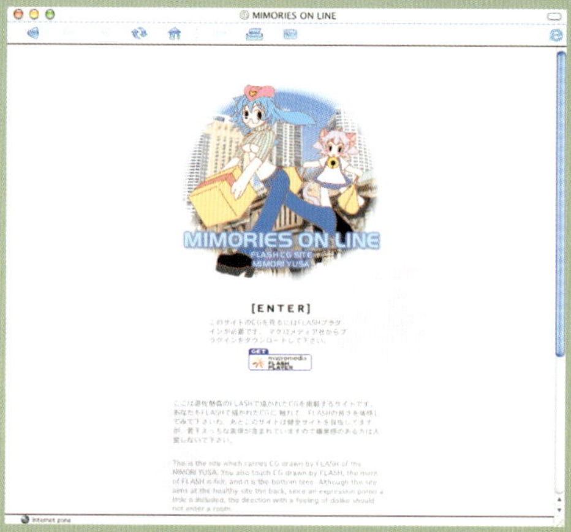

MIMORIES ON LINE
http://homepage3.nifty.com/mimoriesonline/

Favorite Bands
hide, Iron Thumb, Manowar, Arkenemy, Led Zeppelin

Favorite Anime
Marin & Meran, Mobile Suit Z Gundam, Furi Kuri

Favorite Manga Art and Artists
Hiroshi Tamaru("Choaniki," "Alps no Densetsu," "Legend of Black Heaven," "Rabu Yan")
Kunio Aoki ("Unicorn Maiden")
Natsuki Takaya ("Fruit Basket")
Nanpei Yamada ("Koucha Ouji")
Kan'on Yamazaki ("Keroro Gunso")
Kengo Yonekura ("Pink Sniper," "Yellow Hearts")
Miyuki Obayashi ("Hyaku Man Kai Kikasete Yo," "Angel Hunt")

Favorite Video Games
The Guilty Gear series
Metal Gear Solid
The Final Fantasy series (7 and up)

Machine Stats
OS: Windows 2000
CPU: 1.6 GHz AMD Athlon(tm)
Memory: 512MB
Monitor: 19" (1280x1024, 16 bit)
Devices: Wacom Tablet

Frequently Used Software
Flash 5
Flash MX
Fireworks 4
Photoshop 5.5

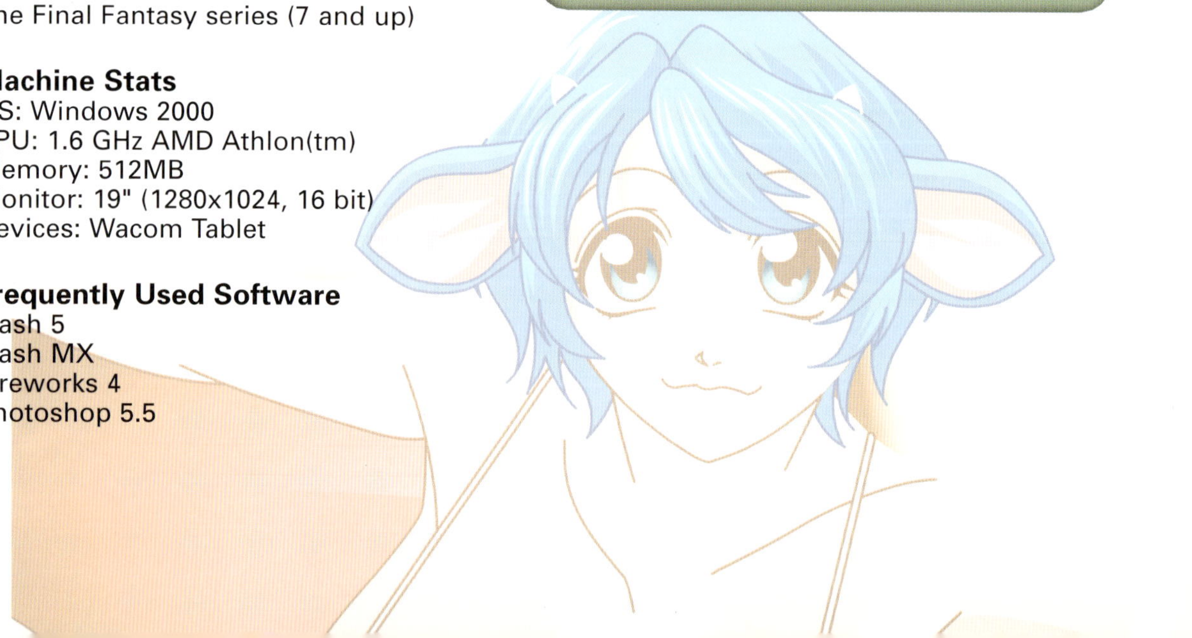

Preparing the Rough Sketch

Decide how big your project will be.

In Flash, the white part of the screen is called the Stage, and the size of it will be the size of our project (actually a Flash movie).

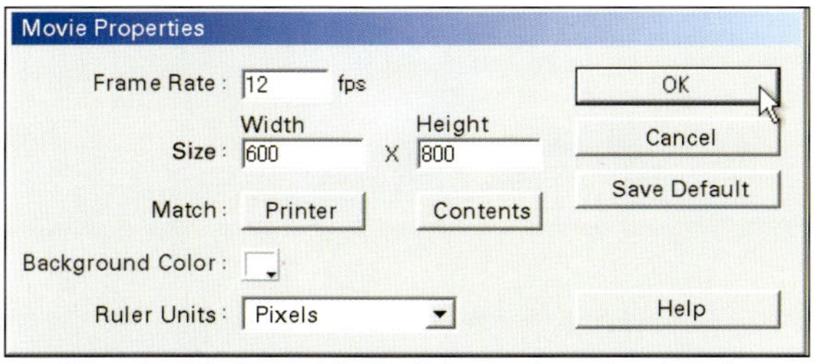

▲ Open the Modify → Movie dialog and set the size of your project.

Point
In Flash MX, set the project size in the Modify → Document → Document Properties dialog.

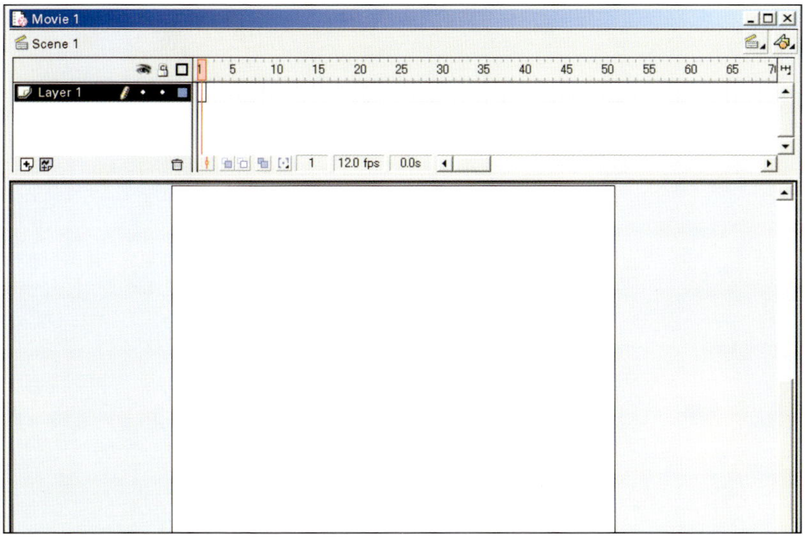

▲ I have successfully resized the Stage.

Point
By changing the Magnification, you can magnify detailed areas or look over your entire piece.
If you set the Magnification to Show All, it will auto adjust so that you can see everything.

Scenes?

Flash movies are composed of separate units called "scenes." Just like a movie or a TV show is made up of several different scenes, longer Flash movies can be made by splitting them up into scenes.
When create a new Flash file, one scene is automatically defined—this is what the "Scene 1" displayed in the upper left of the Scene window represents. This book doesn't deal with animation, however, so we will continue as is without creating any more scenes.

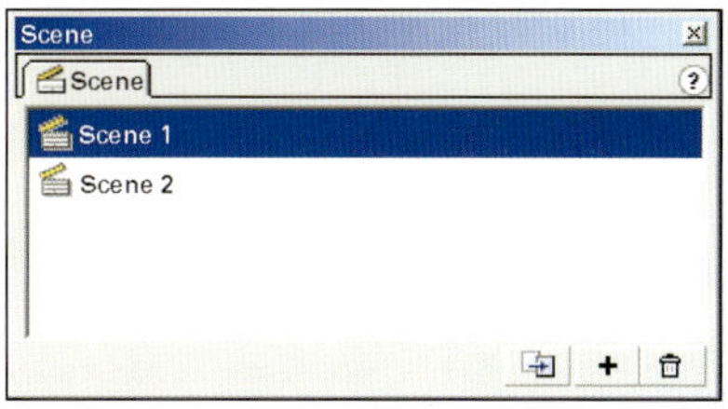

▲ Choose Window → Panels → Scene (in Flash MX, Scene is in the Window menu) to open the Scene window. In this window you can change which scene you want to edit, rename scenes, etc.

Convenient Management of Complex Composite Illustrations through Symbols

First, create symbols for the character arrangement.

In this illustration, I've decided on a four character arrangement of girls. To make modifying composite illustrations where multiple characters appear, such as this one, we'll turn each character into a symbol.

Before starting the rough sketch

Instead of rushing into drawing the rough sketch on the Stage, we'll create some symbols and sketch in those.

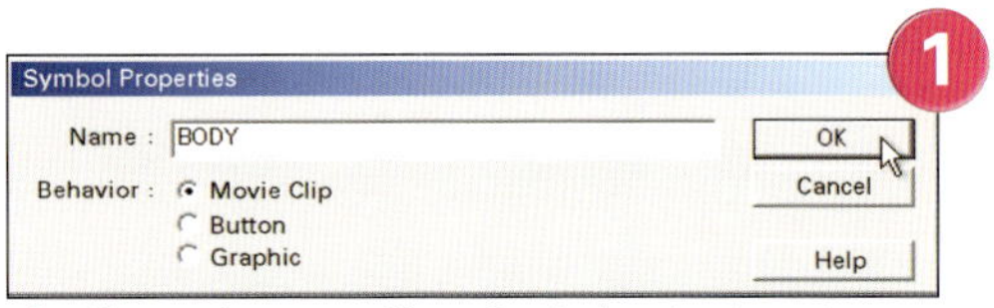

▲ Choose Insert → New Symbol and select the Movie Clip radio button to create an empty symbol. Be sure to assign a clear name to the symbol (I've used "BODY" here) and click the OK button.

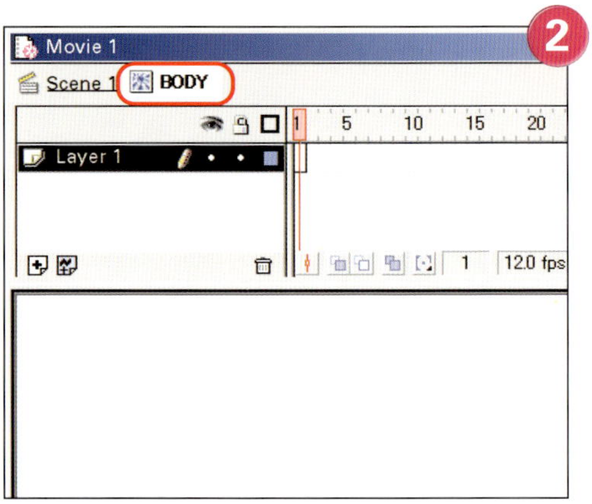

▲ Since you are now in Edit Symbol mode, click on Scene 1 to go back to your movie.

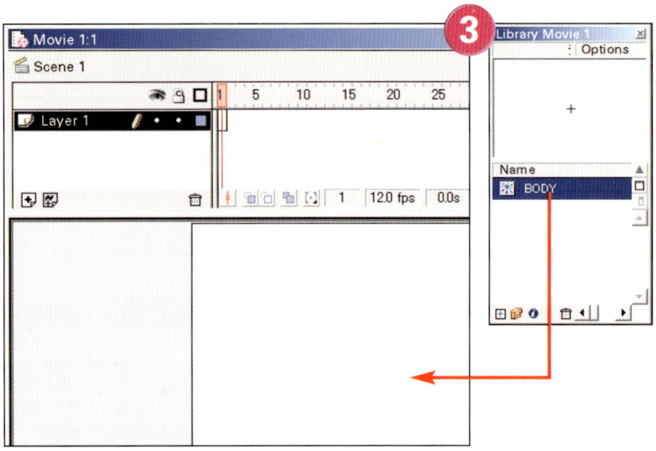

▲ Here, choose Window → Library, drag the BODY symbol to the Stage, and drop it.

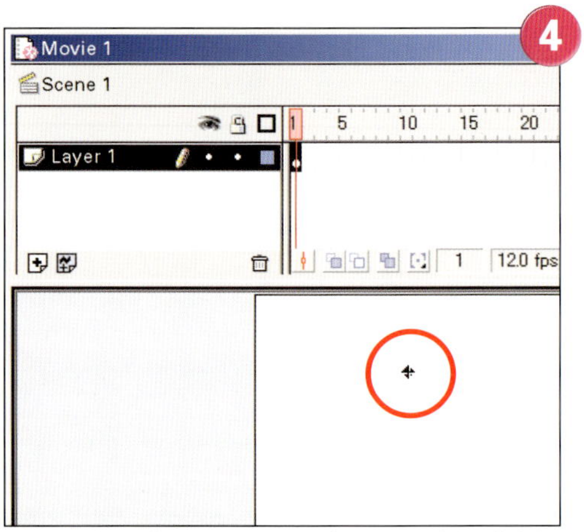

▲ A point will appear on the Stage. Double-click it.

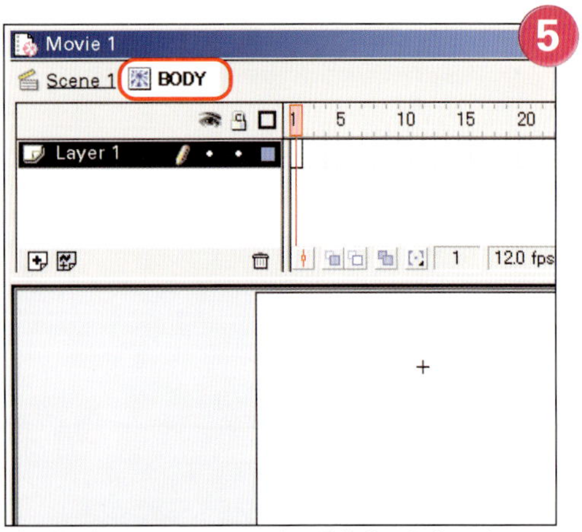

▲ We have now returned to Edit Symbol mode. Notice BODY is now displayed at the upper left.

Point

All this seems repetitive, but by doing things this way you can work in Edit Symbol mode and still clearly see the Stage size. That means you can draw your characters and still keep the size of the Stage in mind. However, immediately after creating a new symbol, or after double-clicking on a symbol in the Library, you will not be able to see the Stage.

Symbols?

In Flash, animation is usually accomplished by registering each moving part as an object, and then giving that object commands: move, turn, change, etc. Even animation involving lots of separate pictures can be done with just a few individual images. This is very space efficient since you can also shrink your file size this way. These objectified images are called "symbols." Symbols are registered in the Library, where they are assigned names and managed.

For unanimated Flash pictures like the ones in this book, there is no real necessity for using symbols. However, for pieces composed of multiple characters, like this one, turning them into symbols, assigning them names, and managing them as such is convenient.
Finally, be sure to choose a symbol type other than "Button."

When you have an image in mind, sketch it out.

Now we'll start the line drawing. We won't be coloring these drawings as they are when we finish them at this stage, so just draw with an eye toward just getting your characters' pose and composition right. To make it easier to separate them into symbols later, put each character into its own layer.

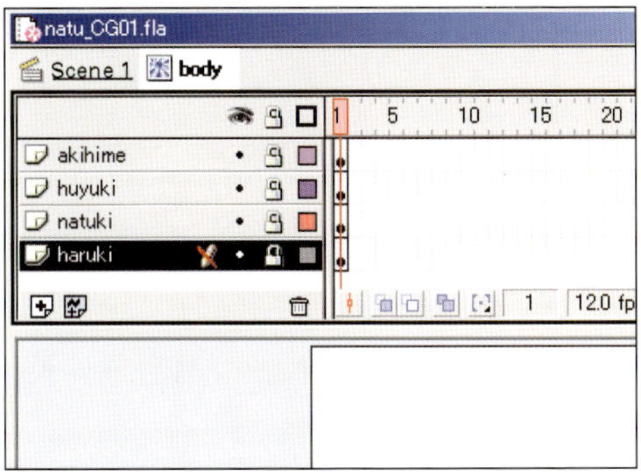

▲ Be sure to assign clear names to your layers, too. Double-click on a layer's name to change it.

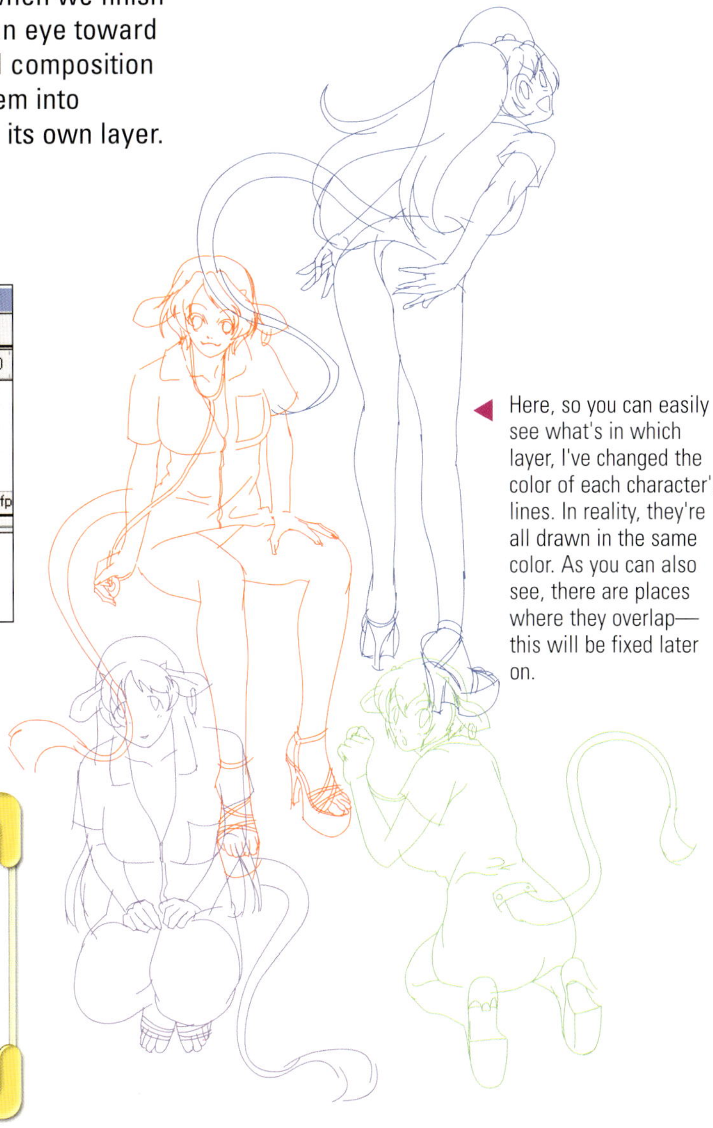

◀ Here, so you can easily see what's in which layer, I've changed the color of each character's lines. In reality, they're all drawn in the same color. As you can also see, there are places where they overlap—this will be fixed later on.

Point

Each time you finish drawing in a layer, remember to click on the dot next to the layer name, below the lock icon. This will protect the layer from being affected by what you do in the next one. Don't forget to do this!

Line Drawing Revisions

Be detailed but don't hold back; erase a rough face to redraw it later.

Now, we're going to stack another layer on top of what we drew earlier and turn it into a well and proper line drawing. You can use the Arrow Tool to adjust your lines, but even if you do a beautiful job of it, you're still going to end up with minor overlaps in some areas. So, our last step should be zooming in on those details and cleaning them up. Whether you properly take care of this now or not will have a powerful impact on your finished work.

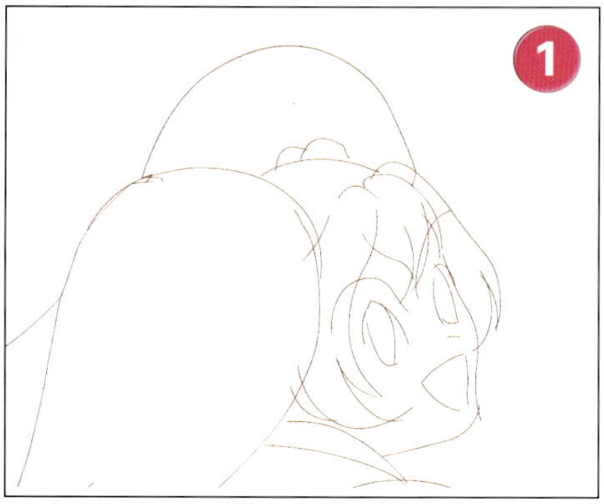

▲ This is the unrevised image. It's certainly a rough picture, isn't it?

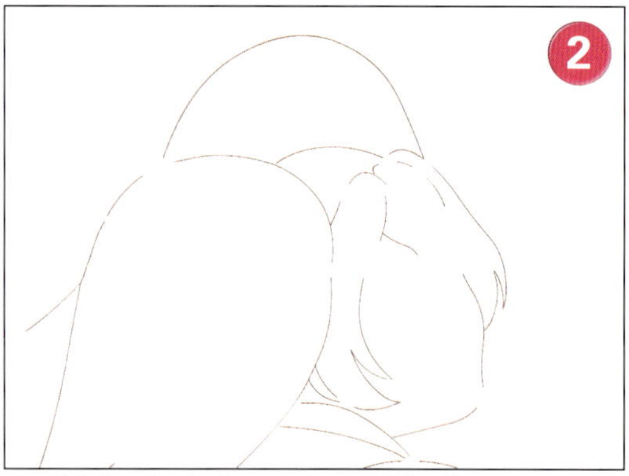

▲ This is a basically complete revision. I've cut away nearly all the unnecessary lines and parts. Since I'm going to do the eyes and other facial features in a different layer, I've erased them here.

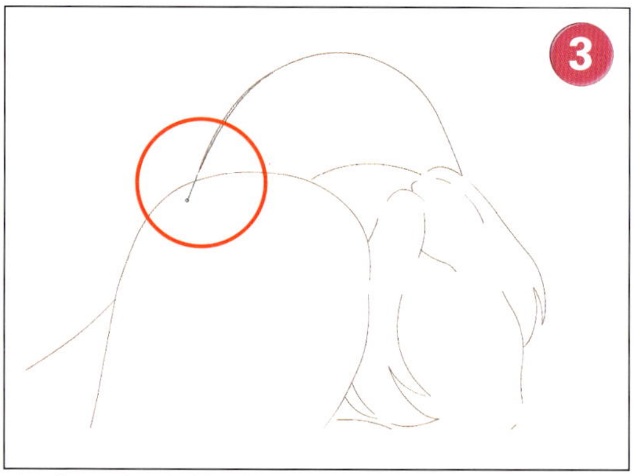

▲ Just when I think I'm done, I do a detail check. If I find any gaps or breaks in my lines, I use the Arrow Tool to pull one broken end over to the other. Once that's done, I bend the line into place and repeat the process for the whole drawing.

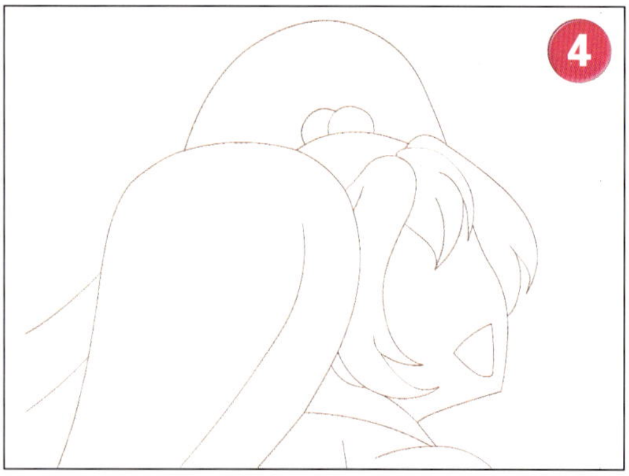

▲ All the revisions are finished. Having come this far, it is now a complete line drawing, and is ready to be colored.

Post-revision

All the character revisions are now complete. If you can get really good with the Arrow Tool, you'll be a Flash master! Probably. The eyes and mouths are still missing, but we'll draw those in later. ▶

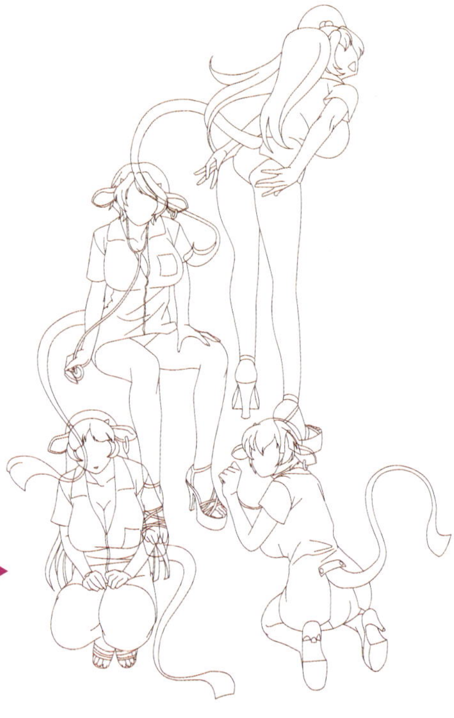

Turning the Line Drawing into a Symbol

Turning all the characters into symbols makes future editing and management easier.

When all our line drawings are complete, we'll finally change all our layers into symbols. By doing so, the characters won't affect each other and we'll be free to arrange them as we wish.

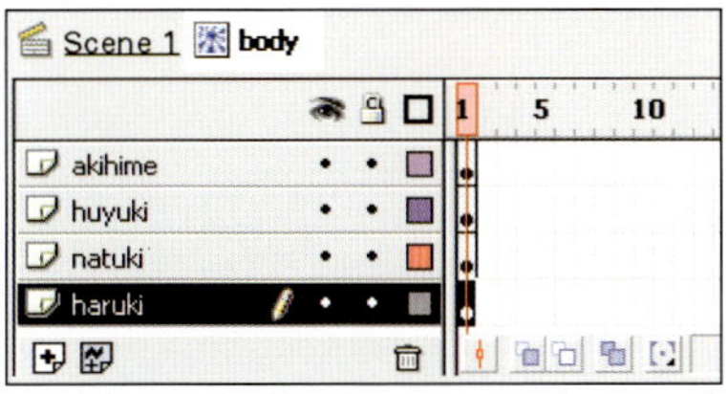

▲ I'll use the first layer we made to explain the process. Choose a layer and click on the lock icon next to the layer's name. The line drawing in the layer you chose will now be selected.

▲ Leave the line drawing in its selected state and choose Insert → Covert to Symbol. Click the Movie Clip radio button, give the symbol a name, and click OK. Here, I've given my symbol the same name as the layer, and I've done the same thing with the other three characters.

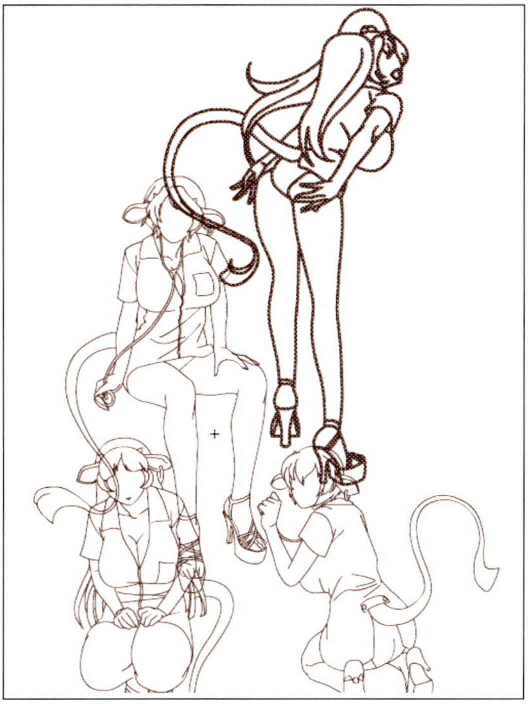

All the characters are now symbols. Double-clicking on a character emboldens it and fades all the other characters—this makes it so that only the bold character's symbol can be edited.

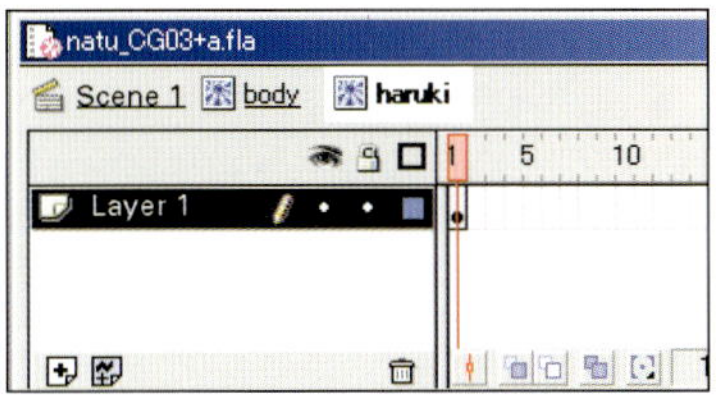

▲ All the character symbols are now arranged within the BODY symbol.

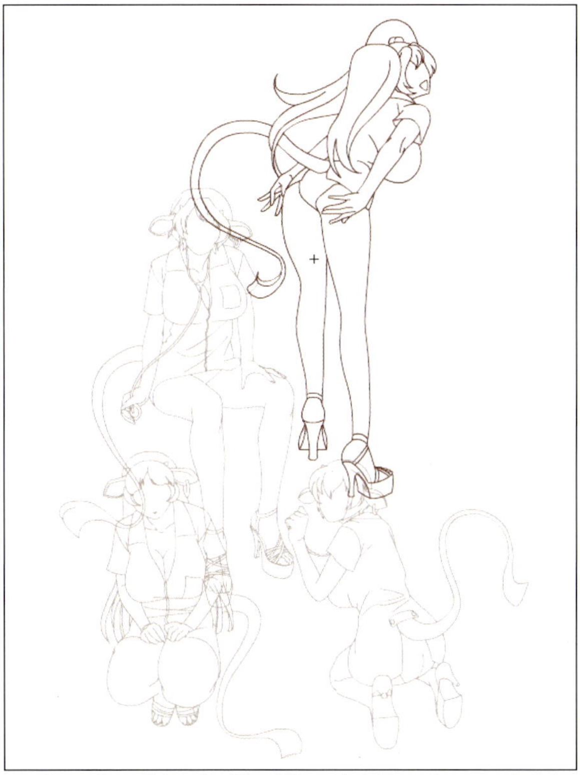

▲ Here, I'm editing the "Haruki" symbol. The others are faded out-this means they cannot be edited in this state.

Point

On page 58 we made the BODY empty symbol, and then created symbols within it by drawing pictures there. Selecting pre-existing pictures and turning them into symbols involves a different process.

Introductory Level Flash with Anime-Style Fills

Keep the light direction in mind and fill liberally.

Next, I'll introduce a method for anime-style fills that's easy even for a Flash beginner. There are also ways that make heavy use of gradations, but you can use shadows and create depth even with the minimum of colors available to anime-style fills. In any case, the more advanced gradation methods all require mastery of the basic anime-style fill techniques.

Shading using circles and triangles

Set the Pencil Tool's Stroke Color to red (it's easy to see) and draw guidelines for the shaded sections. As one of the basic tricks to anime-style coloring, separating shaded areas into circular and (acute) triangular sections is essential. Round out curvy sections and use acute triangles on other surfaces—wrinkles, creases, and what have you—for a "deeper" feel. At this point, the coloring lines for the clothing and skin are drawn as well.

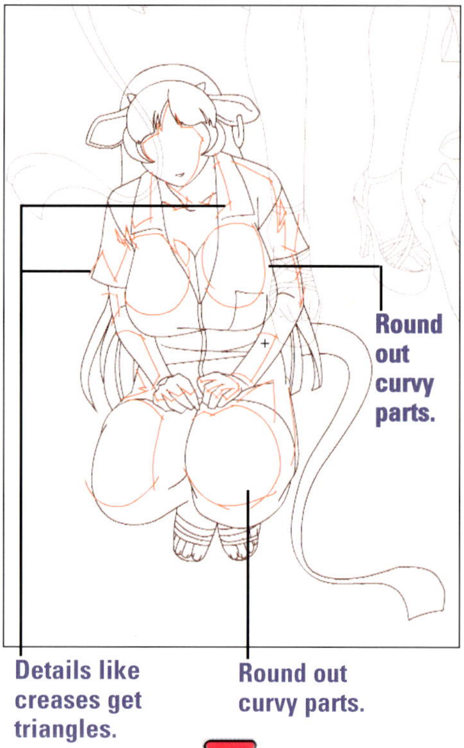

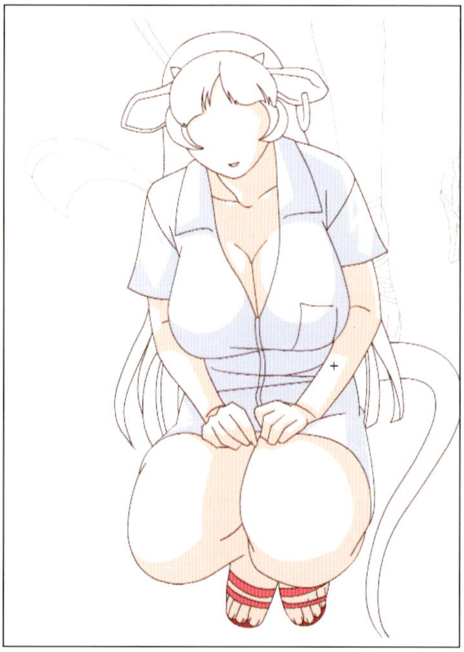

▲ I'm coloring this one relatively close to completion. Even at this early stage, it looks pretty anime-like, doesn't it? When I'm done coloring, I'll use the Arrow Tool to select all the red lines and hit the Delete key to get rid of them.

What's an "anime-style fill?"

It's a way of solid coloring in 3 or 4 stages, from shading to highlighting. For televised anime, for example, the artist has to draw a lot of pictures. Those artists use this technique as an ideal way of increasing their efficiency, and so coloring done this way came to be called an "anime-style fill." The often heard term "cell shading" comes from the fact that cells are used for drawing anime. Back when computers could only create 8 or 16 colors, anime-style fills drew a lot of attention as a means of expression using only a few colors. These methods have come to be used in modern computer graphics as well, especially in Japan. Despite the fact that computers can display things in full color, anime-style fills are still used today as a means of expression. Recently, ways of blurring the lines between solid colored areas are being used to achieve a greater sense of realism. This allows for expression beyond simple anime-style fills, and some people maintain that therefore, strictly speaking, they can no longer be called such.
In this book, I've claimed that doing anime-style fills in Flash is easy. This is because using fills in Flash is basically just a way to paint in solid colors.

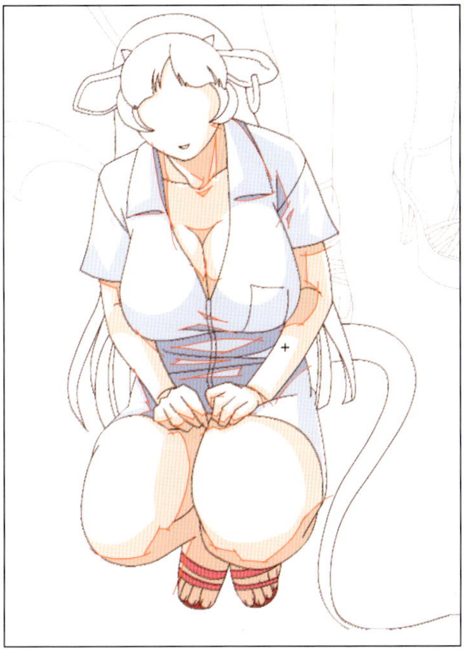

▲ Further shading of some of the darker areas is now complete. If you overdo this, your piece will start to look odd, so pay attention to the overall image as you color.

Point
Normally, I can complete my shading in two stages, but just this once I thought I'd add a third stage and try to take her beauty to the next level.

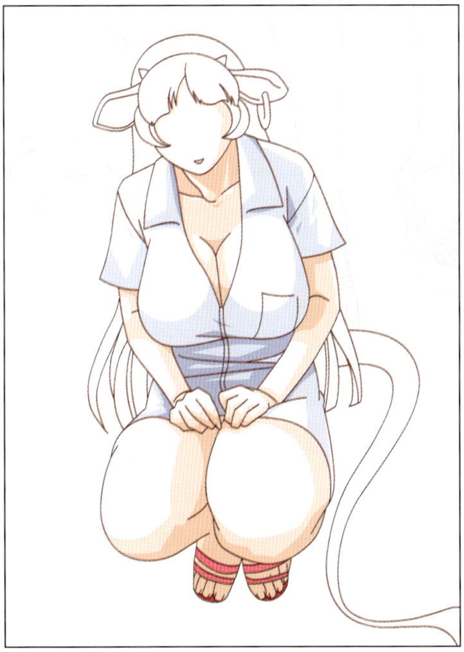

▲ As before, I've double-clicked the red lines with the Arrow Tool and hit the Delete key to get rid of them.

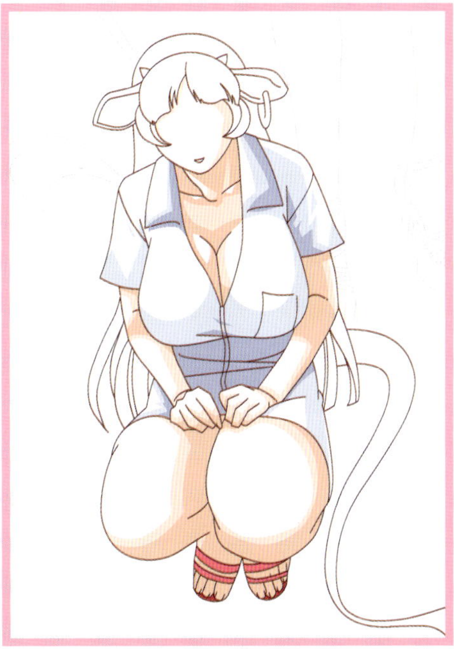

▲ Here, I've tried changing the darkest area a bit. The result is the impression that the light hitting the other areas appears stronger. I ended up not using this image, however.

Highlighting the Hair and Adding Shadows for a 3-D Feel

Picture the flow of the hair and then draw. This is the trick.

To achieve a sense of depth and luster in the hair, give it some highlighting and shading.

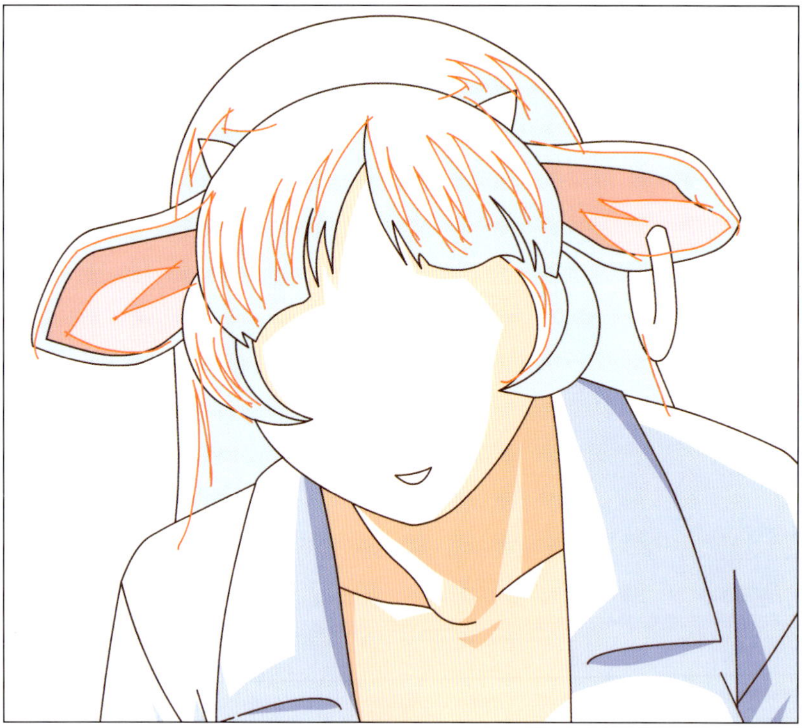

Shading

To get realistic hair, draw a series of little "mountains," as shown here. But be careful not to overdo it, because if your piece is displayed at a lower size, the effect will be ruined. When the "mountains" are complete, fill them in.

Point
Since this girl has white hair, I added a touch of green to it so that it won't overlap with the blue shade of her clothes. When you're drawing a picture, you have to pay attention to this kind of balance.

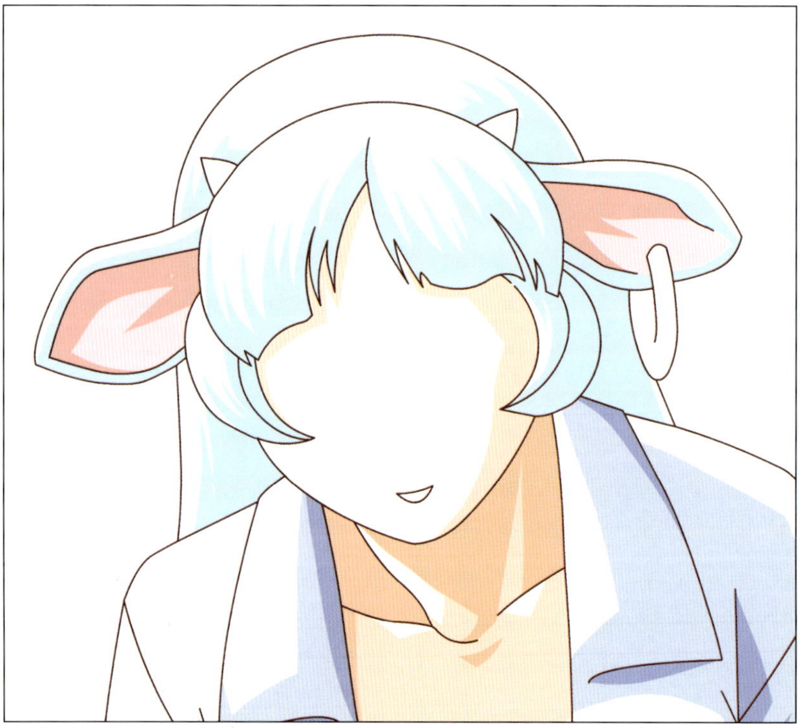

After I erased the red fill lines, her hair looked a little light, so I made the colors a touch darker. Now the hair has been filled up to the second stage.

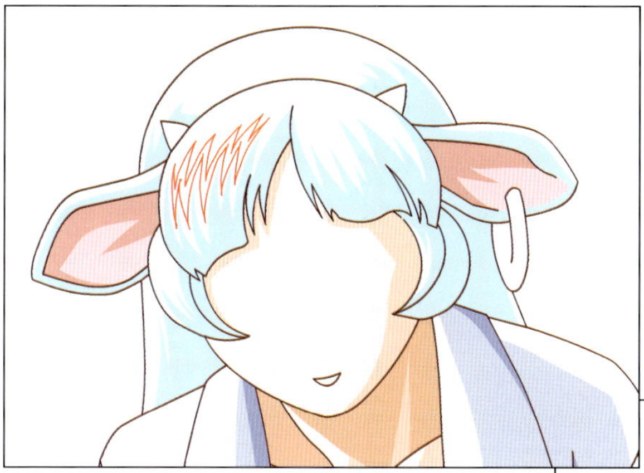

Highlighting

There is a certain pattern to how highlights take shape, but in this case I'm going to make some red mountains to match the blue mountains I've just added. I'll pour white into these for highlighting and erase the red lines when I'm done.

Add highlights in the same way to other areas as well.

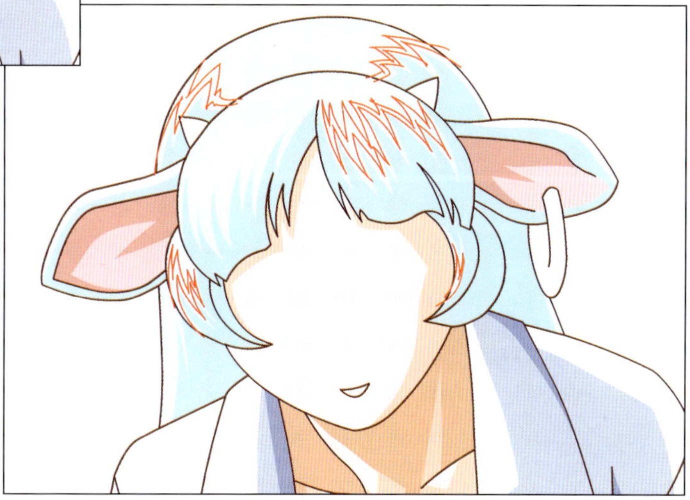

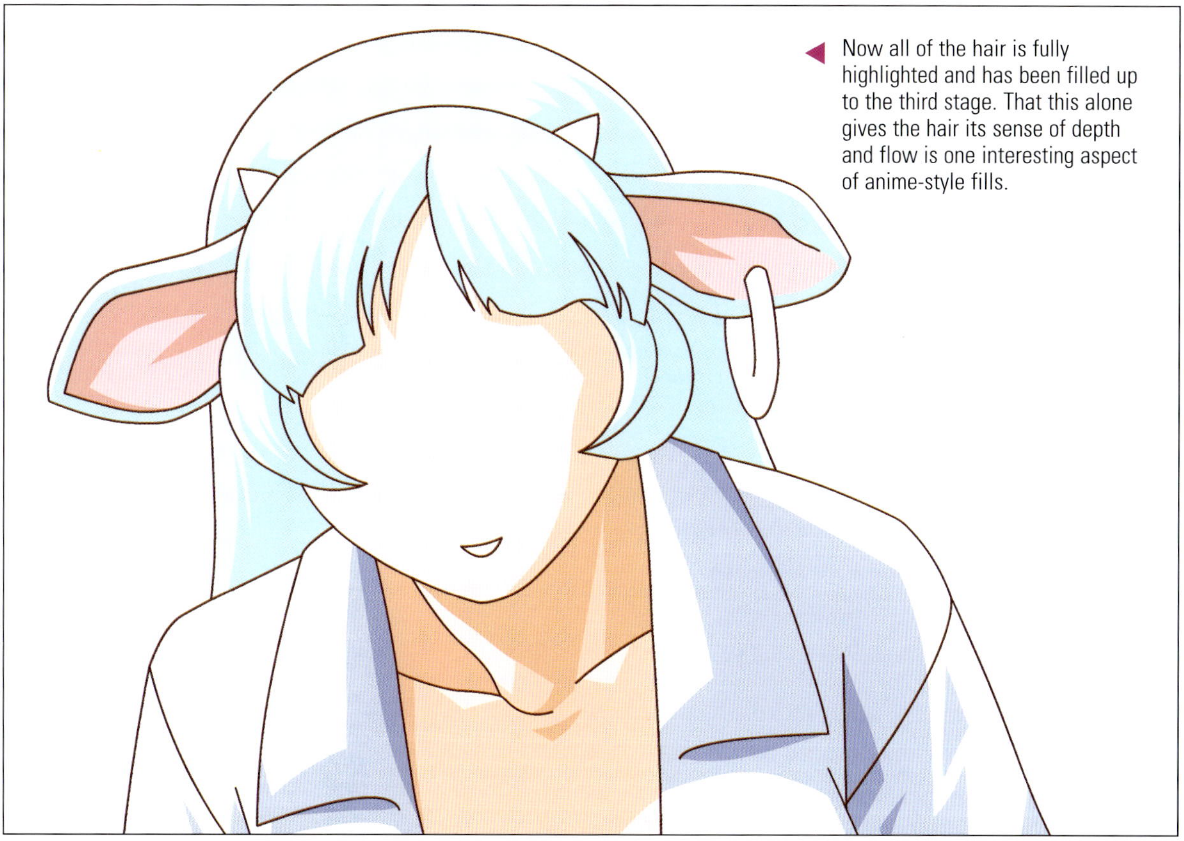

Now all of the hair is fully highlighted and has been filled up to the third stage. That this alone gives the hair its sense of depth and flow is one interesting aspect of anime-style fills.

Combining Anime-Style and Gradational Fill Techniques

Fine tune your solid and gradational fills to connect the body and the tail smoothly.

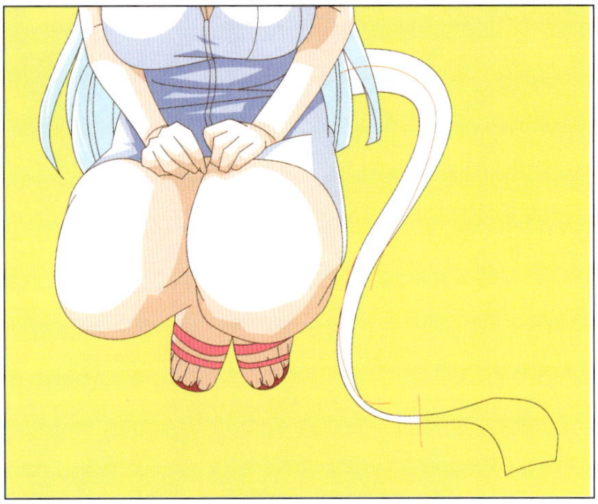

The body creates atmosphere with the anime-style fill in place, but let's try using a gradation to soften the tip of the tail.

◀ Other than the tip of the tail, I've painted the whole thing with the same anime-style fill. So you can more easily see the white and uncolored sections, I've colored the background. In actual projects I work with the white background.

How to create a gradation

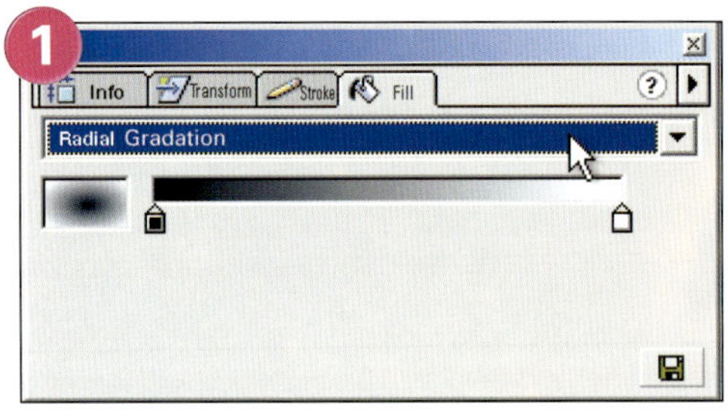

▲ Click on the Fill tab in this panel and select Radial Gradation in the pull-down menu. Initially, a black/white gradation will be loaded.

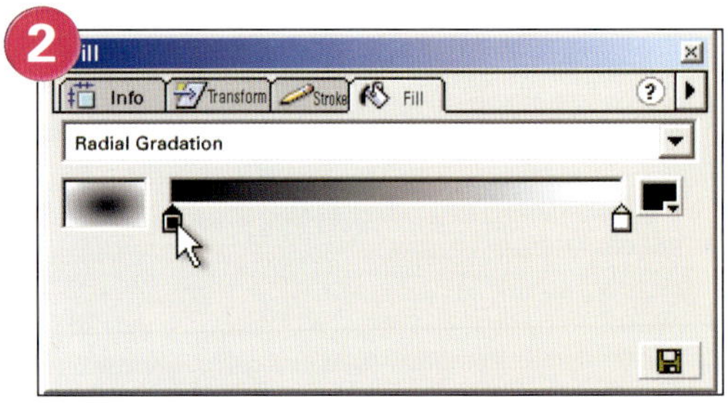

▲ Click on the markers, starting from the left (the black one). The tip of the marker will turn from white to black, so you can easily tell which marker you've selected.

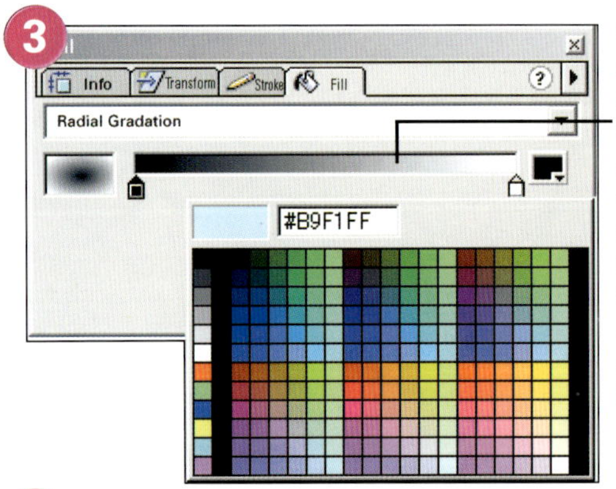

When you click on the color swatch, your cursor will turn into the Eyedropper Tool and a Color Palette will open. Without selecting anything from the palette, drag your cursor over to your picture and sample the shaded hair color.

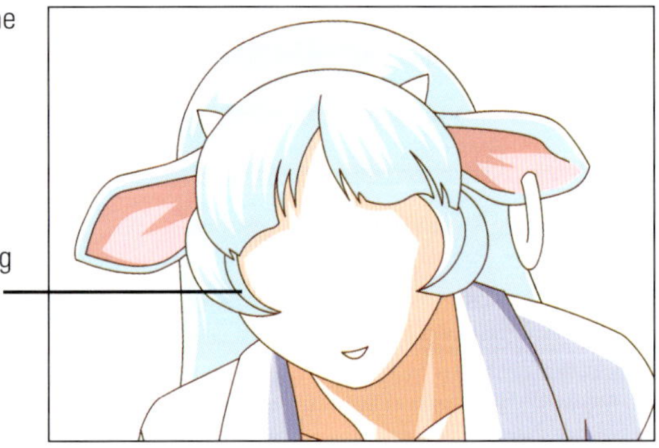

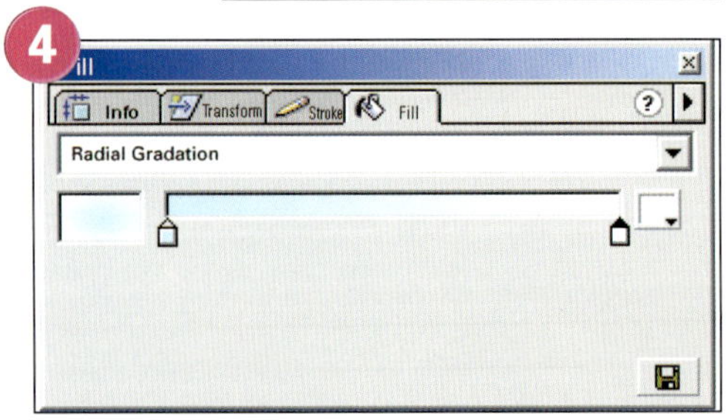

▲ Now select the right marker and click on the color swatch. This time, select white from the Color Palette. You have now successfully created a gradation using the same colors as your character's hair.

Point
In Flash MX, you can use the Color Mixer panel in the same way to create a gradation.

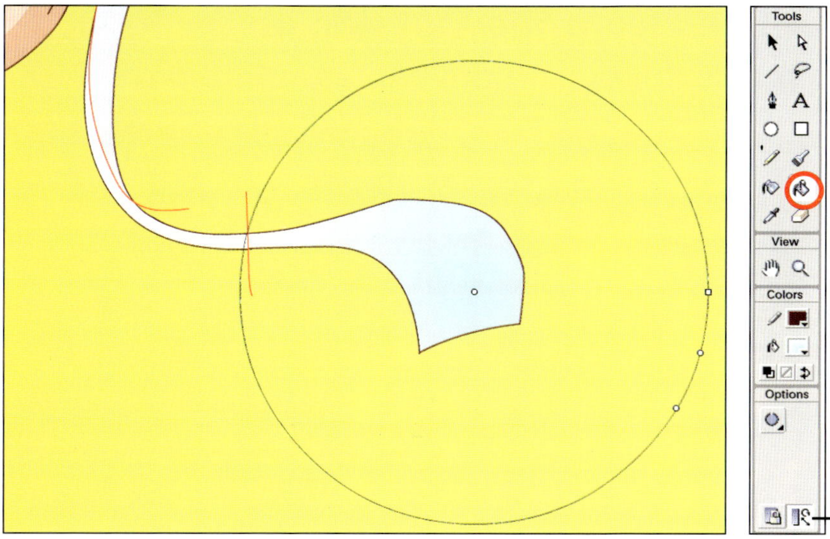

Transform Fill

▲ Use the Bucket Tool to pour on the gradation you've made. When you're done, click on the Transform Fill button at the bottom of the Toolbar and select the gradation on the Stage. Now you can move or change it as you like.

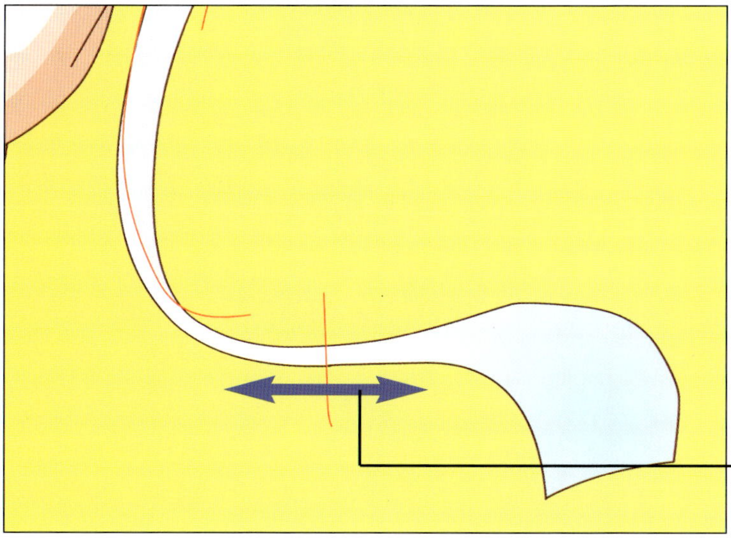

Adjust the gradation so that it blends smoothly.

Point

Connect and blend the gradation smoothly from the portion previously filled in white for a natural feel.

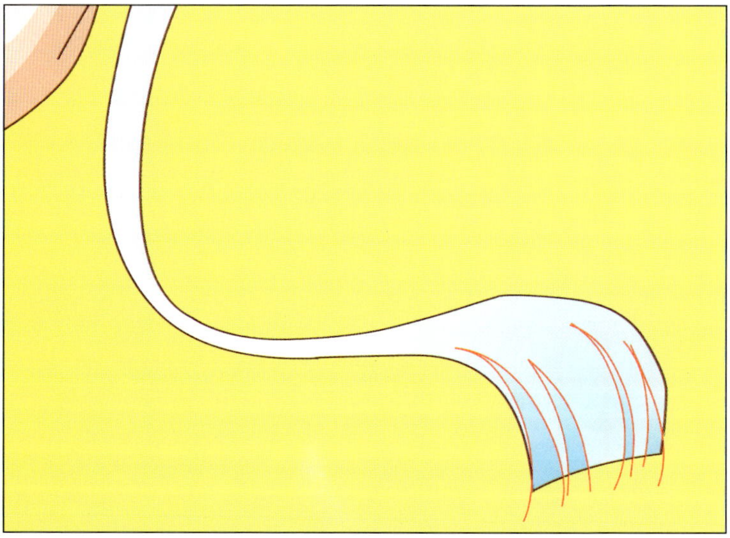

◀ Next, to make the tail appear more realistic, I'll draw some "mountains" just as with the hair. I'll create and apply a slightly darker gradation as before, too.
When you're done painting, be sure to adjust its size and direction with the Transform Fill modifier.

How You Can Draw Eyes from the Outside In

Separate the eyes into pupils, irises, and the whites, and then paint them.

At last, we're going to put in the as-yet undrawn eyes. People tend to think drawing the eye and all its parts is difficult, but if you break it up into the pupil ("inside"), iris, ("center"), and the whites ("outside"), you can easily draw them. First, let's stack on another layer just for the eyes.

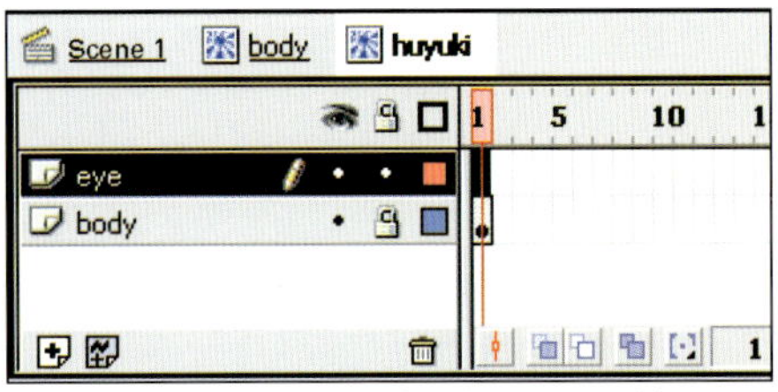

▲ Stack on a layer just for the eyes and be sure to give it a name. I've named mine "EYE." I've locked the BODY layer to protect the EYE layer from any interference.

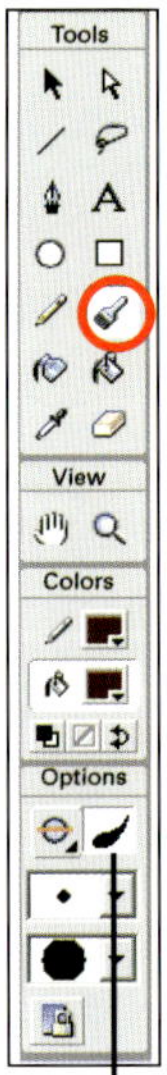

Pressure modifier

◀ Return to the EYE layer, and select the Brush Tool from your Toolbox. From the Options, select the Pressure and Brush Size modifiers, and set the Fill Color to whatever color your main lines are. Your preparations are now complete.

Point
If you're not using a pressure-sensitive tablet, then the Pressure modifier will not be displayed for the Brush Tool.

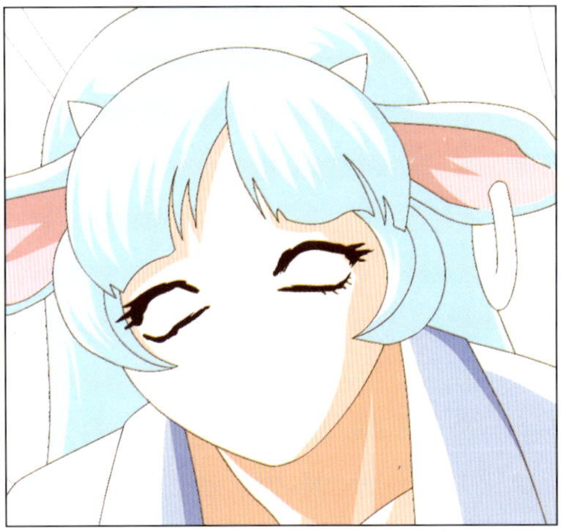

◀ Draw the upper and lower eyelids. Try to adjust the tilt and separation of the eyes one at a time. Use the Arrow Tool to drag a box (a "marquee") around the eye, and right click on it while it is selected. From the pop-up menu, choose Scale or Rotate to adjust the eye's balance.

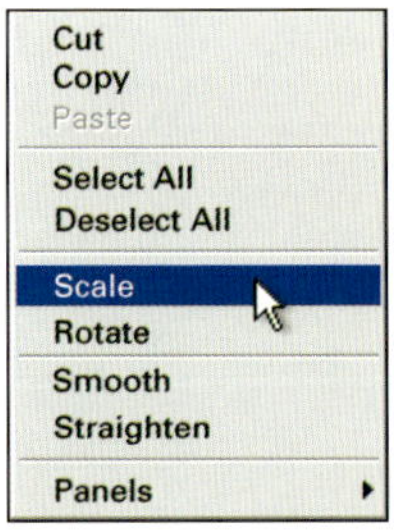

◀ Adding a crease to the upper eyelid completes the frame for the eye.

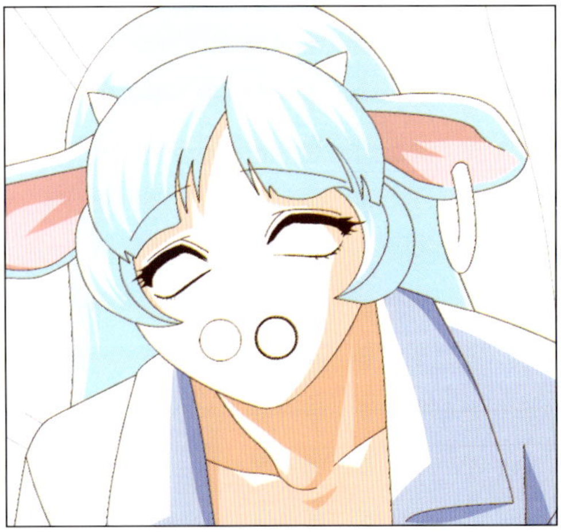

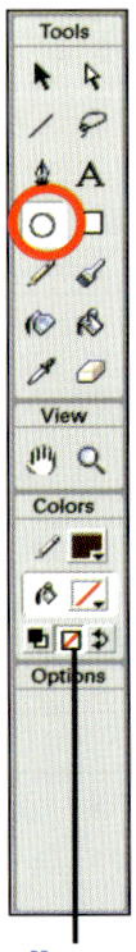

"None" as a Fill Color

◀ Now draw the irises. Select the Oval Tool and click the None button to set the Fill Color. This will let you draw an unfilled circle-only the shape line will be drawn.

If you draw the circle too big or too small, select the circle and right click on it. Select Scale or Rotate from the pop-up menu to adjust the circle. Once you've drawn one circle, use Copy and Paste to make another one for a pair of irises.

Point
You can draw a proper circle (as opposed to an oval) by selecting the Oval Tool, holding down the Shift key, and dragging your mouse.

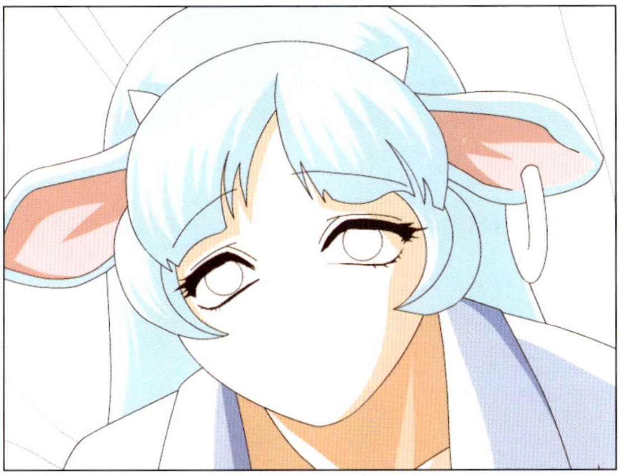

▲ Once you've created the irises, drag them over to the eye sockets and align them properly. Be sure to erase the parts of the circle that stick out past the eyelids.

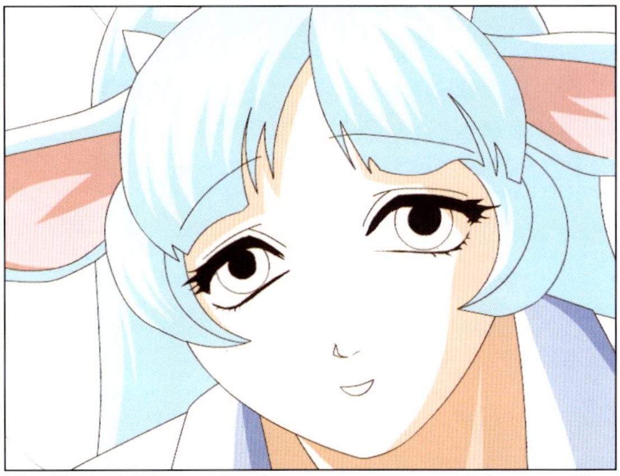

▲ Now add the pupils, the centermost part of the eyes. Be sure to paint them in with the Brush Tool. When you're done with that, add a cute little nose and mouth.

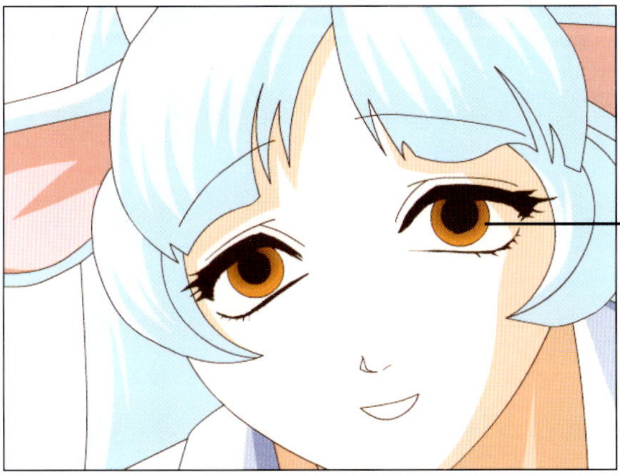

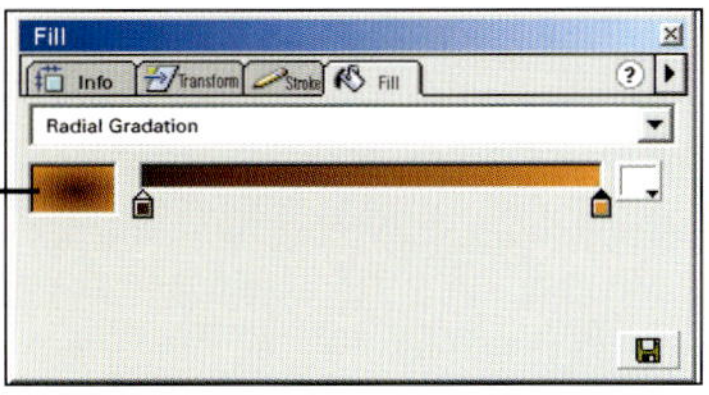

I've painted the irises with a gradation (Upper Limit: RGB = 51, 0, 0; Lower Limit: RGB = 204, 102, 0). It's good to make the dation seem to converge on the center of the eye.

The whites of the eyes are bound by coloring lines and then painted in with the Bucket Tool. Add some judicious highlights to the eyes with the Brush Tool to finish them off. Adding a little color to her mouth and some shading around the nose completes the face, too.

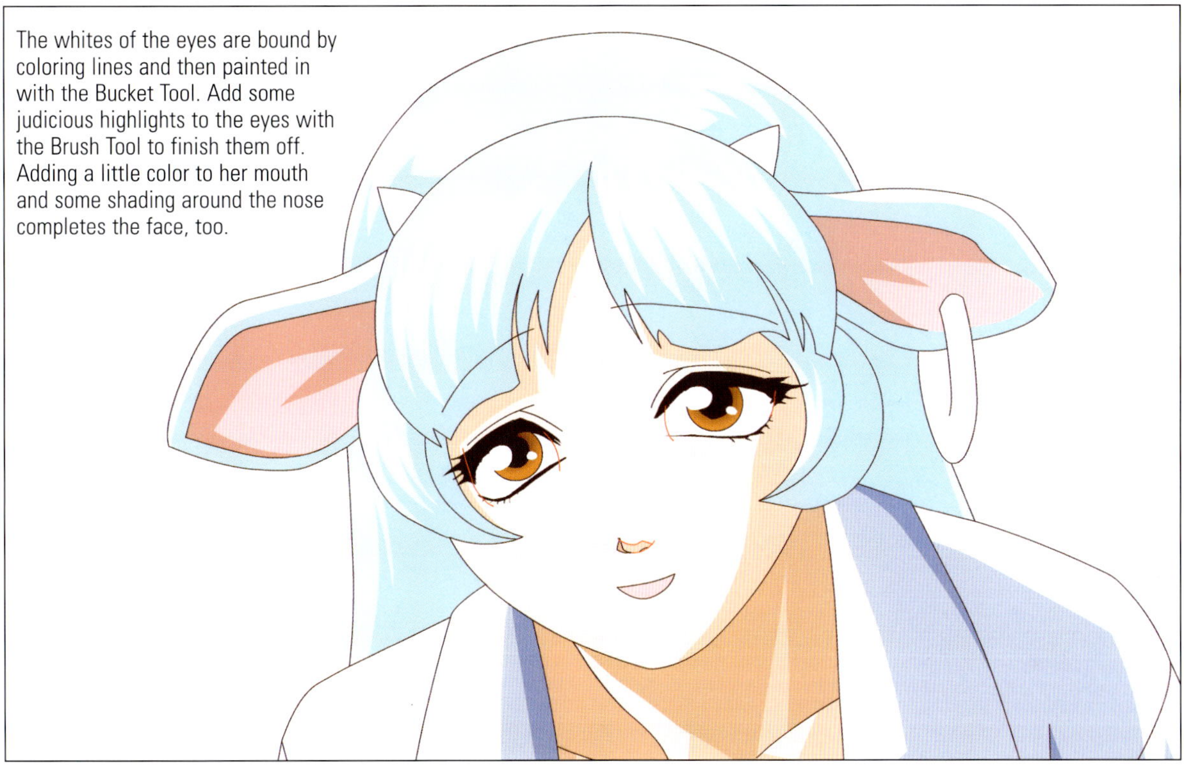

Add a Natural Blush and Luster to the Cheeks

Use a translucent gradation to put some pink on her cheeks and make her even cuter.

Using Alpha values to change a color alters its RGB values as well. Even if we lower the Alpha to 0%, it won't be completely transparent—the original color will still faintly show through.

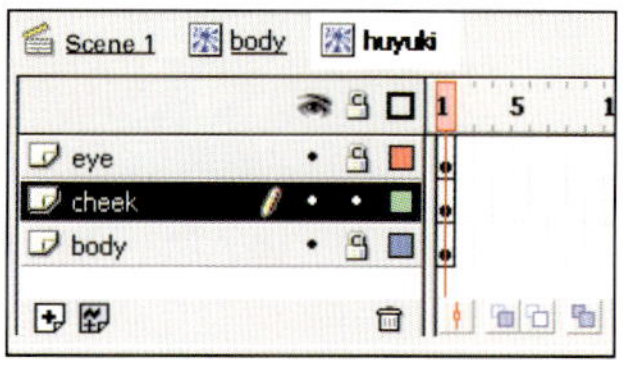

Lock the EYE layer to keep it from interfering with the original picture. Add a new layer in between the EYE and BODY layers and give it a name, like CHEEK. All the work described hereafter will be done in the CHEEK layer.

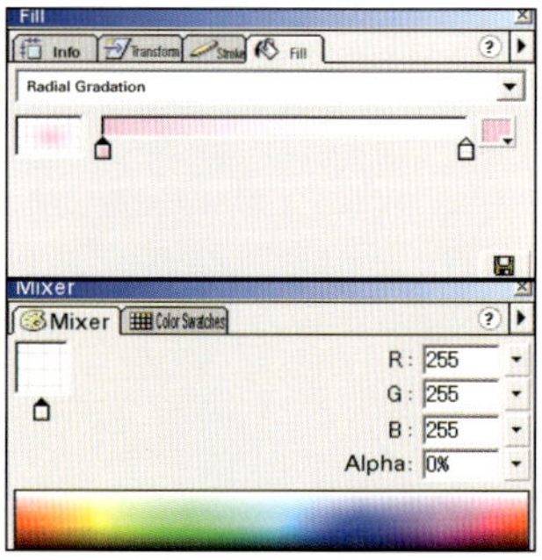

In the Fill panel, after you select Radial Gradation in the pull-down menu, set the left marker to pink (RGB = 255, 153, 204) and set the right marker to white. Then, in the Mixer panel, set the Alpha value to 0%.

Point
As you lower a fill's Alpha value, the color becomes more and more transparent. However, even lowering it to 0% won't make it perfectly clear—the original color will still be faintly visible. Match this effect well with the underlying color for a beautiful finish.

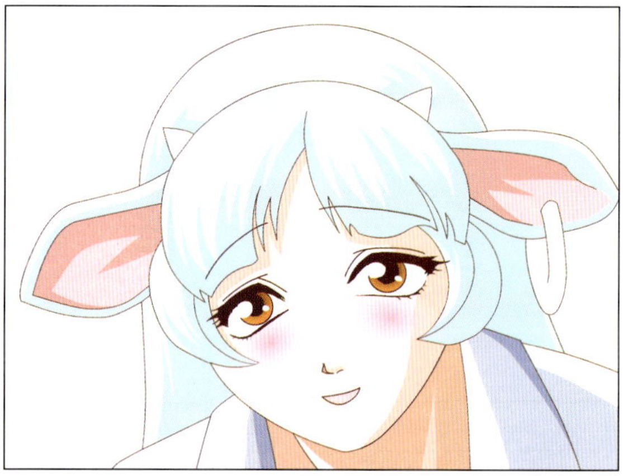

Set the Oval Tool's Fill Color to the gradation at the left and draw a couple of wide ovals around the character's cheeks. Pictured here are the results. One of the nice features of Flash is being able to adjust the gradations' position as you like afterwards.

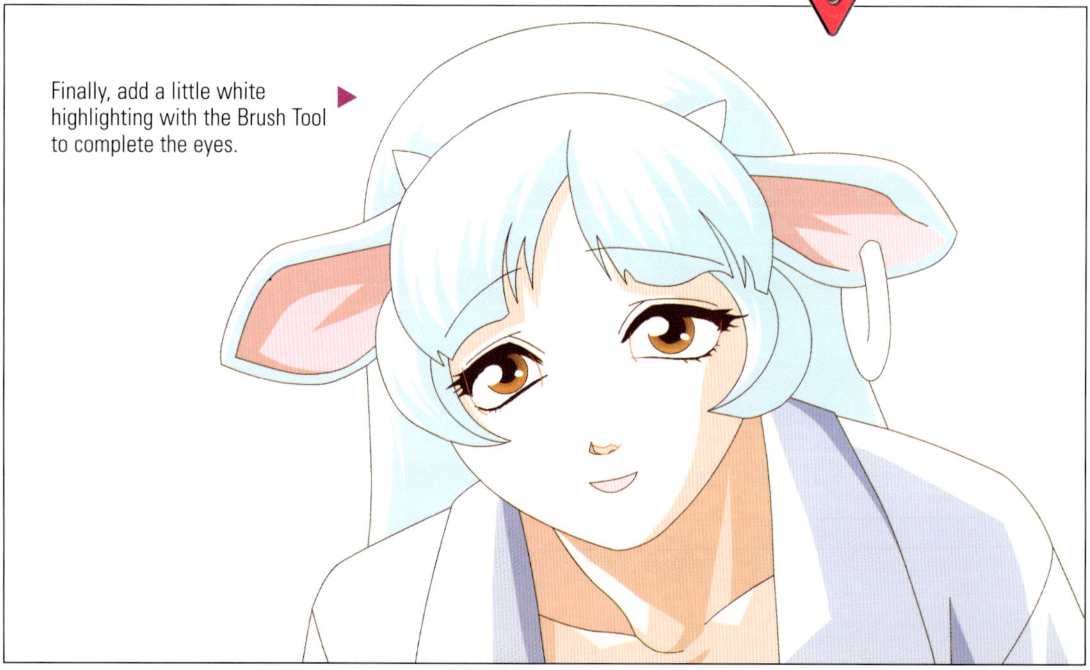

Finally, add a little white highlighting with the Brush Tool to complete the eyes.

Add Highlights to Get Snow-White Skin

Your girls will look sexier.

Stack on a highlight layer and add some highlighting to the skin. Here, I've so far drawn red highlight boundary lines with the Pencil Tool. Now I'll make a white version of the same transparent gradation I used on the cheeks and fill the areas bounded in red with it for snow-white skin.

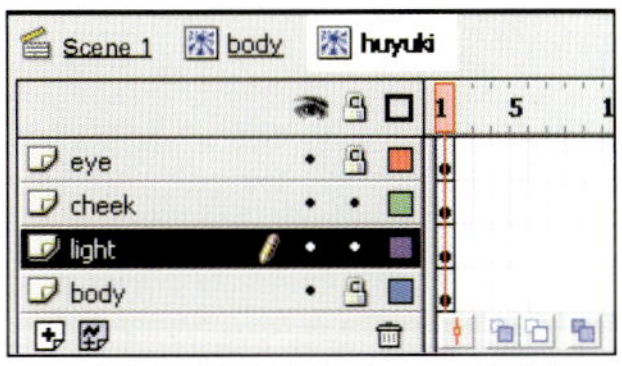

▲ Add a highlight layer, LIGHT, on top of the BODY layer.

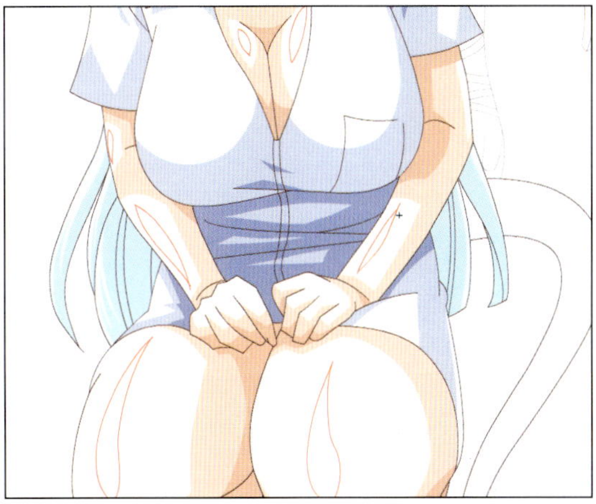

▲ Draw fill lines for your highlights.

Here, I've added a barely (0% Alpha) white transparent gradation to the skin. Tight, white, clear skin is the result. ▶

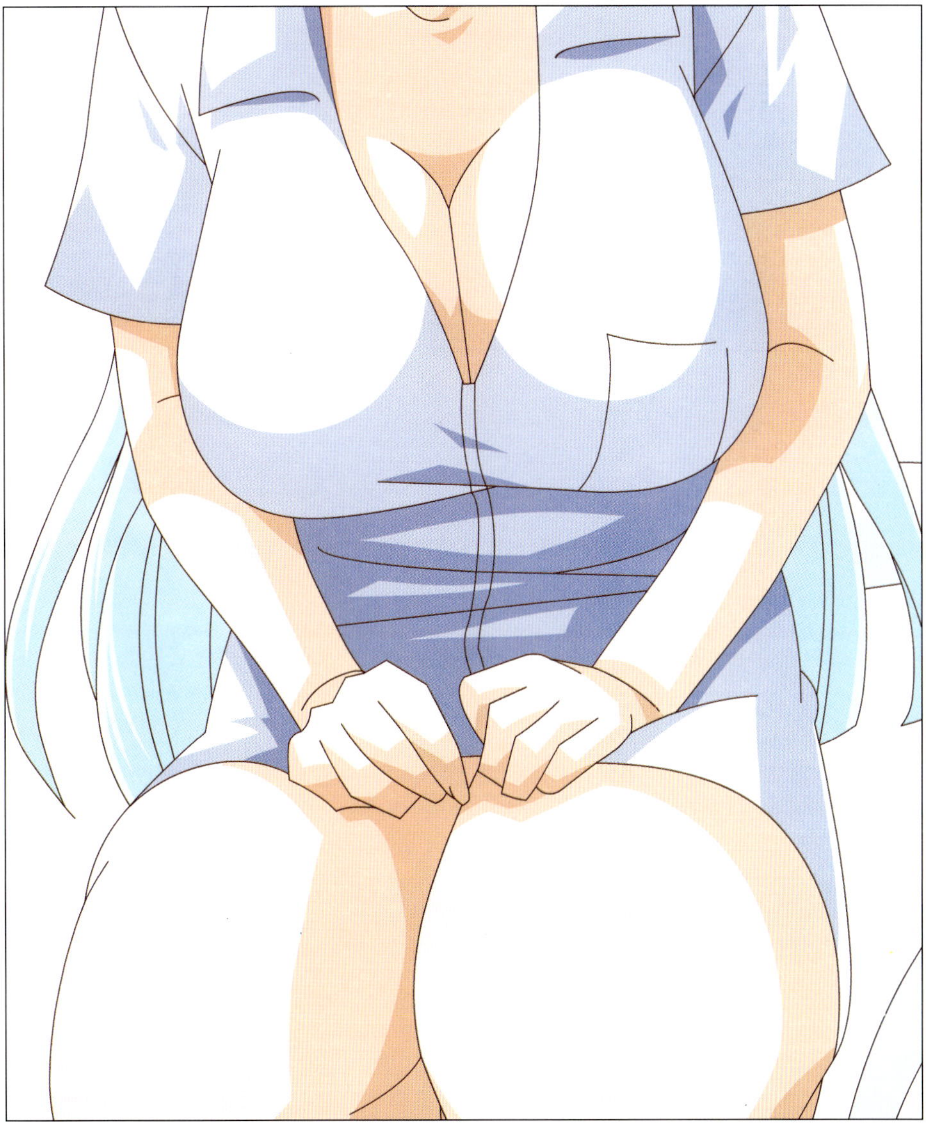

Did You Forget to Paint Anything? Time for the Final Check!

To make sure you haven't left anything unpainted, choose Modify → Movie to bring up the Movie Properties dialog. (In Flash MX, choose Modify → Document to get the Document Properties dialog.) Change the background color to something that will stand out. Anything you've forgotten to paint will take on the color of the background, and you'll know right away if you missed anything.
Remember to zoom in on those areas and paint them over carefully.

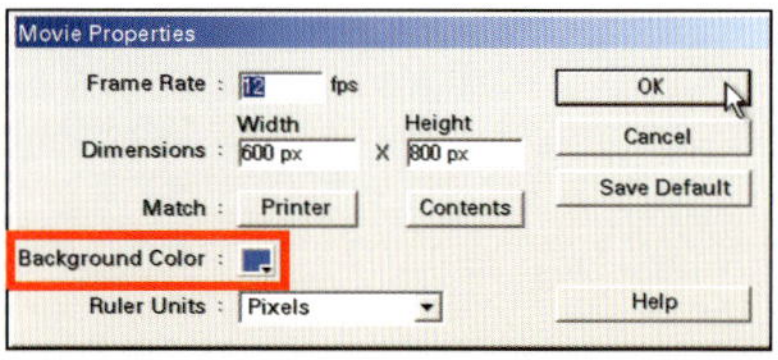

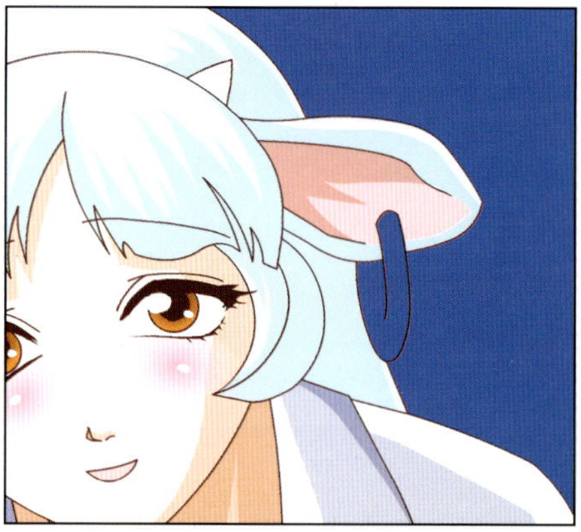

In Flash, even sweeping changes are simple.

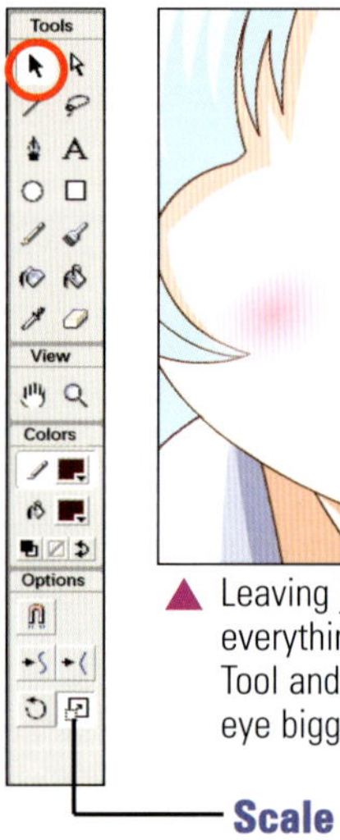

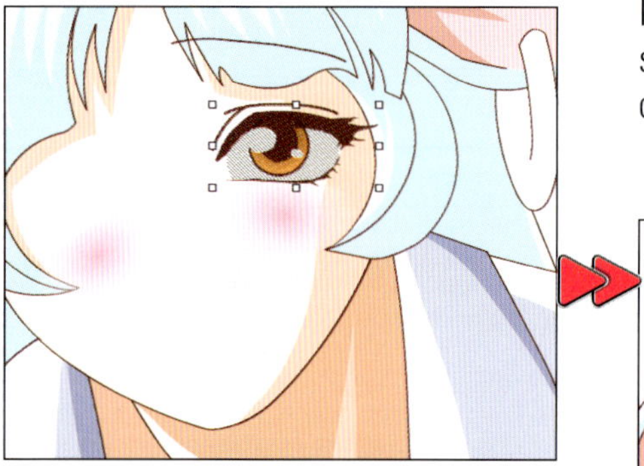

▲ Leaving just the right eye, I've erased everything else. Now I'll use the Arrow Tool and the Scale modifier to make the eye bigger.

I'm not really pleased with the face I've drawn so far. At times like this, modifications aren't difficult in Flash.

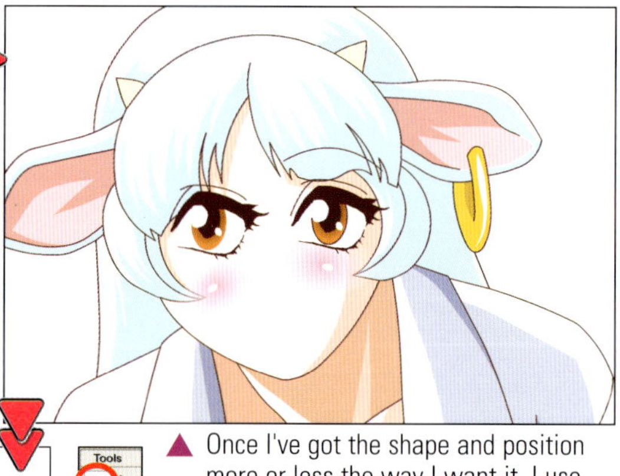

▲ Once I've got the shape and position more or less the way I want it, I use Copy and Paste to make the left eye.

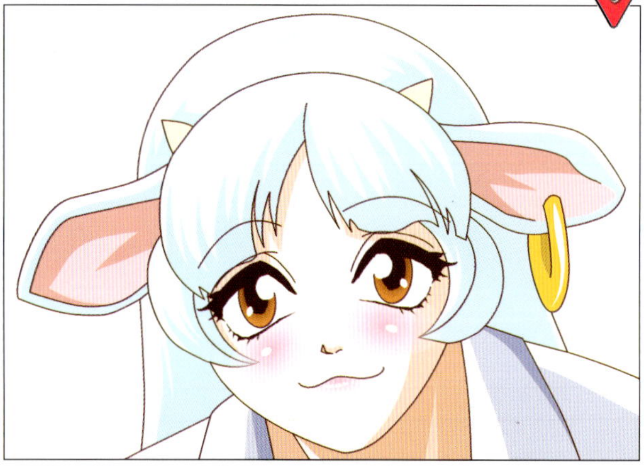

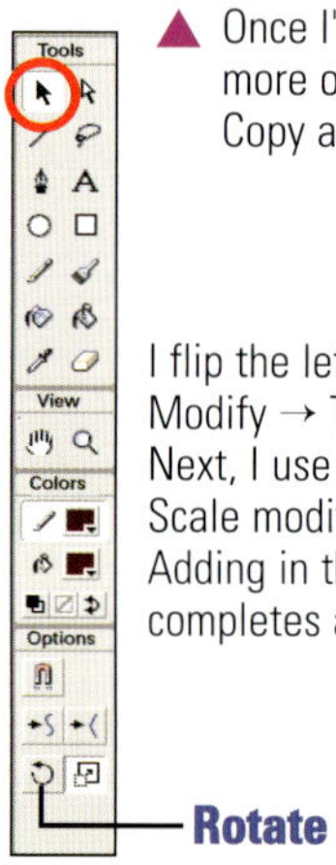

I flip the left eye around by choosing Modify → Transform → Flip Horizontal. Next, I use the Arrow Tool's Rotate and Scale modifiers to get the right balance. Adding in the eyebrows, nose, and mouth completes all my modifications.

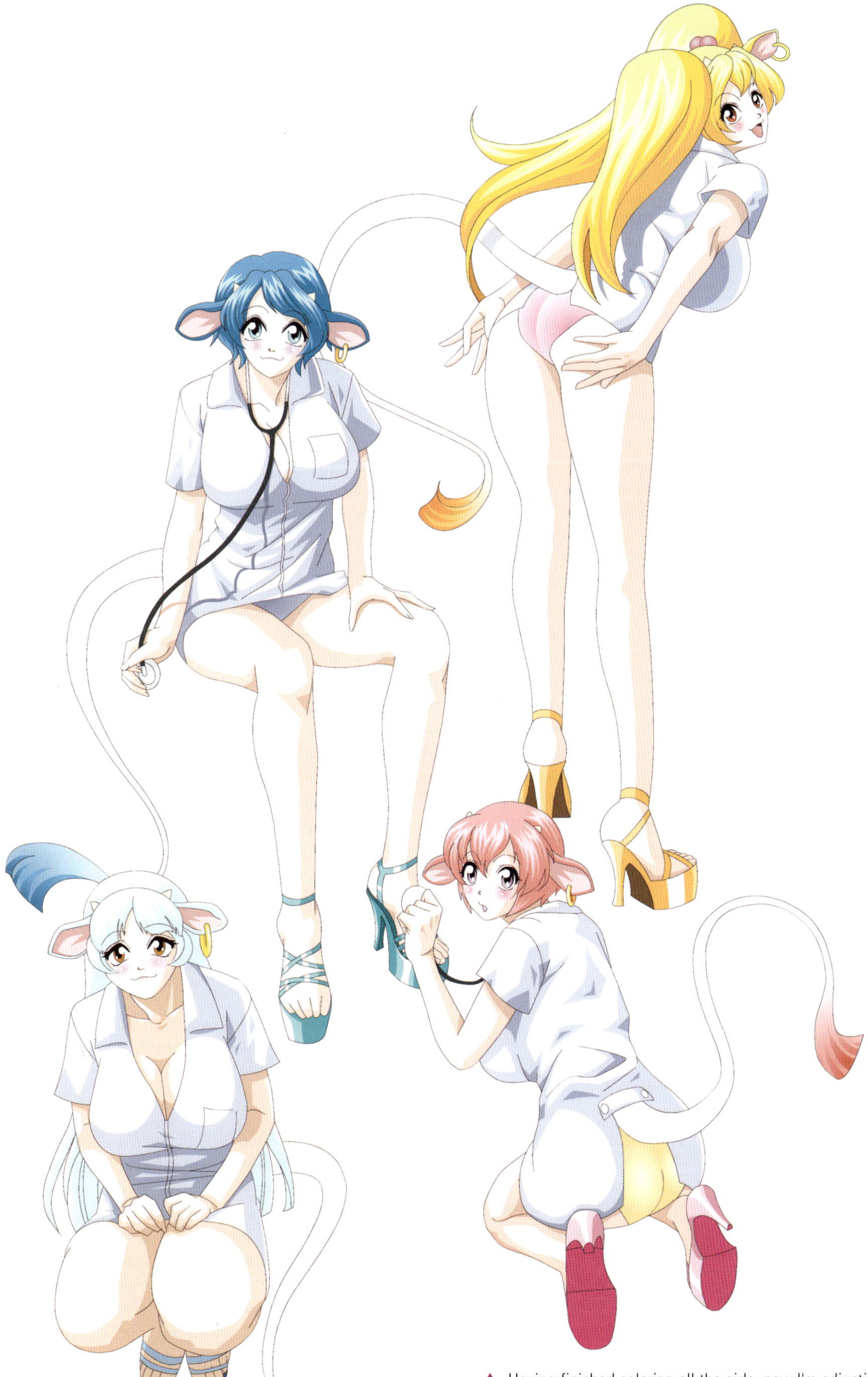

▲ Having finished coloring all the girls, now I'm adjusting their placement. Ever since step one, the characters have been packed in tight, so now I'm spreading them out a little.

Giving the Characters Shadows to Enhance the "View from Above" Look

Take a base image and turn it gray to make a shadow.

Now we'll make the final background pieces. I want the basic background tone to be white, so without drawing in too much I'd like to accent the artwork just using some shadows and a title.

Reproducing a character

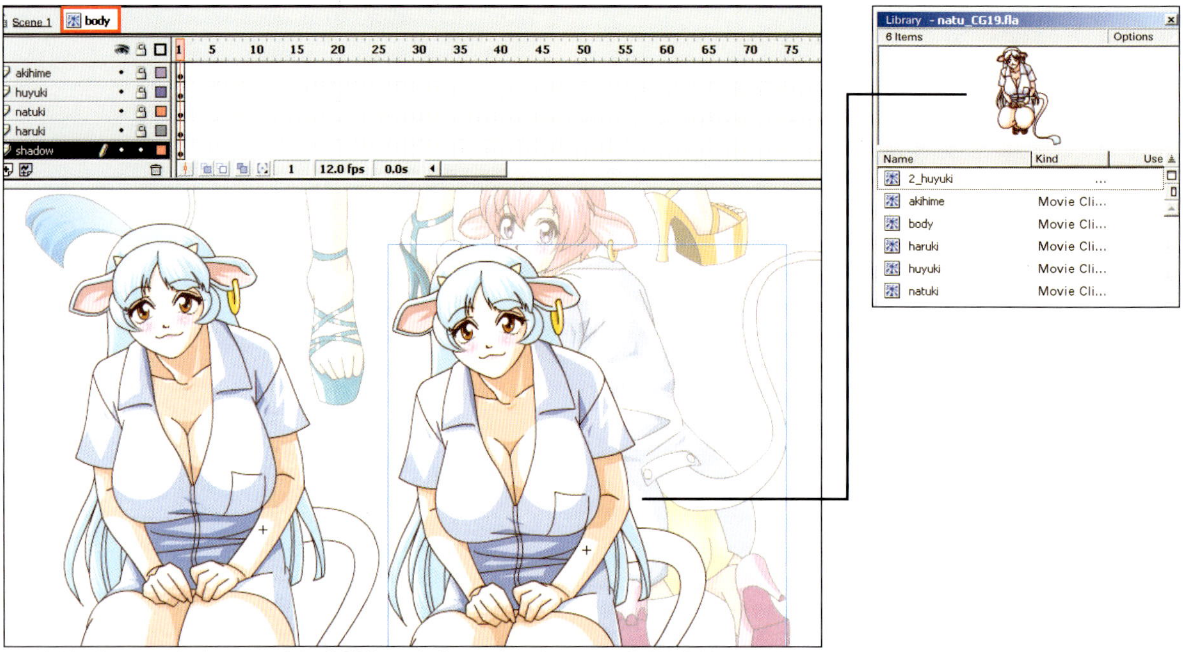

▲ Add a layer to the bottom of the BODY symbol's stack and name it SHADOW. Here, I've used the mouse to drag and drop 2_HUYUKI from the Library to my new layer. This will be the base for the character's shadow.

Eliminate all the unnecessary parts of the character copy.

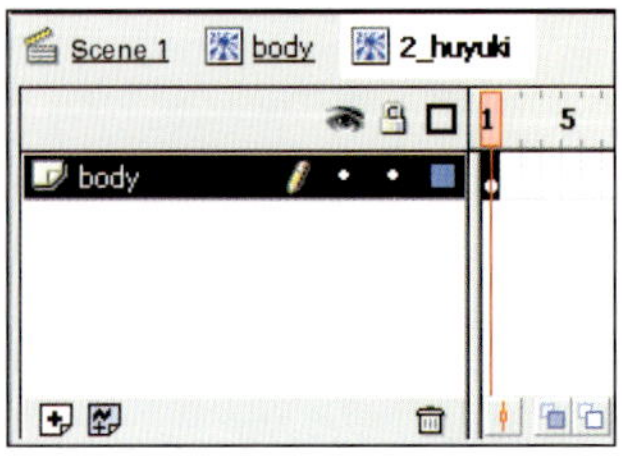

▲ I've deleted all the layers in the 2_HUYUKI symbol except the BODY layer.

With everything in the BODY layer selected, make the Fill Color gray. This will paint the entire character gray in one swipe. ▶

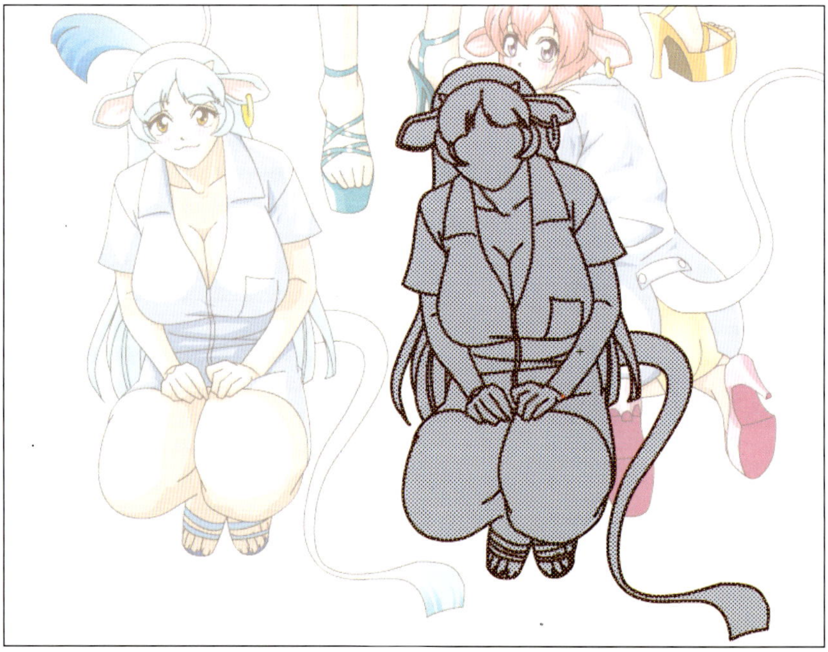

Making a Realistic Shadow

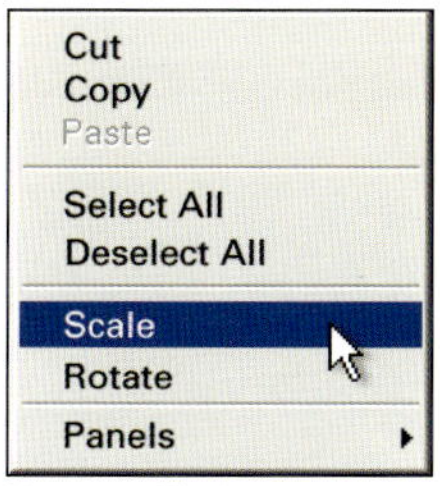

Now we'll place our shadow and make it more realistic. Right click on the image and use the Scale and Rotate modifiers in the pop-up menu on the shadow.

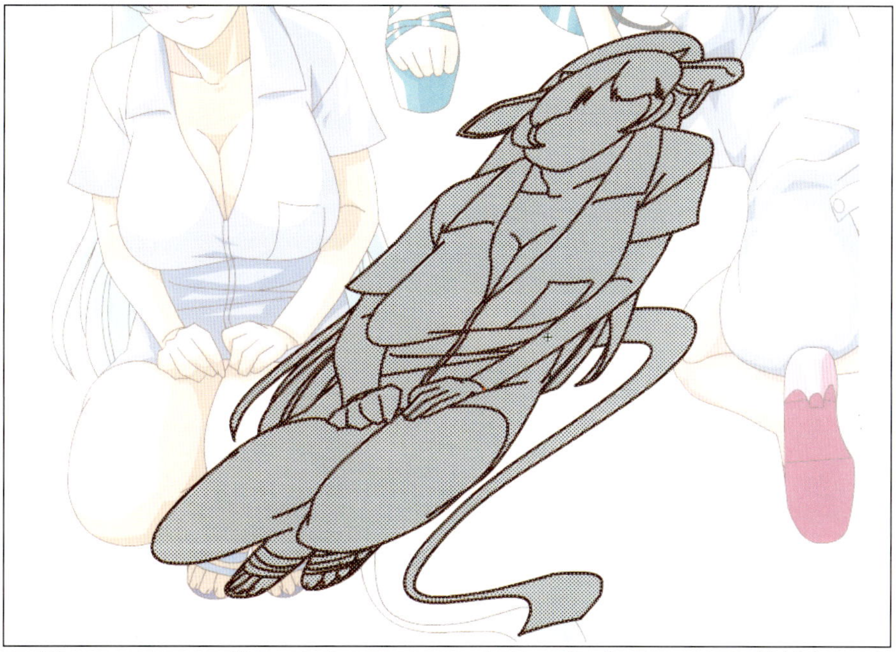

▲ When you give something a shadow, you have to decide on its direction with the highlights and shading you've already done in mind. In other words, you have to pay close attention to the light source, and you should clearly see the light's direction. Erase the remaining lines by double-clicking on them and hit the Delete key. Now it's starting to look like a real shadow.

The light is coming from up and to the left in front of these characters.

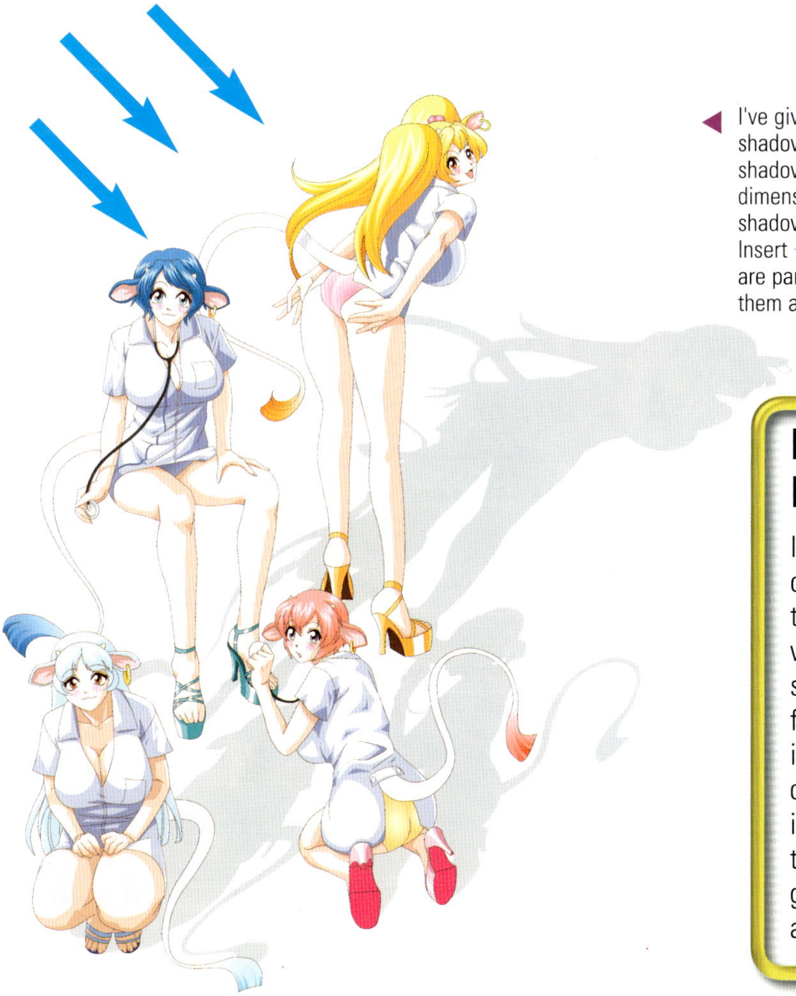

◀ I've given the other characters the same kind of shadow—this is what it looks like with all the shadows added. Now it looks fairly three dimensional. When you're done with all the shadows, click on the SHADOW layer and choose Insert → Convert to Symbol. Now all the shadows are part of the same unit, and you can manage them all as one.

Is it better to have shadows?

It's necessary to shade the characters themselves, but I think it's alright to decide whether or not to put shadows in based on how you feel about that particular illustration. Then again, I could be wrong. Maybe your illustration is better without the shadows. Computer graphics are all about trial and error.

Laying Out Text

Break apart text to display it exactly as you like, regardless of the browser environment.

All that remains is the title. My goal is to make my title appear as though it were written on the ground. Let's give it a try.

Insert another layer below the SHADOW layer and write on it with the Text Tool. Here, I'm using the title of my home page, MIMORIES. When I've decided on a position and angle for my title, I'll select the text and choose Modify → Break Apart.

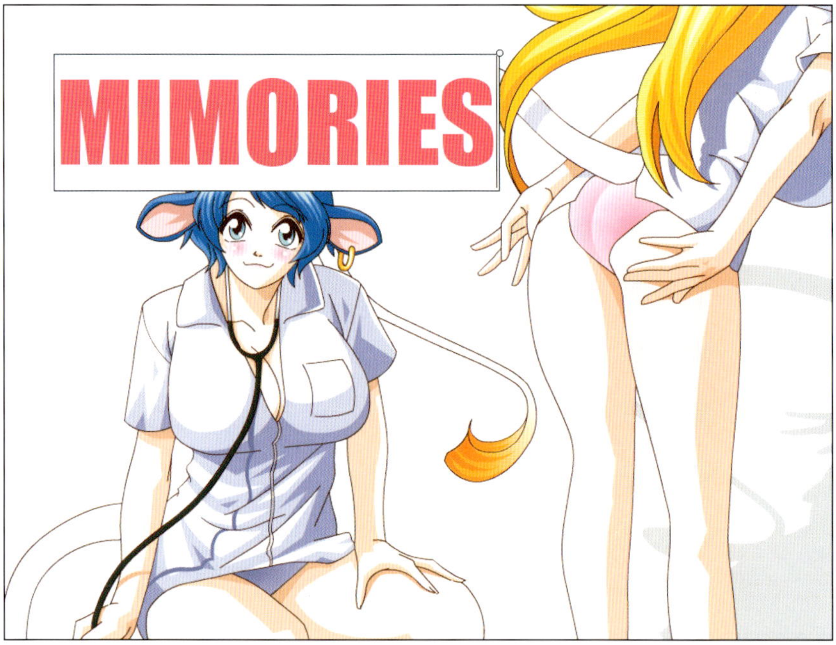

Point

The purpose behind breaking apart your text is to control how it appears on any PC. If you don't break apart your text and it's viewed from another PC, it's possible that it will not display properly. Your viewer might then not be able to see it as you intend, so to be safe you should be sure to break apart your text.

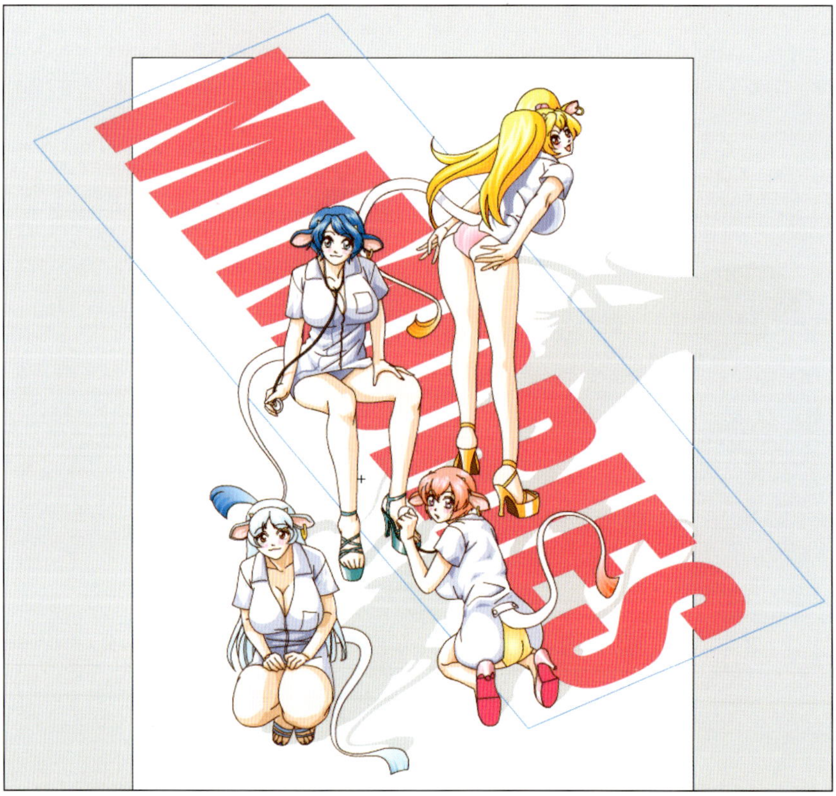

Now apply the Scale and Rotate modifiers just as you used them before on the shadows. The upper left part of this picture seemed a little empty, so I stuck my title in there at an angle to fill up the space.

Making the Shadows More Realistic

To make the shadows appear to fall across the text as well, make them transparent.

By putting the text in the very bottom layer, the shadows that lay in the layer above obscure it. Making them transparent will make the title easier to see, resulting in a more realistic shadow effect. Click on the SHADOW layer and select the entire SHADOW symbol. Since we can't adjust its Alpha value as is, choose Modify → Break Apart and break the shadows up until you can break them no further. Now lower the shadows' Alpha value (making them transparent) in the Mixer Panel until the title beneath them becomes visible.

Completion!

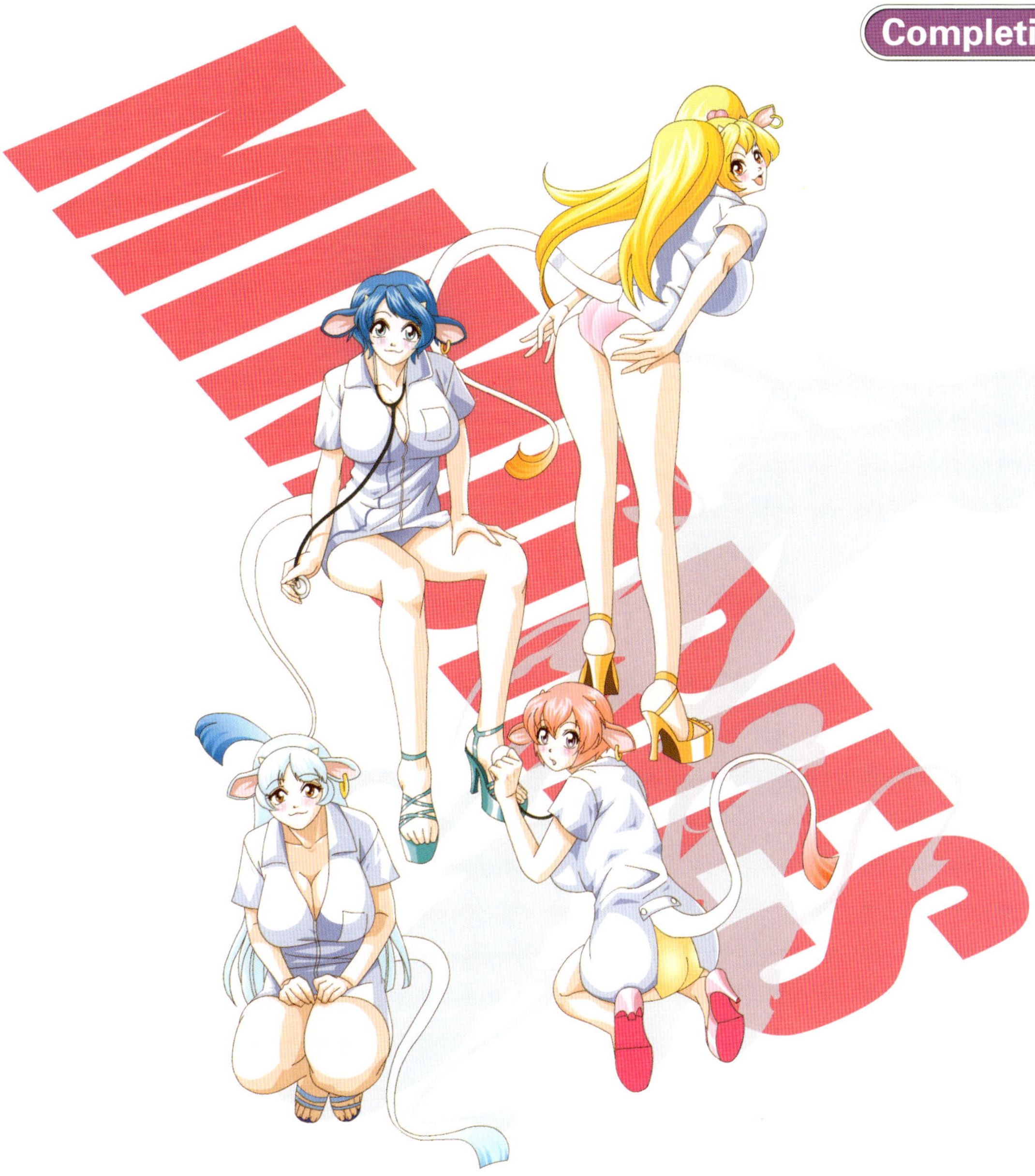

▲ This piece is now complete. It was a long way coming this far, but check out the slick finish! I love being me. Thanks for coming along for the ride.

Gallery

This isn't a limited run Christmas piece or anything, but just something I made for kicks. The bunny girl on the right with the blue hair is ūshi, and the one on the left is Pelipanna.

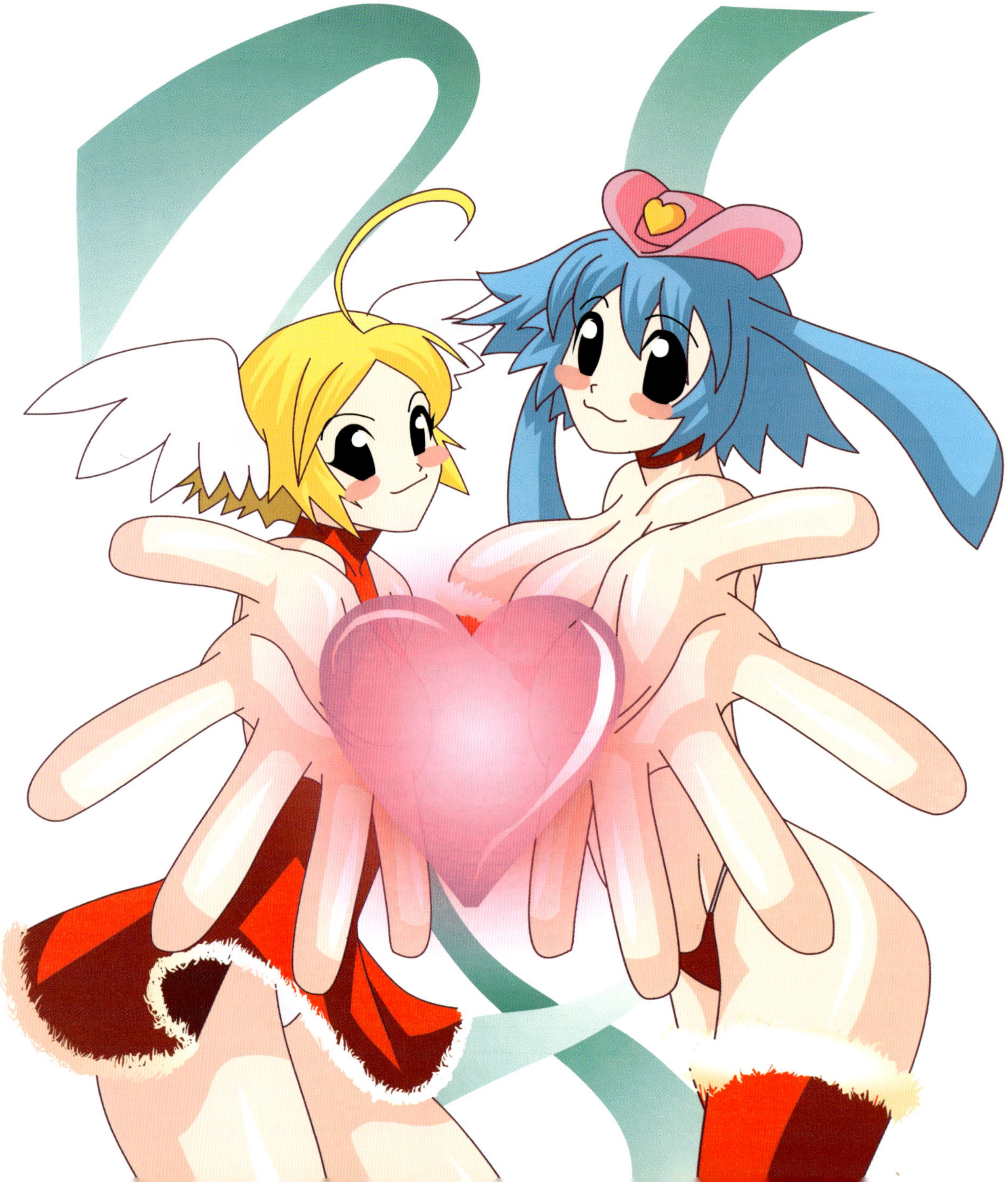

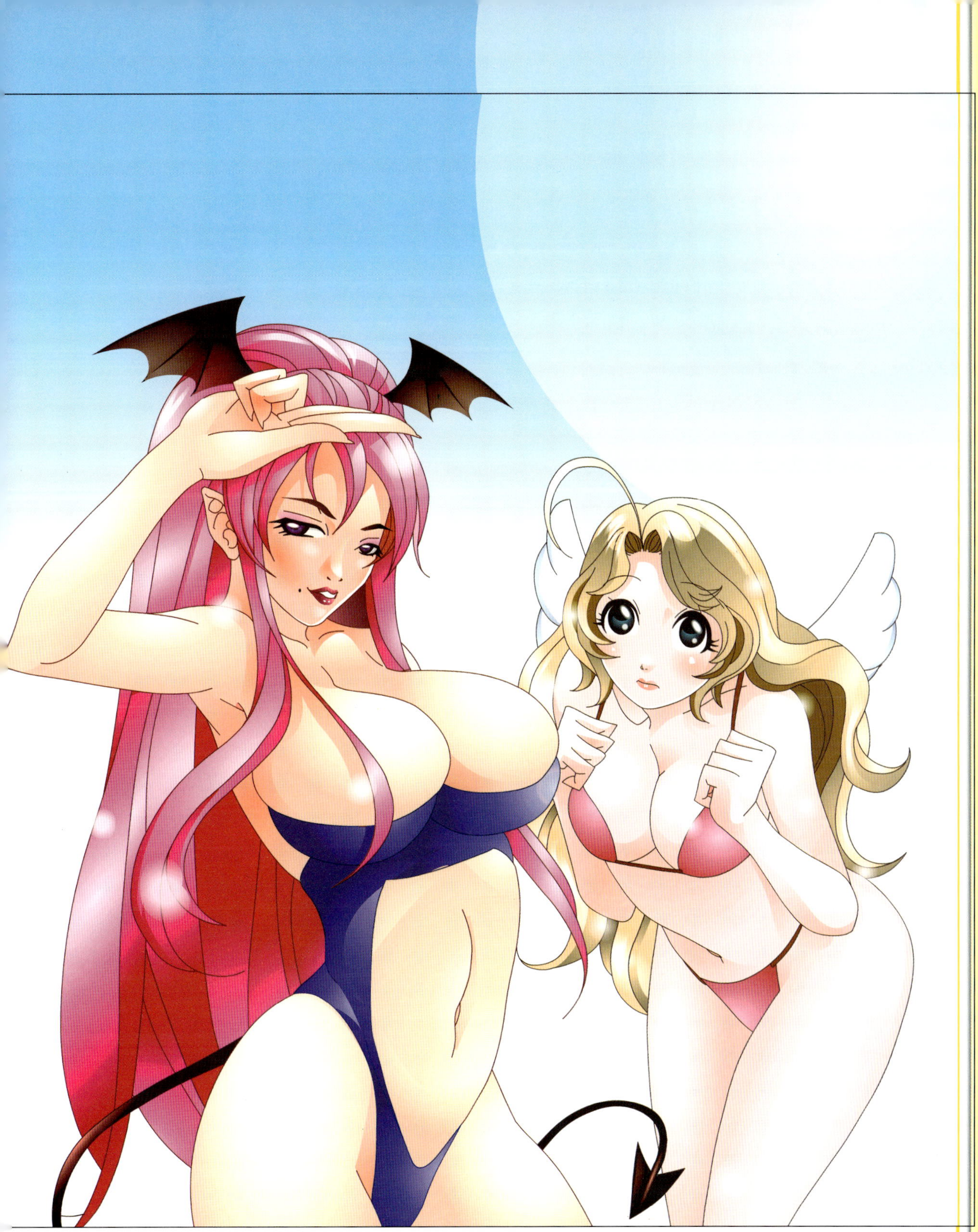

This one is a collaboration piece I drew with Teru for the top banner on his Bishoujo search site. I drew the character on the right; Teru drew the one on the left and did all the coloring.

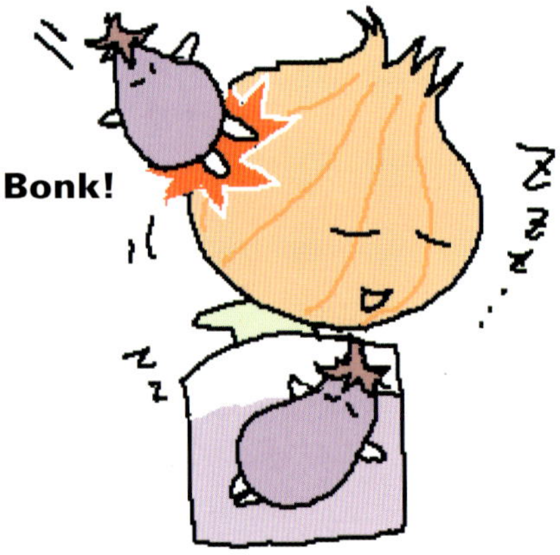

Machinery
My handmade machine, Joanna:
Athlon 1.7GHz CPU, AOpen AK77-333 motherboard, 512MB PC2700 RAM, 64MB GeForce 4 MX420, 40GB hard disk, floppy disk drive, DVD-ROM, CD-RW
OS: Windows 2000
Monitor: 19" Sony G420
Tablet: Wacom ArtPadFan
Printer: Canon BJF850
For drawing pictures, this setup is overpowered, and I love it.

Software
Flash MX (for creating graphics), Fireworks 4.02 (for converting graphics files), Dreamweaver 4.0 (for creating web pages)
So long as I have these three apps, I'm not much at a loss-for now.

Goals
To master American comic-style animation and take the world by storm! Just as soon as I set up my home page, that is.

Favorite Artists
None. I'm really just in love with my own work.

Internet Connection
Flets 8M ADSL

Teru

Sex
Male

Age
I've not aged at all since I was 27.

Personality
I get really into things easily, but I get bored with them just as easily, too.

Hobbies and Interests
Other than drawing, I chat a lot on the Internet. I'm always looking for friends, and I try to respond to foreigners even with my incomprehensible English.

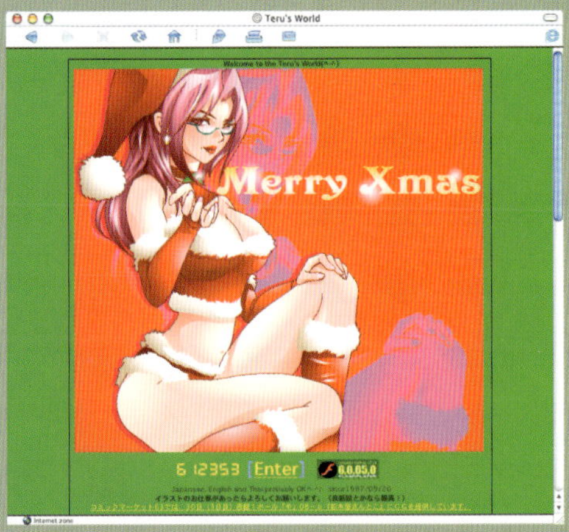

Teru's World
http://www.pluto.dti.ne.jp/~dtino004/

The Line Drawing

The Smooth modifier is your key to drawing neat lines.

Before you begin, make a few preparations before you start working. First, select the Pencil Tool's Smooth modifier to neaten up the lines you draw. Then, so your lines don't start sticking to everything else, click the magnet icon and turn off Snap to Objects.
Using the Pencil Tool opens the Properties panel, where you are free to change the line color, type, and thickness. In my case, when I'm drawing graphics I select the absolute lowest thickness. When I'm drawing animation images I set it to 1.0.

Point

Just like version 5 did, there are windows that do not open on startup with MX. Before you get started, be sure to choose the following: Window → Toolbars → Main, Status, and Controller; if Window → Tools isn't checked, check it as well.

Turn the Magnet (the Snap to Objects function) off to keep your lines from sticking together.

Set the Pencil Tool's option to Smooth.

The image your work gives off changes according to the line thickness.

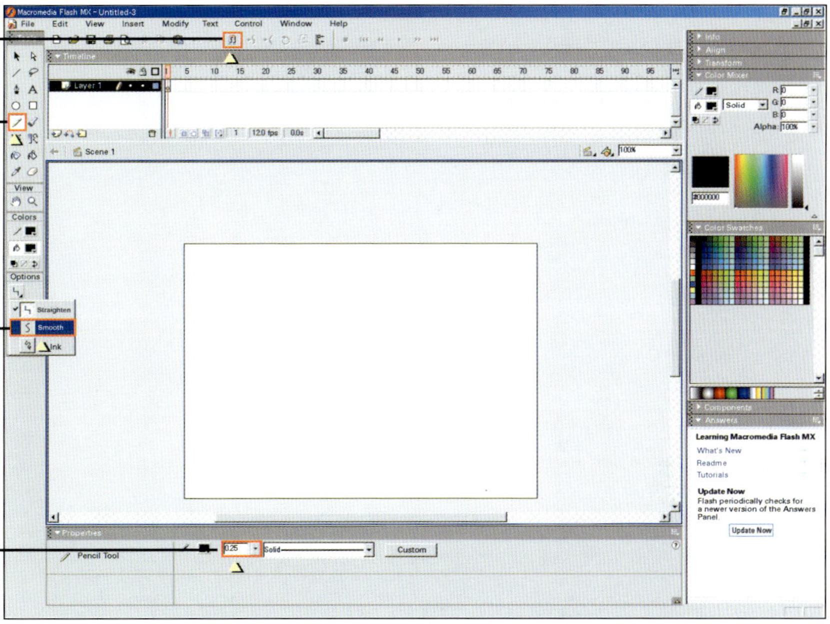

▲ Make the preparations described above before you make your rough sketch.

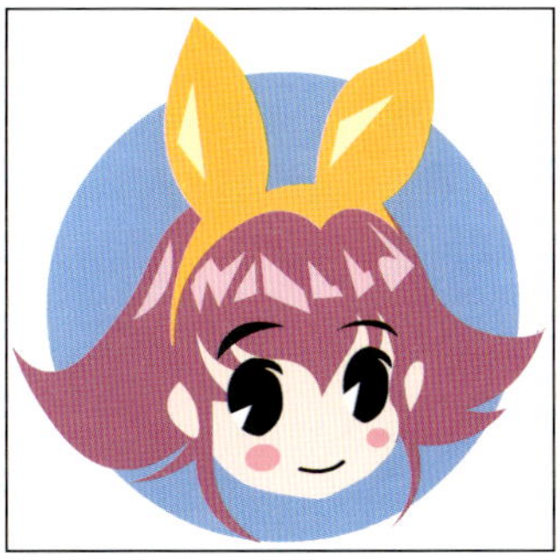

Hello, everyone! I'm Fal.
As the site mascot, Master makes me cosplay. The truth is, I like it so, I'd probably do it myself, anyway.

This time around, Master says he's writing a book on making Flash computer graphics, and he's been working on it all through the night. I haven't seen him like this in a long time, and I'm pretty excited about it. But, uh, this is the first time Master has ever tried using Flash MX, so I hope it turns out alright.

Oh, by the way, this is my "American Waitress" costume. Like it?

Tracing Layer and Preparations

You are free to draw your rough sketch in Flash, and then adjust the screen size to match later.

In Flash, you draw a rough sketch using the Pencil Tool. I might otherwise adjust my lines as I go, but sure enough, this time I've got so many lines to work with, I'm just going to trace it now. Use your Pencil Tool for tracing as well.
Once your rough sketch is done, decide on a screen size that will make your work easier and create a layer for your tracing. When you decide on your screen size, make the upper left corner of the white workspace a reference point and imagine the height and width of your drawing from that point. Choose Modify → Document to bring up the Document Properties dialog, click the Contents button, and click OK to close the dialog. The dimensions of the white portion of your screen now match the size of your rough sketch.

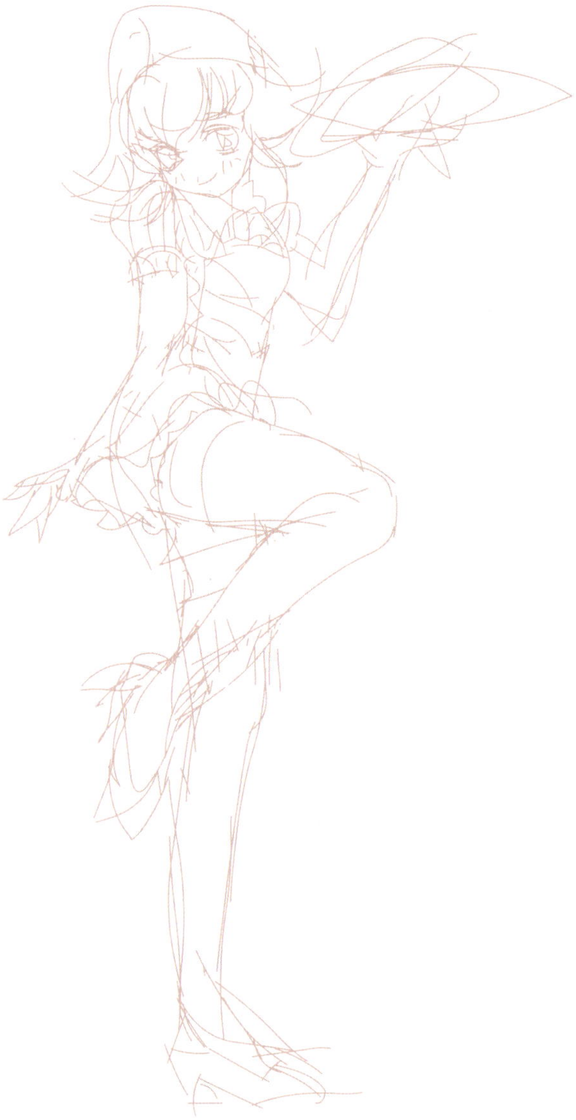

Reference Point

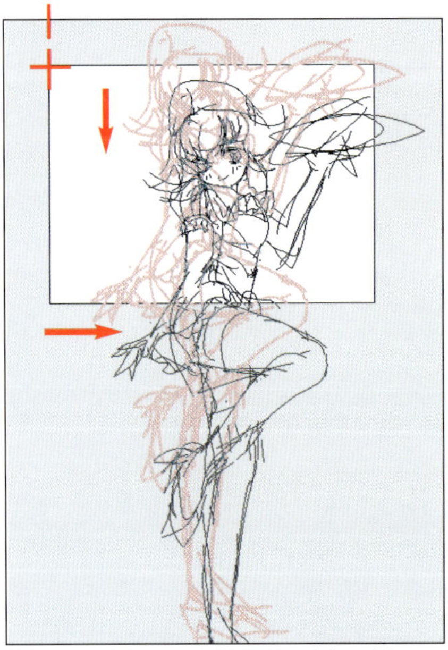

▲ Make the upper left corner of the white area your reference point and imagine how much more space the overhanging rough sketch (the pink lines) will require (the black lines), and position it accordingly.

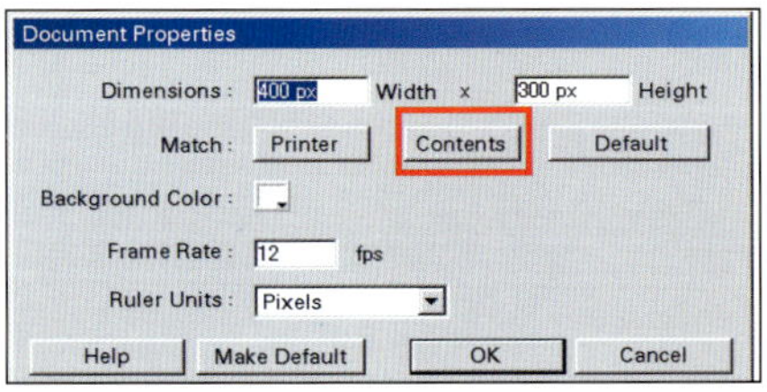

◀ Click the Contents button in the Document Properties dialog to change the Dimensions setting to match your image.

Lock icon

Insert Layer button

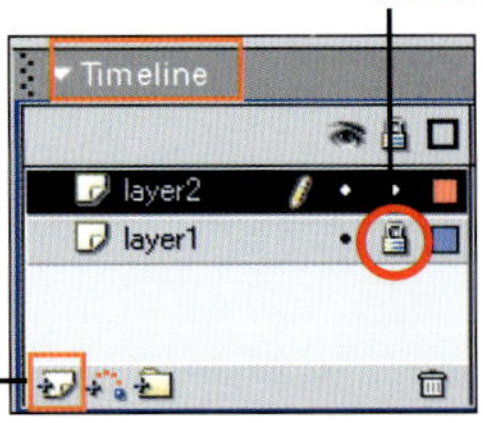

◀ Lighten the color of your rough sketch to make it easier to trace. Then stack a new layer on top it by choosing Insert → Layer or clicking the Insert Layer button. Click on the dot in the Lock column of Layer 1 (the rough sketch) to keep it from interfering with Layer 2 (the trace) and click on Layer 2. When the Pencil icon appears in it, your preparations are complete.

Finishing the Line Drawing: Eyes

To tighten up your image, paint the eyes in ahead of time.

Now we'll start to finish off the line drawing. There are two points to keep in mind about your trace. One is the constant use of the Zoom In and Zoom Out functions to make drawing your lines easier. The other is making sure all your lines fully intersect each other to make cleaning up the excess later on easier.

I'm in the habit of painting in the eyes first. After that I get rid of the eye lines. The point of erasing the lines is to prevent the eye color from being lost when the picture is shrunk. Choosing Erase Lines from the Eraser Tool's options makes removing them easy.

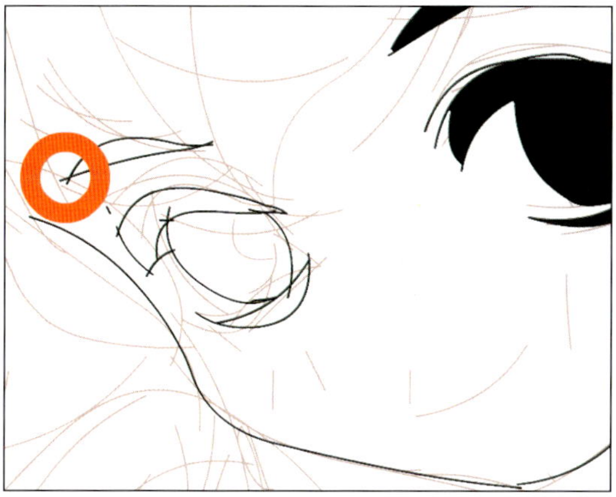

▲ Make sure all lines fully intersect each other. This makes them easier to erase later. Here, I'm working with my sketch displayed (zoomed in) at 800% magnification.

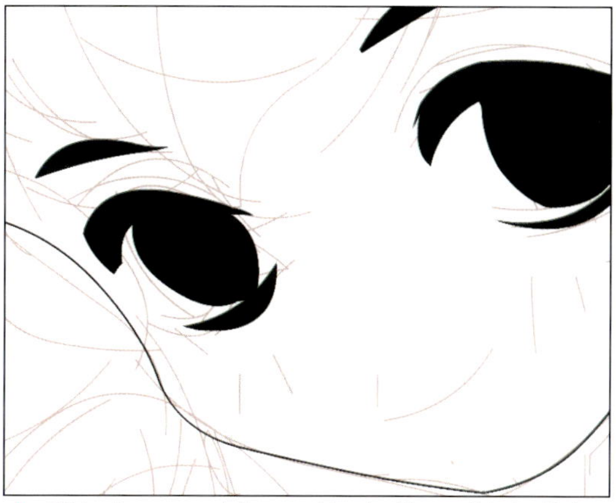

▲ Fill in the areas delineated by the lines with the Paint Bucket Tool. When you're done coloring, erase all the eye lines.

Point

Even if your lines are not completely overlapping and closed off, selecting Flash's Paint Bucket Tool options, Close Medium Gaps and Close Large Gaps, lets you fill their areas in anyway.

To leave your fills untouched and erase only your lines, Select Erase Lines from the Eraser Tool's options.

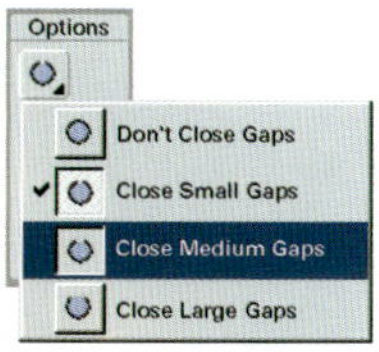

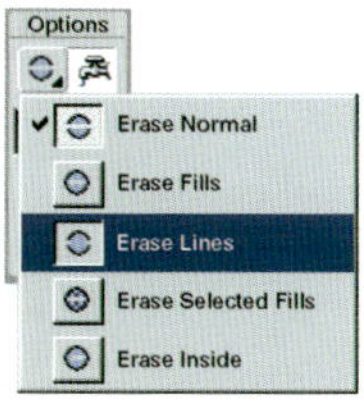

What's a "Layer?"

If you lay a clear sheet on top of a drawing, you would be able to draw on it or erase things from it without affecting the drawing beneath it. This effect is reproduced on the computer with a "Layer." Regardless of how many layers you create, you can easily stack and shuffle them around. This functionality is commonplace in modern graphics software tools.

In Flash, lines connect to one another just by intersecting, but you can also avoid this effect by drawing them in different layers.

Techniques Using the Tool Palette

The Lasso Tool: It works for modifications, too.

One important element in reproducing femininity in a drawing would be the hand.

For times like this when you have to do fine detailing, make an oversized sketch of the area in a different layer and shrink it to fit afterwards. Keep this convenient technique in mind: you can use it for improving things you've already sketched, too.

Incidentally, my wife provided the pose for this picture. ▶

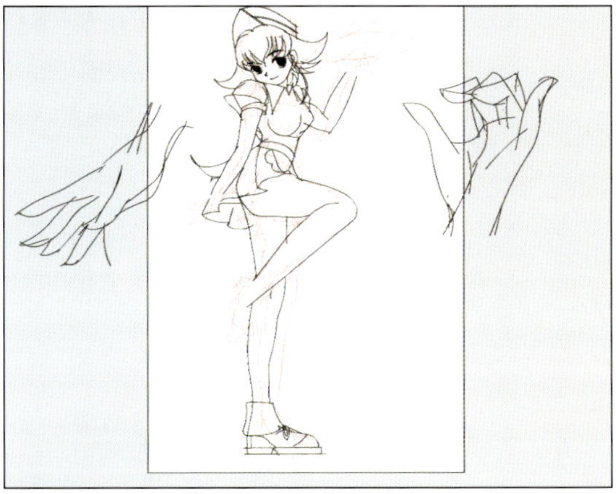

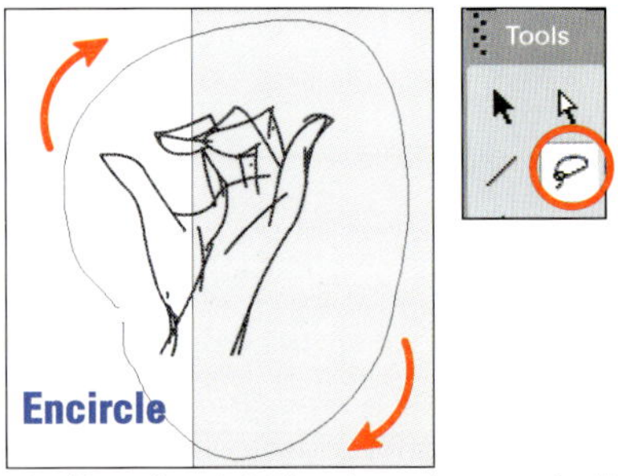

▲ Here, I'm shrinking down the oversized hand I've drawn to match Fal (the girl) here on my screen. I'm also using the Lasso Tool to encircle and select the hand.

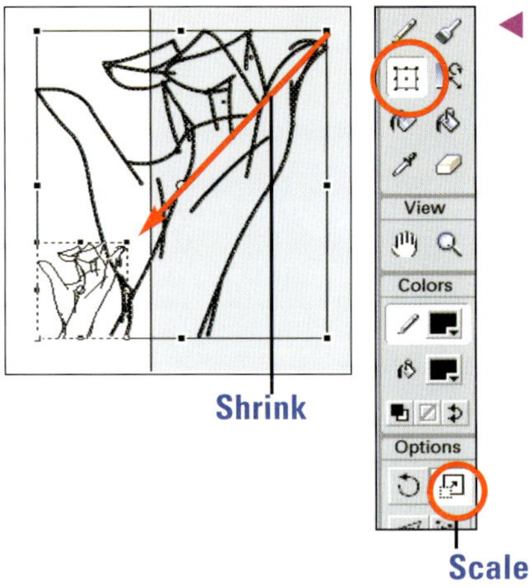

◀ Next, use the Free Transform Tool to select your image, hit the Scale button, and drag the handles on the corners of the selection box to enlarge and shrink it. Once you're happy with the size of your image, lay it atop your drawing and align it, adjusting the connecting sections as necessary. Using the Scale function this way does not change the length vs. width ratio, so it is useful in cases like this.

The Rotate and Skew function: Transforming objects freely

To make the as yet undrawn other foot, I first encircle the one I've already done with the Lasso Tool, choose Edit > Copy, and then Edit > Paste. Finally I use the Rotate and Skew function and position the foot.

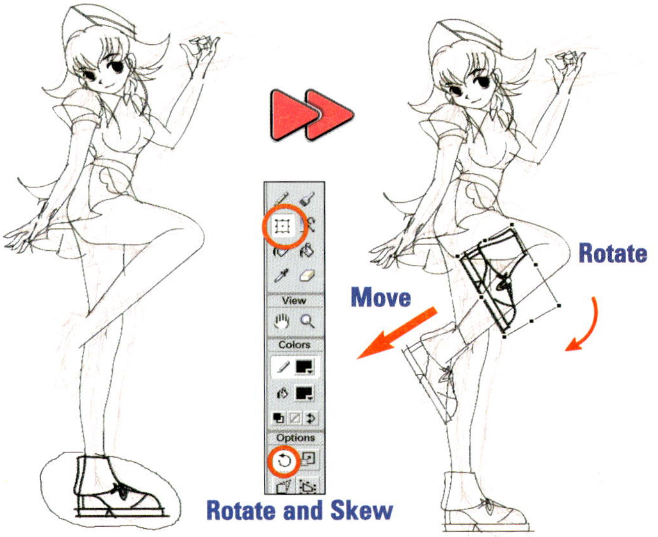

▲ Use the Lasso Tool to select and copy the foot that we've already drawn.

▲ After you use the Rotate and Skew function on it, line the foot up to match the angle of the leg.

Point

The Free Transform Tool lets you do exactly what the name says: transform certain objects freely. Using the Scale function lets you enlarge or shrink images and the Rotate and Skew function lets you rotate objects. Both leave the selected object's structure intact.

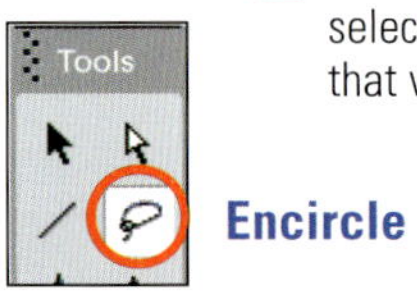

Cleaning Up the Line Drawing

The Eraser Tool: Snip away overhanging lines.

Once you're done tracing your rough sketch, delete Layer 1 as it is now unnecessary. Now, we move on to the final stage of finishing your line drawing.

First, we'll erase the bits of line we don't need and clean them all up. Try using the Eraser Tool's Faucet modifier to neatly erase unnecessary lines. At the same time, be sure to add in any missing lines you come across.

This is what my illustration looks like after deleting the rough sketch and leaving behind just the tracing. Now it's on to the cleanup. ▶

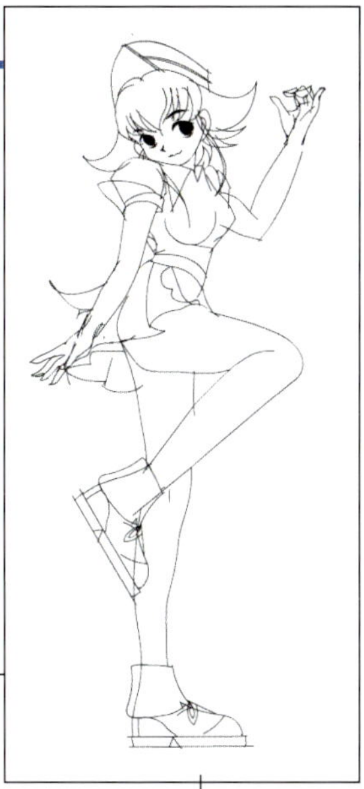

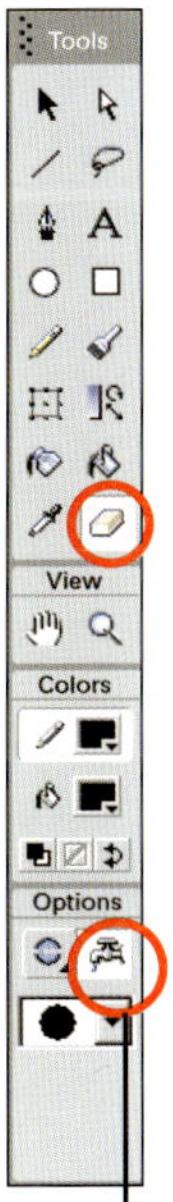

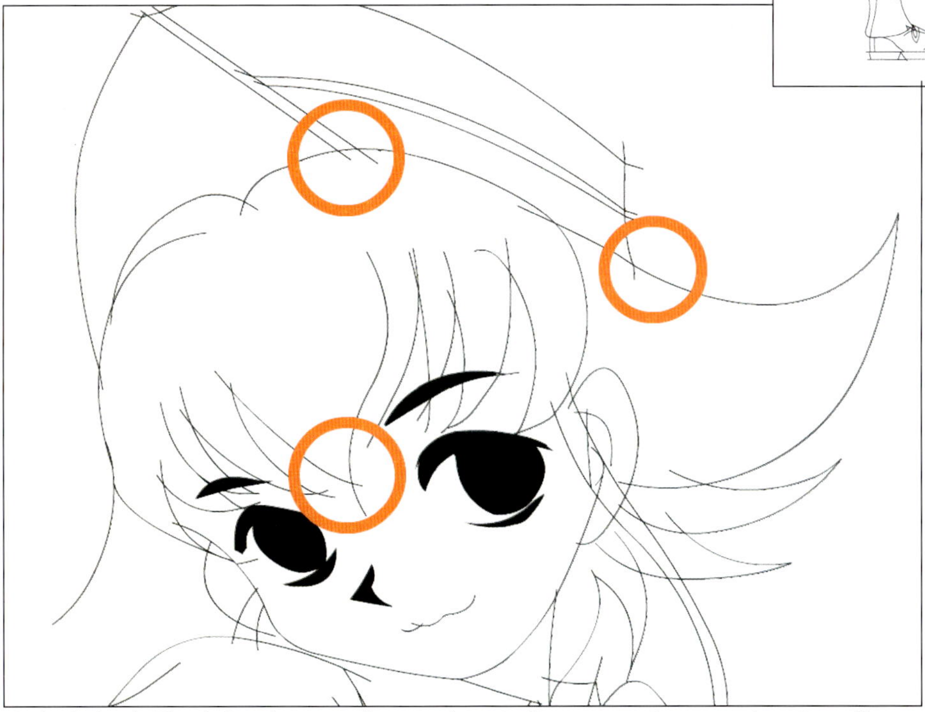

▲ Look closely. The circles above are all areas where the lines are too short or too long-they will get my careful attention.

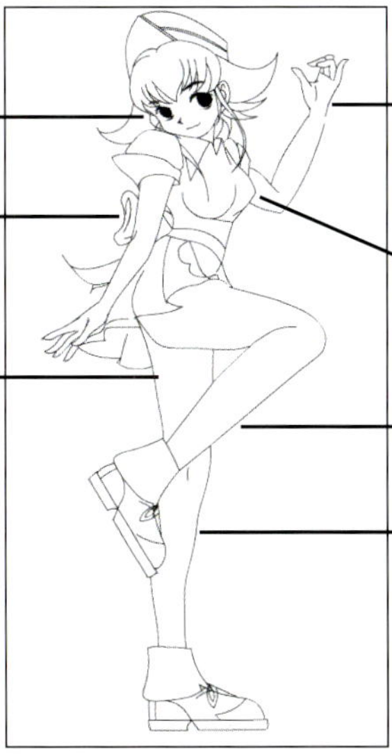

In practice, after the cleanup, I take a few notes on things I observe. Then I go down the list and take care of each one. ▶

The timing of layer deletion

When your trace is relatively complete, right click on the name of the layer you want to delete in the Timeline. Select Delete Layer in the pop-up menu.

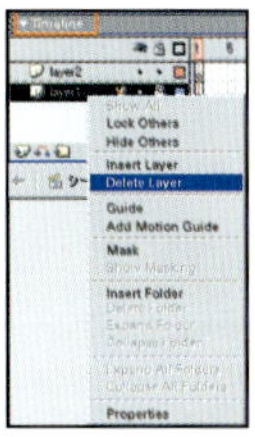

Line Drawings: Super Technique 1

Applying the Magnet: Securely connect lines to one another with Snap to Objects.

After finishing the trace of your rough sketch, you would do well to remember that Magnet icon's function: Snap to Objects. Here, I'll introduce how to use it to fix any disconnected or shifted lines.

Point

You can securely connect your lines to one another by using the Arrow Tool with the Magnet icon (Snap to Objects) set in the On position.

Moving shifted lines

When the lines in your tracing aren't quite connected properly, as with this cuff, you can select the Arrow Tool and click the Magnet icon in the toolbar to drag your lines wherever you please.

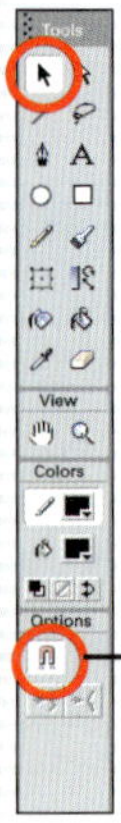

Snap to Objects is on.

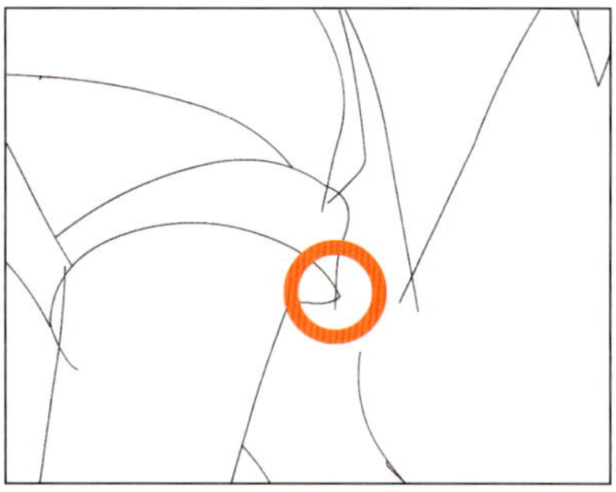

▲ One of the lines on this cuff is shifted to the inside. I hit the Magnet icon and move it with the Arrow Tool.

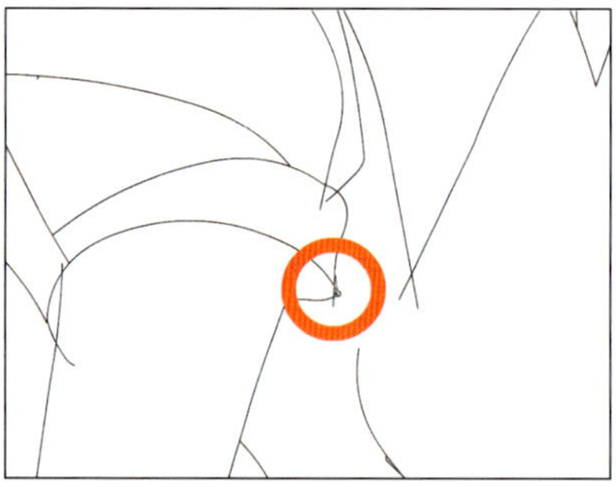

▲ With your cursor over the center of a line, click and drag the line to a position you like. Let go when you've securely joined the two lines.

Lengthening lines drawn too short

The Magnet icon's function can also be applied when your lines are too short and don't connect well. In that case, drag the end of one line and pull it to where you want to connect it on another line. Let it go when you're sure they're connected properly.

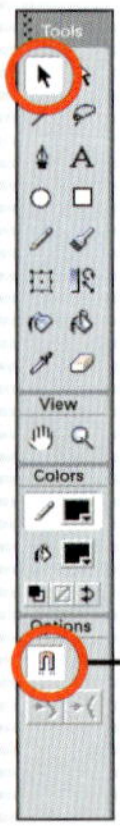

Snap to Objects is on.

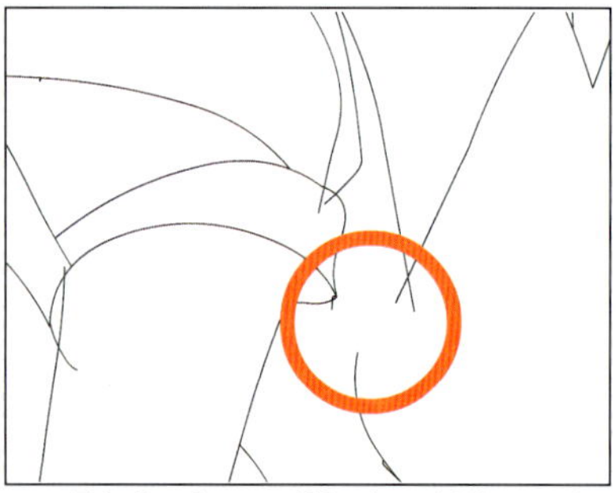

▲ This line is cut off in the middle, as though I didn't draw it at all when I was tracing. So, I hit the Magnet icon.

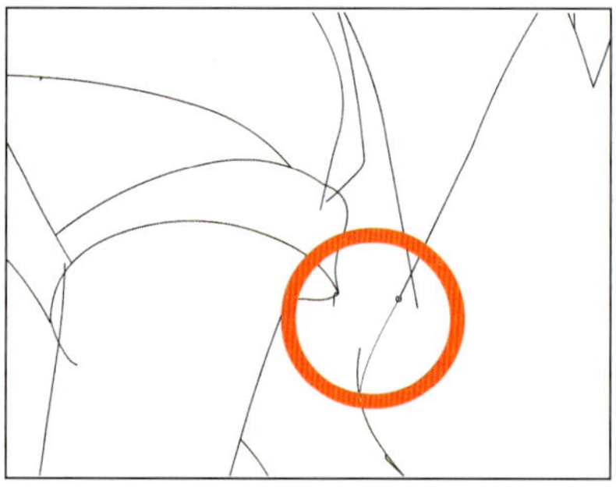

▲ Now I drag the end of the line I want to lengthen, holding on until I get to where I want to place it on the other line.

Affecting naturally wavy hair

When I draw hair or any other small, curved lines, I stop drawing them halfway through and use the Arrow Tool to pull the ends of them as I please. Then, if you float your cursor near a line you want to curve, it will turn into a round bracket. You can then drag and pull the line to make a nice wave. Be sure to turn the Magnet off for this.

Point

With the Magnet icon (Snap to Objects) on, you can securely connect your lines to one another. However, since moving any line at all close to another one makes them stick together, making fine adjustments becomes impossible. In situations like that, set the Magnet icon to Off.

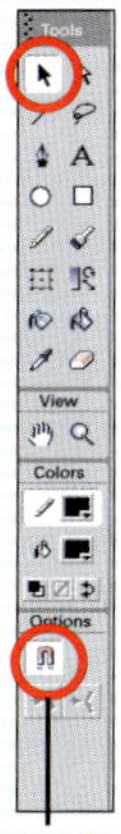

Snap to Objects is off.

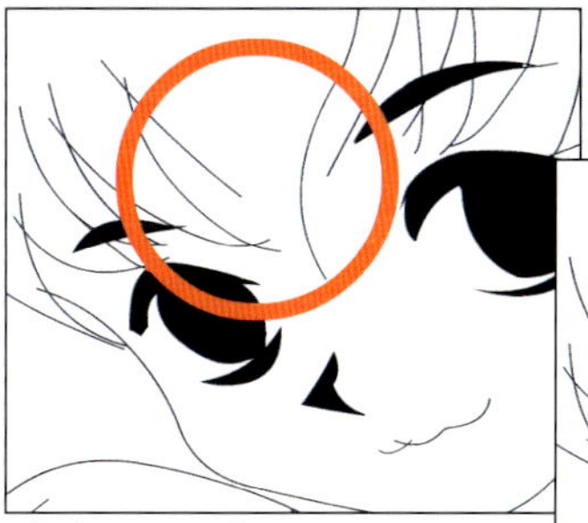

▲ I want to draw some wavy lines here with a natural feel and finish to them. So, I draw some hair halfway down and then switch to the Arrow Tool.

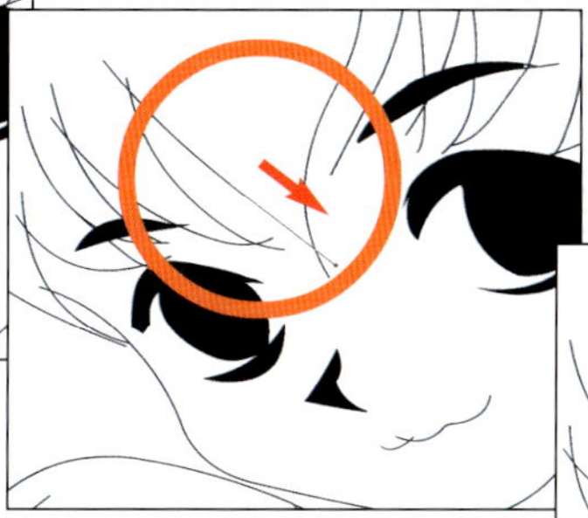

▲ Next, I grab the end of the hair and pull it until I like the length.

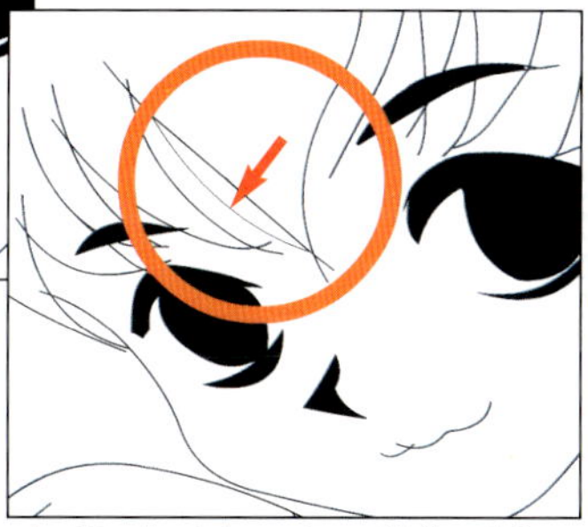

▲ Finally, I drag the middle of the line to curve it.

Warping a straight line into a large curve

When you want to draw a large curve, first use the Line Tool and draw a straight line. Then you can use the Arrow Tool as described above to bend it. Being able to freely change the angle of the line based on where you grab it is another convenient feature of the Arrow Tool.

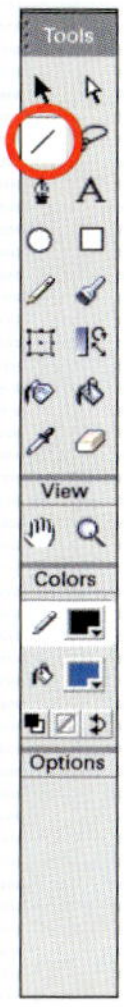

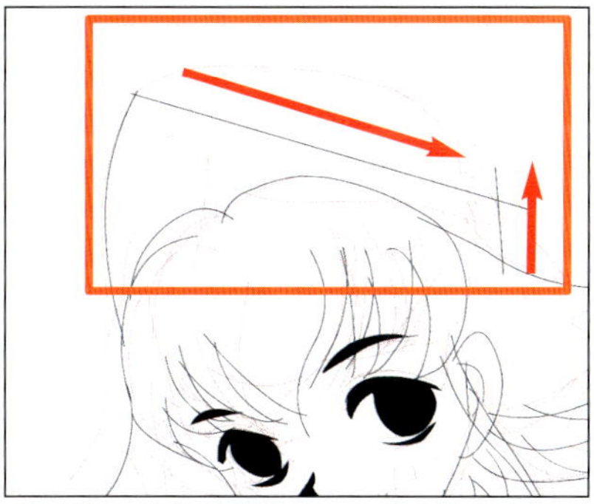

▲ When I draw large curves, such as the rim of this cap, I start by first drawing a couple of straight lines with the Line Tool.

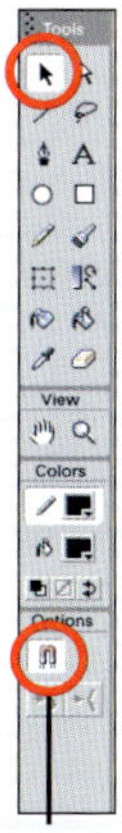

Snap to Objects is off.

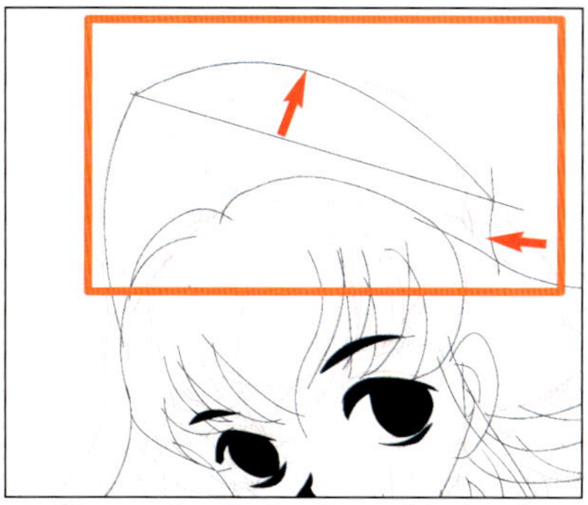

▲ You can bend a line by positioning the Arrow Tool cursor over the middle of it and dragging the mouse. This way, you can easily draw neater curves than if you'd tried to draw one from scratch.

Line Drawings: Super Technique 2

Neat curves and sharp lines with the Smooth and Straighten functions.

Lines drawn on a tablet or with a mouse are almost always shaky—they can hardly be called "neat." But, one of the great things about Flash is being able to go back and modify the shakiest of lines with ease. Don't worry if your lines are all crooked. Just draw, draw, draw! When you want to neaten everything up later on, use the Arrow Tool's Smooth and Straighten functions.

Point
Use the Arrow Tool's Smooth function to make your lines appear natural

Smooth out subtle curves

Even crooked lines drawn with a trembling hand can be made even by using the Smooth function afterwards.

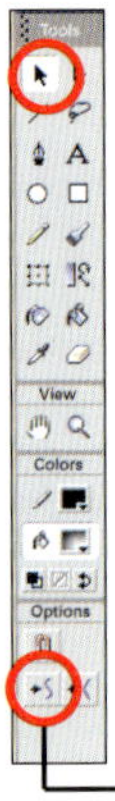

Smooth

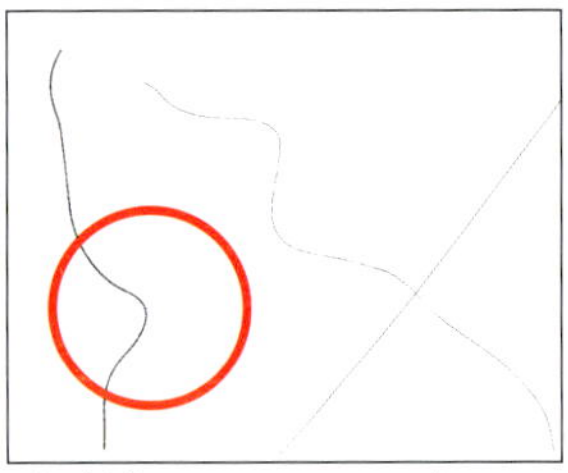

▲ When you want to draw a smooth curve, click on your freehand line with the Arrow Tool to select it. Then, click on the Smooth icon in the Toolbar. You can click it as many times as you like to repeat the effect.

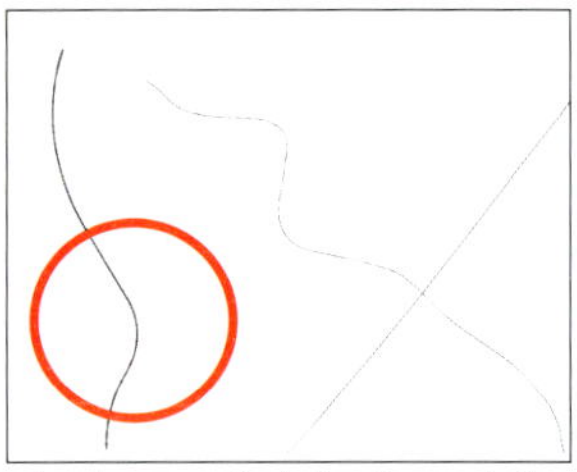

▲ I've applied the Smooth function to this line 6 times, and now it's changed from being too uneven to being a natural, neat curve. To reverse the effect, hit the Undo button in the Toolbar. Hit the Redo button to repeat the effect. At its default setting, Undo can remember the last 100 actions you've taken.

Straightening out erratic lines

Drawing a straight line is really difficult. Just as we did earlier, select the line with the Arrow Tool. This time, hit the Straighten button in the Toolbar to flatten out the line. You can hit that button as many times as you like, too. Keep it up until you're happy.

Point
Use the Arrow Tool's Straighten function to make any line even.

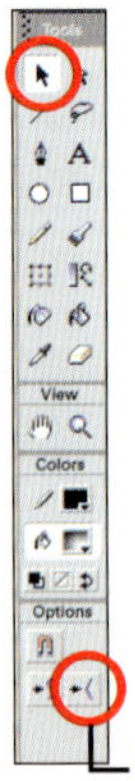

Straighten

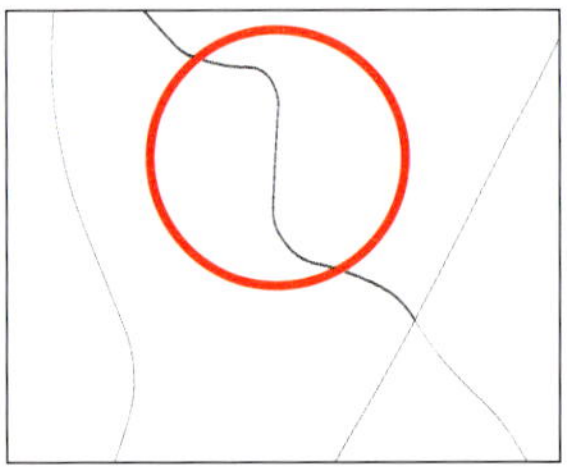

▲ When you want to straighten a crooked line, click on it with the Arrow Tool to select it. While the line is selected, hit the Straighten button on the Toolbar.

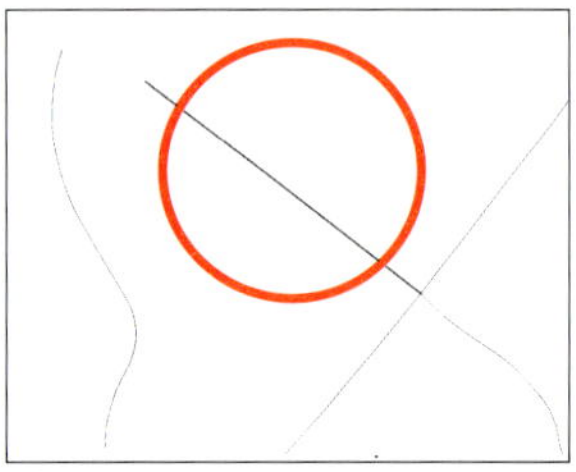

▲ This crooked, wiggle of a line is now straight—you can modify your lines as many times as you like. I straightened this line, by the way, after using Straighten 3 times. I've made no further transformations.

Add a Final Finish to the Line Drawing

Drawing accessories out of basic shapes and optimizing for a smaller file size

Lastly, now that we're done modifying all the areas that needed our attention on the main body, I'd like to create a little tray for her to hold.

Since the tray is circular, I'll draw it with the Oval Tool. The Fill Color is set, so any lines you draw with it like that will get filled accordingly. Hit the No Color button to clear the Fill Color.

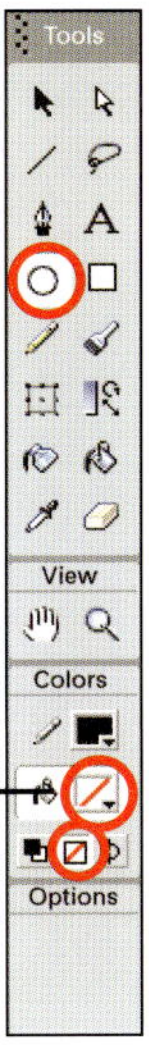

The "No Color" fill

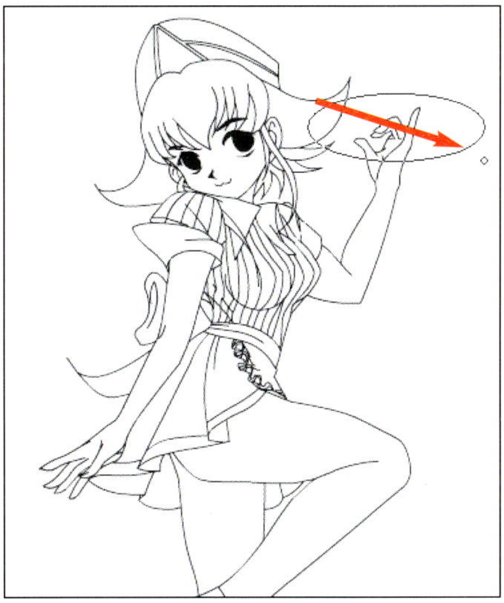

When you're certain that your trace is 100% complete, use the Optimization function to get rid of overlapping lines in your work that don't show up on-screen and to decrease your file size. From the Menu bar, choose Edit → Select All to highlight your entire drawing, and then choose Modify → Optimize.

An Optimize Curves dialog box will appear—check both options. Move the Smoothing slider all the way to None and hit click on OK. This will put your file on a diet without sacrificing much of your work.

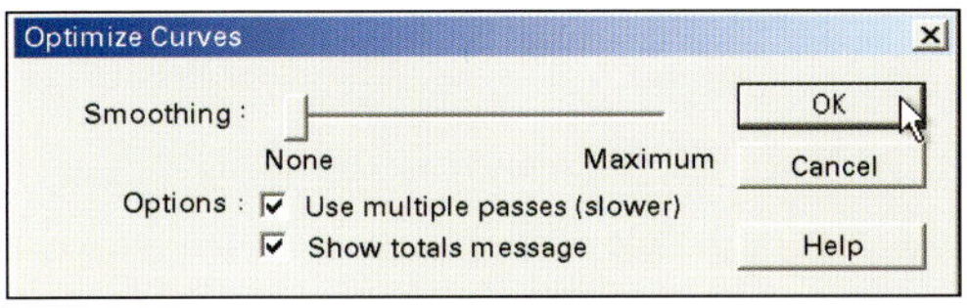

▲ Checking Use Multiple Passes automatically makes this function repeatedly optimize your work until no more can be accomplished.

Point
Optimize reduces file sizes by reducing the number of anchor points needed to define a curve.

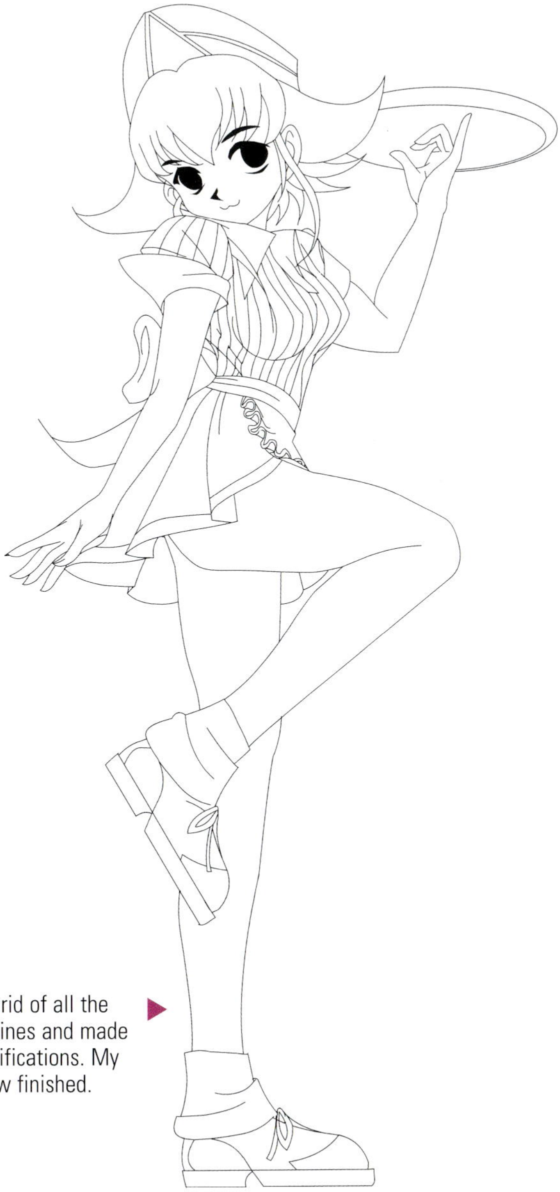

I've gotten rid of all the unneeded lines and made all my modifications. My trace is now finished. ▶

How to Paint Base Colors and Add Shading

Decide where your light source will be, and broadly fill in cell animation-style shades and shadows.

Now that the tracing is complete, it's time to apply the base colors. With the overall image of your piece in mind, select the Paint Bucket Tool, choose a Fill Color shown below on the Toolbar, and get to painting.

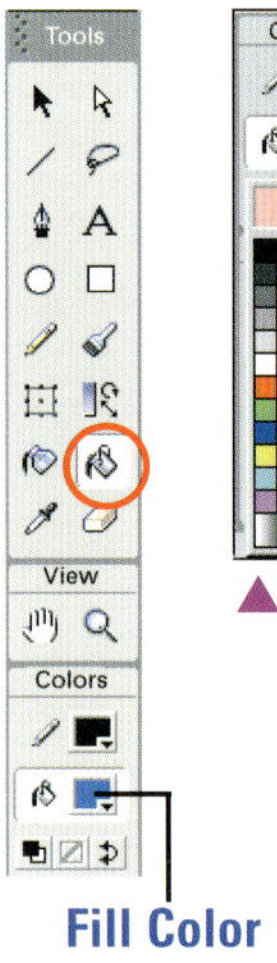

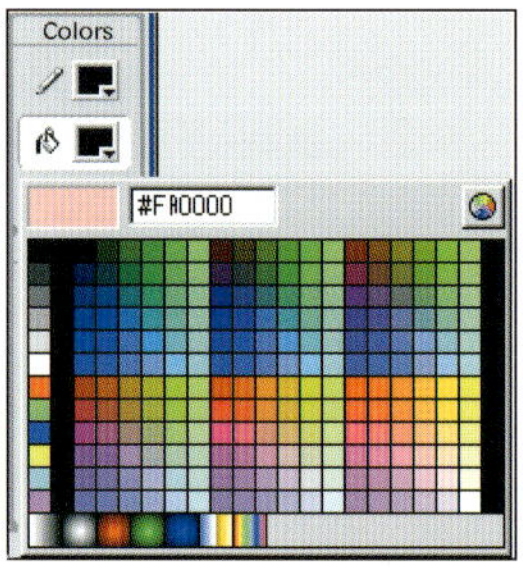

▲ Click on the color swatch next to the paint bucket icon in the Colors subpanel to open the Color Palette. Choose a color that goes with the mood of your piece, and if you don't see one you like, create a new one.

Point

If you can't get the Paint Bucket Tool to behave the way you want it to, it could be because some of the lines in your trace aren't fully closed. You can close them off and try the fill again, or you can select the Close Small Gaps option and try again. Go down the list in order and give each one a shot. In Flash, you can fill in areas even if there are small gaps in the fill lines.

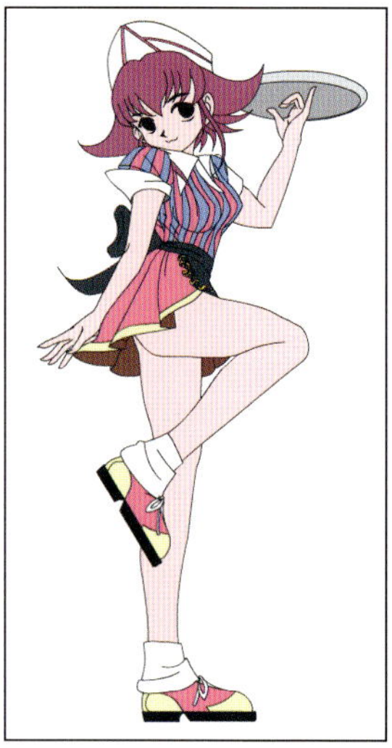

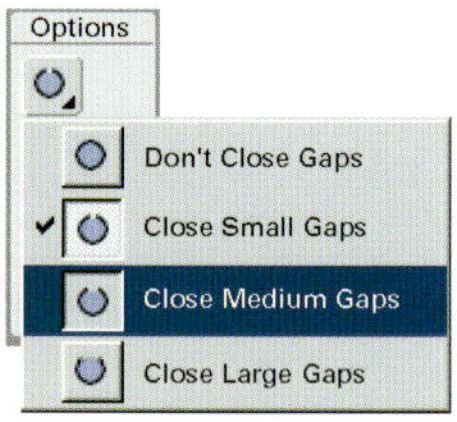

Creating a shade color

Base colors are no different, but by using the following process, you can easily create shade colors by making subtle changes to the ones already used in your work or in the Color Palette. Here, I'll demonstrate how to make a shadow fill based on the skin color. When you use the Eyedropper Tool to sample a color, make sure the cursor automatically changes into the Paint Bucket Tool. (Note: If it turns into the Ink Bottle Tool, then you've sampled a line color, not a fill color.)

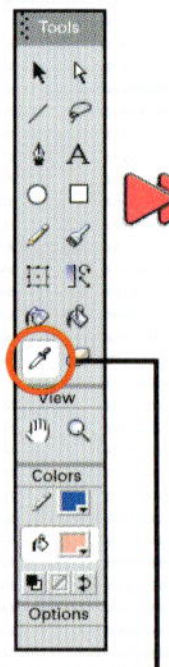

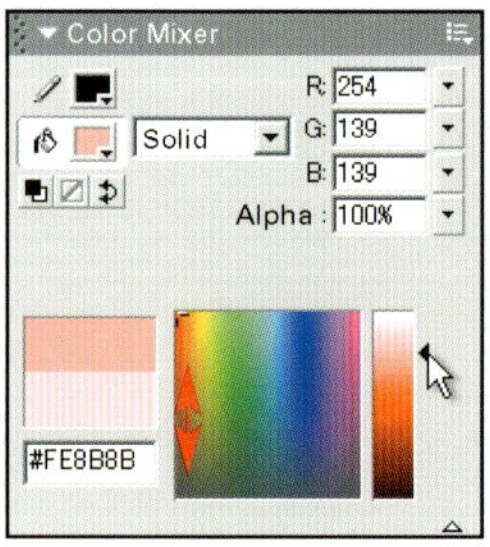

▲ The color you've sampled will show up here, in the Color Mixer. Move the Brightness control slider to change the color's shade.

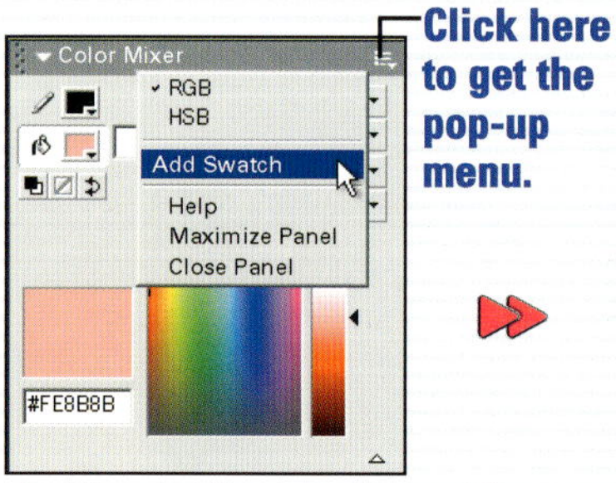

▲ When you're created something you like, be sure to click on the pop-up menu in the upper right corner of the Color Mixer panel and choose Add Swatch to save your color.

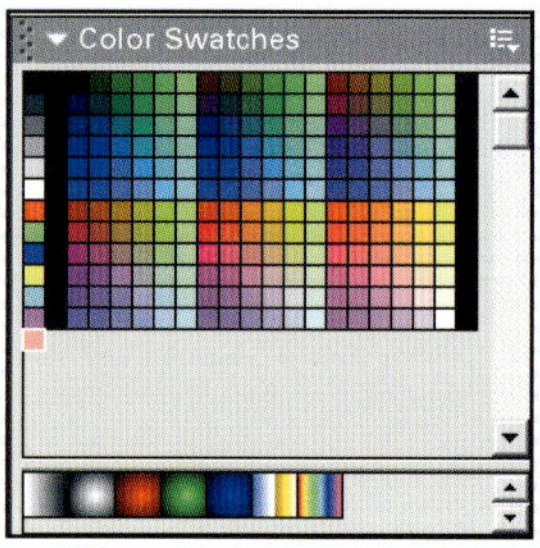

▲ The color we've made is now saved in the Color Swatches Panel (or "Color Palette").

Thoughts on shading methods

To finish the base coloring, add shading. But before we get to that, we have to decide exactly from which direction our light is shining. Then, once you know which areas on our character to shade, go ahead and mark them off with fill lines. Choose a fill line color different from the ones you've already used—here, I've chosen blue—and set your line thickness to 1.0. We want the fill lines to stand out, so erasing them later on will be easier.

Just as when you drew your tracing, set the Magnet icon to the Off position.

1

Establish the light direction

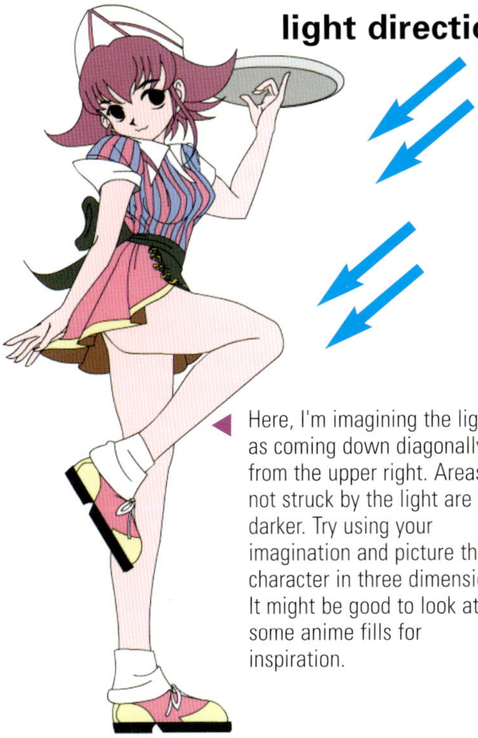

Here, I'm imagining the light as coming down diagonally from the upper right. Areas not struck by the light are darker. Try using your imagination and picture the character in three dimensions. It might be good to look at some anime fills for inspiration.

2

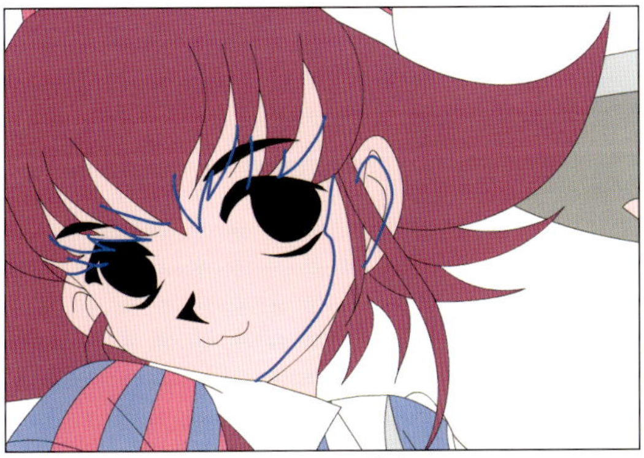

Use the Pencil Tool to mark off the areas you want to shade. Apply the same drawing techniques and principles we used earlier with the line drawing.

3

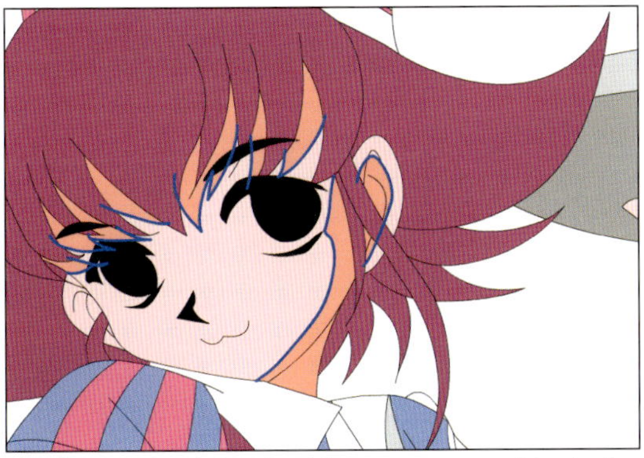

Once you've determined the areas you want to shade, set the fill color to the one you made earlier and use the Paint Bucket Tool to fill them.

4

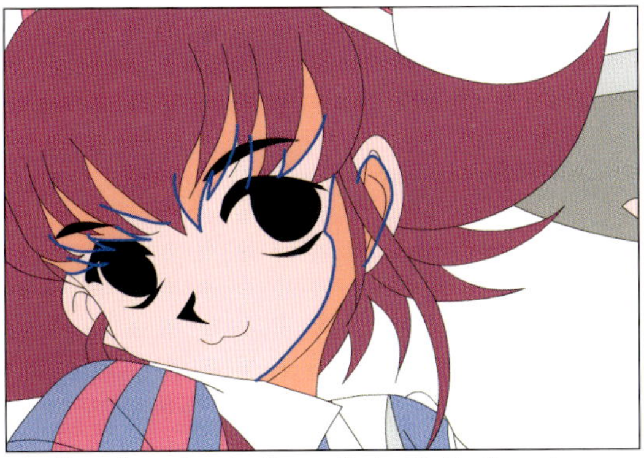

Here, I'm using the Eraser Tool with the Faucet modifier to get rid of the blue fill lines.

5

Done!

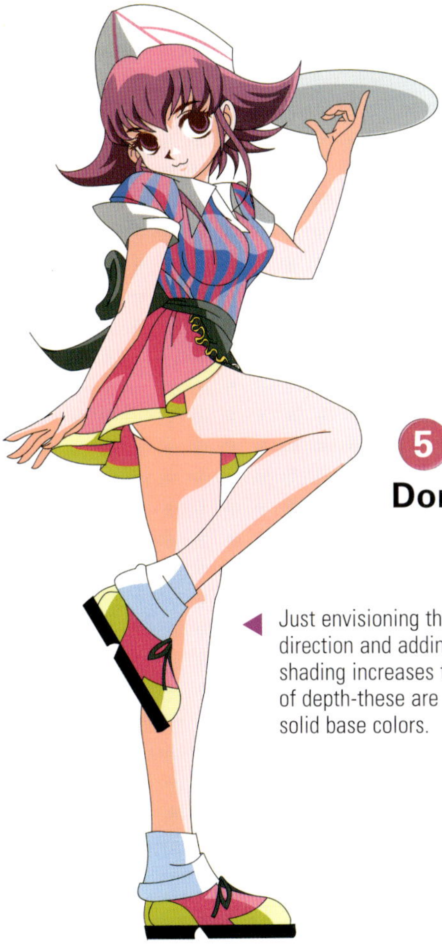

Just envisioning the light direction and adding some shading increases the sense of depth-these are still only solid base colors.

Mastering Gradations: The Royal Road to Coloring

Expressing supple curves for increased charm

Try making a gradation.

While we can say that our character looks more three dimensional as a result of our progress, it still seems somewhat flat and cold. By gradually changing a color over a given surface, we can express softness and depth. So, applying some gradational fills is our next step. But first, here are a few comments on creating gradations.

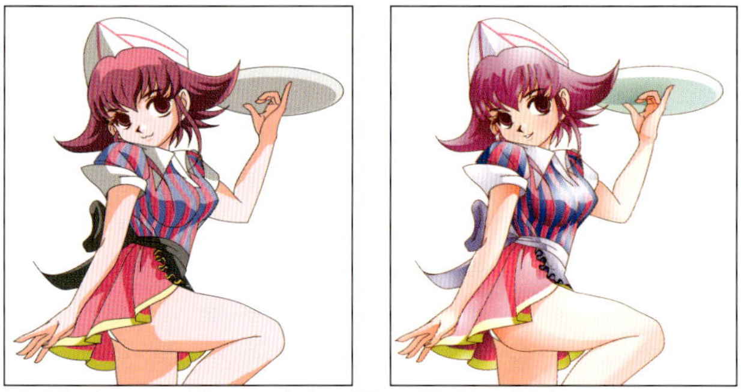

▲ The image with a gradation fill applied (at right) appears altogether softer and curvier than the image with only added shading (at left).

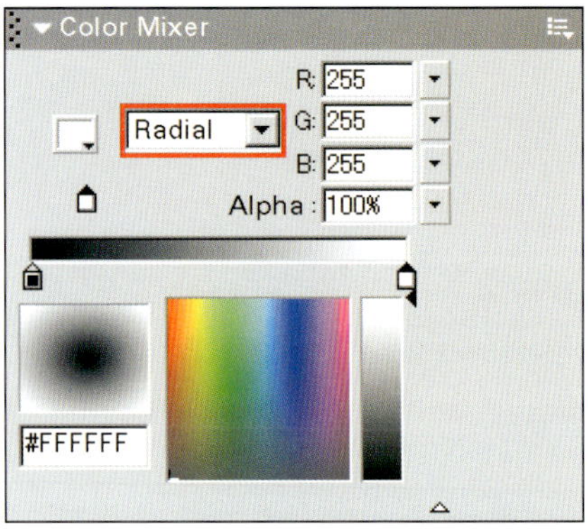

▲ Select Radial Gradation from the Fill Style pull-down menu in the Color Mixer panel, framed in red above. The initial settings show a gradation with white outer edges and a black center. First change this color and then make an original gradation.

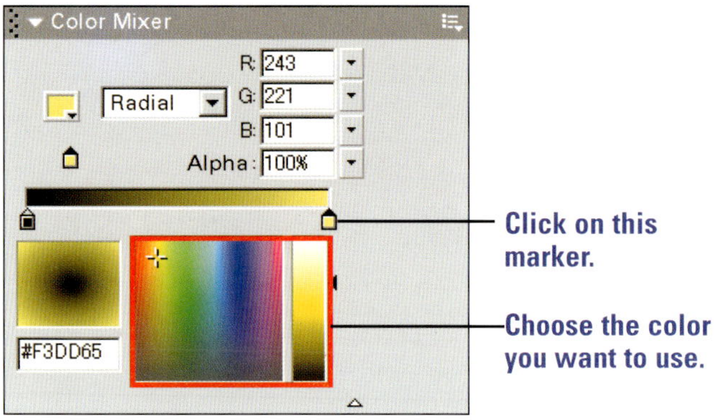

▲ Try changing the white outer edge first. Click on the white marker and choose a color you like from the Color Space. You can further fine-tune your choice by using the vertical Brightness slider.

The two gradation types

There are two varieties of gradation in Flash: linear and radial. Linear gradations are appropriate for flat or cylindrical surfaces while radial gradations are best suited for giving a spherical or curved appearance.

For drawing human characters, you will use radial gradations most often. They are especially important for expressing the supple curves common to female illustrations.

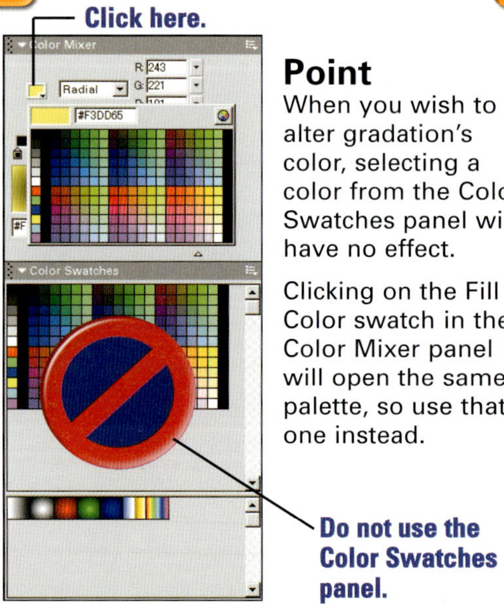

Point

When you wish to alter gradation's color, selecting a color from the Color Swatches panel will have no effect.

Clicking on the Fill Color swatch in the Color Mixer panel will open the same palette, so use that one instead.

Creating three-color gradations

When something about the nature of your project or the lighting isn't right, a two-color gradation might just not be enough. Try adding extra colors and using a more complex gradation. You can create a gradation with up to eight colors, but three is sufficient in most cases.

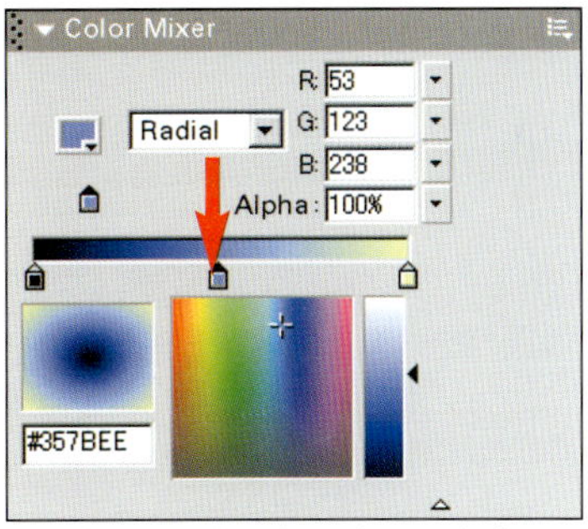

▲ Clicking directly underneath the gradation bar in the Color Mixer will spawn a new marker. Modifying this marker lets you create a new, complex gradation. You can remove extra, unnecessary markers by dragging them down and away from the bar.

Transparent gradations are also handy.

Colors have an "Alpha" transparency value. Making a color transparent allows the color beneath it to show through. An opaque color has a 100% Alpha value, while an almost invisible color has a 0% value.

You can change the Alpha values of the colors used in gradations as well—this is especially useful for highlight and shade filling.

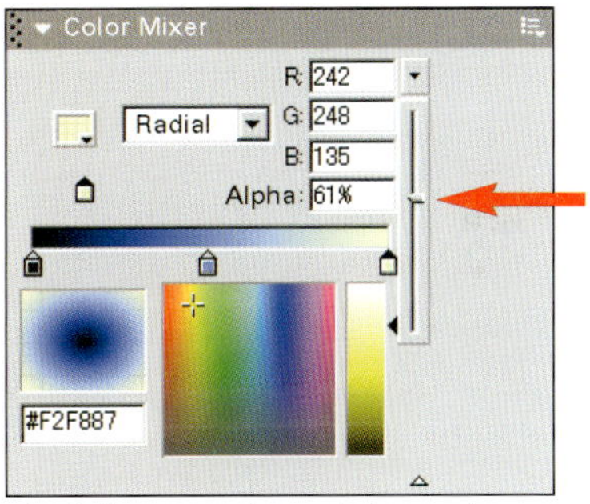

▲ Select a marker and change its color's Alpha value, and you can create a (semi-)transparent gradation.

Custom gradations and colors are an artist's treasure.

Be sure to save any gradations you create the same way you've saved your custom colors (see page 90).

Further, those original gradations and colors are essential to your work, so be certain to save them separately to disk.

In Flash, every time you create a new file, the various palettes are reset. If you load a color file you've saved in advance, then your custom gradations and colors will be immediately available for you to use.

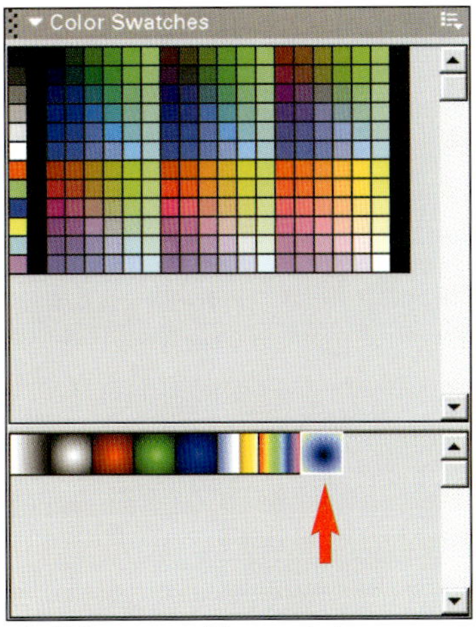

▲ When you add a gradation swatch, it is displayed in the bottom of the Color Swatches panel.

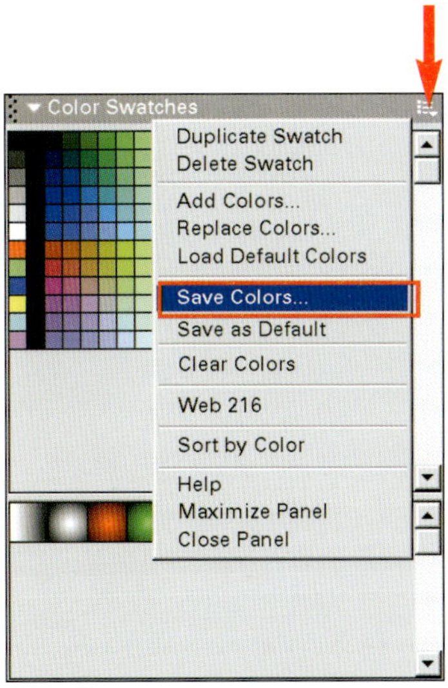

▲ Click on the pop-up menu in the upper right corner of the Color Swatches panel and choose Save Colors. Save your file with the .clr extension, and next time you can load your colors by choosing Add Colors in the same menu.

Practical Gradational Application: Part 1

Use gradations to draw eyes with feeling.

Now, we'll try actually applying a gradational fill. Here, with drawing an eye as an example, I will show you how even a beginner can easily apply gradations and create mood.

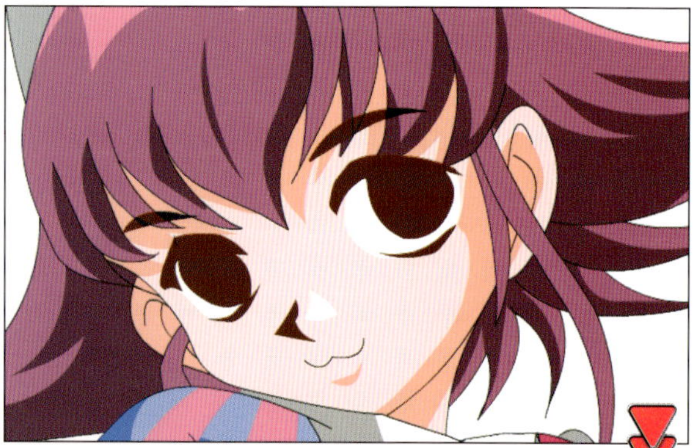

First, change the eye from its traced color state, black, to the desired base color (here: dark brown; color code #333300) with the Paint Bucket Tool.

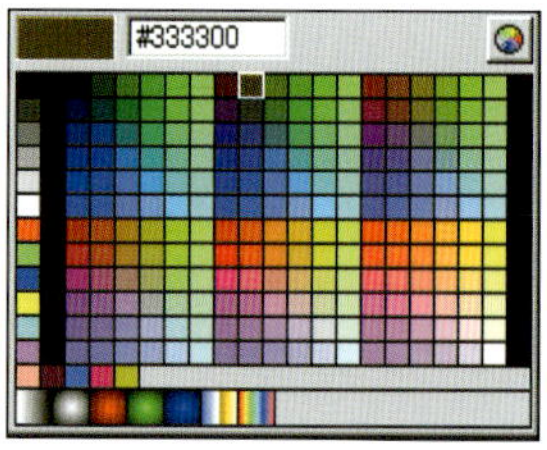

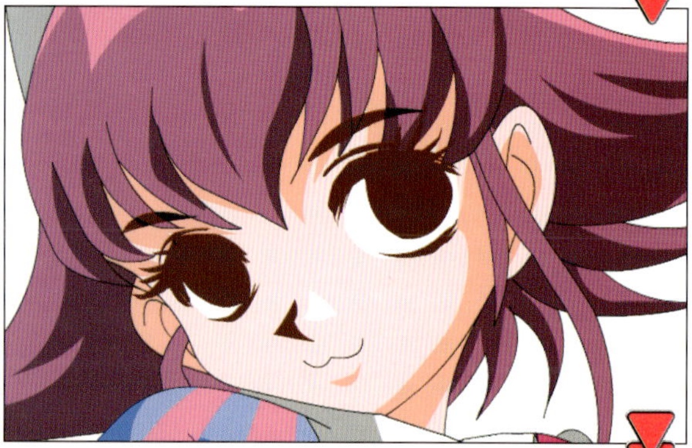

When that's done, choose the Brush Tool—tablet users should adjust the Brush Pressure settings—and paint in the eyelashes and eyebrows. Now it's starting to look a little more eye-like.

Mouse users should try adjusting the Brush Size and Brush Shape settings.

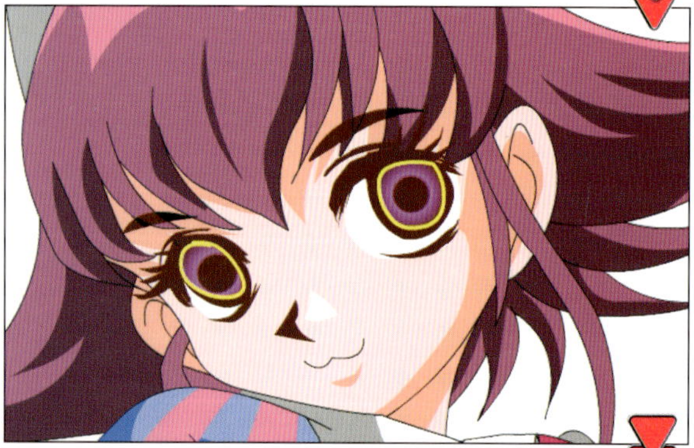

To paint a gradation on the eyes, first draw fill lines with the Pencil Tool. Here is where I'll use my three-color gradational fill. The inside and outside (left and right, respectively) markers are both set to #333300, and the middle marker is set to #B028A0 (reddish purple). Slide the inside marker as shown here and apply the fill.

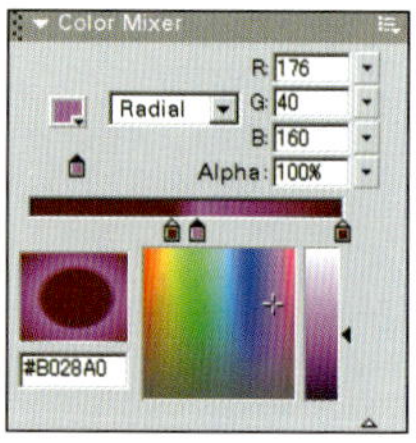

Point
Make sure the Lock Fill option on the Paint Bucket Tool is set to Off.

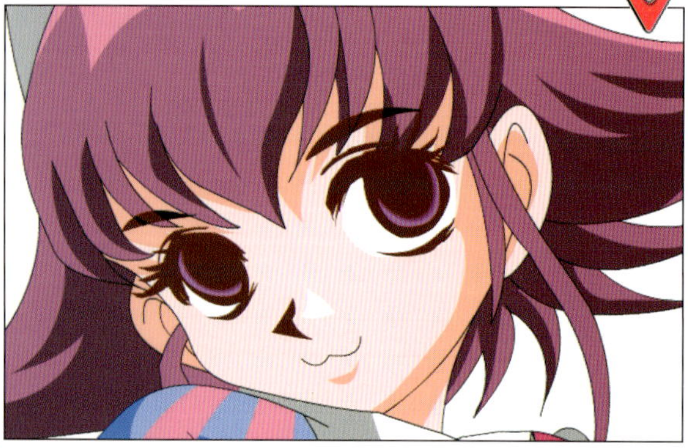

After using the Eraser Tool with the Faucet option engaged to neatly erase the fill lines, fine tune the gradation to make a more realistic eye with the Fill Transform Tool. Tuning methods are discussed on the next page.

Gradational Fill Transformation and Movement

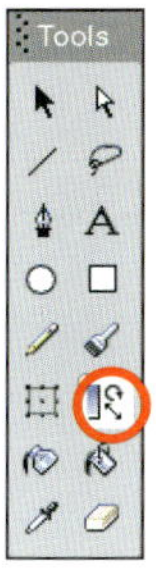

Even gradational fills in Flash can be transformed as you please and moved around at will. Using the Fill Transform Tool to fine tune your gradation can add to it increased subtlety of expression.

Select the Fill Transform Tool, click on the center of your gradation, and a circle with four handles will appear. This is called a Bounding Circle. Using our eye fill as an example, I'll explain how to use the various handles.

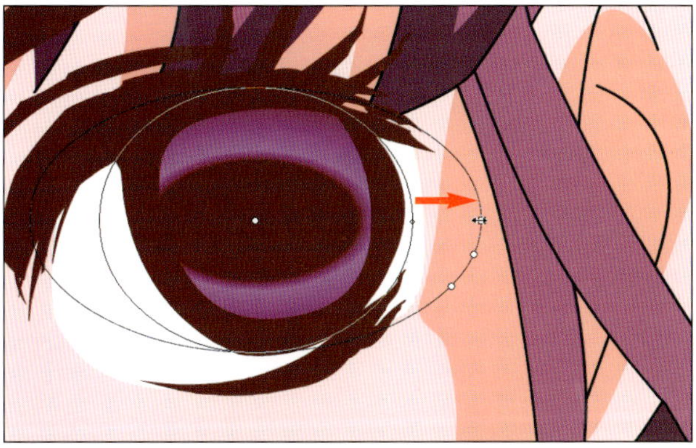

The Width Handle

Use the Width Handle when you wish to pull the fill horizontally, expanding or contracting it.

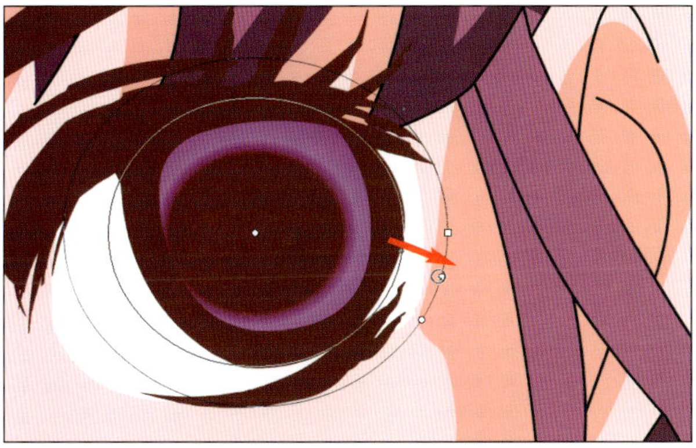

The Scale Handle

Using the Scale Handle can also expand or contract your fill, but in all directions.

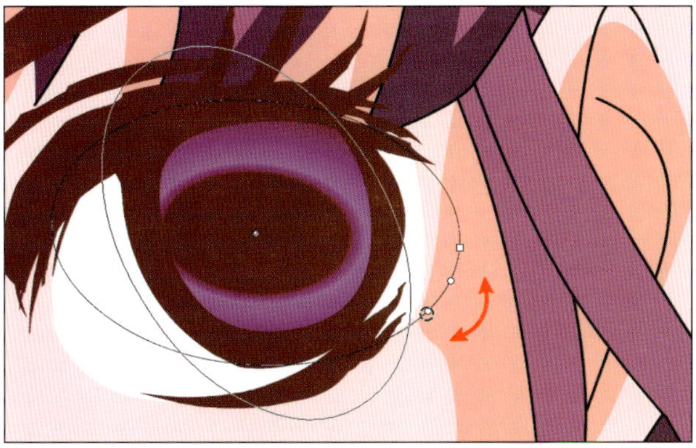

The Rotation Handle

Moving the Rotation Handle lets you spin your gradient fill around in place, changing its direction.

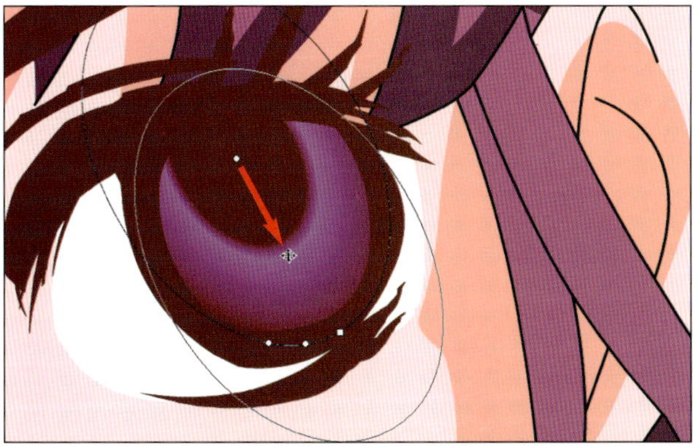

The Location Handle

The last handle is used to move your fill around the stage.

Practical Gradational Application: Part 2

Highlight the eyes with gradations, too!

Now we move on to highlighting the eyes. This captivating technique will really make your character come alive.

Insert a new layer here—choose Insert → Layer to add one to the stack. Remember to give it an easily recognizable name, such as "highlight."

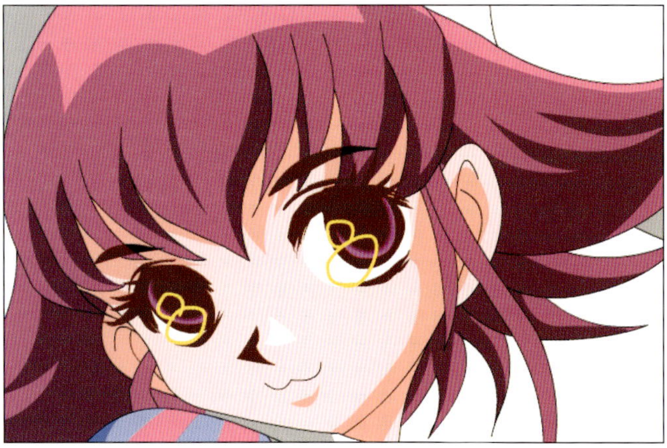

In the new layer, draw borders for the highlighted areas with the Pencil Tool.

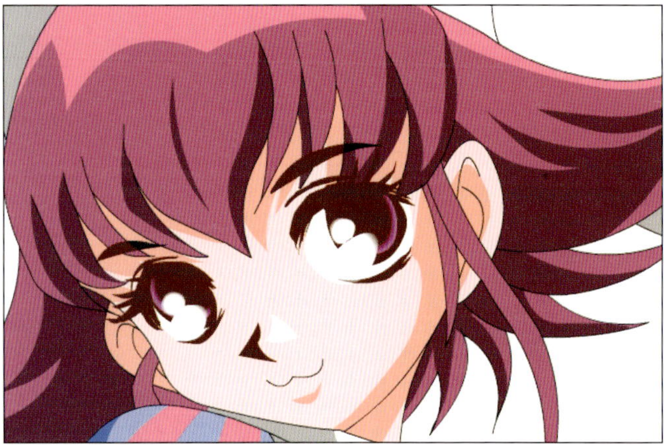

For the highlight color, create a gradation with the outside marker set to 0% Alpha white and the inside marker set to plain white. The highlight should melt into the surrounding color at its edges. When your fills are done, erase the borders you drew earlier with the Eraser Tool. Just as we did earlier, use the Fill Transform Tool to alter and improve the appearance of your highlighting.

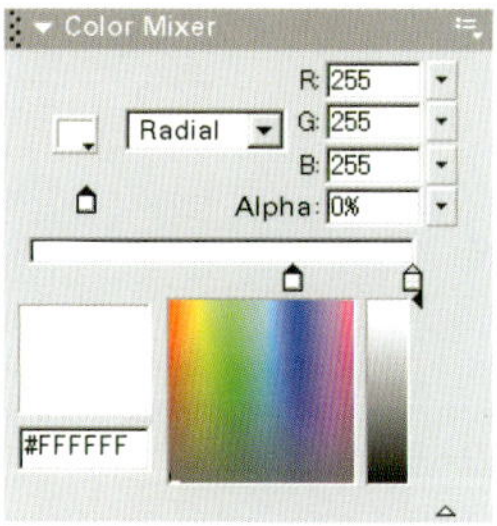

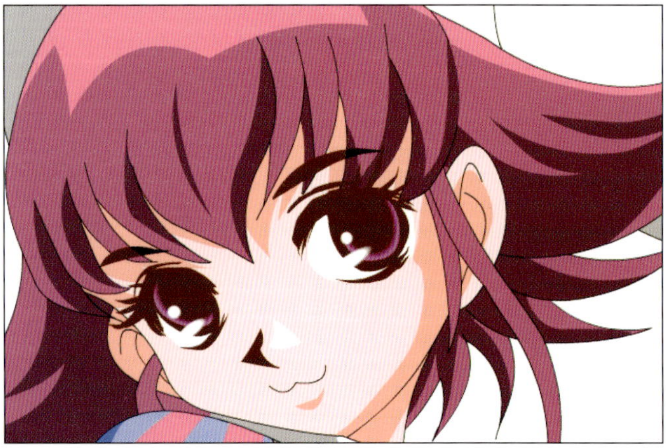

In the previous image, I thought the brightened areas were too big, so I've shrunk them down here. By changing the placement of this highlight, you can also change the direction of a character's gaze. Experiment with this process a bit, balancing the highlights with the shading you added earlier.

Point

Highlights done with transparent gradations have a natural finish to them. That's why we make separate layers on top of our characters to hold them.

Practical Gradational Application: Part 3

Make beautiful skin with a gradation.

Now for the skin gradational fill. Notice how many colors we're using this time. Also note that we're applying on a single gradational fill pattern for the entire skin—everything from the jaw to the shadows cast by her hair. It's tempting to create and use a wider variety of fill patterns, but skillfully using just a few patterns results in a piece with a strong sense of harmony.

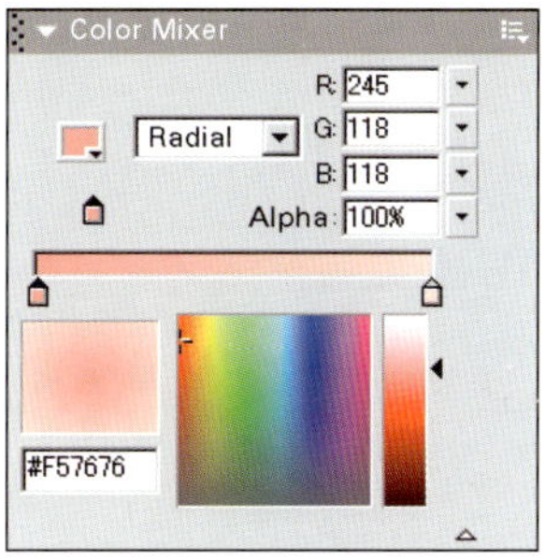

For the gradation I'm using this time, I've set the outer marker to a lighter skin tone (#F57676) and the inner marker to a darker skin tone (#F8C5B1). Using this gradation, I can handle everything, even the shadows around the jaw.

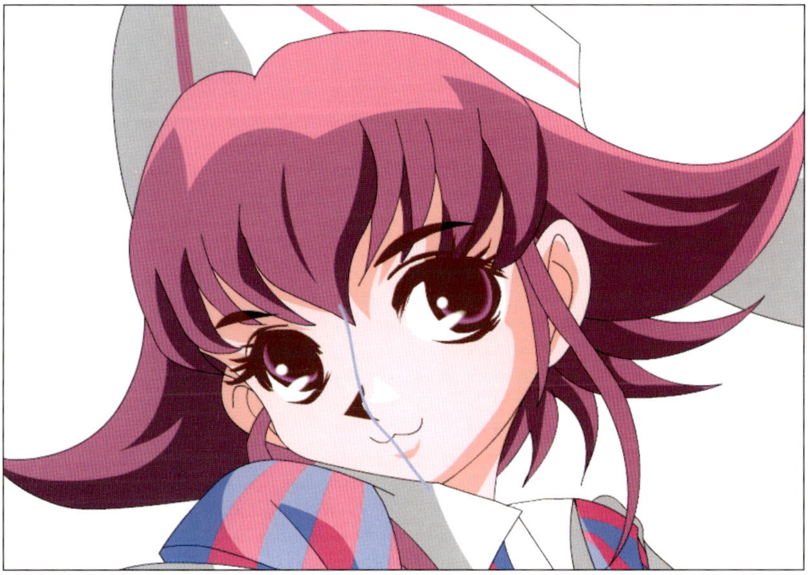

I want to separately fill the jaw area, so the first thing I do is draw some fill lines and split the face in half with the Pencil Tool. Once that's done, I'll switch to the Paint Bucket tool and fill in both sides with the above gradation.

Point
When you use the Paint Bucket Tool here, make sure the Lock Fill setting is in the Off position.

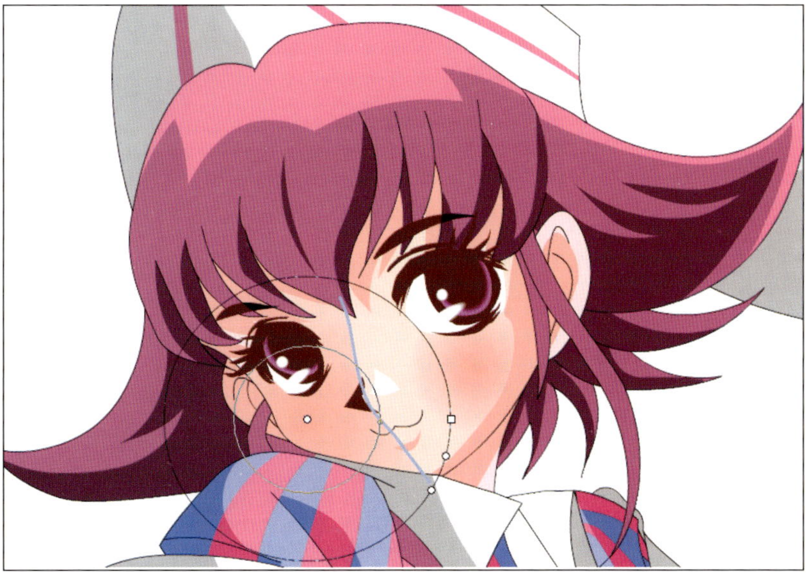

Once the filling is done, choose the Fill Transform Tool again and adjust the shape of the gradation. Pay attention here: make sure the left and right halves of the face connect smoothly.

Practical Gradational Application: Part 3

Combining multiple locations and filling them with a single gradation

Now we'll fill in the shadows cast by our character's hair. There is a certain technique for combining fills, and knowing it will make applying fills easier.

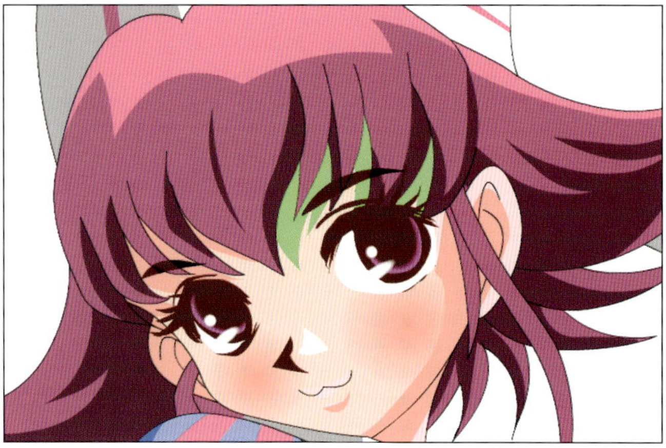

The section shown here (colored green for explanatory purposes) is actually split into different areas. So, we will lock them together into a single gradation. This will allow us to transform the entire area fill in one pass, and give the shading a natural look.

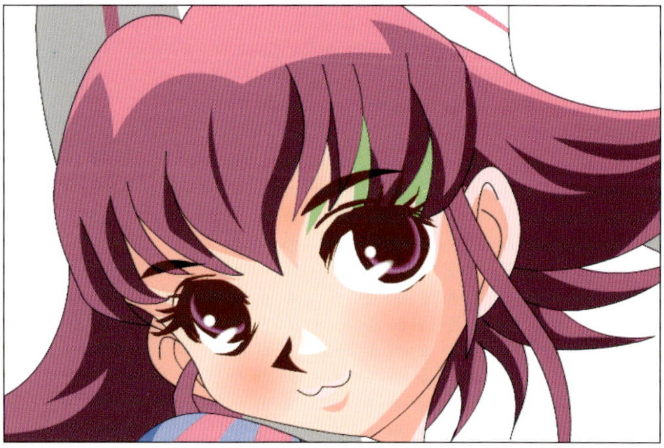

Apply the same skin gradational fill to a single area.

Point
Before you apply your fill, make sure the Lock Fill is set to Off.

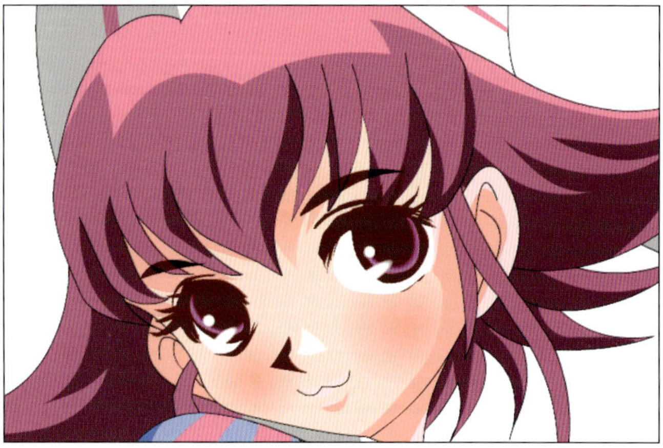

Switch to the Eyedropper Tool and sample the filled area. The cursor will change to the Paint Bucket icon. Now fill in the remaining areas.

Point
Here, the Lock Fill will be switched on. Leave it as is and apply your fill.

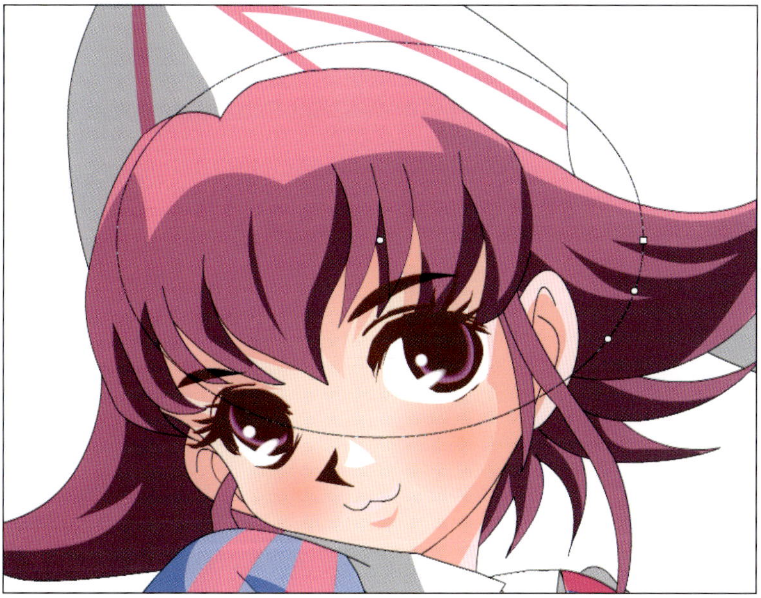

◀ When you apply gradations like this, they're all connected to one another. This allows you to use the Fill Transformation Tool to adjust them all at once, and fine-tune them to be more shadowlike.

Point
Unifying a gradation across multiple areas means setting the Lock Fill to On and applying a fill. It can be done easily by using the Eyedropper and Paint Bucket Tools to sample and fill them in separately.

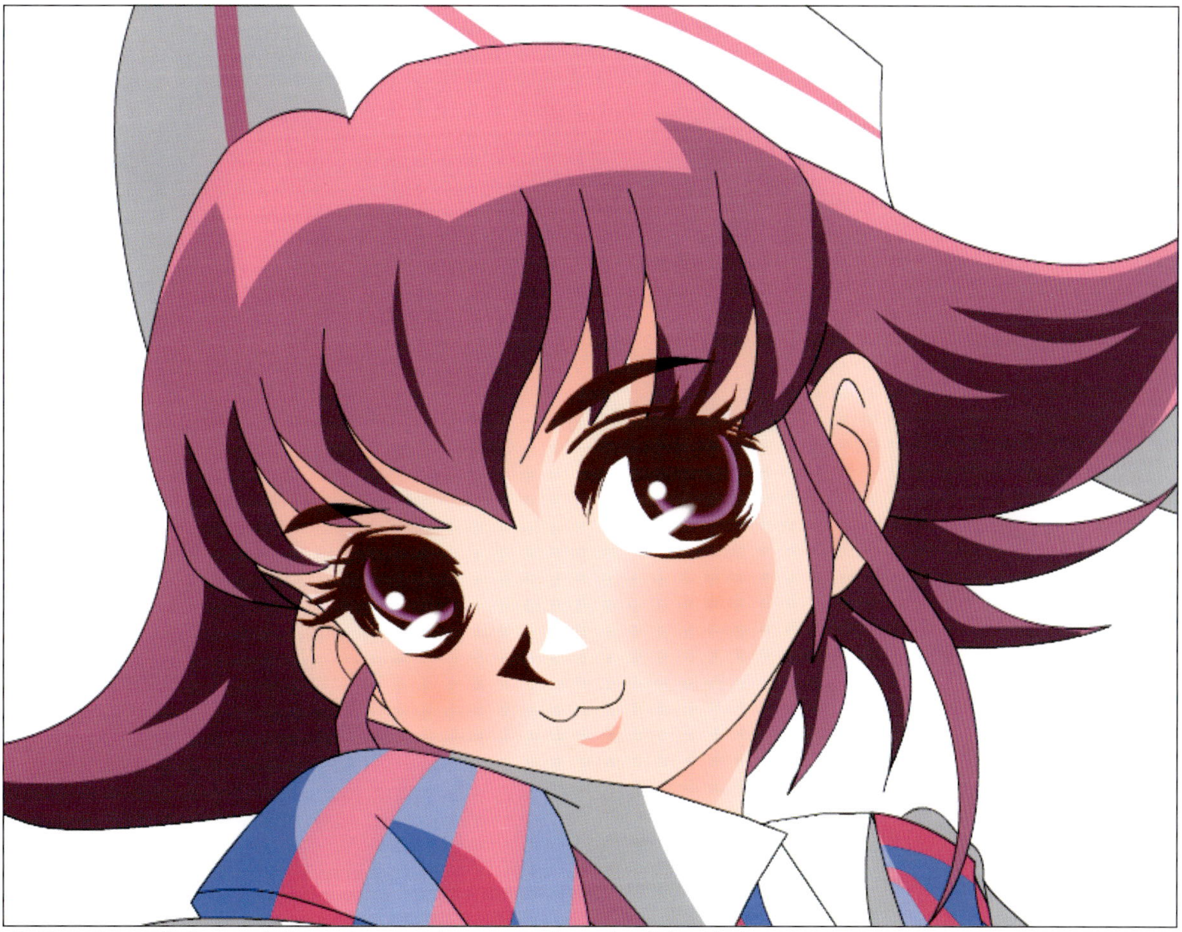

▲ Here, I've applied my gradation to the remaining areas and completed the skin. It doesn't look like it was done with one big gradation pattern, does it? You, too, can achieve this kind of natural finish.

Practical Gradational Application: Part 4

At last! A simple way to paint hair.

Our last gradation process covers the hair. Here as well I will be expressing how light hits the hair with a gradient. Dealing with hair is usually an aggravating experience. But there's an easier way to an attractive, neat finish, and I'm going to show it to you now.

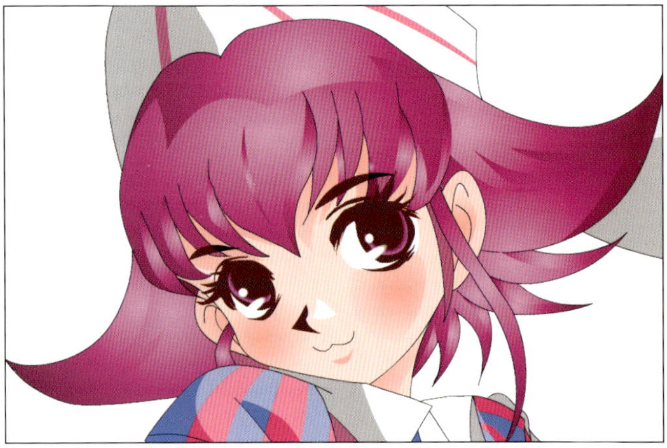

Here, I'm creating a purplish three-color gradation (inner marker: #F15CC9, middle marker: #990066, outer marker: #58012E). This is the gradation I'll use on the hair. Note that Lock Fill should be set to Off at this point.

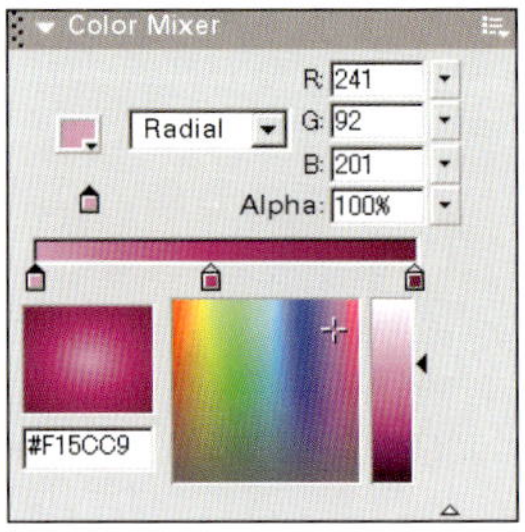

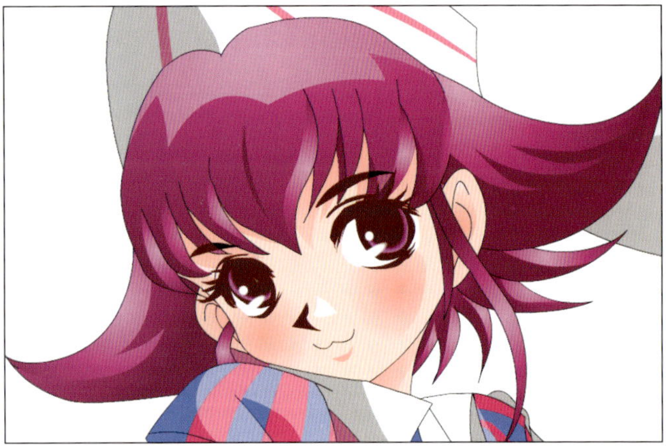

Now, with the light direction in mind, I adjust the freshly applied gradation (pictured above) with the Fill Transform Tool.

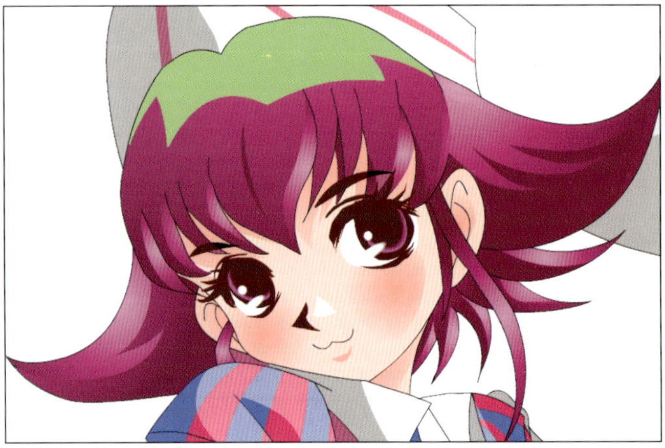

This area (painted green for explanatory purposes) will get highlighted. After selecting this area with the Arrow Tool, I choose Edit → Copy.
Next, I move to the "highlight" layer we created for the eyes earlier and choose Edit → Paste in Place.

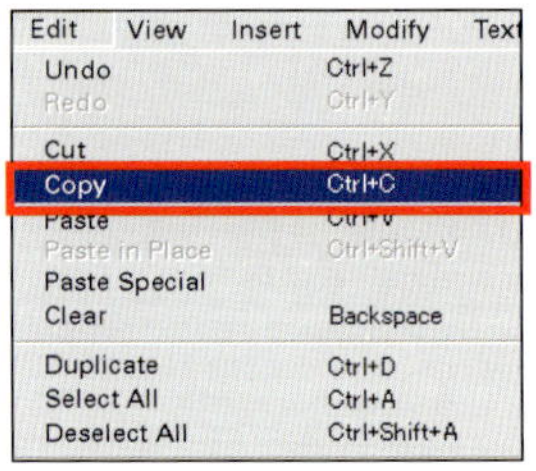

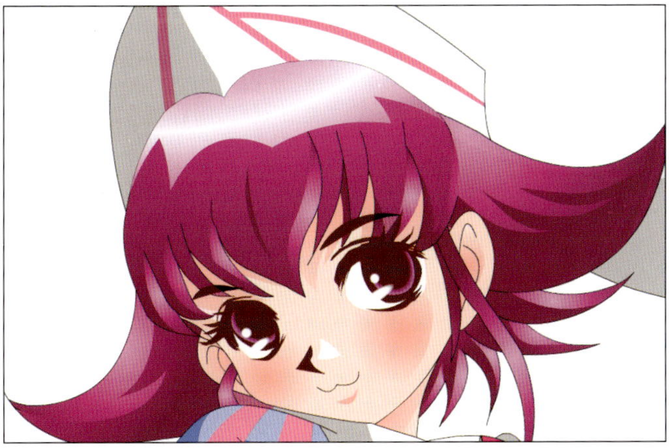

Then, I apply a doughnut-like gradient (inside and outside markers: #EF59C6 at 0% Alpha, middle marker: #FFFFFF at 100% Alpha) to the highlight area I've just pasted.

Pictured here is the gradation after I've adjusted it to add shine to her hair with the Fill Transform Tool.

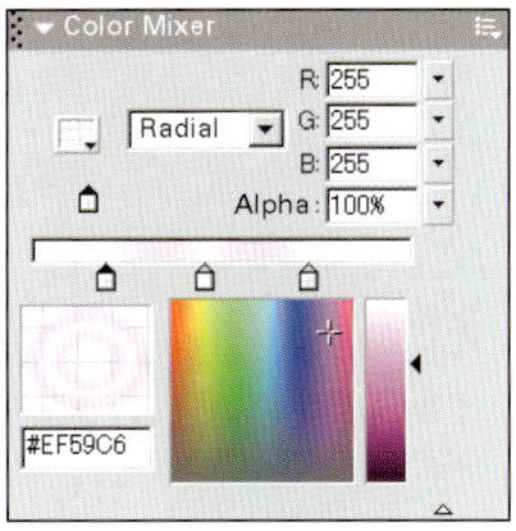

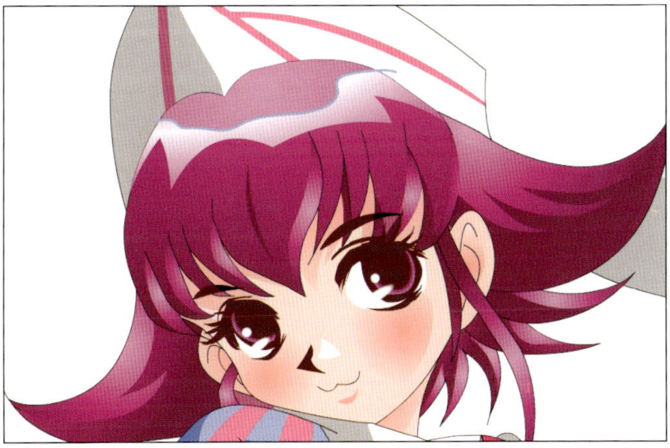

Using the Pencil Tool, I mark off section as the light would fall and erase the upper portion with the Eraser Tool. This lets the color in the layer beneath it to show through.

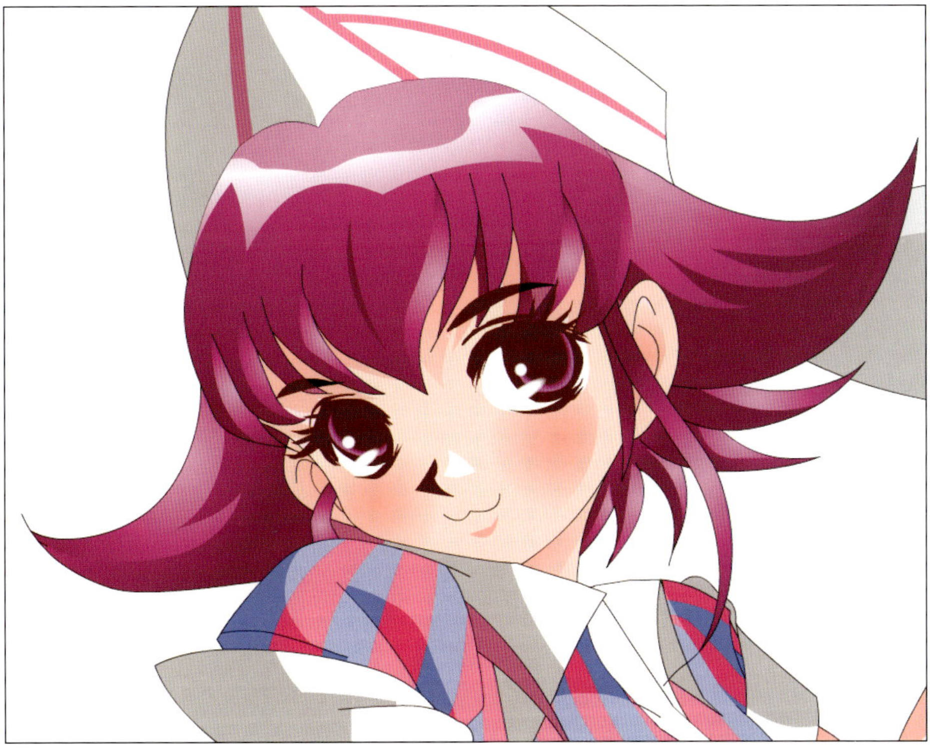

Thanks to added shading and highlighting, this character is considerably more attractive than her base color version.

Transforming hair highlights

We made highlights for the hair on the previous page, but now I think their impact is a little lacking. So, I got rid of the old ones and redid them. Now I'm going to transform the newly rehighlighted areas.

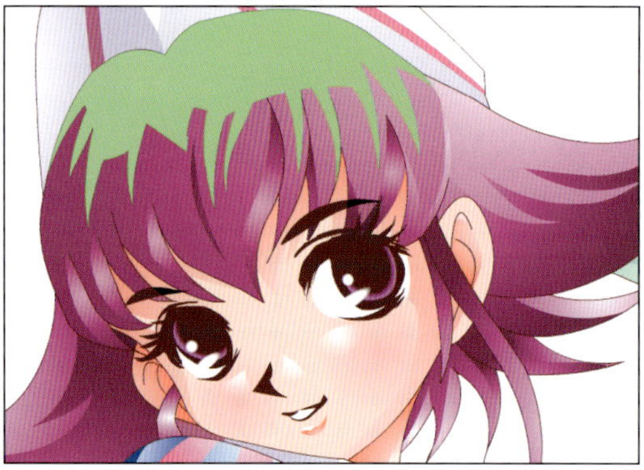

▲ Here, I've changed the area I want to highlight by pulling on the fill lines with the Arrow Tool. I've done this because I want to make the highlights follow the way her hair flows. The area is colored green here for explanatory purposes.

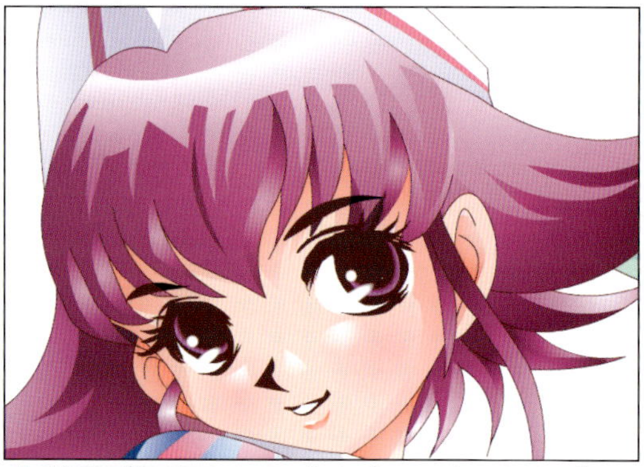

▲ Repeating the process from the previous page, I've copied the highlights onto the "highlight" layer and applied my gradient.

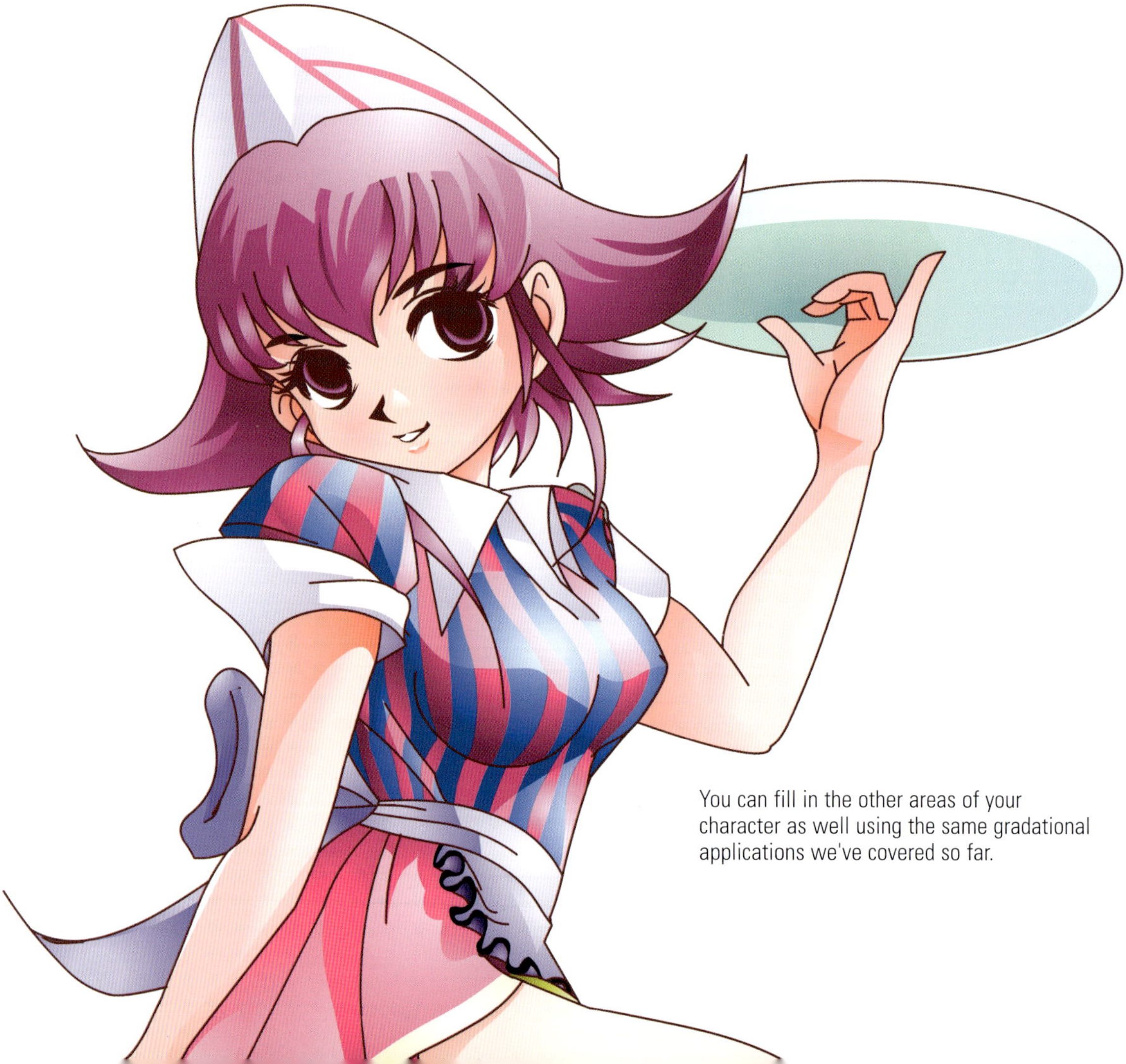

You can fill in the other areas of your character as well using the same gradational applications we've covered so far.

Backgrounds, Accessories, and Completion

Change the background to pink and sprinkle some flowers

I've added a background and drawn in some flowers and other accessories. How to draw *those* is something I'll save for next time. The project is now complete.

When I started drawing *bishoujo* graphics in Flash (around 1998), there were about 2500 related graphics sites on the Net. Among those, I could count on one hand the number of friends I had who were working with Flash. Since then that number has increased, but it's still a miniscule figure. If you want an easier way to create high-quality computer graphics, by all means, please join our ranks and give Flash a try.

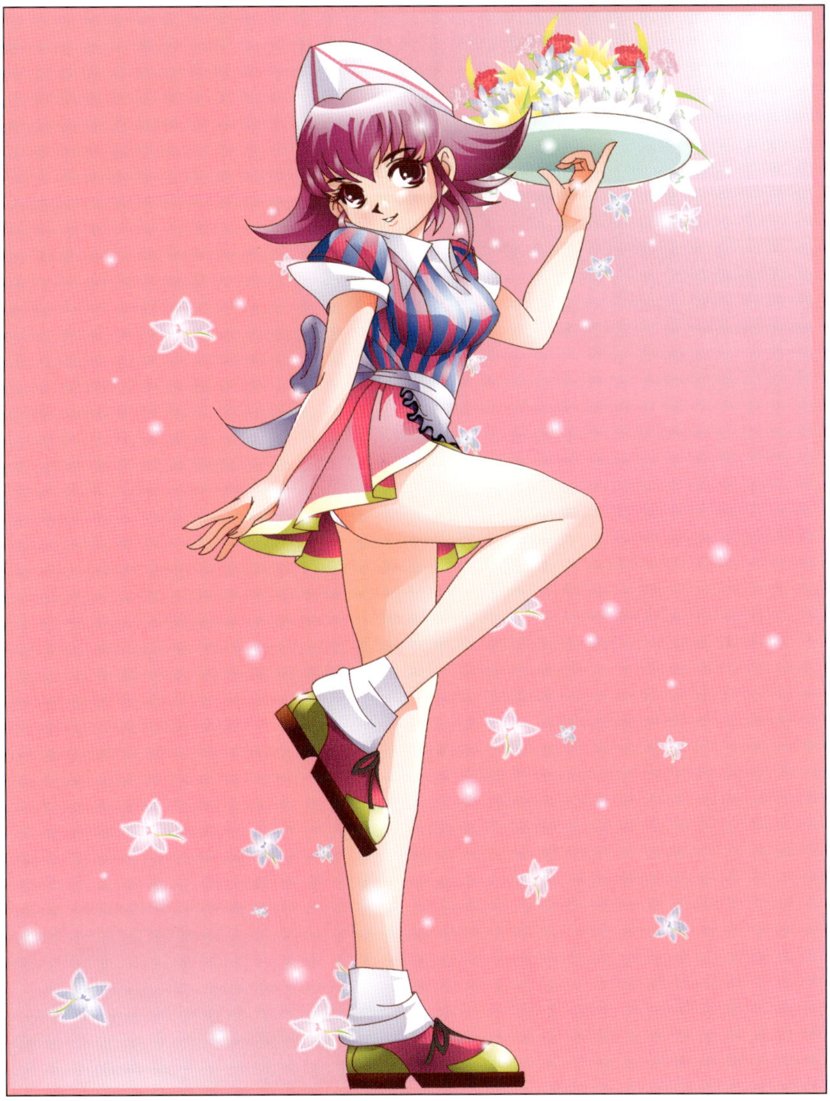

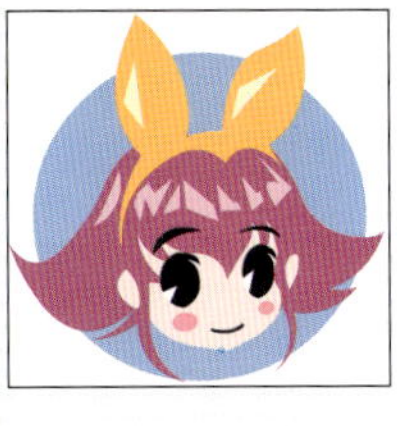

Thank you, Master!! *smooch*
I just can't take my eyes off this new outfit.
I'm sorry, but I look hot! I'm sure to pick up a lot of new fans with this.
You guys are all going to come over and play with me at Master's site, right? I've got a lot more to show off, you know. Well, I guess this is good-bye for now.
Thanks for coming along for the ride, you guys! Bye-bye!

Gallery

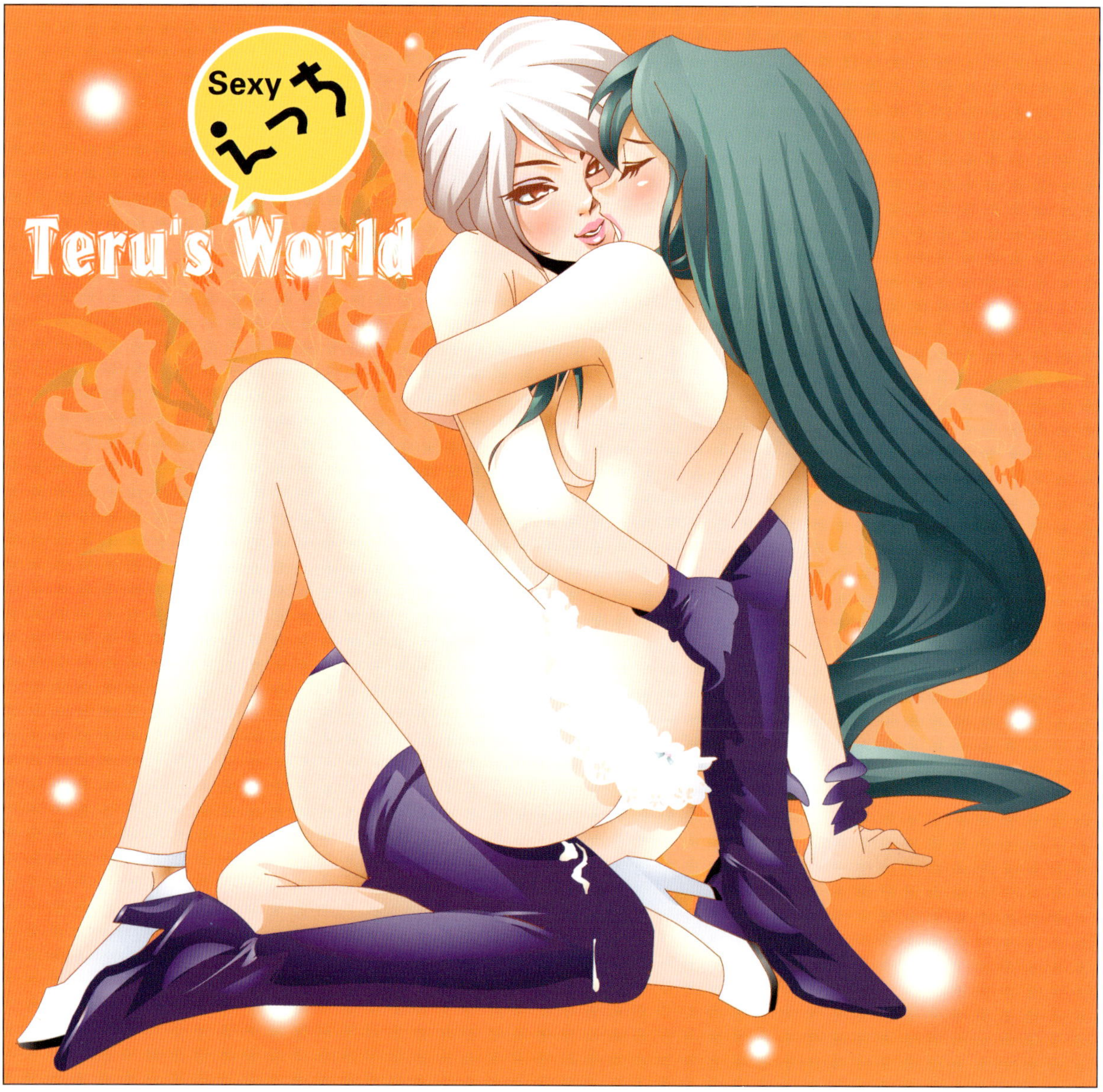

When I made this I hadn't done any adult illustrations at all for several years. But I thought this piece (a collaboration with a friend of mine over an artist's Internet chat) was pretty good so I Flashified it. It's not technically groundbreaking or anything, but if I may be so bold, this piece certainly has a refreshingly erotic feel, does it not?

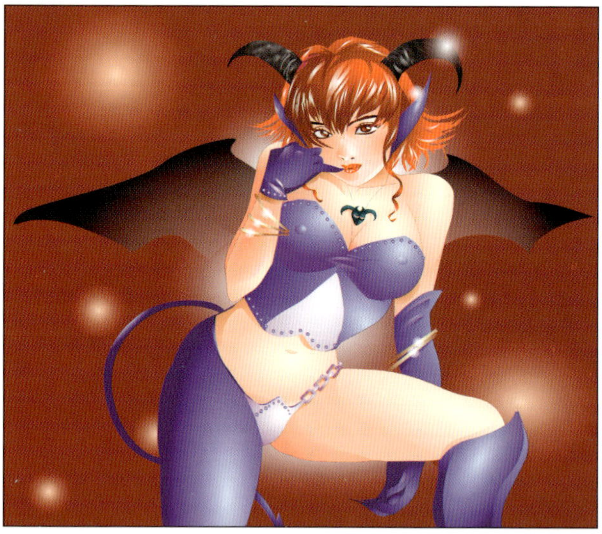

This is a realistic version of my site's mascot, Fal. Stuff like this in Flash or any other drawing-oriented application is fairly difficult, but I gave it a shot. Getting the different gradational boundaries to agree with each other was easily the most challenging step. Still, taking the same character and coming up with different ways of expressing her is all part of the fun.

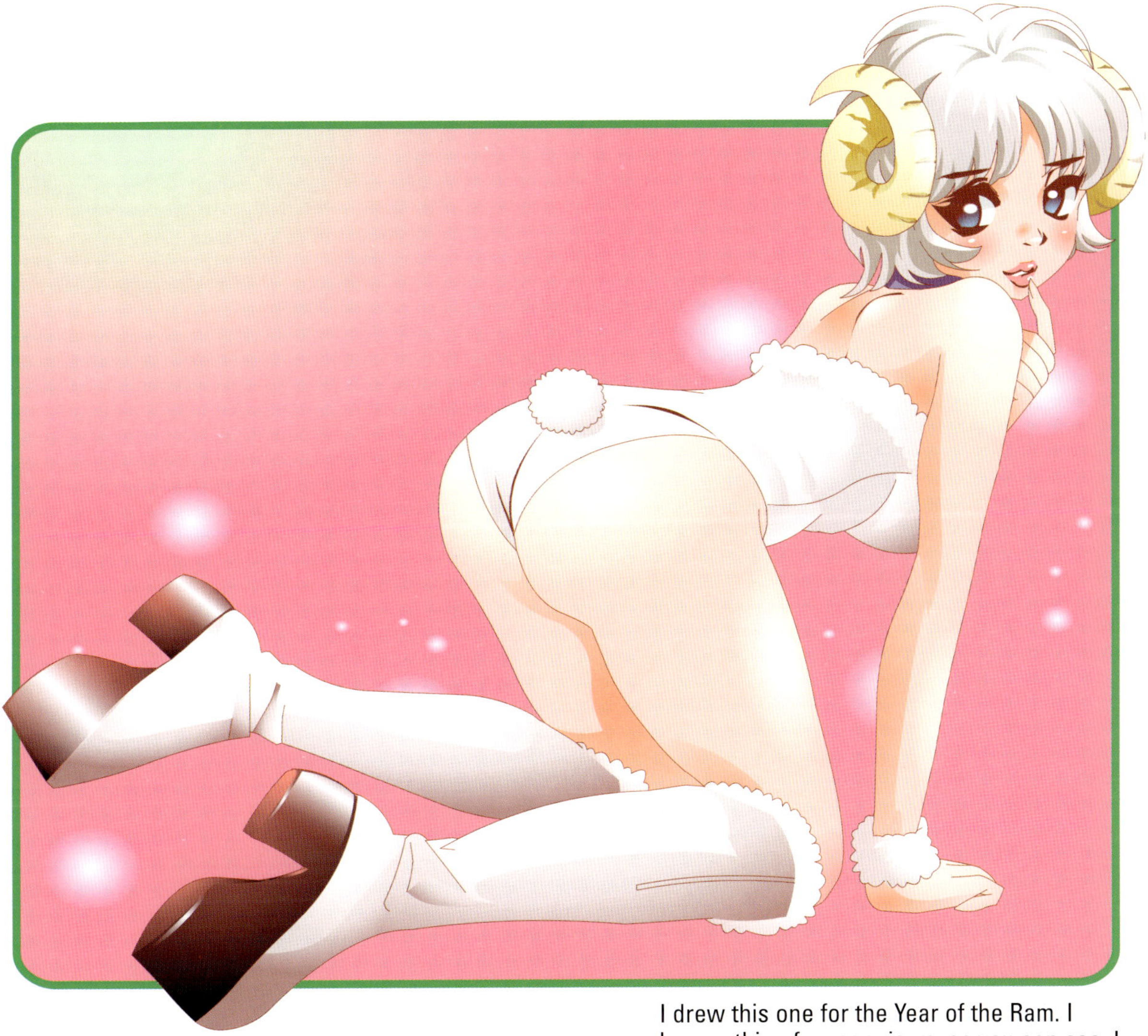

I drew this one for the Year of the Ram. I have a thing for rear views, as you can see. I used to draw outlines in and around the hips and leave it at that. But when the image was shrunk down a bit, the lines all mashed together into a big mess. So I tweaked the whole area a bit, making some lines bolder and others weaker.

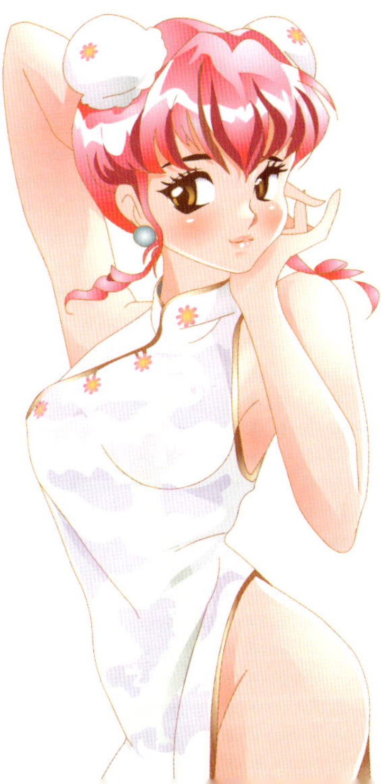

Here's my mascot again, Fal, wearing a Chinese dress this time. The pattern for the dress is Alpha-adjusted (for transparency) and lies in a separate layer. Really, the hair highlights and what have you should be in a separate layer, too. But when I drew this piece, I hadn't yet acquired that technique.

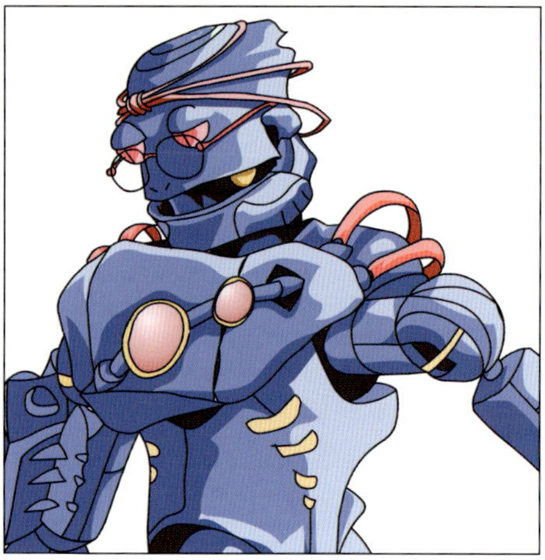

Machine Specs

Compaq Presario
Athlon 4 850MHz CPU, 384MB RAM, 20GB hard disk, Windows ME, 1024x768 display, Wacom Intuos A6 tablet (Grape)
I love notebooks. They suck up so little juice! But, I'm always crying about "Insufficient Resources." I usually just give up and use a freeware app, AllKill, to indiscriminately open up more resources.

PowerMac G4/400
PowerPC G4 400MHz CPU, 1.5GB RAM, 110GB hard disk space (spread over 4 disks), MacOS 9.2, Wacom Intuos A6 tablet
This one sucks up a lot of power, however. It's also slow, but very reliable. Flash MX is a little too much for it, so I use version 5.

Monitor

Mitsubishi RDT 172M
at 1280x1024 resolution

Peripherals

Alphus MD-5000 printer, SmartMedia Reader/Writer (since I'm not on a LAN)

Software

Flash MX and version 5, Expression 2, Poser 4.0.3, and HexaSuper 3

Penname
Gaten Boya

I thought I'd attached this thing so it wouldn't bust on me again! Ah well, that seems to have already gone awry. My new third generation right arm, you see, is under construction being expanded. These weird plugs aren't really giving me as much of a boost as I thought they would, considering how much time this is taking.

Speaking of time, I would love to have a Castle of Time [as in "Laputa: Castle in the Sky"]. I believe that if you don't give up on trying to master time, on making it your ally, then you can become anything you desire.

Date of Birth

June 29, 19XX

Favorite Things

Things I want, and things I like. I think there're a lot of those. What I really need is unfading brilliance, something I think I've actually been running away from as of late.

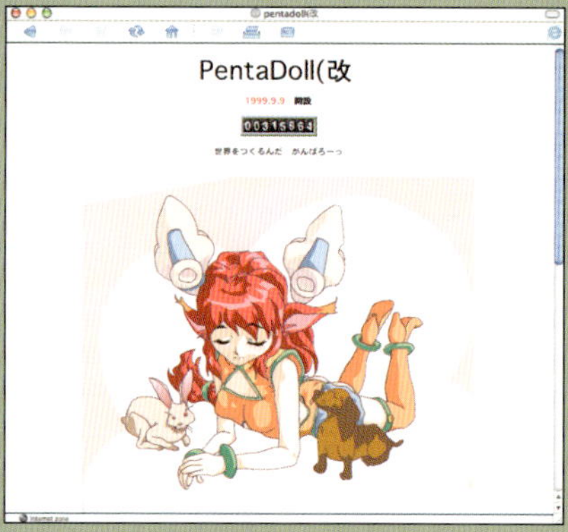

Pentadoll
http://www.interq.or.jp/snake/gboya/

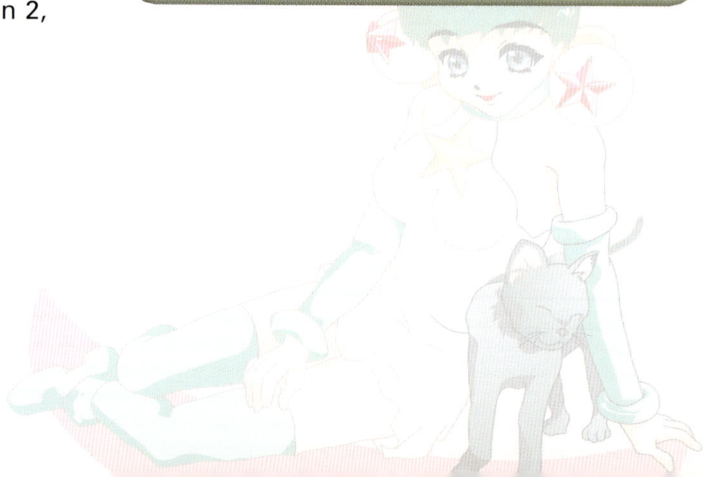

Pre-Drawing Preparations

Set the size of your piece and turn Snap to Objects off.

Before you draw any character, you have to get the rough sketch done first. But, before we do that, we need to prepare the Stage. Choose Modify → Document (or Modify → Movie in Flash 5) and set the Dimensions of your project. I usually use a wide stage (550 x 400) or a slightly narrower, taller one (320 x 440). Next, choose View → Snap to Objects to uncheck it.

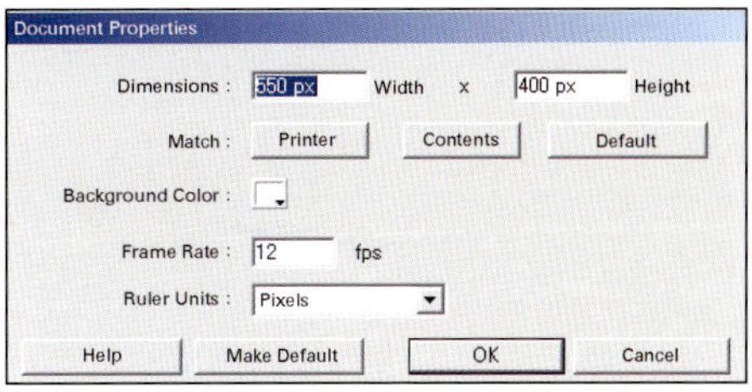

▲ Choose Modify → Document to determine the size of your stage.

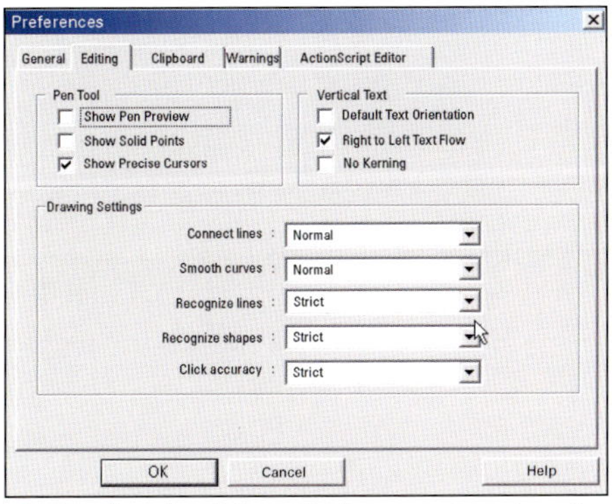

▲ Try choosing Edit → Preferences to set up the Tool windows and other details as you like.

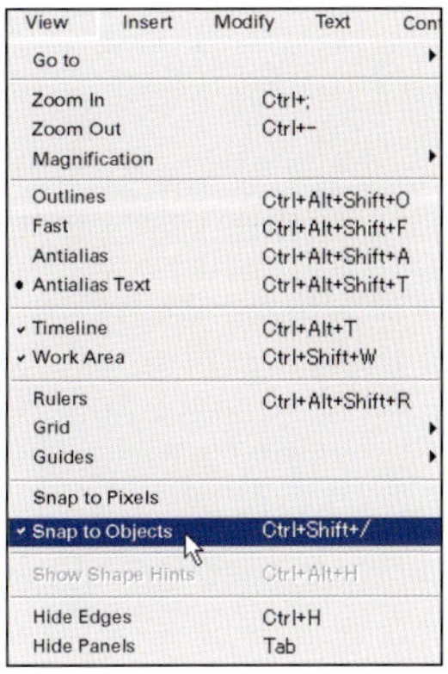

◀ Be sure to turn Snap to Objects off-the keyboard shortcut is Ctrl + Shift + /. Now let's get on to making your rough sketch.

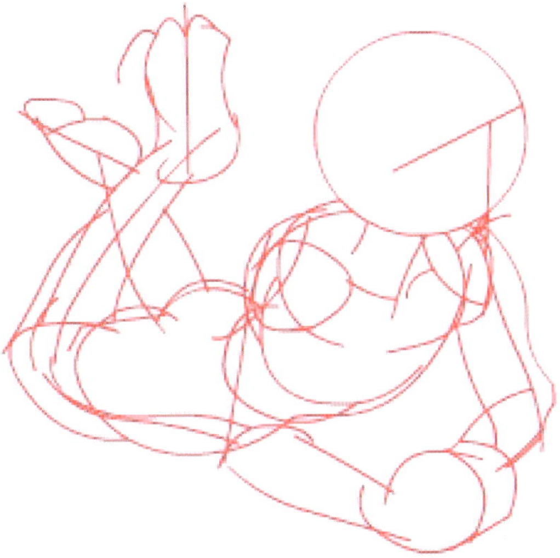

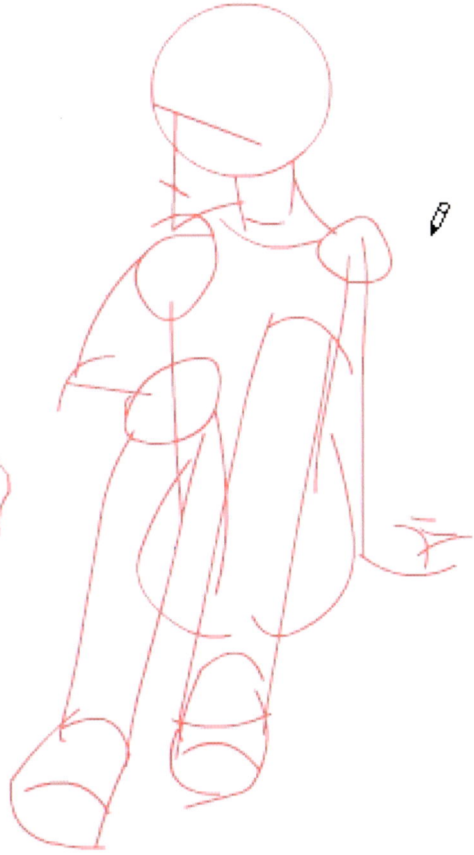

▲ You can draw on regular paper and scan it if you like, or you can draw your rough sketch directly into Flash. That's the way I did mine, so that's what I'm going to explain next.

What are the Keys to Drawing a Quality Rough Sketch?

Get good with the Pencil Tool and make liberal use of the Group function.

Now we're going to get down to drawing the rough sketch. First, I'll explain two things you need to know to make more efficient progress.

Master the Pencil Tool, the detailing implement of choice.

I recommend the Pencil Tool for drawing the rough sketch, because using the Brush Tool tends to make your file a lot bigger when you save it. The Pencil Tool has three modifiers: Straight, Smooth, and Ink. Choose whichever one strikes your fancy. Here are my impressions on the characteristics of each one.

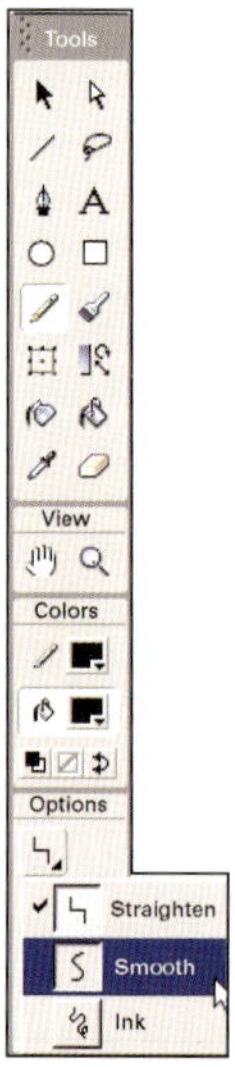

Straight:
I don't use this cumbersome modifier much. I can only ever really use it when I want to draw with mostly straight lines, and I've never used it for drawing bishoujo.

Smooth:
It's not so good for drawing hemlines and the like, but I use this setting the most. Zoom in on your work and the Pencil will do what you tell it to.

Ink:
With this modifier, the Pencil Tool will track exactly like a pen would. Unfortunately, it will pick up your hand shaking, too.

Make use of the Group function for increased efficiency.

When you draw in Flash, using the Group function improves your efficiency and lets you make better progress.

Grouping takes things you draw in Flash, like lines or fills, and lumps them into a single unit. Pictures you draw in Flash are all made up of independent parts, but when you group them together, they become single object you can then manipulate. So for example, with a single click of the Arrow Tool, you can select and move the entire group.

Further, when you group things together, they cease to affect or be affected by the lines or fills around them. Therefore, the skillful use of this function eliminates the bother of splitting lines and fills into different layers. As with layers, it is also possible to change the stacking order of Groups afterward.

The benefit of being able to draw without necessarily affecting the other things in your piece is the same as with layers, but I think if you make use of the Group function to handle your lines and fills as a single unit, you'll dramatically increase your efficiency.

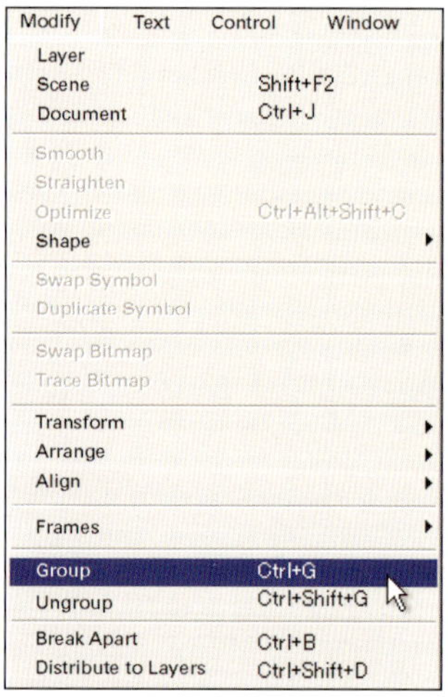

▲ Select the lines and fills you want to Group together and choose Modify → Group. You can also combine different groups together into an even larger group the same way. To split a group up, choose Modify → Ungroup.

Creating a Line Drawing

Use your rough sketch for reference and draw your main lines in a separate layer.

After your rough sketch is complete, stack a new layer on top of it (Layer 2). Layer 1 holds your rough sketch—lock it down so you can't change it and switch to Layer 2. As you look at Layer 1, start with the easier lines and quickly draw the main lines.

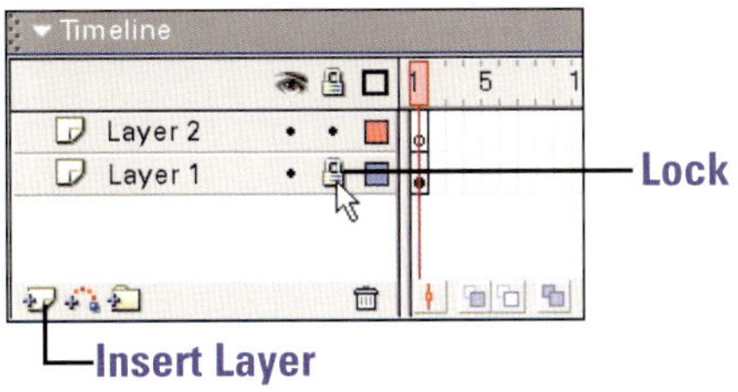

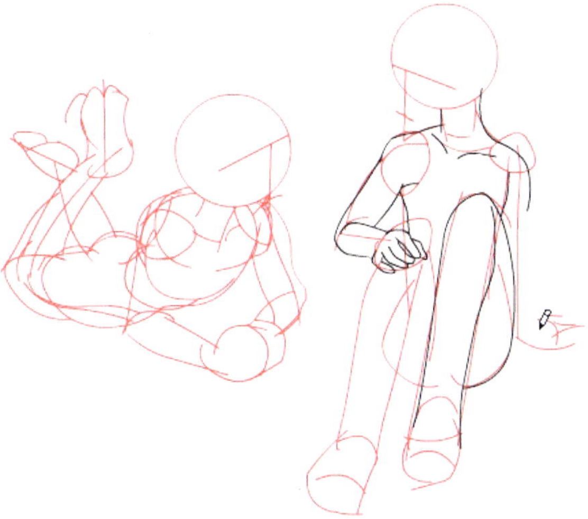

The red lines are Layer 1, and the black lines are Layer 2. Start tracing. If your trace lines deviate a bit, don't worry, just keep going. Select the bits you don't want with the Arrow Tool and hit the Delete key.

Once you're done tracing, use the Arrow Tool to drag, move, and otherwise adjust your trace until the line drawing is complete.

From time to time, it's a good idea to hide your rough sketch from view so you can check just

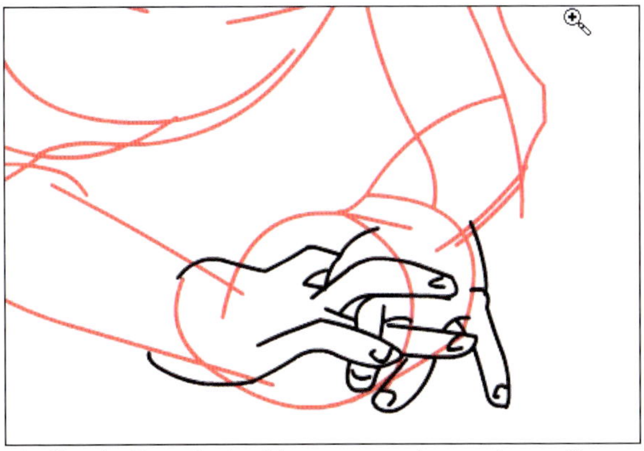

▲ Use the Zoom Tool to blow up areas that require small, detailed work, such as the hands.

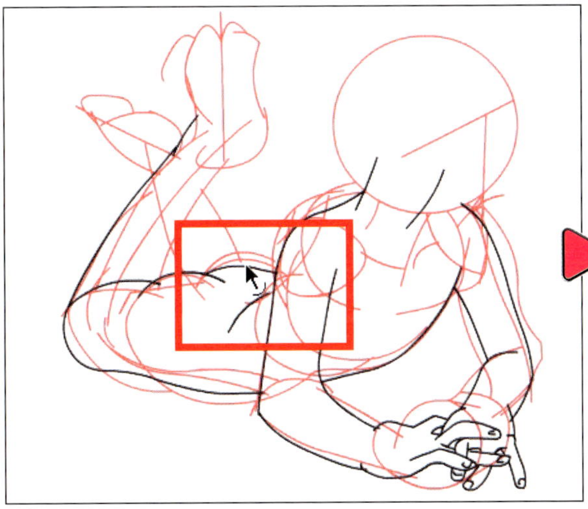

▲ Move the Arrow Tool cursor close to a line, and a little arc will appear next to it. Now drag the line.

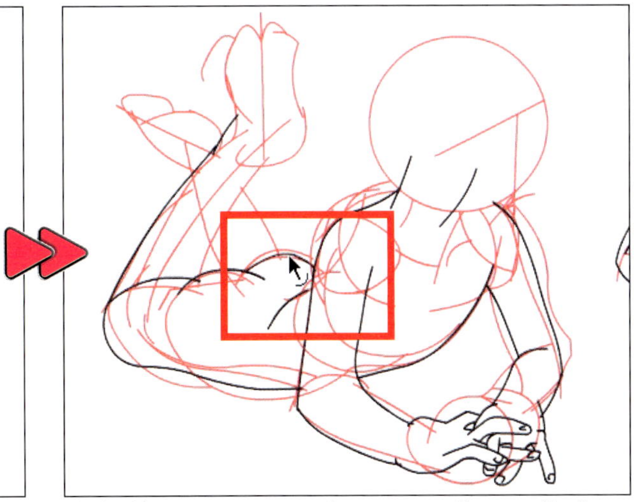

▲ In this way, you can transform contours. However, if a line is selected, you'll instead move the whole thing around. Deselect the line first and then try transforming it again.

Break your Piece Up into Groups

Once you've made some progress, start grouping thing to make modifications easier.

Even if you go overboard using of the Eraser Tool, you can erase only the ungrouped portions of a piece without touching those that are grouped. This is a lot easier than putting things in separate layers. Later, when you're adjusting balance, you can readily move things about your piece in groups.

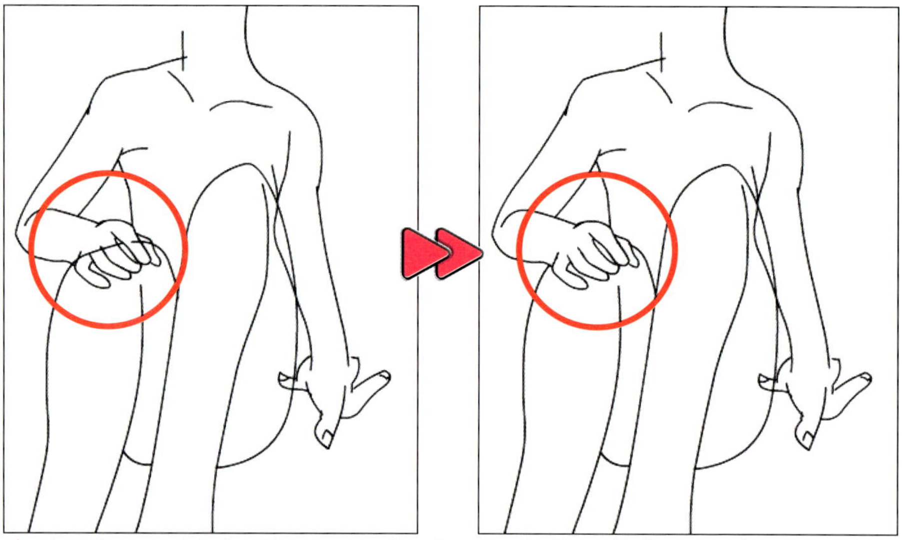

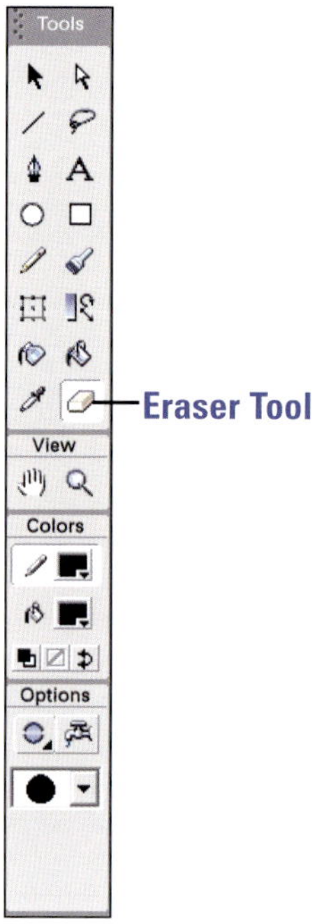

▲ Here, I've turned the hand into a group. Now I can use the Eraser Tool to erase the unwanted knee line beneath without touching the fingers. If the hand weren't grouped, the fingers would get erased, too. In that case, I would have to use the Arrow Tool and select all the little bits of line I wanted to erase, or go a little bit at a time with the Eraser Tool's Faucet modifier.

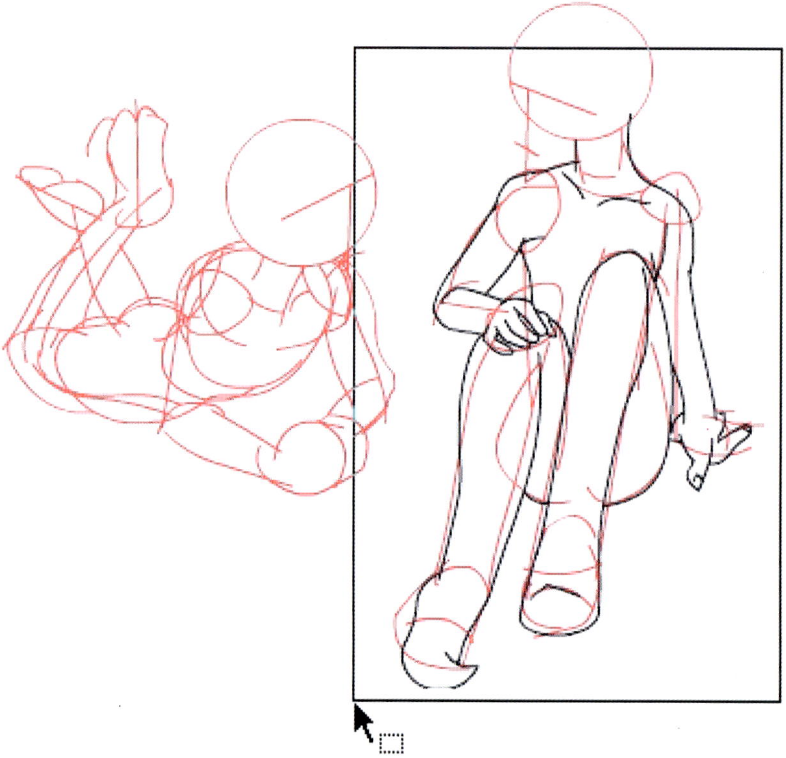

◀ Here, I've made everything from the neck down into a group. Now I can work on the face without affecting any overlapping areas, such as the neck.

Draw the Back of a Character's Head with the Oval Tool

Drawing an oval and cutting it in half makes an elegant arc.

Drawing the face from the easier parts first is a good idea.
I recommend you break things up into groups here, too.
Here, I've used the Oval Tool to draw the back of the head.

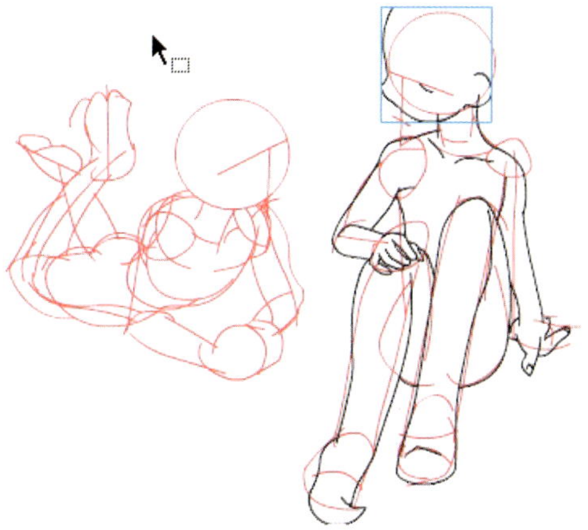

▲ Once you've draw the outline for the face, Group it.

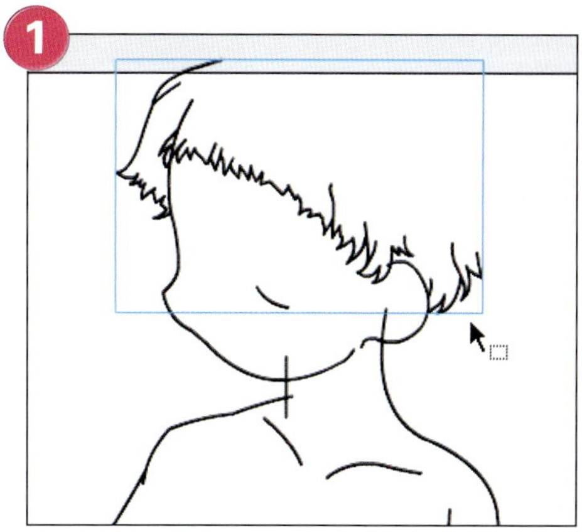

▲ Draw the hair and Group that, too.

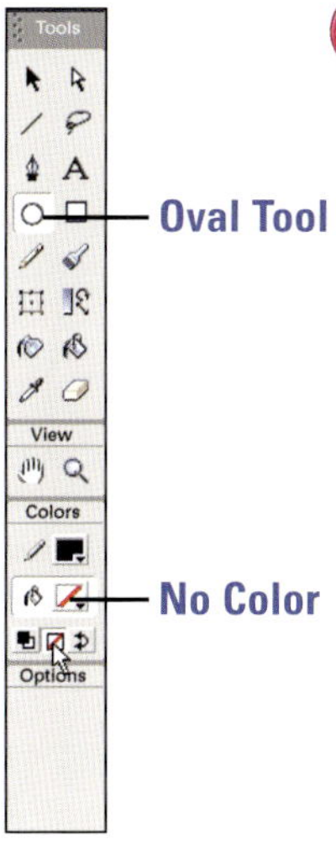

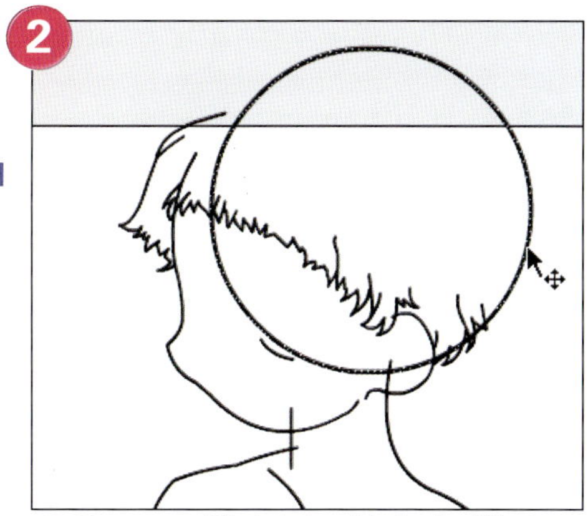

▲ Draw an unfilled circle with the Oval Tool.

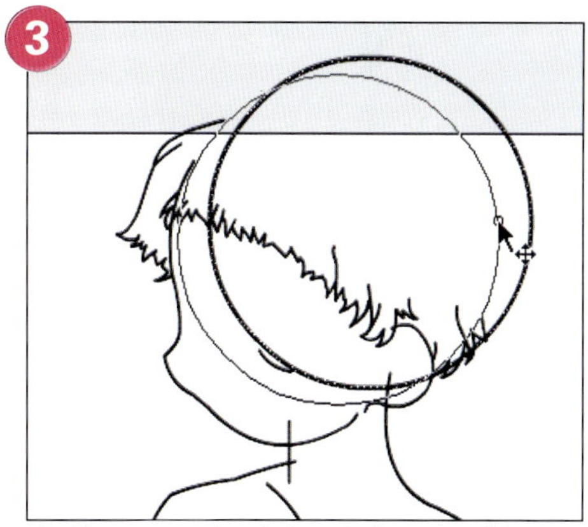

▲ Now, move the circle so it lines up with the head.

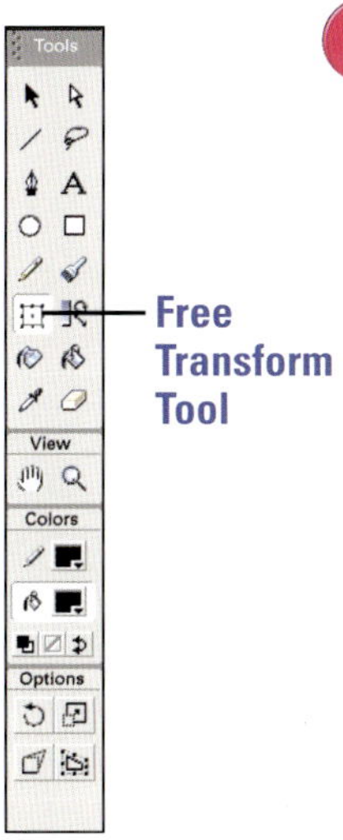

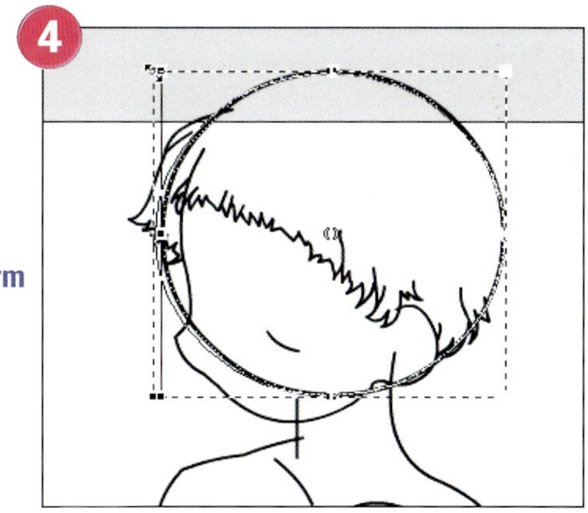

▲ Use the Free Transform Tool to adjust the circle to match the curvature of the back of the head.

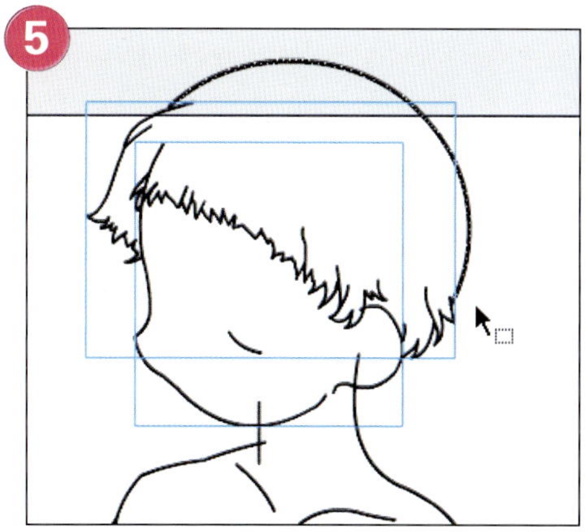

▲ Erase the unnecessary portions. As before, because the facial outline and the hair have been grouped, this is simple. Finally, gather the outline, the hair, and the back of the head and Group them together.

Use the Brush Tool to Add Expression to the Eyes and Eyebrows

Lines drawn with the Pencil Tool have a detached, lonely feel to them, so use the Brush Tool to accentuate your drawing.

Now that you've grouped together the outline of the face and the hair, draw the eyes, mouth, and eyebrows. Subtle expression is easier with the Brush Tool, and that makes your character come alive. When you're finished, you can smooth over the rough spots.

All the same, you're still free to draw with the Pencil Tool as you see fit.

Point

Using the Brush Tool in combination with a pressure-sensitive tablet lets you vary the thickness of your lines according to brush pressure. In Flash, while what you draw with the Pencil Tool are treated as "strokes," things drawn with the Brush Tool are treated as "fills."

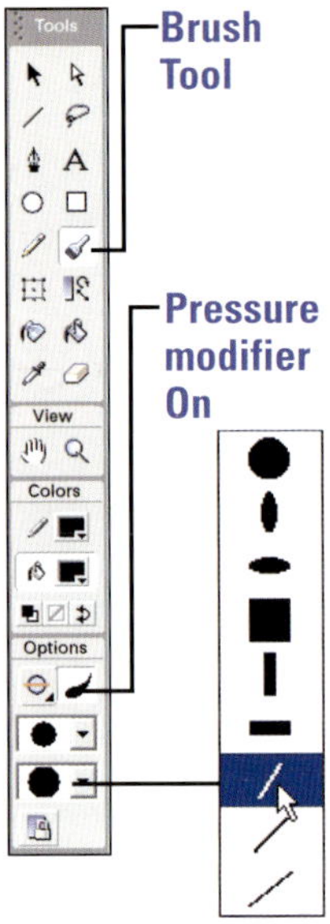

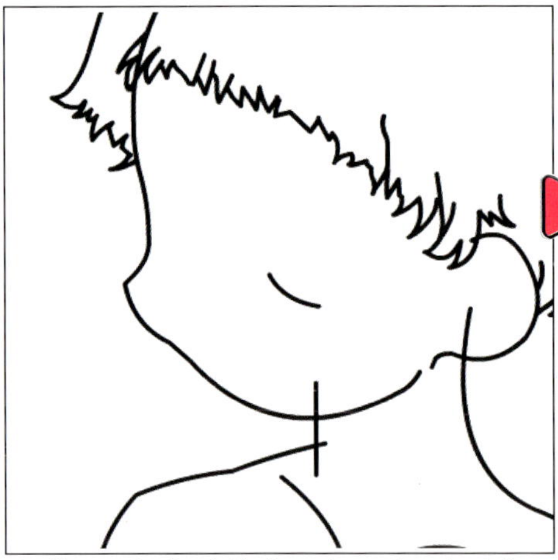

▲ Set up the Brush Tool as pictured on the left, and draw the eyebrows and eyelashes. If you're using a pressure-sensitive tablet, the Pressure modifier button will appear. Turn it on.

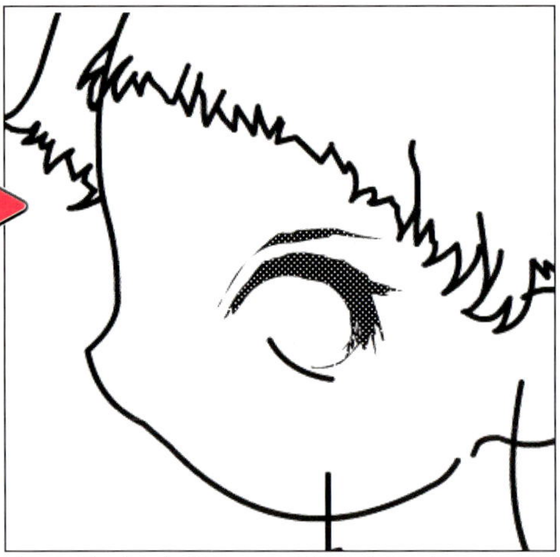

▲ Find a Brush Shape and Size that suits you and draw boldly.

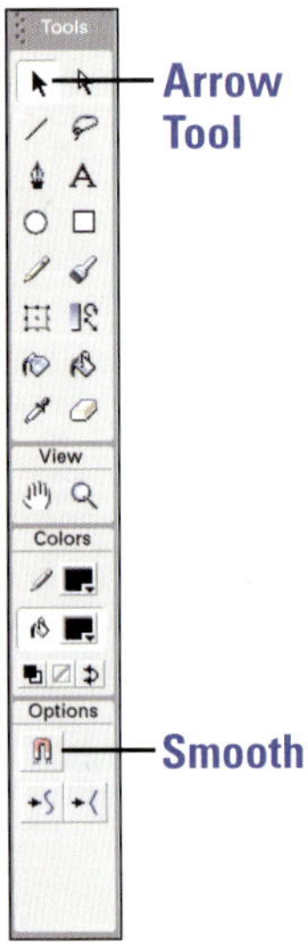

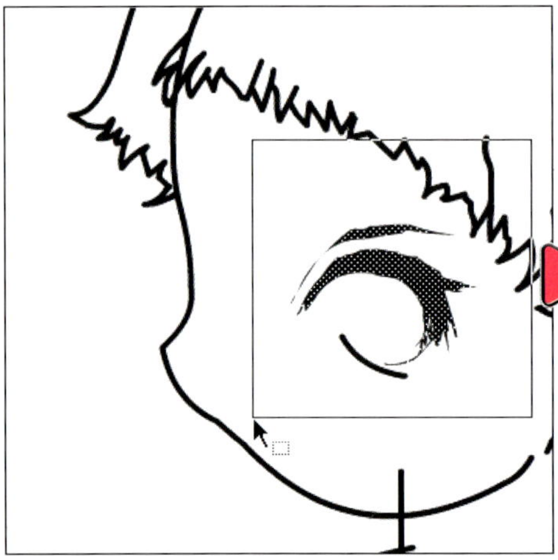

▲ Select the eyebrows and eyelashes with the Arrow Tool.

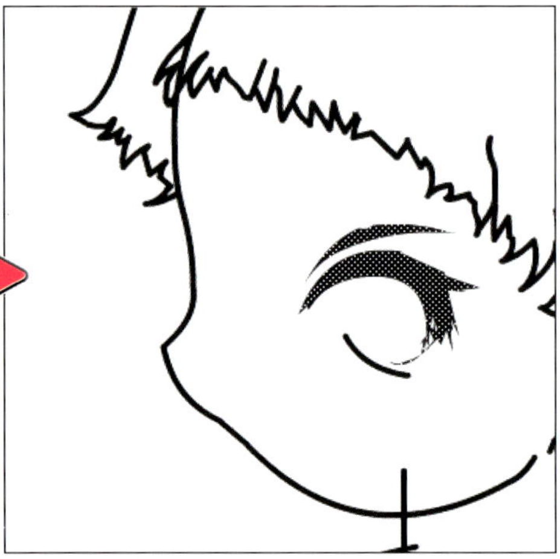

▲ Hit the Smooth button a few times to soften them up.

How to Draw Eyes in Flash

Introduction to drawing eyes by combining basic shapes

The eyes will determine the whole expression of your character. You must be especially sensitive to this. In this section, I will introduce a way to draw eyes in Flash that makes full use of its features.

Point

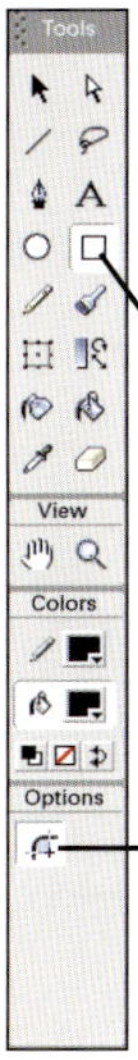

Here, I'll draw the eye based on a rounded rectangle shape. You can draw rounded rectangles by using the Rectangle Tool's Round Rectangle Radius option. I've set this rectangle to 20 points.

Rectangle Tool

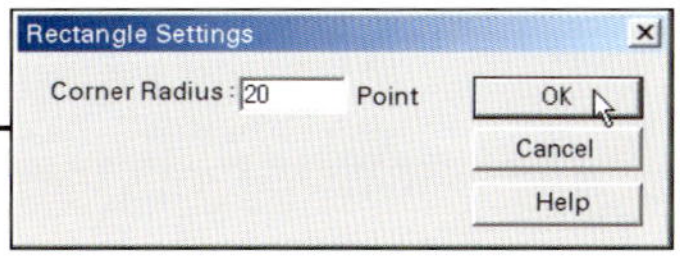

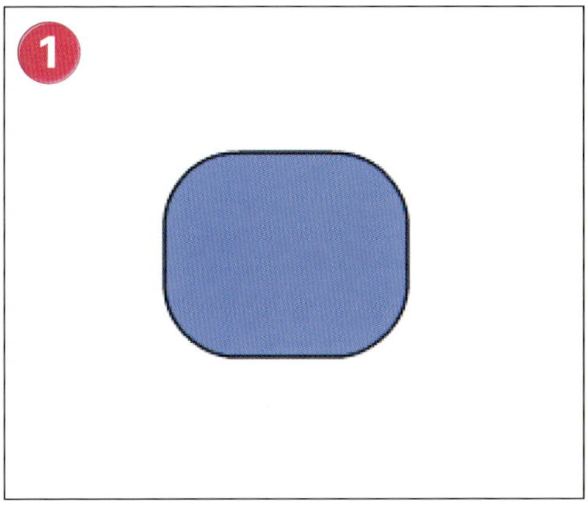

▲ Create a rounded rectangle with the Rectangle Tool. I'll make the base color black in the end, but I've changed it here to make it easier to understand this process.

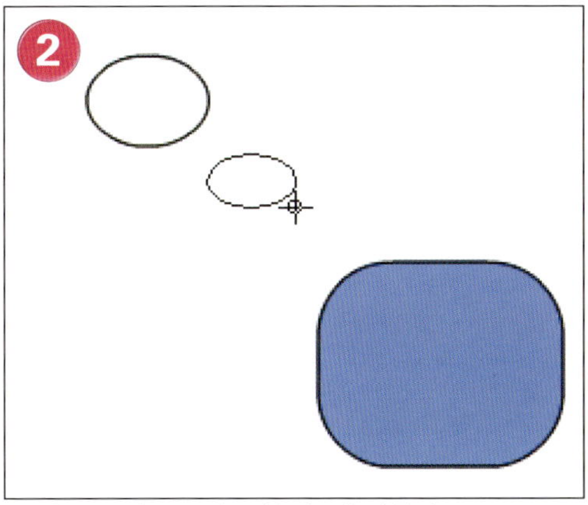

▲ Draw a few ovals with the Oval Tool to serve as highlights for the eyes.

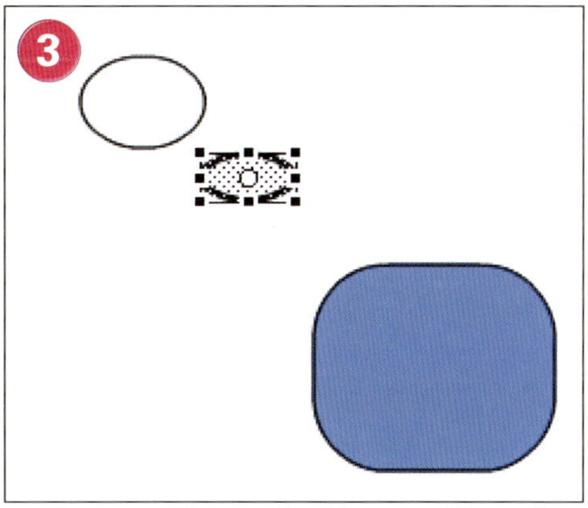

▲ Be sure to fill the ovals with a color different from the rounded rectangle. Here, I've chosen white.

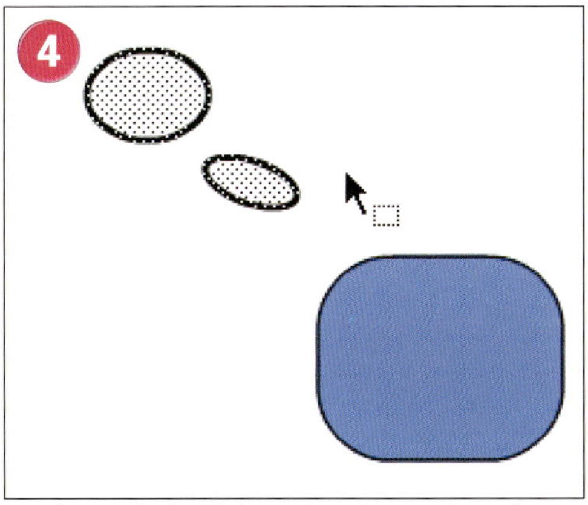

▲ Rotate the highlight ovals and move them about with the Free Transform Tool.

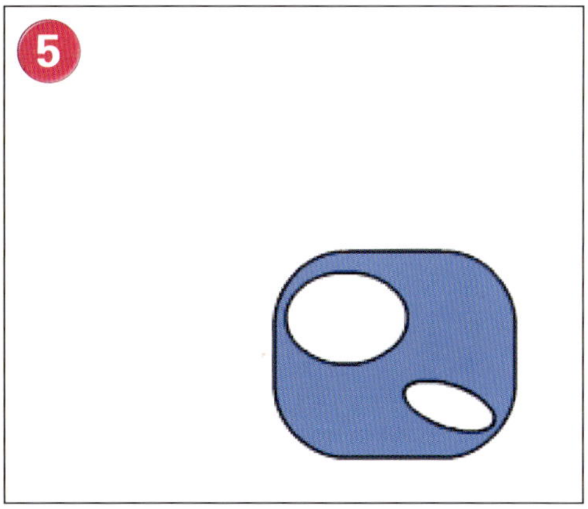

▲ Move the eye highlights to the inside of the rounded rectangle.

How to Draw Eyes, Continued

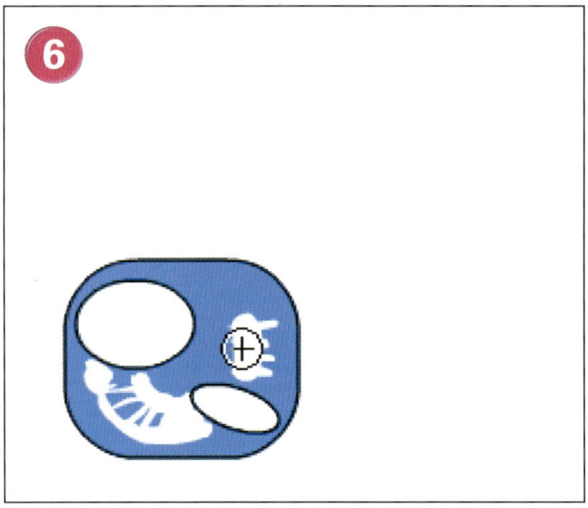

▲ Use the Brush Tool to draw in the iris lines.

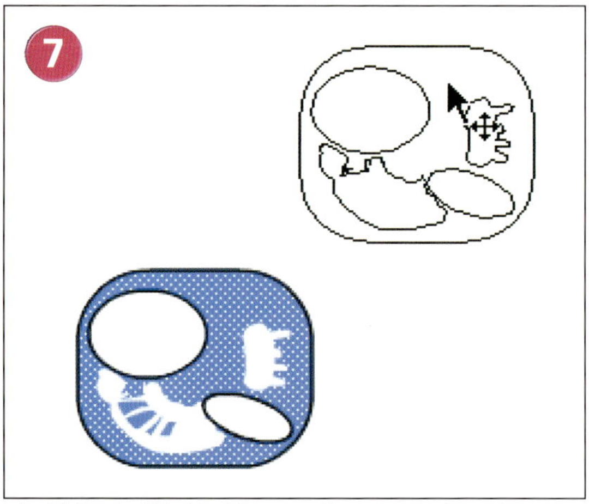

▲ Make the fills (the blue parts) a group and set them aside someplace unoccupied on the Stage.

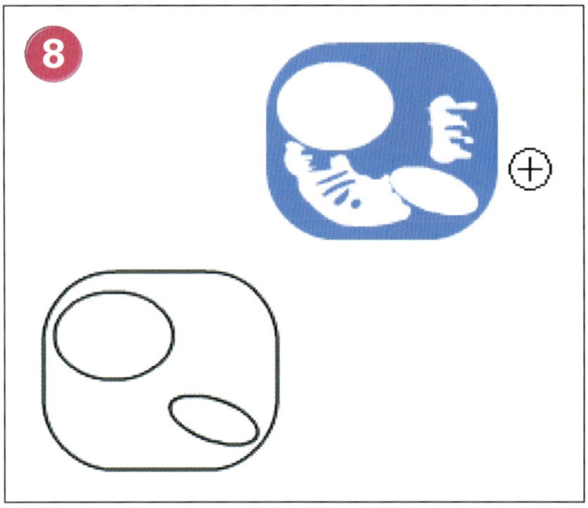

▲ Now you've separated the fills and lines.

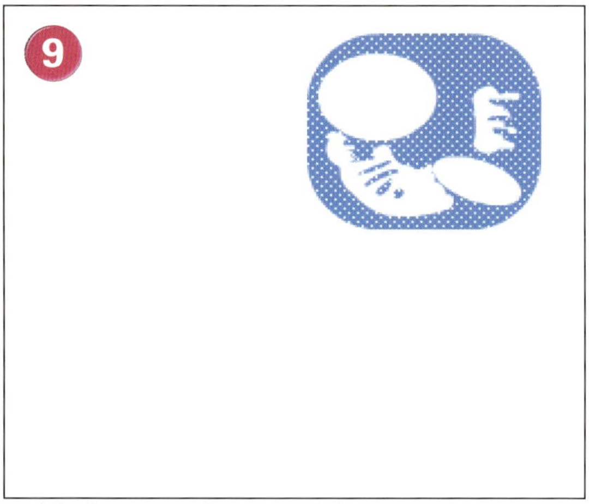

▲ The lines are no longer needed, so erase them.

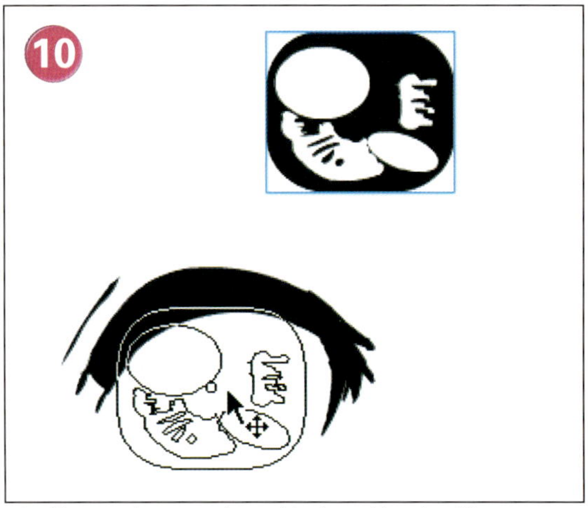

▲ Change the eye color to black, and lay the fill atop the previously drawn eyelashes.

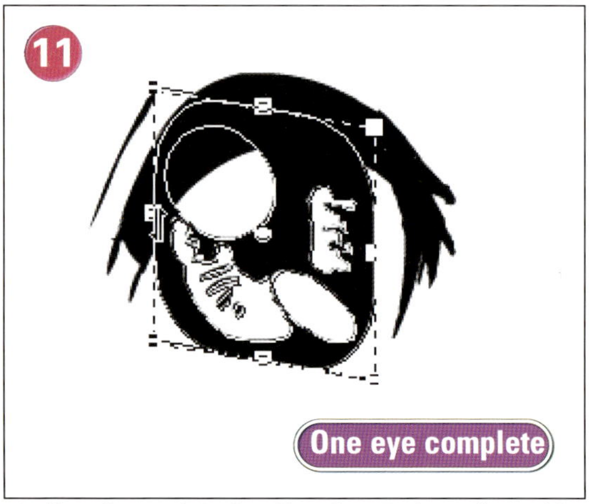

▲ Here, I've used the Free Transform Tool to pull one side of the eye up at an angle. This will affect your character's expression, so try out a few different positions.

Create One Eye from the Other

Copy the eyebrow and flip it horizontally, then copy the eye and use as it is.

Now let's take the eye you made using the process from the last few pages and use it to make the other one. This is an efficient technique because the things you draw in Flash are stored as data (as opposed to an image file), allowing you to freely transform your work without damaging it.

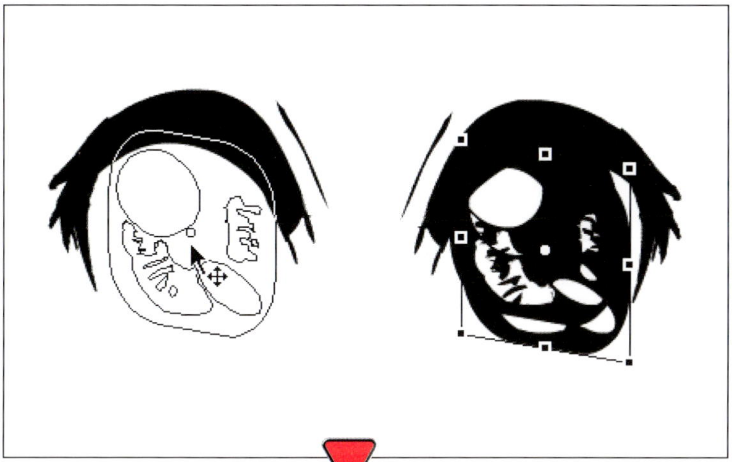

Copy, paste, and horizontally flip the eyebrows. Copy and paste the eye, too, but don't flip it. Use it as is.

Point
Flip things horizontally by choosing Modify → Transform → Flip Horizontal.

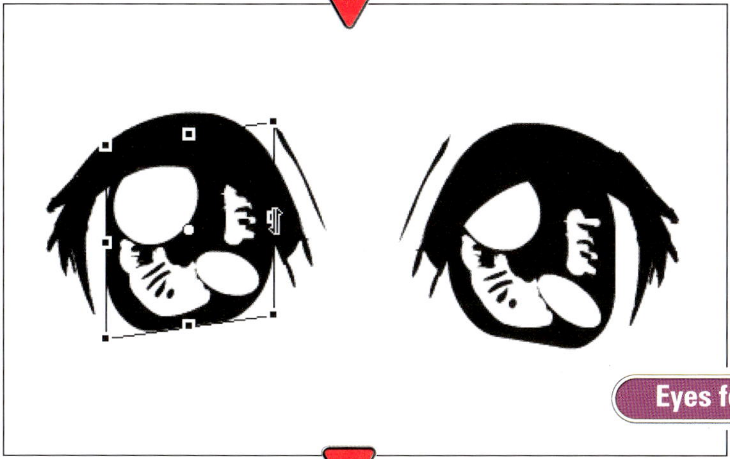

Eyes forward

Make use of the Free Transform Tool to tweak the eye. You could use this layout for a face looking straight forward.

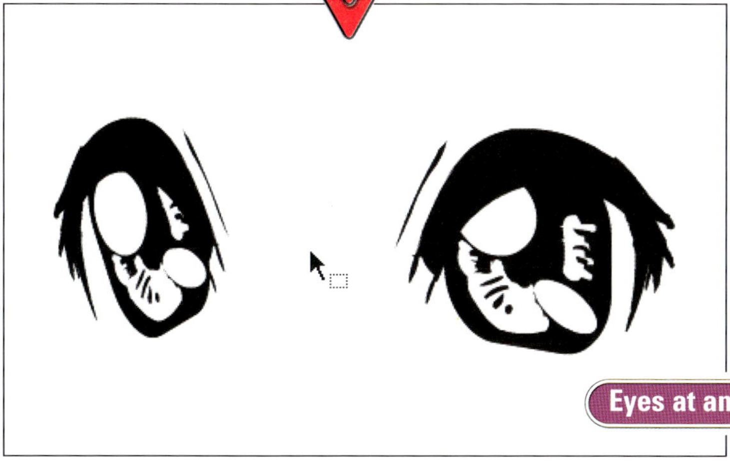

Eyes at an angle

If you shrink one eye to half size with the Scale function, you can make the eyes look at an angle. If something seems odd when you do this, try using the various Transform functions and tools to fix it. Here, I only used Scale, Rotate, and the Free Transform Tool.

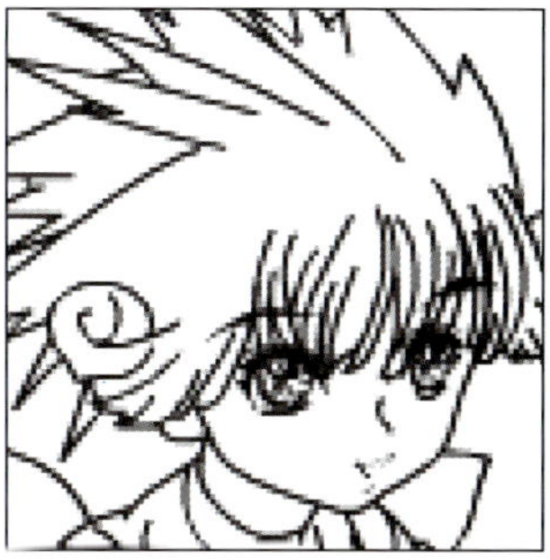

Dressing your Character

Make the body into a group, and draw the costume from the top down.

It's time to give your naked character some clothing, starting from the top. First, don't forget to Group the whole body together. That way, the lines you draw for the clothes won't snap to the body lines or otherwise affect what you've already drawn.

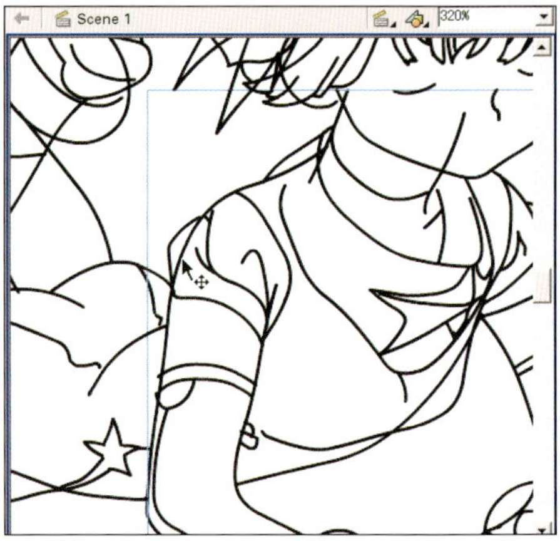

▲ When you want to modify something you've grouped, double-click on it.

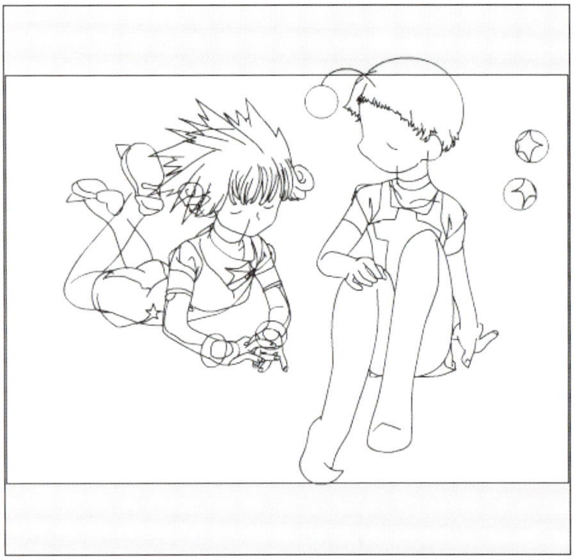

▲ Draw the clothing for your characters right on top of their bodies.

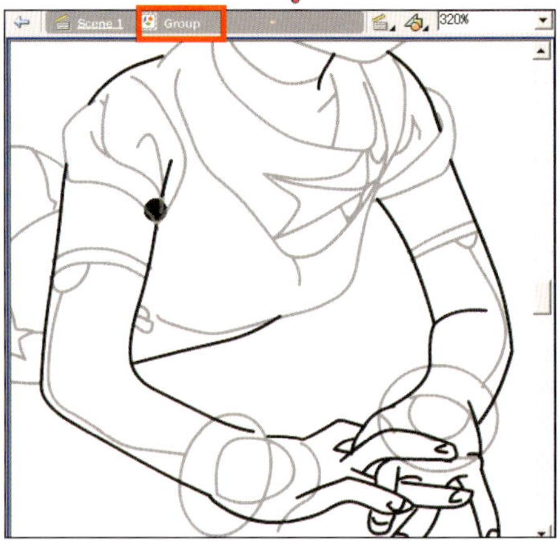

▲ Anything not in the group will be dimmed, and "Group" will appear in the bar directly over the Stage.

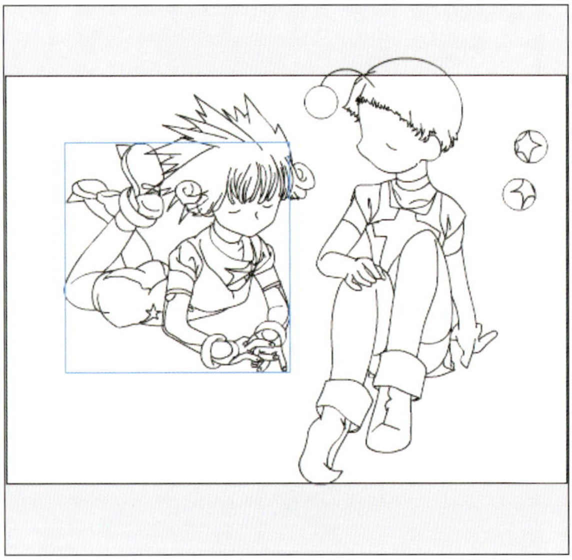

▲ Here, I've just erased the parts of the characters' bodies that are covered by their clothing and grouped them together.

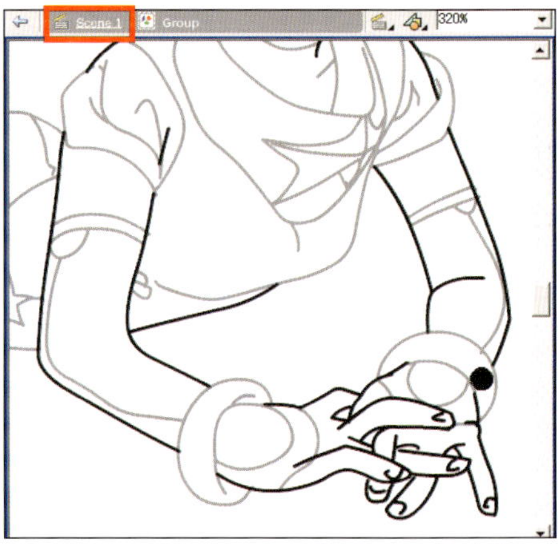

▲ It is now possible to modify only what's in the selected group. Here, I'm erasing the parts of their bodies hidden by their clothing. When you're done editing a Group, click on Scene 1 in the bar above.

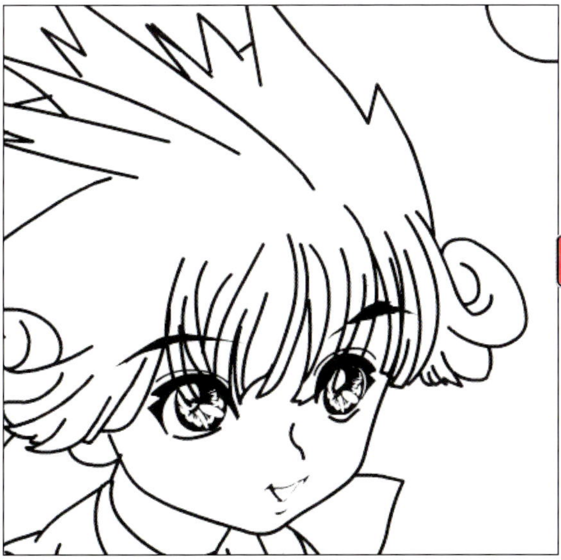

▲ Insert the eyes you drew in the "How to Draw Eyes" section.

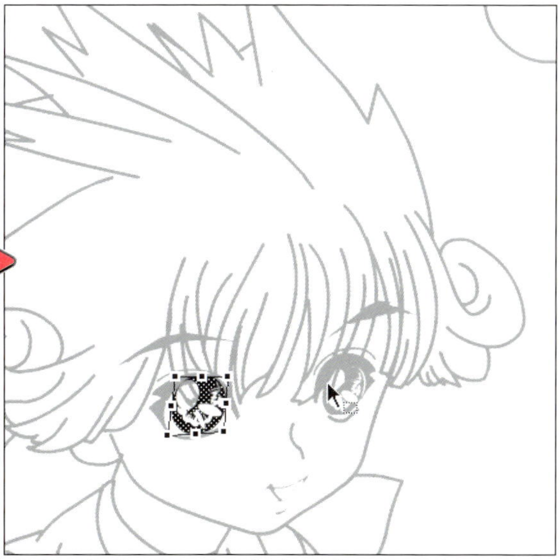

▲ Use the Free Transform Tool to adjust the angle of the eyes.

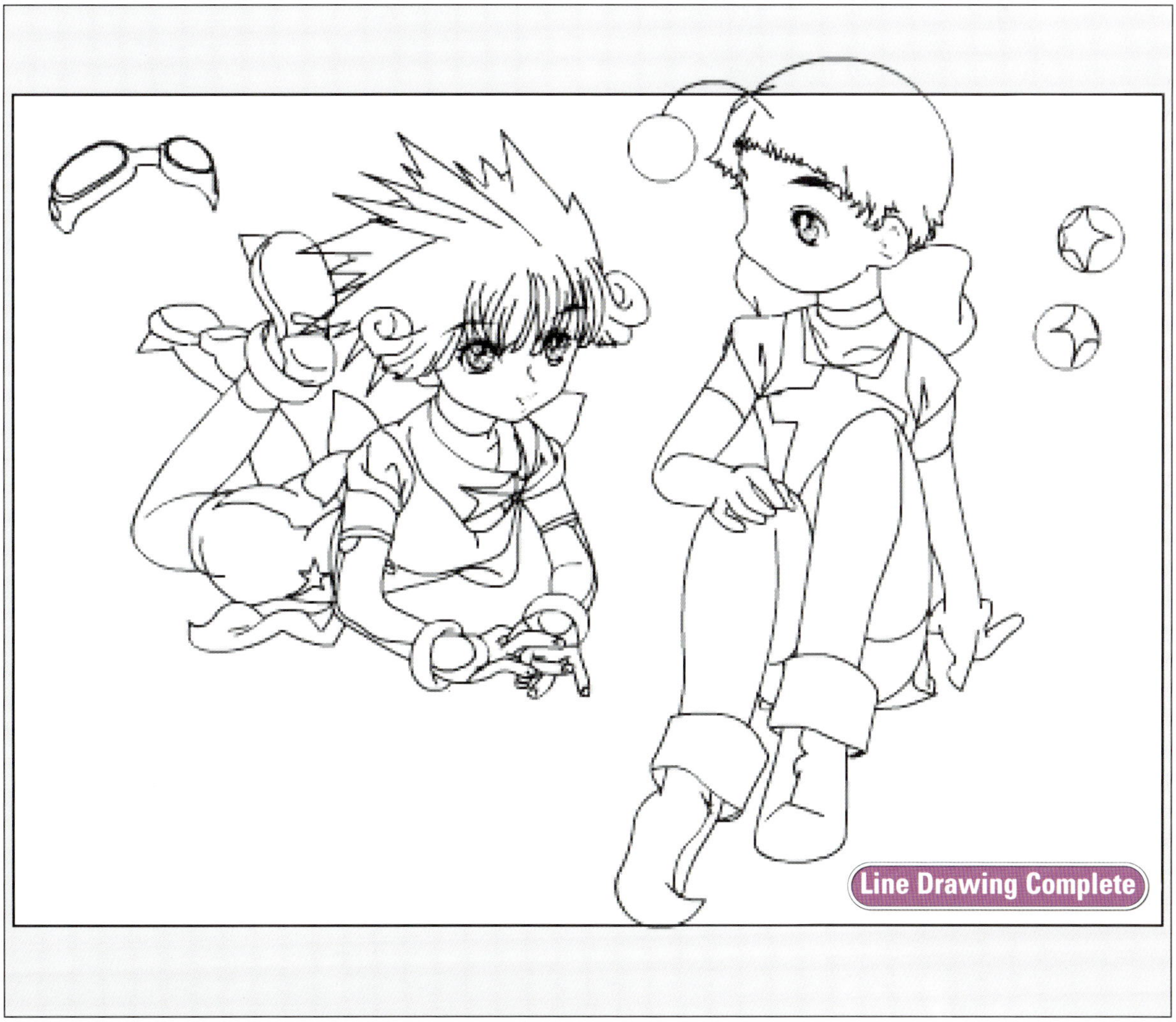

▲ When you're done, Group the bodies and clothing together. Then, since you no longer need it, delete the rough sketch layer (Layer 1).

Things to Remember Before you Start Coloring

The Color Palette

It doesn't really matter if you choose your fills from among the basic colors available or create your own from scratch. When you figure out which colors you use most often, take each one and vary the brightness and hue to make three to five variations. Then, take these variations and create a color set with them. If you save this set as the default palette, then every time you start a new project your custom color set will load into the Color Palette automatically.

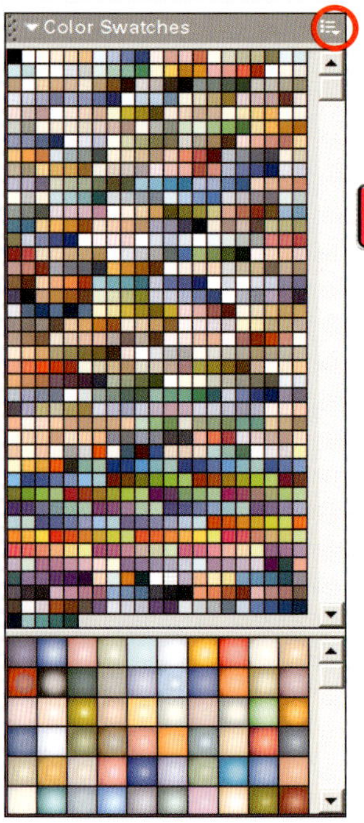

An original palette is a critical asset. By saving it as the default, you can dramatically reduce your workload. To save you palette, click on the upper right corner of the Color Swatches panel.

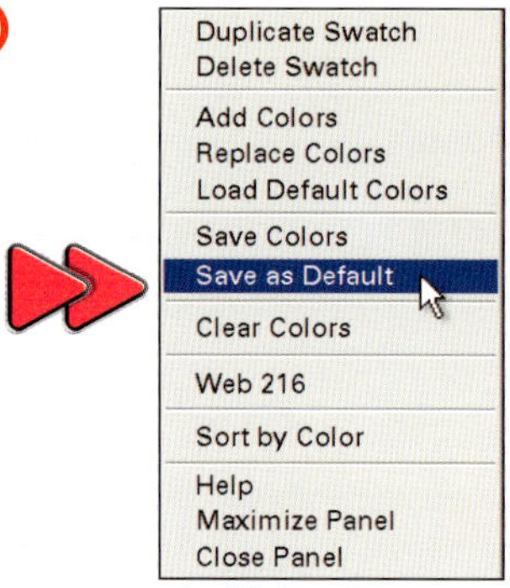

Click on Save as Default.

Gradations

I'm not really sure how to put this and I'm in no position to talk about it anyway, but three-color gradations are usually made going from light to dark, or vice-versa. I made mine with the brightest color in the middle. I thought it would look cool that way, but now it doesn't seem so. I'm providing it here as an example of what not to do.

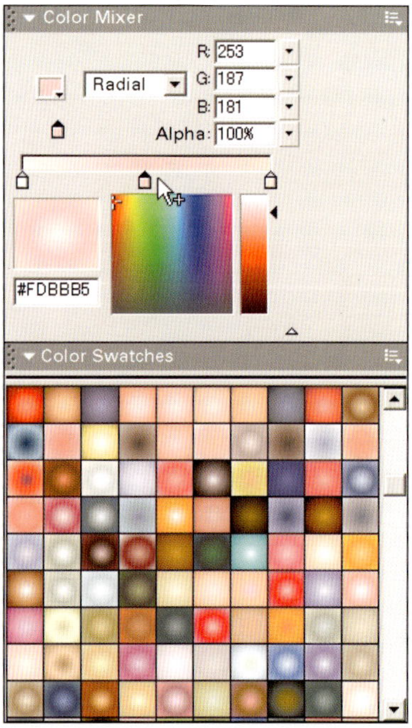

Close the Gaps in your Fill Lines before Coloring

You can still color even with some gaps present, but doing so after you close them is fundamental.

Now we'll start on the coloring. We will be splitting our work into two layers: the line drawing layer and the fill layer. Stack on a new layer now.

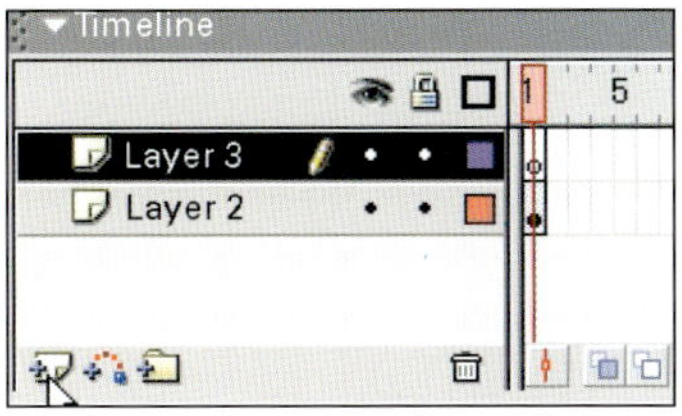

▲ Insert a layer here (Layer 3). In Layer 2, select the entire line drawing and choose Edit → Copy. Then move to Layer 3 and choose Edit → Paste in Place. Layer 3 is now the line drawing layer, so Lock it down.

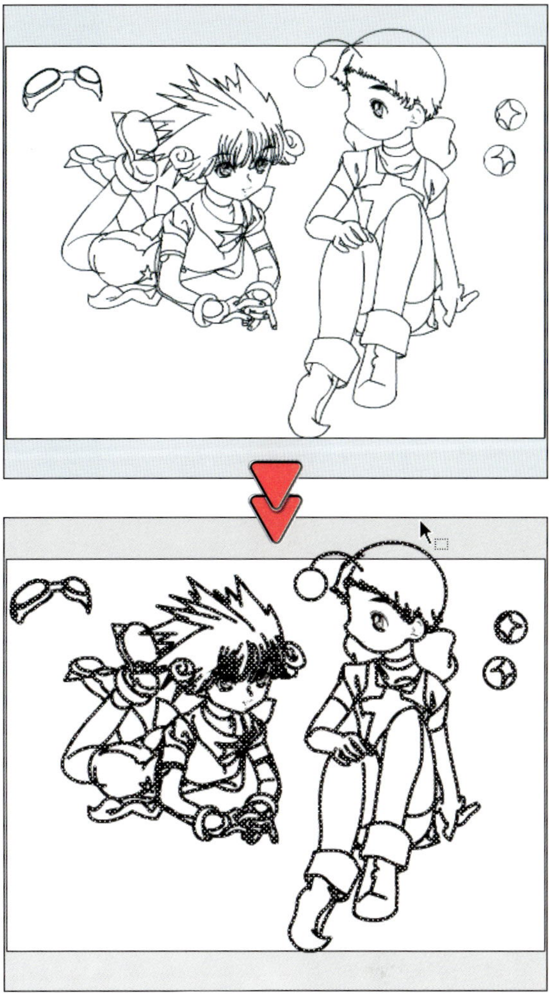

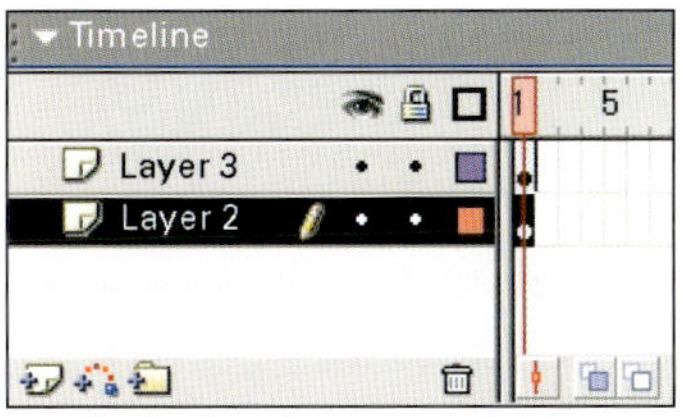

▲ Go back to Layer 2, and delete everything that is grouped together. Your coloring preparations are now complete. We will be coloring in this layer.

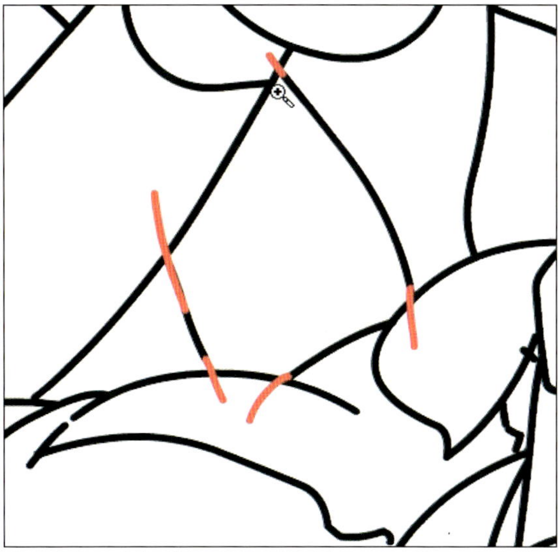

▲ We'll use the Paint Bucket Tool for most of our rough coloring. If your fills overflow the area you're coloring, zoom in on it and close off any broken lines with the Pencil Tool. Here, the red lines indicate areas where I've closed off gaps.

I can't paint anything!!

When you can't get the Paint Bucket Tool to work properly, there's probably an opening in your fill lines somewhere. If your lines are littered with gaps and fixing them all would be a pain, try applying your fill again with the Paint Bucket Tool's Close Medium Gaps option checked.

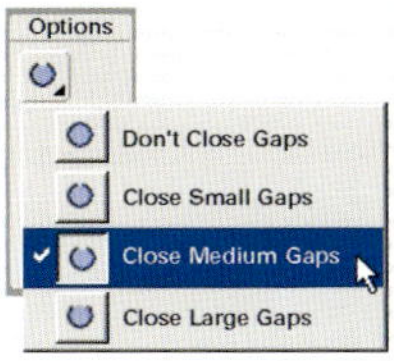

Effective Shading

In advance, prepare a utility palette of colors similar to your original.

Now that your colors are mostly laid out and you're back from closing any remaining gaps, it's time to draw some fill lines for the areas you want to shade. Use the Pencil Tool (set to a stroke color different from your main lines) to draw them.

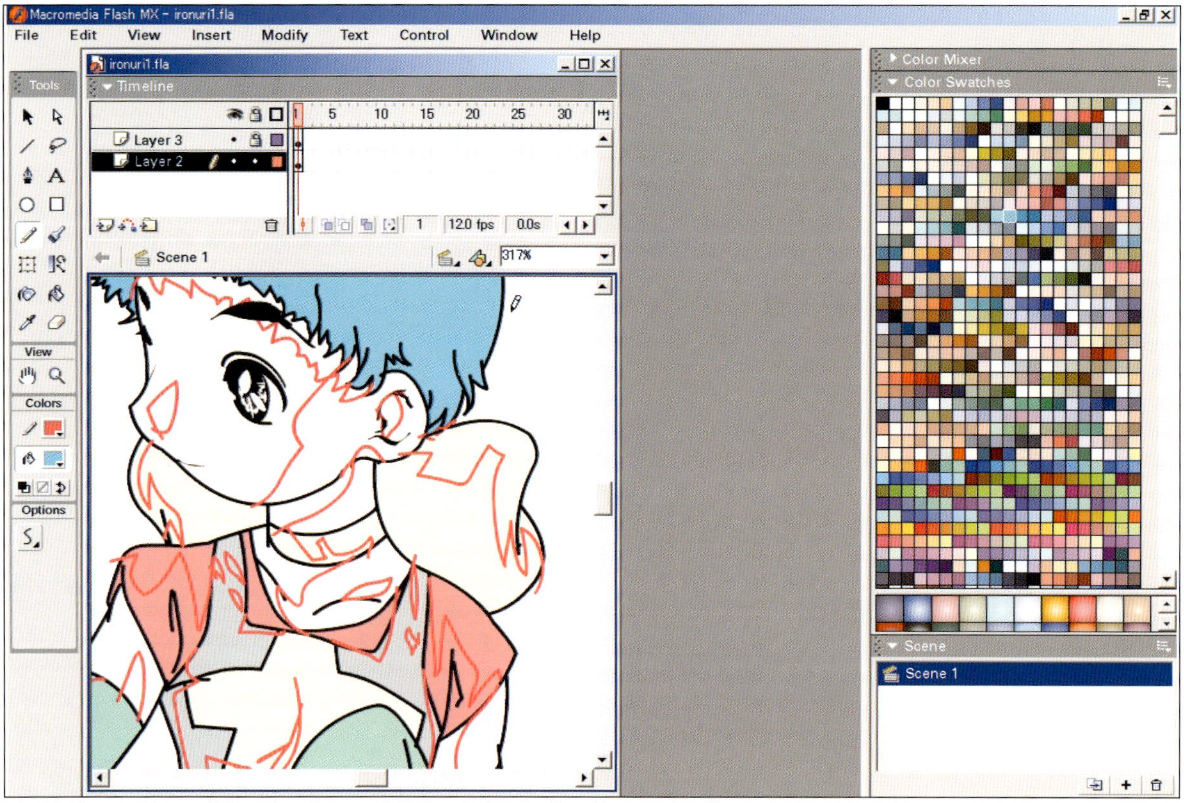

▲ Making a palette of like colors is especially handy for shading. Your work will speed up just by adding colors to this new palette in the order you want to shade your piece. So let's get to working with those colors.

When you're done with the shade lines, scribble them away.

When the shade lines get to be in your way, scribble all over your drawing in the same color as the lines, as pictured here. Then, you can double click on any of the like-colored lines to select them all and hit the Delete key to get rid of them. This will make your work go a lot easier.

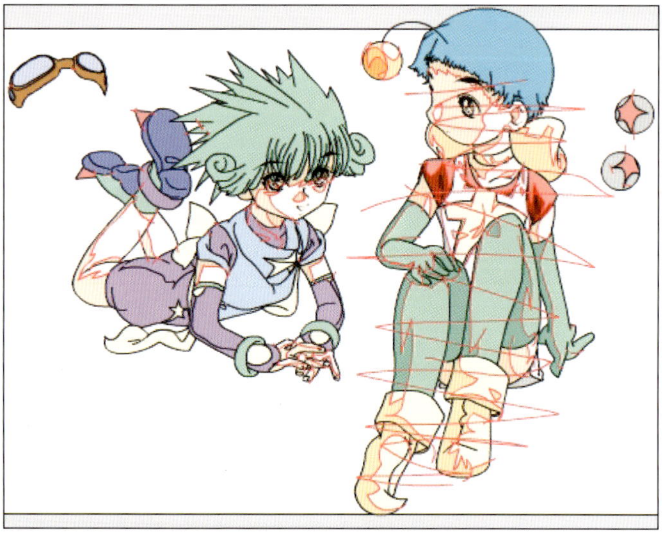

Post-Coloring Modifications

Skilled use of the Copy, Flip, and Rotate functions is the key to easier modifications.

When your piece is just starting to look like it's getting somewhere, you're probably going to want to start fixing things, like repositioning a hand or what have you. Actually, I'm too slow in pointing this out, but that character's right foot is at an odd angle, isn't it? Next, I'll introduce a way to fix things like this.

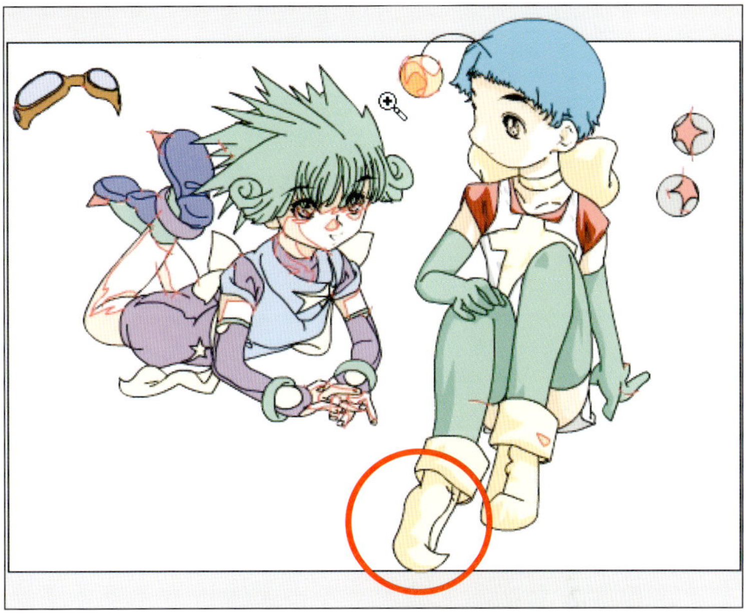

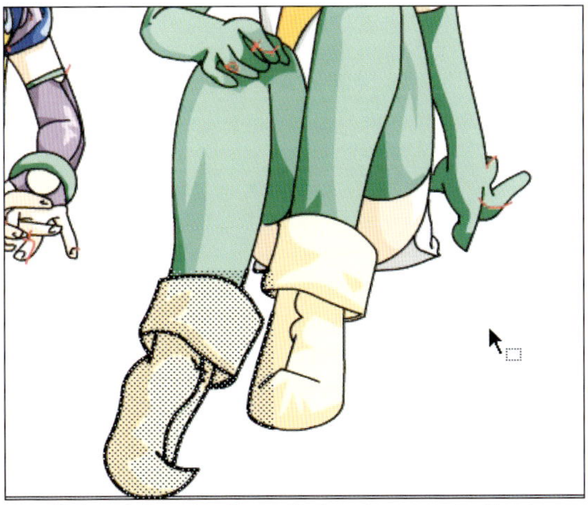

▲ Click and drag the Arrow Tool to draw a selection box a little larger than the target area and copy it.

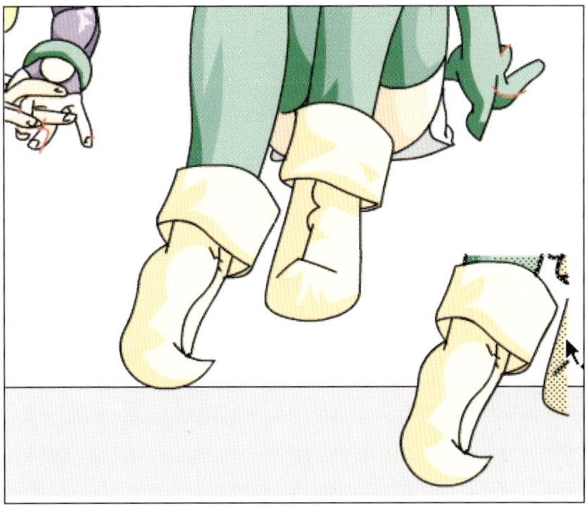

▲ Paste it back in and drag it to an open area.

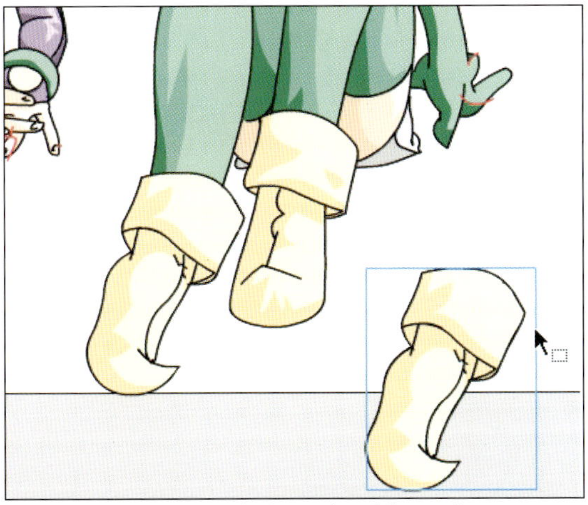

▲ Erase the parts you don't need and Group the rest.

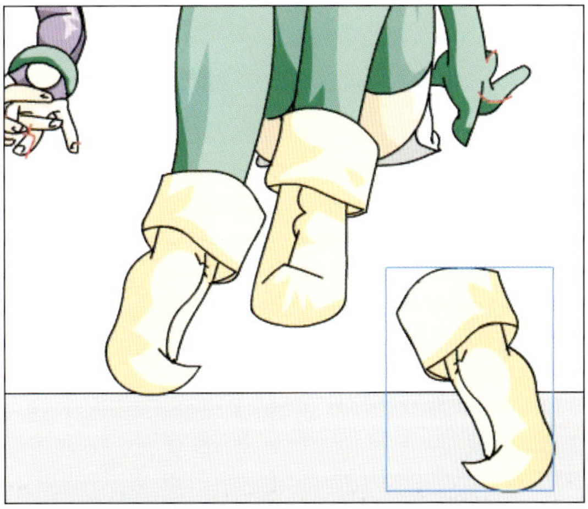

▲ Choose Modify → Transform → Flip Horizontal.

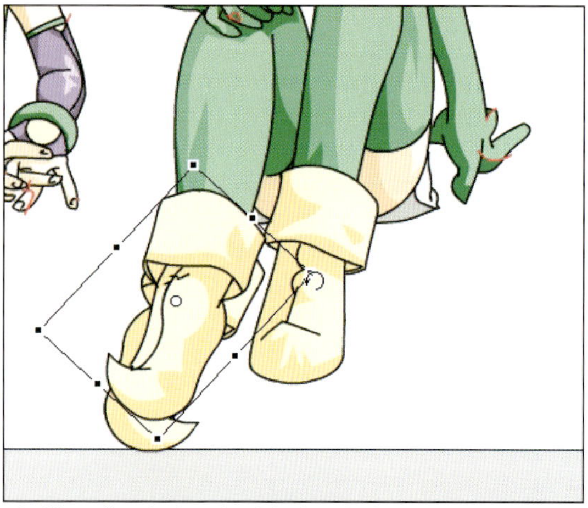

▲ Now, I'm placing the right foot in the proper location. Next, I'll use the Free Transform Tool to Rotate the foot, adjusting it so it looks correct.

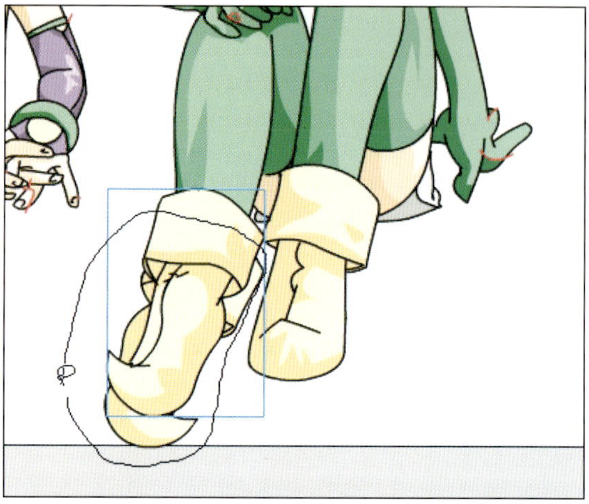

▲ Select the old parts that you don't want anymore with the Lasso Tool, and hit the Delete key to erase them. Here, I'm getting rid of the old right foot.

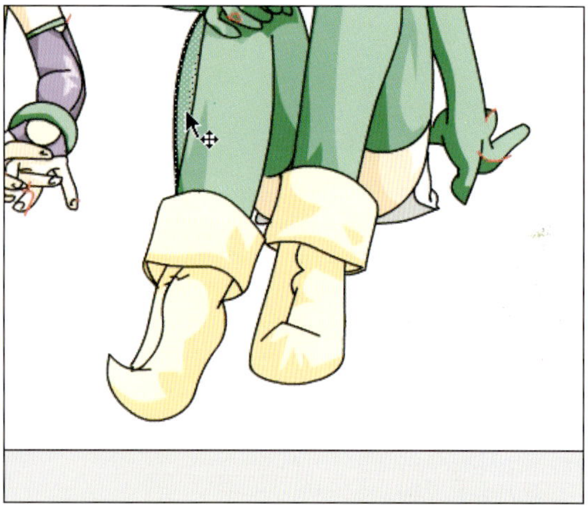

▲ Now the right calf looks fat, so I draw the Lasso Tool delicately around the lines and fills I don't want and erase them.

Erase Fills? Erase Lines? Erase selectively.

An image editing necessity, the Eraser Tool will, at its unaltered default settings, wipe out anything and everything you've drawn. However, by changing some of the options, you can engage special erasing modes-erase only fills, only lines, etc.

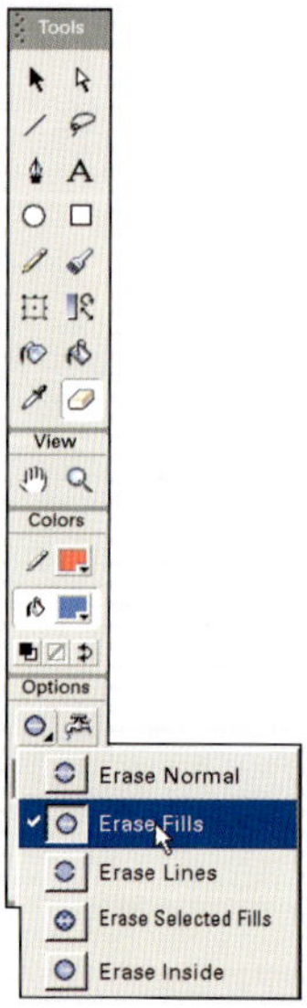

Erase Normal (Default):

Erase both lines and fills.

Erase Fills:

Erase only fills. Things you've drawn with the Brush Tool are fills, too. You can erase them with this.

Erase Lines:

Erase only lines. With this mode you can erase things drawn with the Pencil Tool.

Erase Selected Fills:

Erase only those fills in a selected state.

Erase Inside:

Erase only the fill on which you begin an eraser stroke.

Post-Coloring Modifications, Continued

Make the line drawing layer reflect the modifications in the fill layer.

The changes we've effected so far are only in the fill layer (Layer 2), so we have to make the same modifications to the line drawing layer (Layer 3) as well.

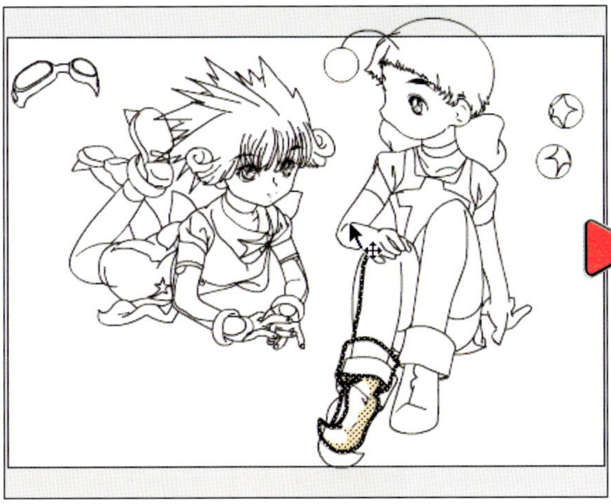

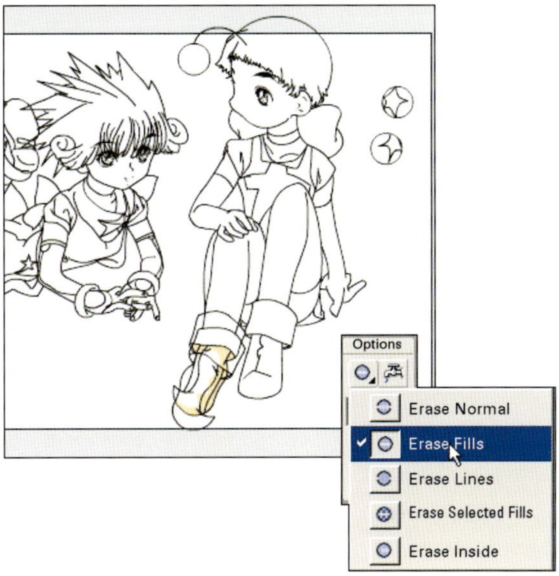

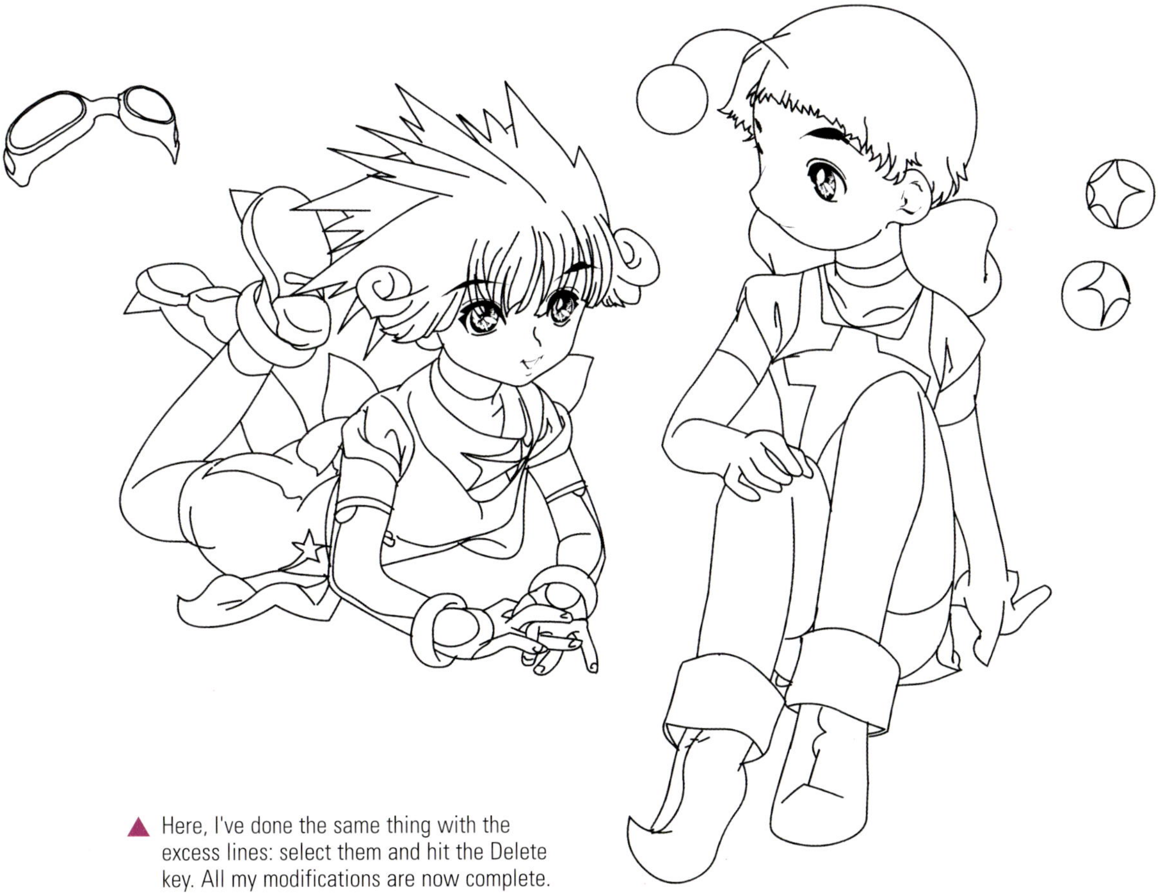

▲ Here, I've done the same thing with the excess lines: select them and hit the Delete key. All my modifications are now complete.

Blush the Cheeks for a Cuter Look

Match an oval to the cheeks, transform it to fit, and fill it with a gradation to add color.

Because she'll look cuter with red in her cheeks, now I'll try adding some. This will complete the coloring stage; since we'll be using a different application to add the final finish to our work, be certain you save your file when you're done here.

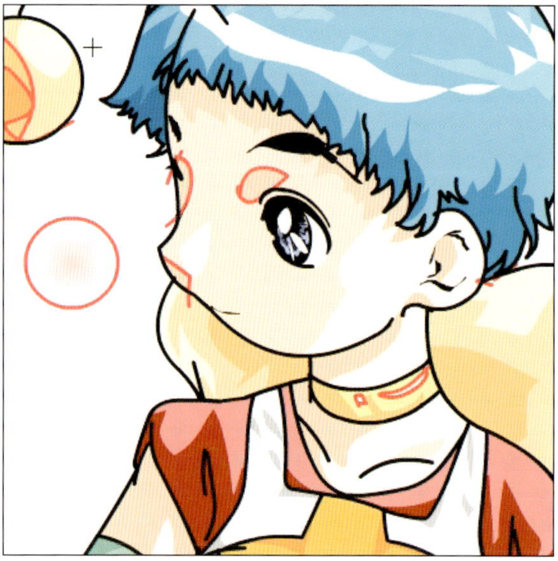

▲ Use the Oval Tool to draw a circle in some open white space and fill it with a reddish color. Use a two-color gradation: make both the inside and outside markers to pink, but be sure to set the outside marker's Alpha value to 0% for a transparent effect.

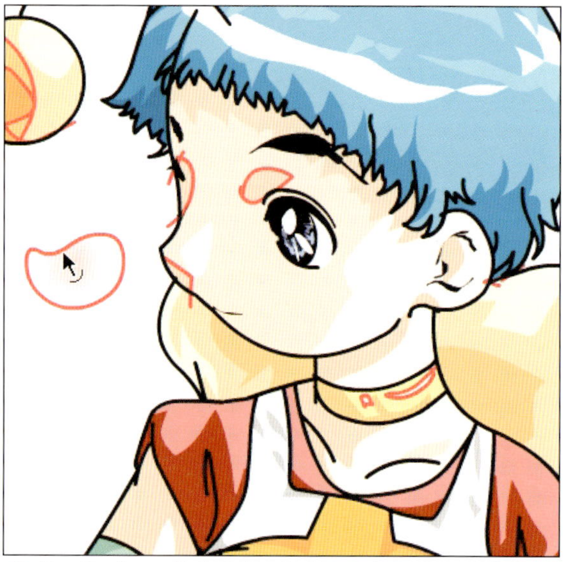

▲ Use the Arrow Tool to dimple the ovals into a rounded triangular shape.

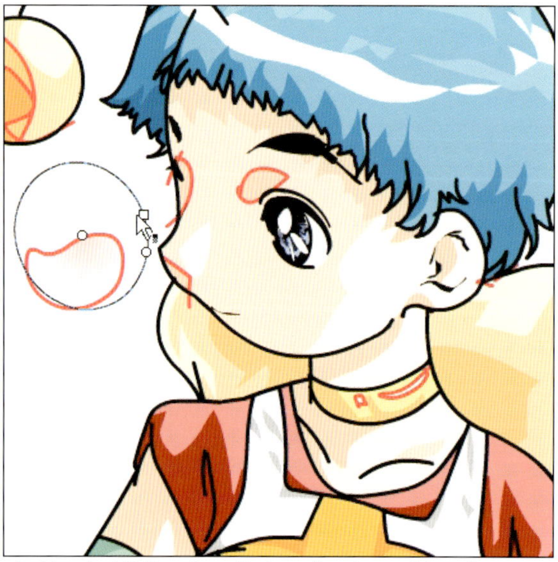

▲ Use the Fill Transform Tool to align the position of gradation and direction with the jaw line.

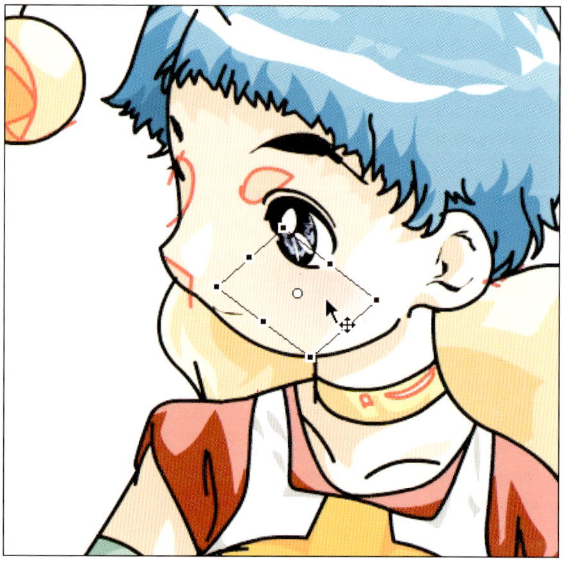

▲ Applying the gradation to the cheeks makes them look blushed and full of life. If necessary, complete this step by using the Free Transform Tool.

The Final Finish: Producing a Realistic Pen Effect

Here is a separate application technique to take the simple lines you've drawn in Flash and accentuate them.

Normally, at this point we'd go straight on to setting up the layout and finishing the project. Instead, I'm going to explain how you can use an application called "Expression" to accentuate the lines you've already drawn in Flash so they look like actual pen strokes. We'll only use the line drawing for this, so be sure to delete the fill layer (Layer 2).

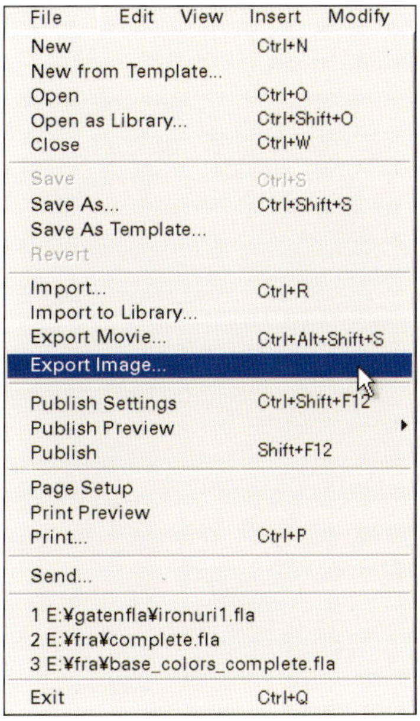

▲ In Flash, choose File → Export Image.

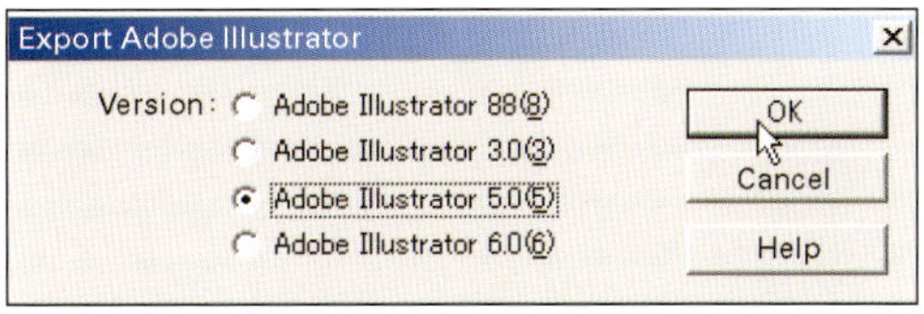

▲ Export your work as an Adobe Illustrator file. (Here, I'm exporting mine as an Illustrator 5.0 file, since Expression 2 can only read files up to version 5.0.)

Point
Do NOT save your file in Flash at this point. The fill layer has been deleted, and if you save your file here, it will stay that way.

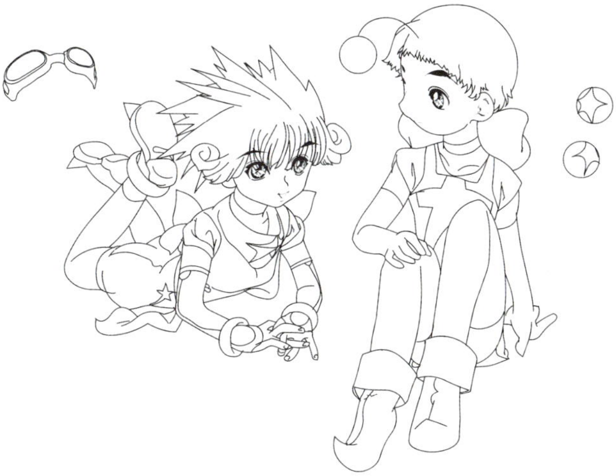

▲ Only the line information is exported as an Adobe Illustrator file.

What's "Expression?"

Expression is a drawing software application made by Creature House. Its most prominent feature is the "Skeletal Stroke," which is a function that can take a plain line drawn in another application and make it look like it was drawn with an actual brush or pen. You can create computer graphics from scratch in Expression, but here we're using as a Flash helper application.

Working with Expression

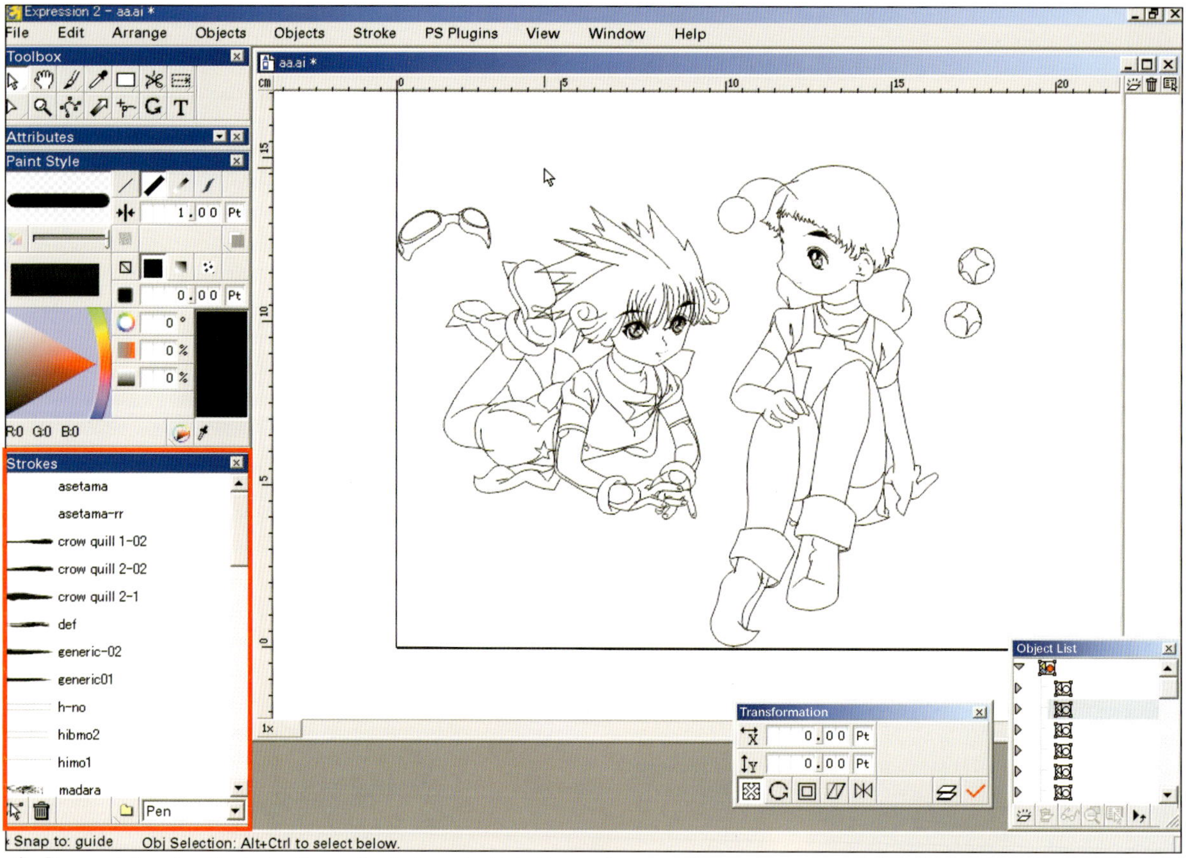

▲ Drag and drop the Illustrator file you've just created into Expression to open it, and choose an appropriate stroke style.

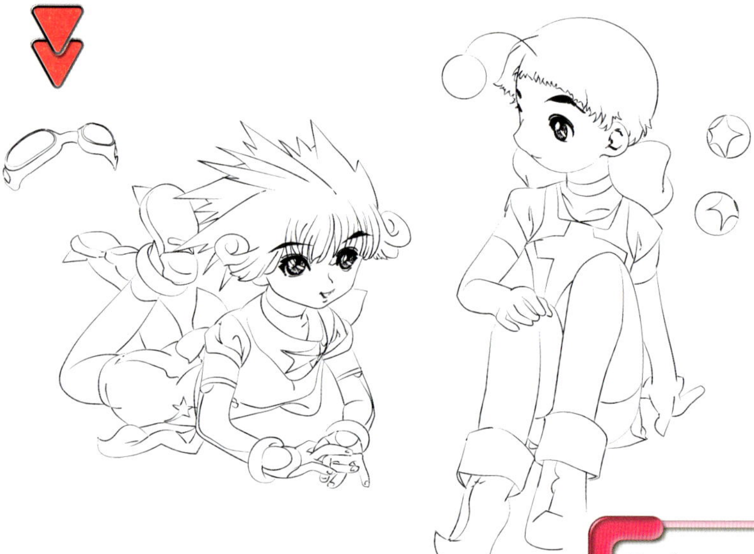

▲ Simple lines become lines that seem to have been drawn with an actual pen.

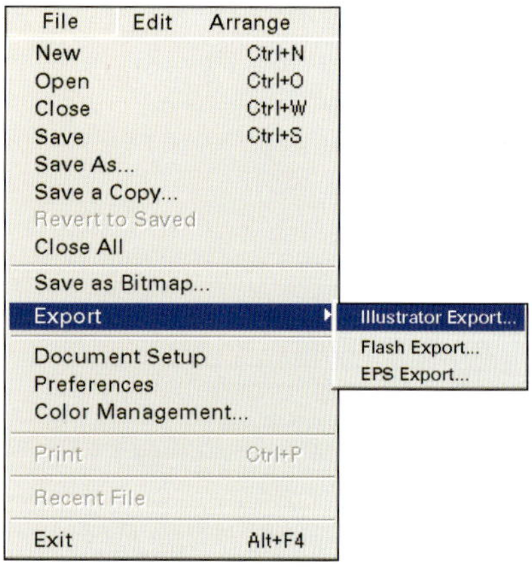

▲ Choose File → Export → Illustrator Export to export your new line drawing.

Point

Choose a format that Flash can read. Flash MX only supports Illustrator files up to 5.0, so that's the one I chose.

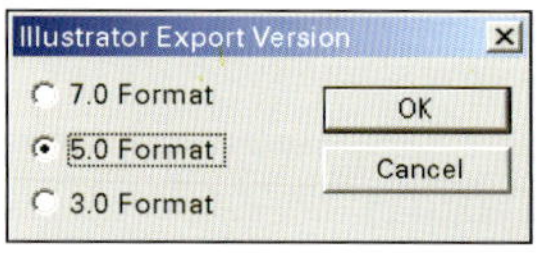

Back to Flash

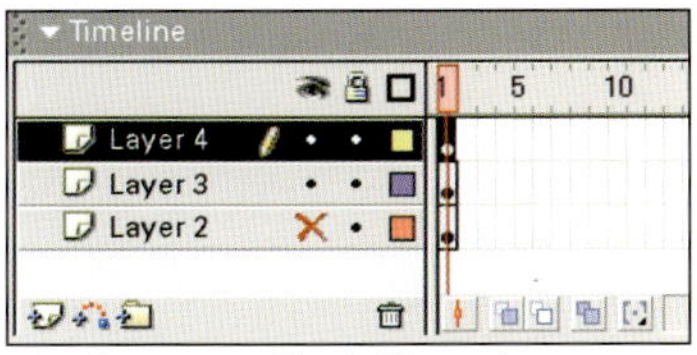

▲ Open your Flash file and create a new layer (Layer 4). Now lock all the other layers, choose File → Import, and open the Illustrator file you just created in Expression.

Point
Make the most of the eyes you've drawn in Flash. Delete the eyes that came with the Illustrator file. Then Copy the eyes in Layer 3, switch back to Layer 4, and choose Edit → Paste in Place.

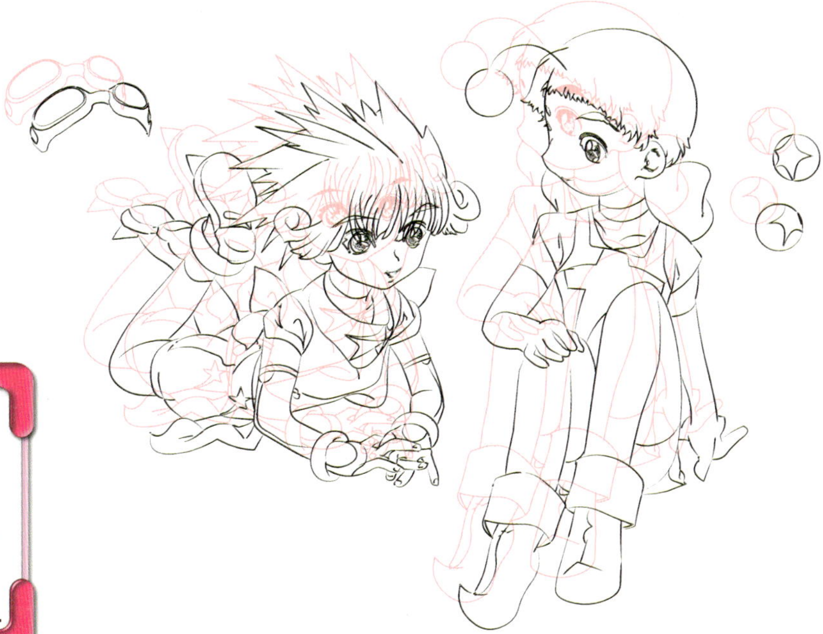

▲ The position of the imported file is a bit off, so I use the Arrow Tool to place it neatly back into position. Hiding the fill layer (Layer 2) makes it easier to do. The line drawing layer (Layer 3) is shown here in red for explanatory purposes.

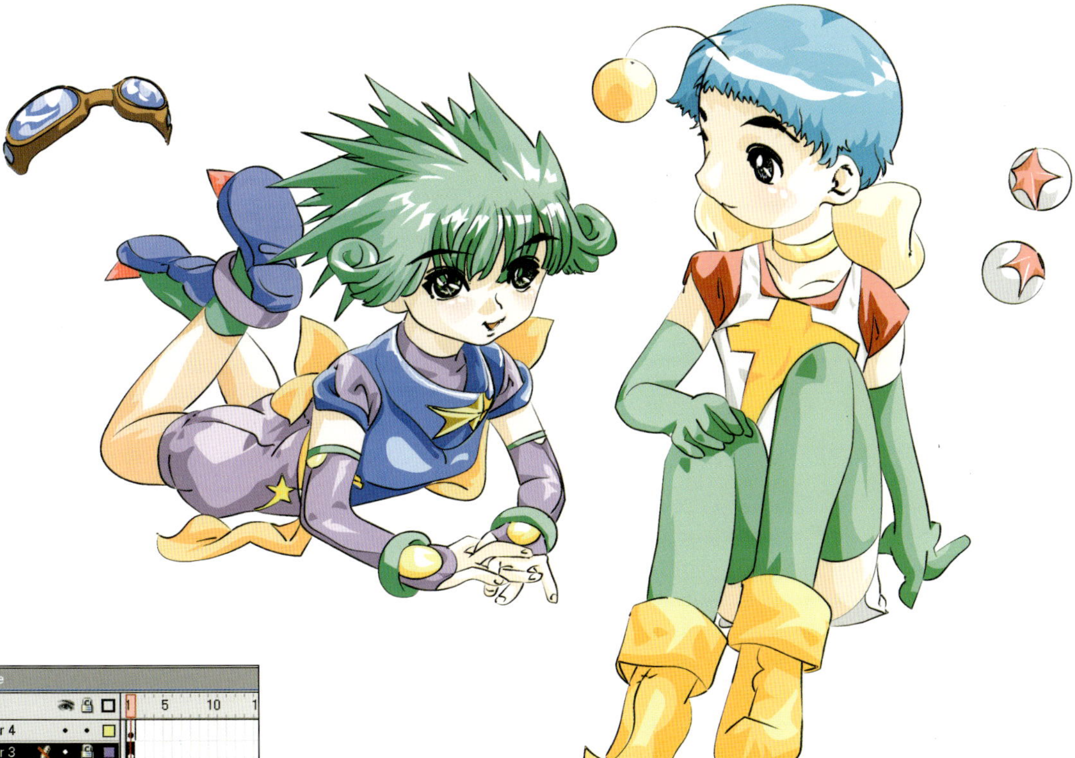

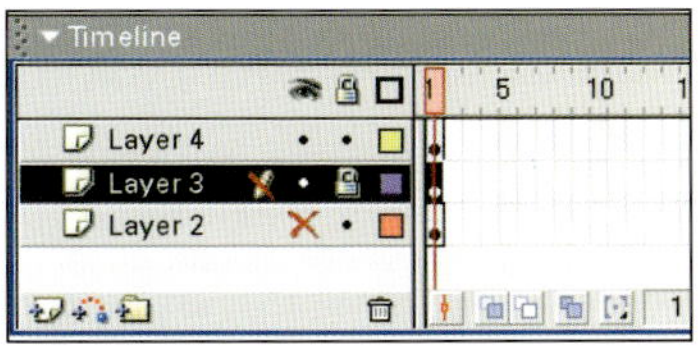

▲ Layer 3 is now no longer necessary. Delete it.

▲ I have successfully switched the Flash lines with the lines created in Expression.

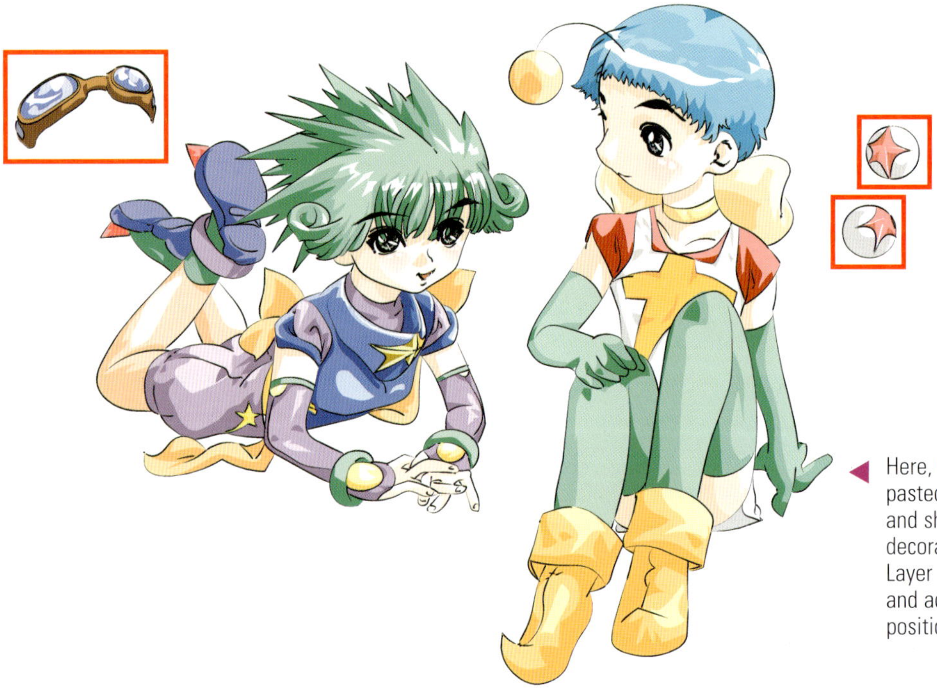

Here, I've cut and pasted the goggles and shoulder decorations from Layer 3 to Layer 4 and adjust their position.

Completion!

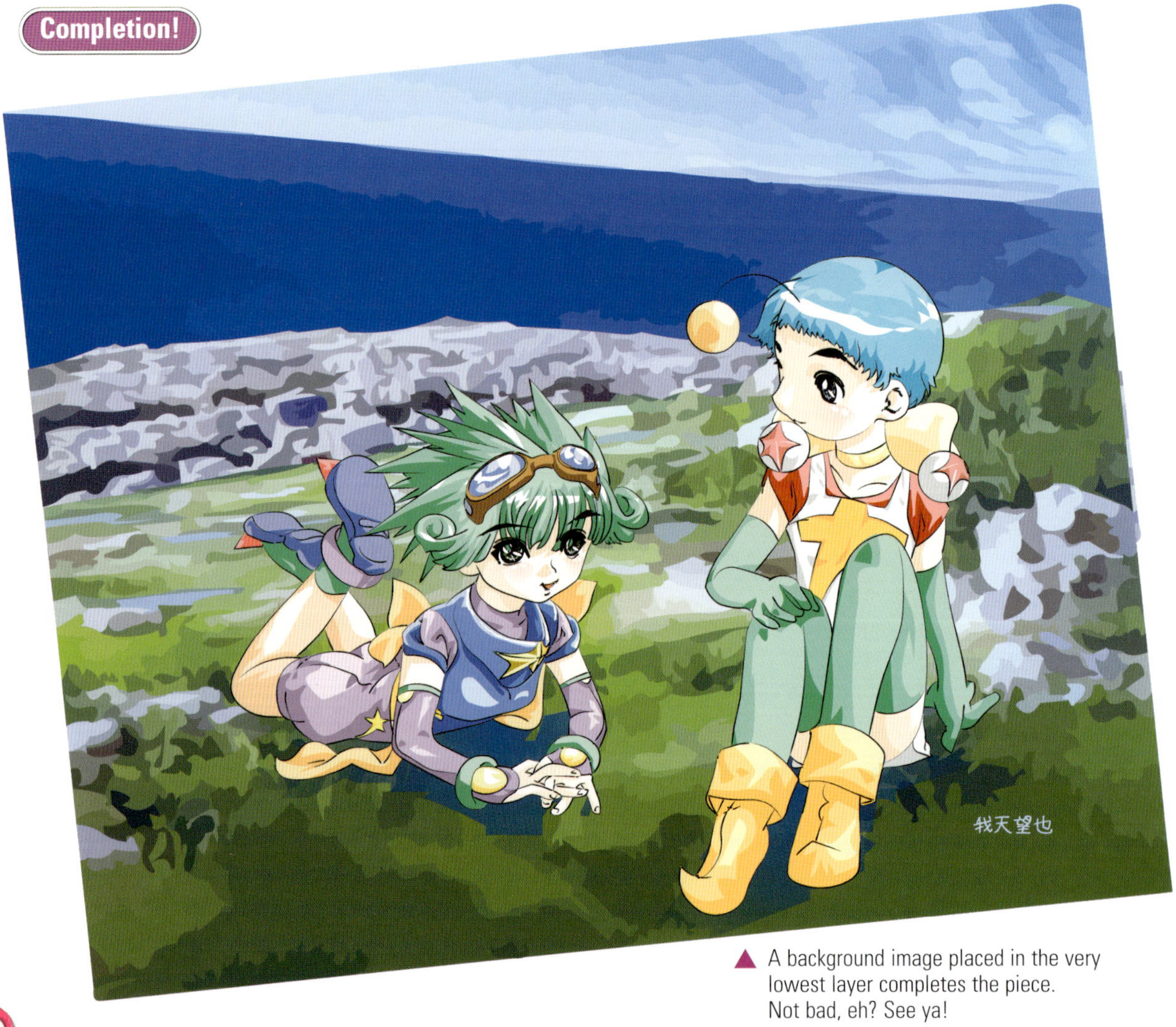

A background image placed in the very lowest layer completes the piece. Not bad, eh? See ya!

Gallery

All the character illustrations in this gallery have a few things in common. First, they were all drawn with the Brush Tool, not the Pencil Tool. On an A4 (8" x 11") paper-size Stage, I used a pressure-sensitive Brush set at 400% to 600% magnification. Also, as an experiment, I used four-color gradients here. I created them in the usual order—lightest to darkest.

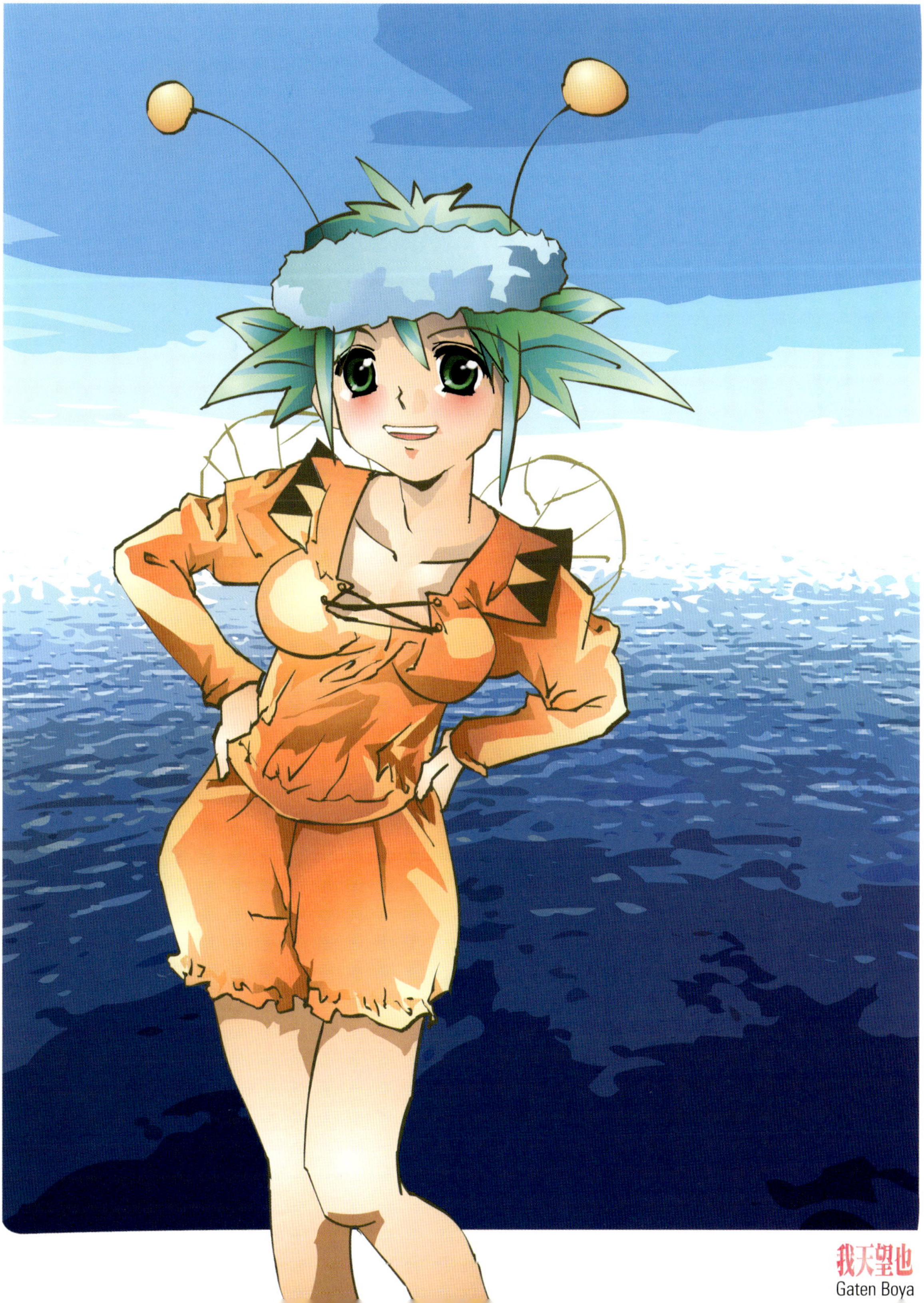

我天望也
Gaten Boya

Gallery

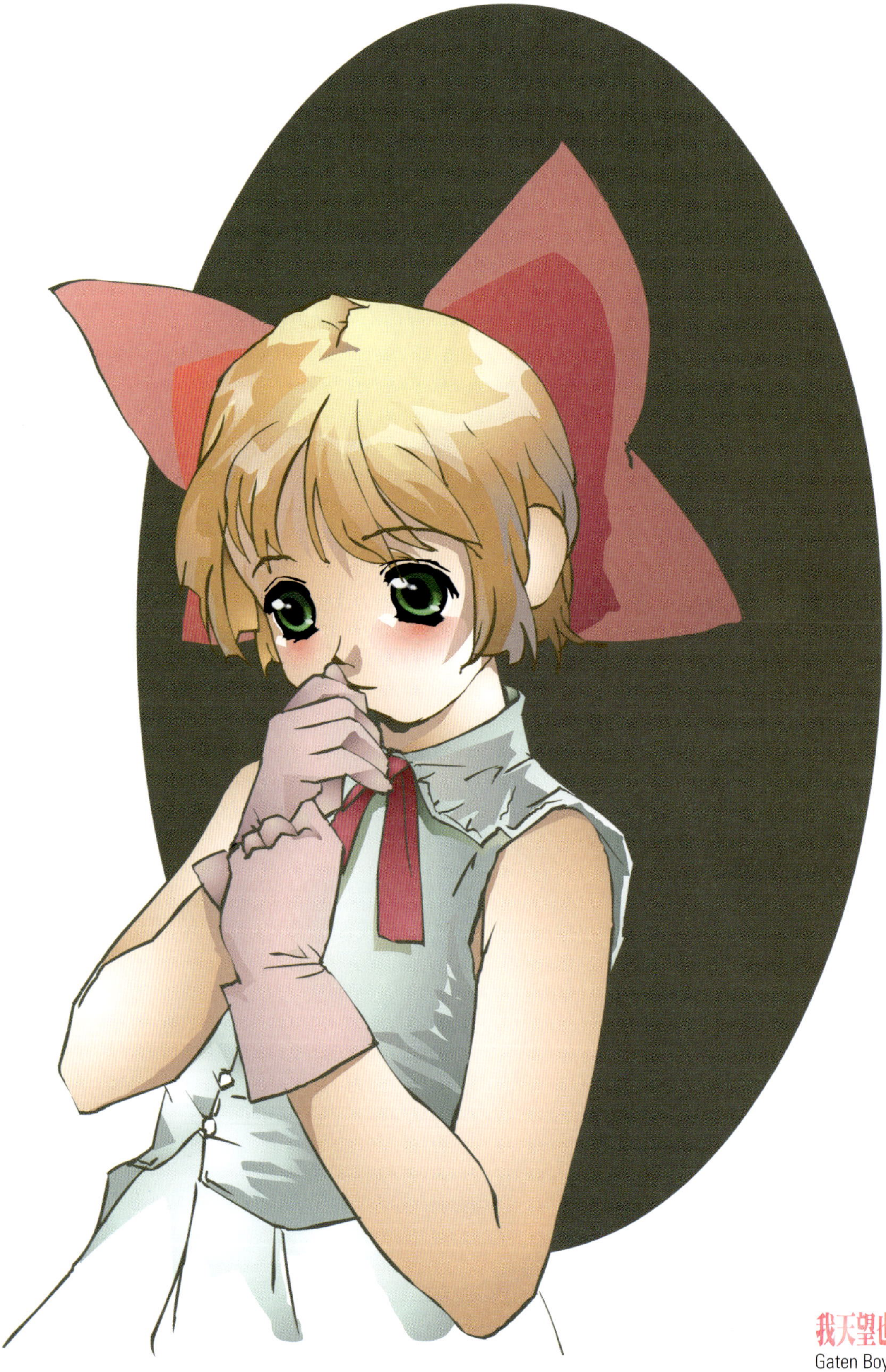

我天望也
Gaten Boya

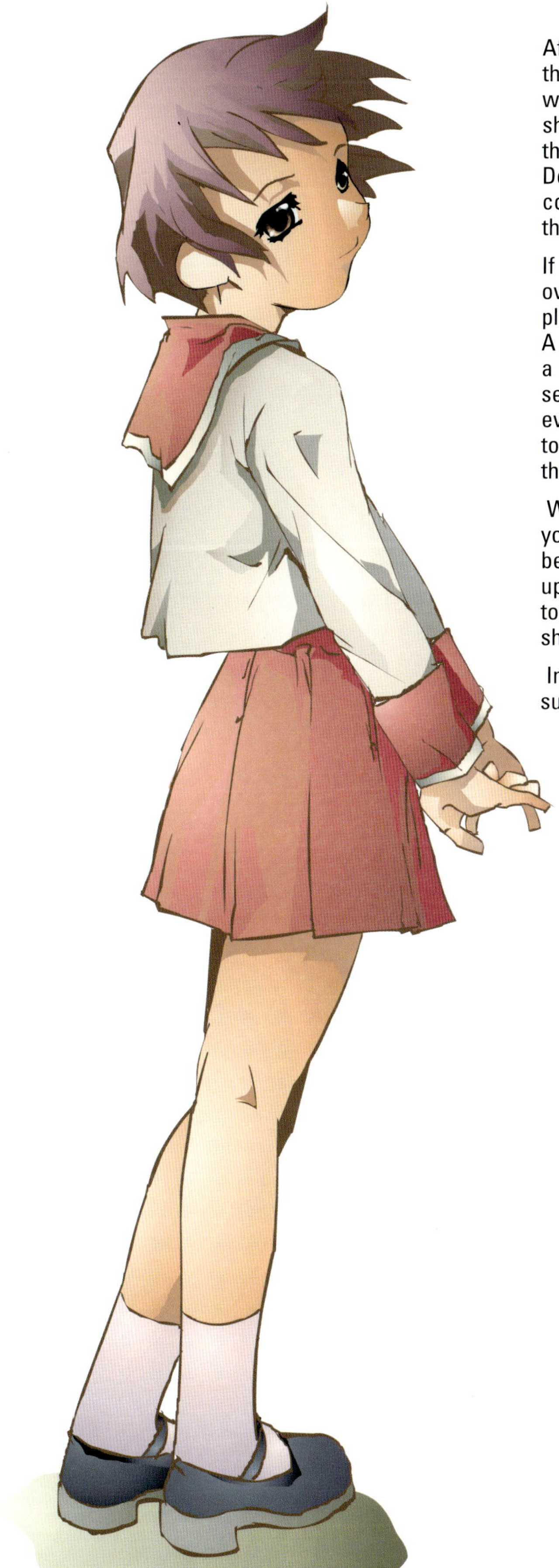

After applying gradations over most of the body, the character is finished off with shading gradations. When you're shading, try shifting your gradations so that they are off-center in the fill space. Doing so can make manipulating four-color gradations about as easy as three-color ones.

If you throw attractive tinted shadows over your character, the result is a pleasing, almost purposeful halo effect. A uniform appearance created just with a relative color set is fine. But if all sense of variation disappears, then even if I'm using relative colors I want to toss in something different. I suppose this is that desire given form.

When you create a relative gradation, you usually go in a 1-2-3 color order (1 being the brightest), but breaking that up with 2-1-3 gradations can be fun, too. Your results may vary, but you should definitely give it a shot.

Indeed, I have hardly achieved any subtlety with this piece. But I digress.

我天望也
Gaten Doya

A Lesson on the Fundamentals of Drawing Cute Characters
—Before you Begin your Flash Illustration

Instructor: Ten Asazuma (http://www.stream.gr.jp/~rhythm/)

How should we go about drawing cute gals? First, understand that manga and anime style pictures rely heavily on deformation, by which we mean exaggerating or downplaying "normal" human features, such as size. In order to draw human deformations in a cute way, it is necessary to know a bit about sketching. Once you've acquired mastery of the base, fundamental sketching techniques used for drawing manga and anime, developing your own deformation style should be easy.

Here, I will introduce to you those fundamental techniques. To begin with, we will touch upon the drawing supplies you'll need. While it doesn't strictly relate to jumping onto a computer with a mouse or tablet and pen, try thinking in terms of pencils and paper. Of course, while you don't need them if you're drawing directly with your computer, but all the techniques are still valid.

Prepare your paper, pencils, and erasers.

Even people steeped in drawing computer graphics should know about these. Choose what's easiest for you.

● Paper

There are many kinds of paper, even kinds that cost several dollars per sheet. There are three kinds of paper you'll need.

1. **Paper you can easily doodle all over when you're thinking up ideas.**
2. **Paper for the final product.**
3. **Finishing paper (for special cases).**

For doodling, any scratch paper will suffice. Printer paper also works well. The point here is to draw out and refine your ideas on paper. Use as many sheets as you need, but don't use up any more than you can afford to toss away.

Paper for the final product should be of a higher quality—something that takes penciling well and is easy to draw on. Normally, what you draw here you will load onto your computer. I use high-quality 110-weight paper myself. Also, although it's a bit expensive, I think Kent paper has a very smooth surface and is really easy to draw on. The requirements of the final product paper are that it be white, have a smooth surface, and not degrade no matter how many times you erase on it.

Finishing paper is used only in certain cases. One example would be using a semi-transparent tracing paper to get the main lines off an overcrowded "finished product" illustration that's been altered too many times.

Point

The lead in wood and mechanical pencils alike can vary greatly, especially in size. Different makes have different feels, so the best way to choose one is to actually go to an art supply store, grab a pencil, and try it out with your own hand.

● Pencils and Erasers

Pencils (including mechanical pencils) have different types of lead in them, such as "B" or "HB." B leads are the darkest and softest, while H leads are light yet hard. It's a good idea to choose lead characteristics according to your drawing pressure.

Mechanical pencil lead can also vary in thickness. There are 0.3mm, 0.5mm, 0.7mm, and 0.9mm sizes. The most common, run-of-the-mill thickness is 0.5mm.

Erasers are used for, well, erasing things. Other than the standard stiff, rectangular erasers, there are also soft, kneaded rubber erasers. These are best when erasing to create a shaded effect. Erasers are available in many colors, but I don't recommend any of them, because the color can bleed off onto your paper.

Types of pencil lead

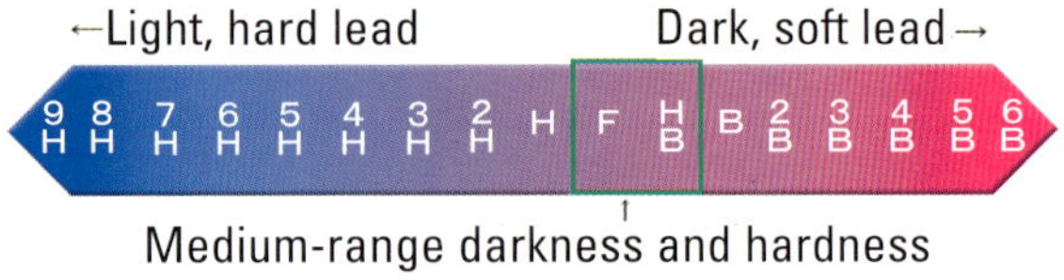

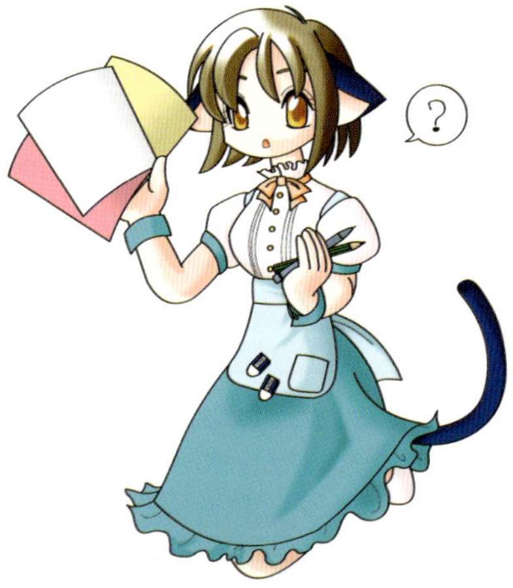

Fill your Page with Cute Imagery to Discover your Picture's Composition

What do you want to draw? Sketch rough and tumble to find out.

First of all, to figure out what kind of picture you want to draw, it would be a good idea to start with a simple theme. Use whatever comes to mind. Something simple like a cat's ears or a diner waitress is fine. Then start doodling and narrow it down from there. What kind of pose is she in? What is she doing? If your theme is based on an object (a letter, or a flower, something like that), framing your piece principally around that object, as if to emphasize it, will make it easy to grasp your theme. If you notice something in a magazine, an advertisement, or on TV that gives you an idea, jot down a quick memo about it for easy reference later on.

Point
When they're working or otherwise busy, some people carry around an "Ideas" memo pad keep quick notes on the things that happen come to them. Then, when they have time, they doodle a picture or two around those ideas. This is one pattern people use to keep up with their work.

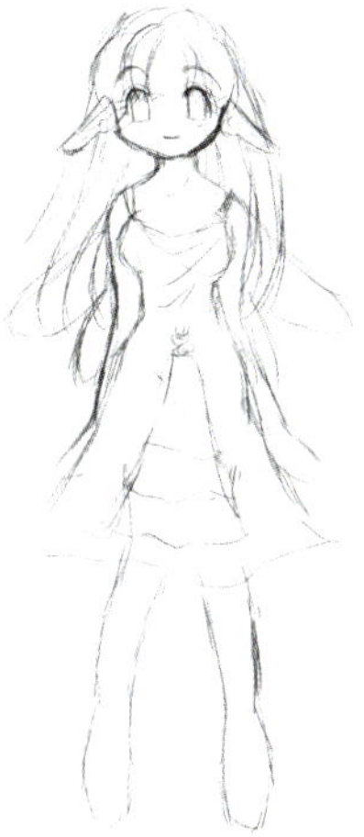

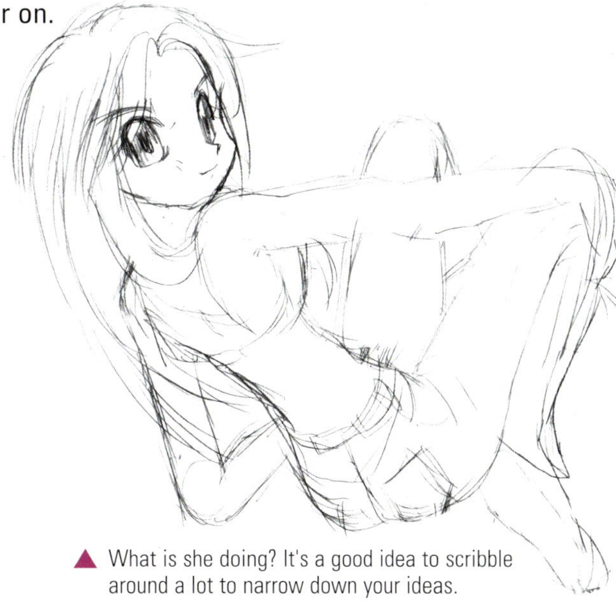

▲ What is she doing? It's a good idea to scribble around a lot to narrow down your ideas.

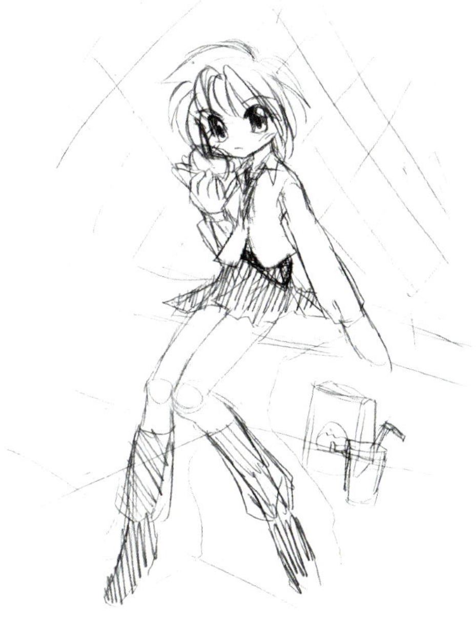

Hints on creating an image

- Watch TV, read magazines, and go people-watching outside.
- Decide on a theme for your characters. Are they students? Are they in uniforms? Plainclothes? Are they working? Etc.
- Think about location and the situation. Are we in school? Downtown? My room? A store? The countryside? Etc.
- How are your characters feeling? Are they happy? Nervous? Sad?
- Gals look cuter and more feminine when they act naturally. How are her head, hands, legs and body positioned?

A Sphere Can Give Depth to that Cute Face

Using crossed lines to visualize the balance of her expression, draw in the details.

It would be fair to say that half of drawing cute characters is getting the face right. Further, conveying a character's age or expression can to a certain degree be done using simplified lines.

Start by drawing a circle approximately as large as the face will be. Decide on a size appropriate to the age and stature of your character. A bustier character, for example, gets a larger size. You can also use placement of the facial features differentiate age and even personality.

Next, draw a cross inside the circle to indicate the center of the eyes and for facial balance. By drawing a rounded (rather than flat) cross, you can give depth to a girl's face, making her seem real.

Basic eye placement

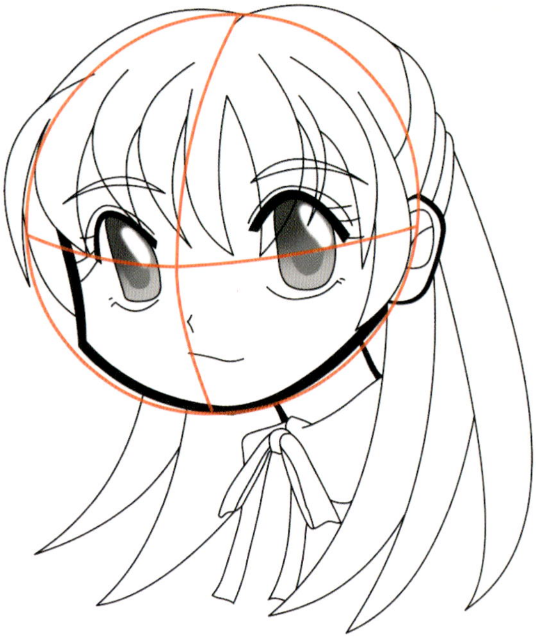

Change her age by changing her eye placement.

Lowering the eye placement makes her look younger.

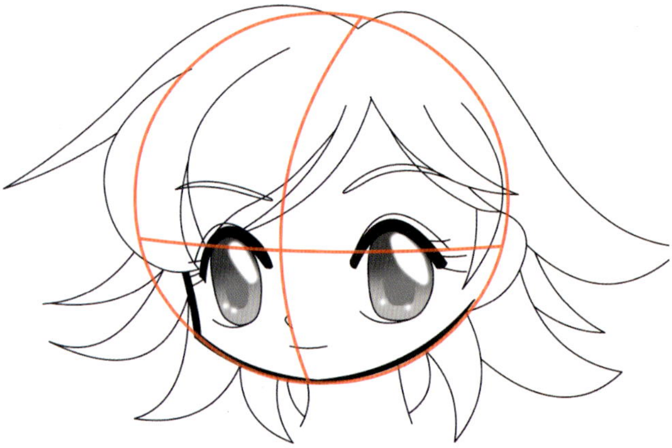

▲ Be sure to figure out the age and personality of the girl you want to draw ahead of time. Then, draw the facial outline rounder, narrower, or wider accordingly.

Raising the eye placement makes her look more adult.

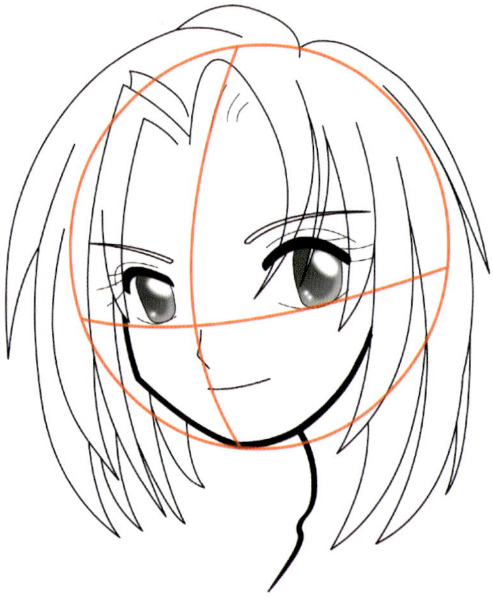

Point

The lead in wood and mechanical pencils alike can vary greatly, especially in size. Different makes have different feels, so the best way to choose one is to actually go to an art supply store, grab a pencil, and try it out with your own hand.

Adding Expression with Plain, Simple Lines

If you think of expressions as having a formula, you can draw them easier than you think.

It is possible to convey an expression using just a few lines. Here, I've tried to show you some formulae for "Happy," "Angry," and, "Sad" expressions. When you're seriously drawing, if you try imitating these, you'll find you can easily convey expression, and hence emotion. It might be a good idea to test these out by doodling several examples and creating a "stock" set of expressions. Going a little overboard with your facial expressions will actually make your characters more easily understood.

Point
Angry people have raised eyebrows and narrowed eyes. Sad people have slightly lower eyebrows and tears. Experiment with these and other expressions using simple lines.

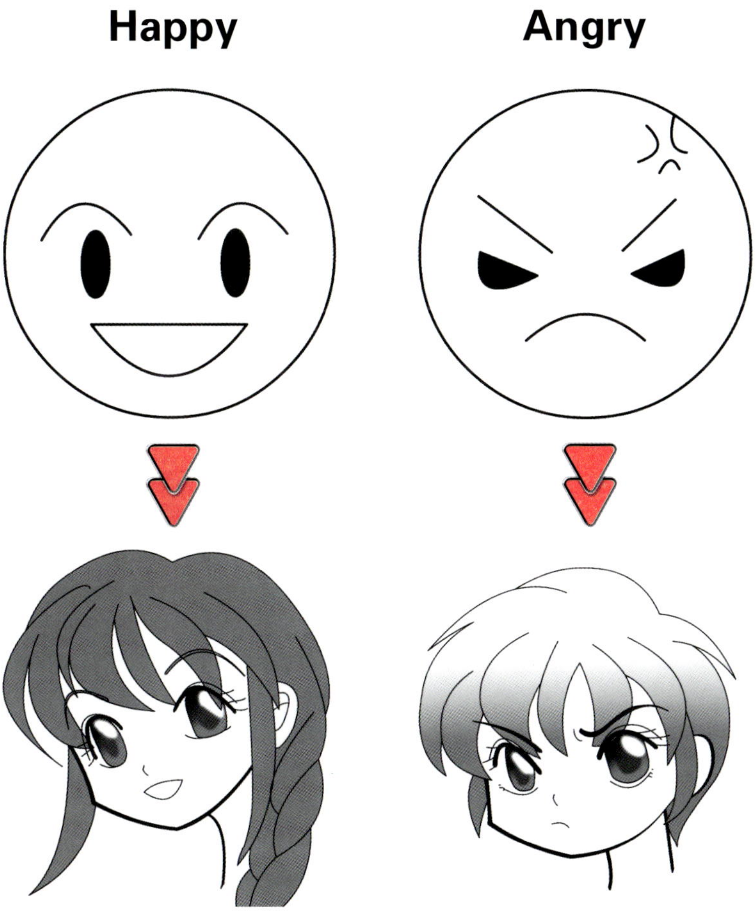

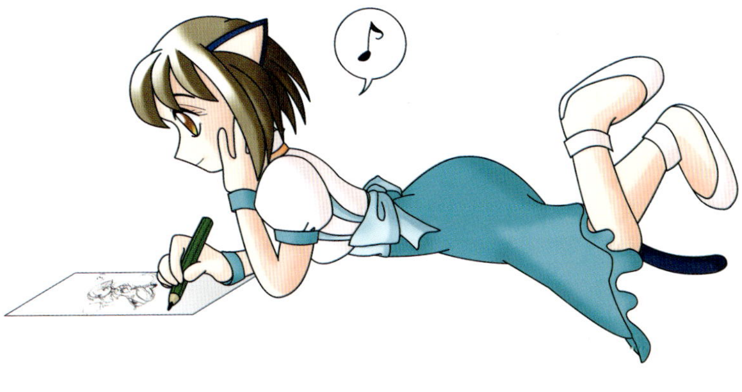

Consider Facial Direction in Three Dimensions

Use the rough sketch's layout to draw faces at an angle.

Here as well, the layout of the rough sketch is done with crosses and circles. Use them to draw faces at an angle according to where they're looking. If a face is looking straight on, leaving the cross centered in the circle is fine. But, if you want to draw a face at an angle, bend the crossed lines in the direction you want her to look, and shift the point the intersection to match her gaze.

The curved cross lines should follow the curves of the closer circle edges as much as possible. Depending on the direction of that cross (and hence the whole face), the eyes, nose, and mouth change direction, too. This all lets you express a three dimensional face.

In order, determine the position of the chin, the size of the eyes, and finally the length of the nose according to the circular and crossed guide lines. Then draw them in accordingly, and you'll make good progress.

Point

Other than the method of bending the cross lines discussed here, you could also draw the cross lines straight and then shift the rest of the lines around it in whatever direction you want. Choose the method that works best. Personally, I draw side profiles and faces at a steep angle starting from an oval going from the top of the head to the chin. Then I place the rest of the lines with the depth of the head in mind—a mixture of the two methods. Try to figure out for yourself which methods of laying out the face are easiest for you.

Diagonally left

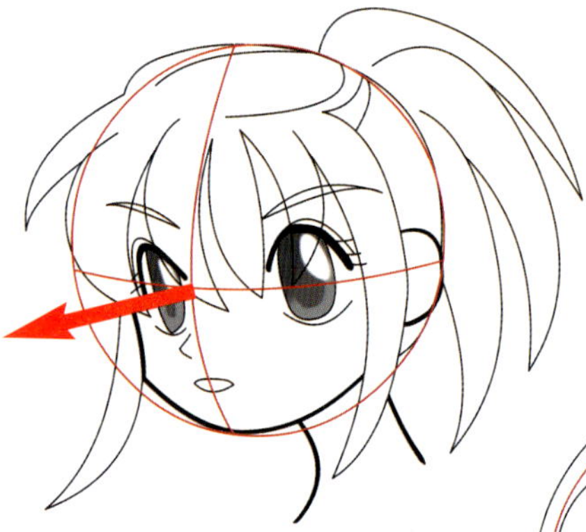

Diagonally right and up

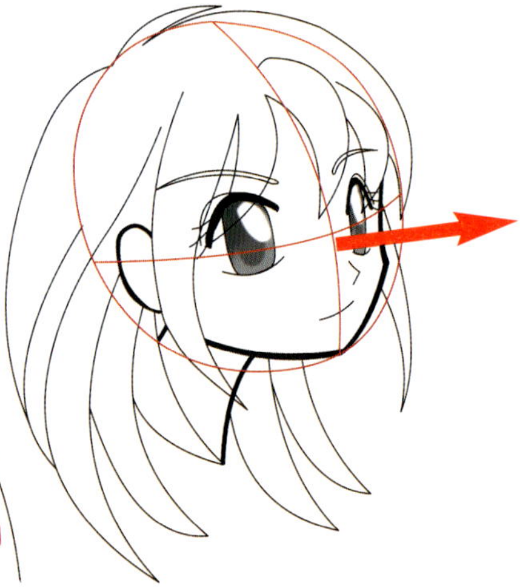

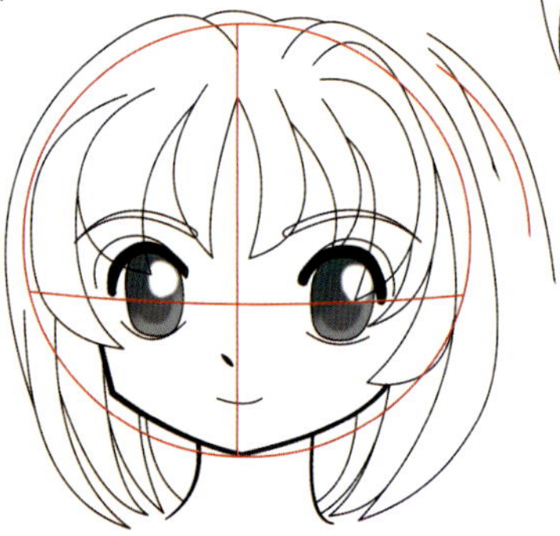

Basic Position — Forward

Forward and down

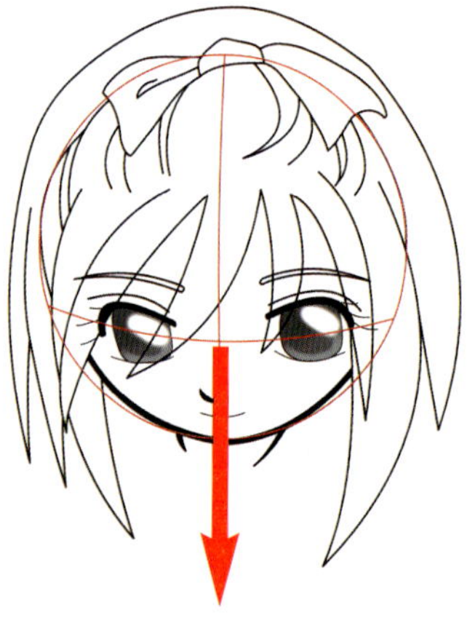

▲ Use the circle and cross to find the direction of your face, and then draw in the facial outline and features.

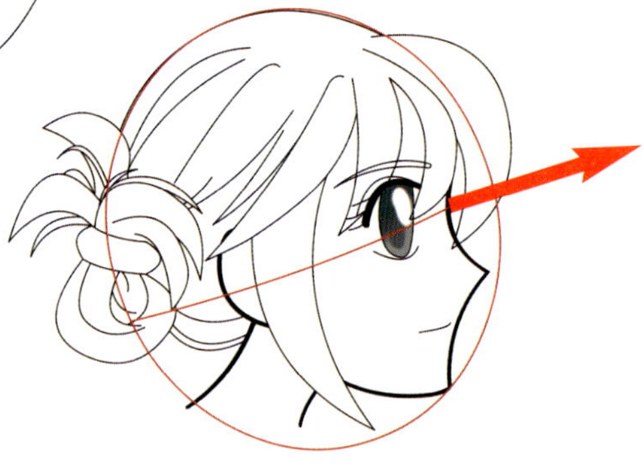

Right and up

Separating and Drawing Feminine Hairstyles into Three Zones

Realize how hair is styled in the real world to unlock this secret.

Hair is another unpredictably difficult area. I don't think we really need to get into often repeated "Her hair is ridiculous!" comment one frequently hears about anime, but in truth, I believe drawing hair that way is necessary for portraying a cute girl. Here, I'll introduce a way to draw hair by breaking it up into parts.

The Hair Zones

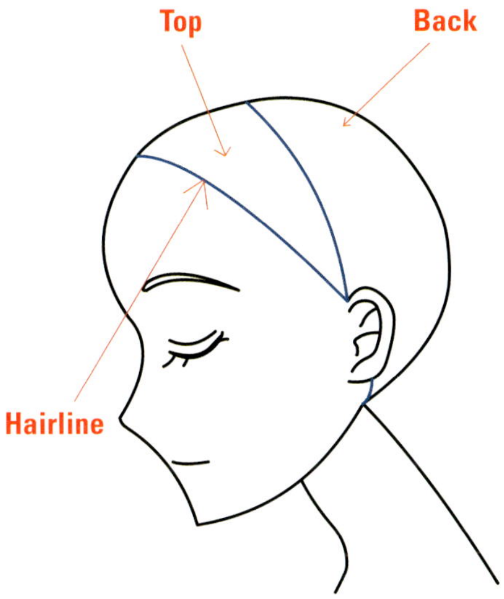

▲ Divide the scalp into three zones: Top, Back, and Hairline. Even if these boundaries aren't strictly followed, as long as the hair is divided up in this fashion, I think it should be OK. Keeping these guidelines in mind, draw in the bangs and drop some hair down the back.

Long Hair Example

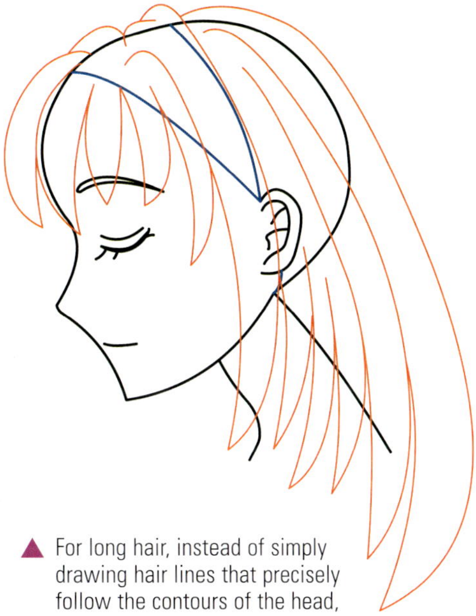

▲ For long hair, instead of simply drawing hair lines that precisely follow the contours of the head, I think lines with a bit of a light, elegant feel to them are cute.

Short Hair Example

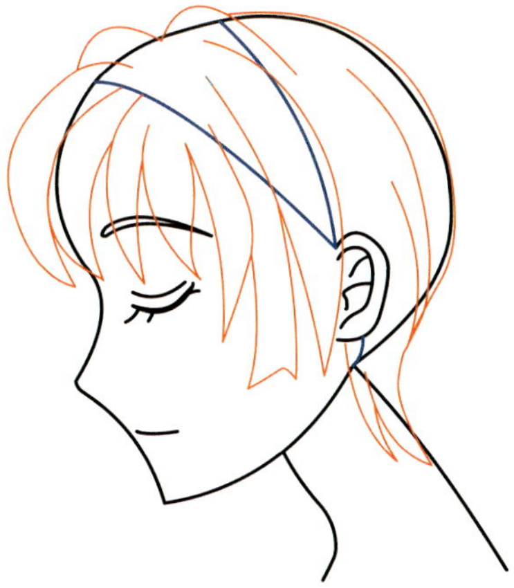

▲ Shorter cuts are done best with lines mostly following the head contours in the back.

Tied Hair Example

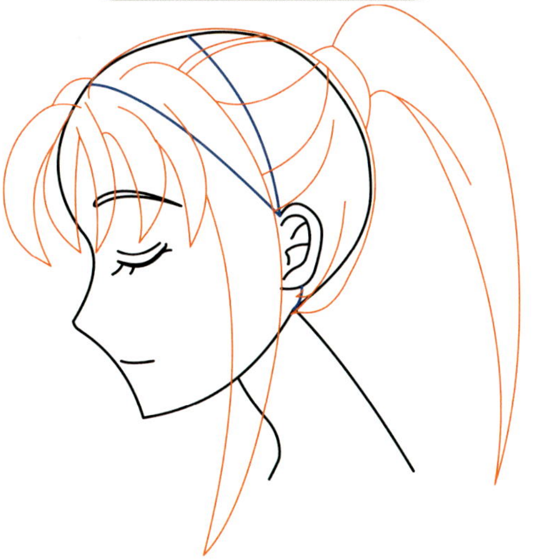

▲ Tied hair cases also have parts that are best drawn along the head contour lines. Please refer to the picture above. At times like this, drawing a few hair lines trailing back to where the hair is tied makes it easy to illustrate tied hair. Keep in mind that the head is basically a sphere and add some more curvy hair.

Body Balance for CG Characters

Drawing a human figure without looking at anything is especially difficult. Instead, use a sample figure for reference.

Pictured here is a sketch I drew by eye, using a dress-up doll sold by a company called Volks, Inc. as a model. If you're wondering why this is here, it's because I find it to be quite useful in approximating full body diagrams. I also love using this doll as a reference for various poses. Now I'll show you how I draw pictures with it.

Thoughts on Body Balance

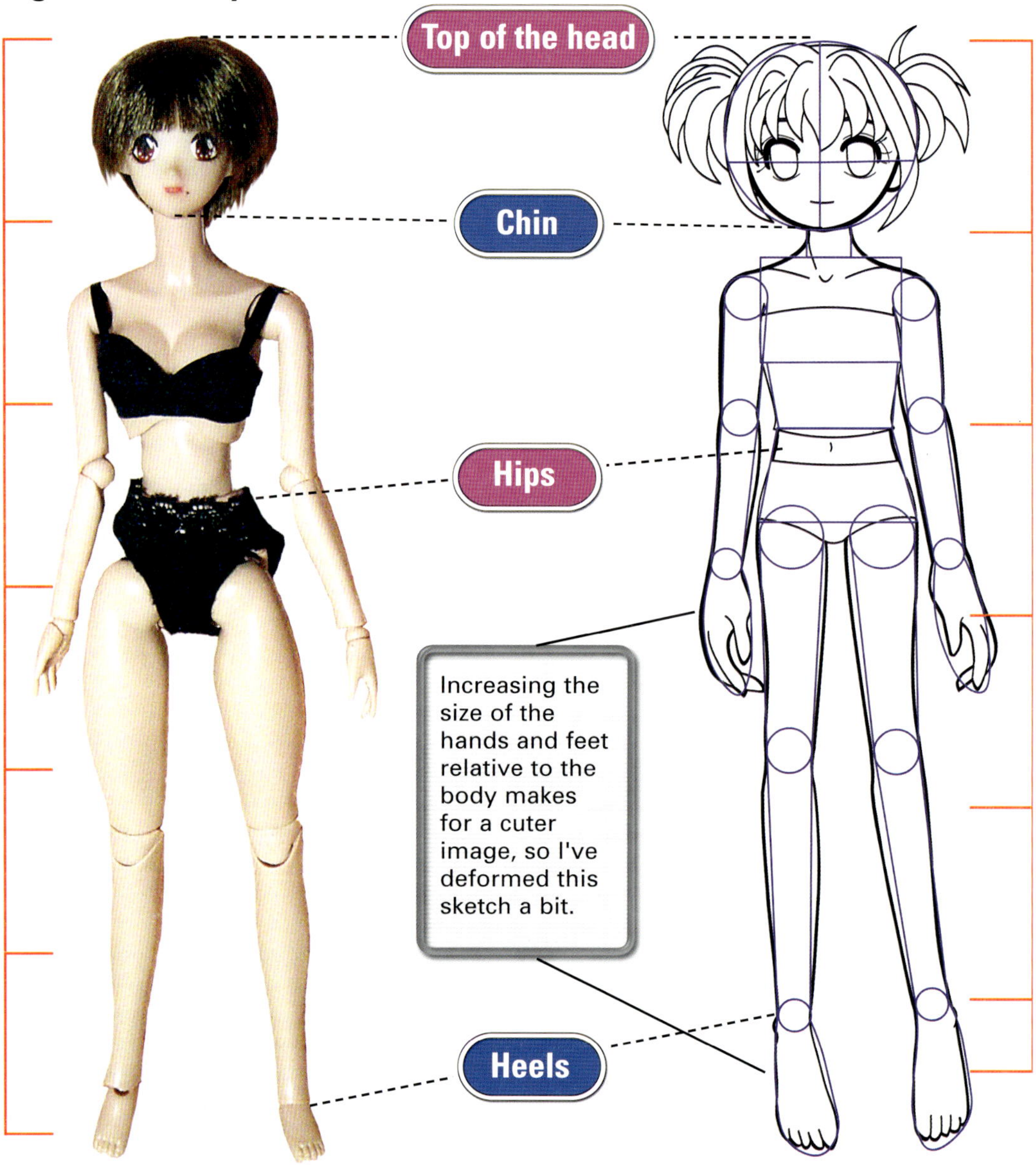

Point

I've approximated all the joints as spheres here. She looks like a robot right now, but don't worry about that—just keep drawing. In this case, I wanted to draw a slightly younger girl, so I drew her head at a slightly higher ratio to her body—the more adult the character, the slightly smaller its head. If you reproduce the doll at a 1:1 ratio, you will end up with a realistic character. Change the balance according to the character image in your mind.

A Character with a Color Scheme to Match her Image Stands Out

Choose a cute-looking color scheme

Keep uniformity in color for an overall cute, neat appearance. In addition, by making a point of using eye-catching colors in certain places, we get an impression of solidity. At this point, we will take a look at some examples of easy-to-make coloring mistakes and explain the best ways to correct them.

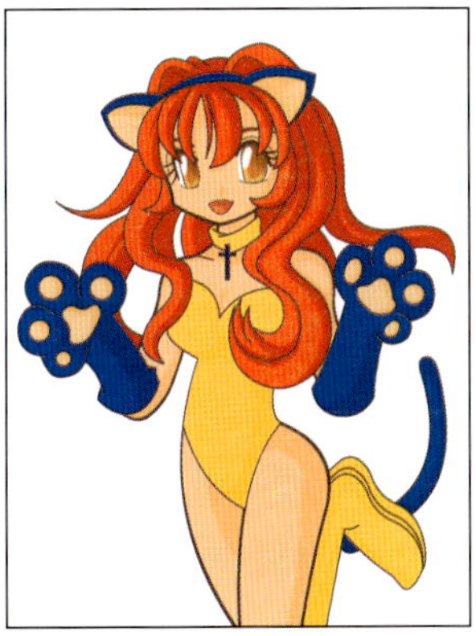

Dark Color Scheme

Problem:

The use of three primary colors (red, blue, and yellow) in such proximity to each other results in a finish that makes the eye jump all over the piece, never resting anywhere.

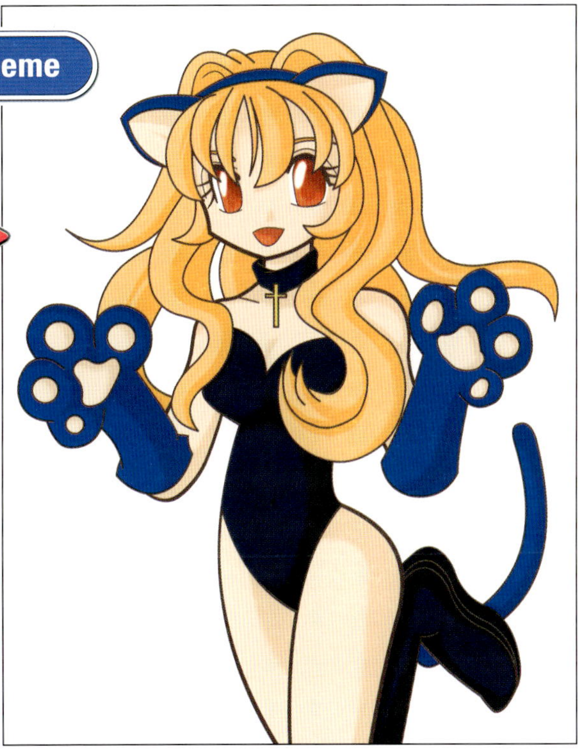

Solution:

I've lightened the color on a wide area of the hair a bit. I also changed the color of the clothing to match the gloves and ears, and tried to catch the viewer's eye by coloring the eyes reddish. Anytime you're applying lots of bright colors, just lowering one of them to a darker shade and using it in one place makes the whole image seem solid.

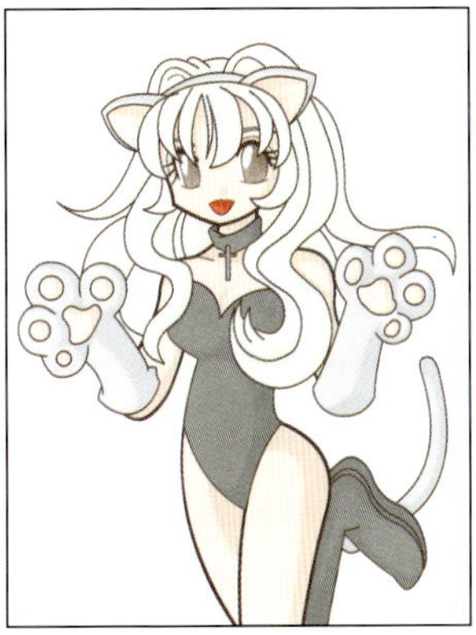

Light Color Scheme

Problem:

Coloring solely with light, dull colors results in a monotonous finish that doesn't say anything. This color scheme leaves a terribly weak impression.

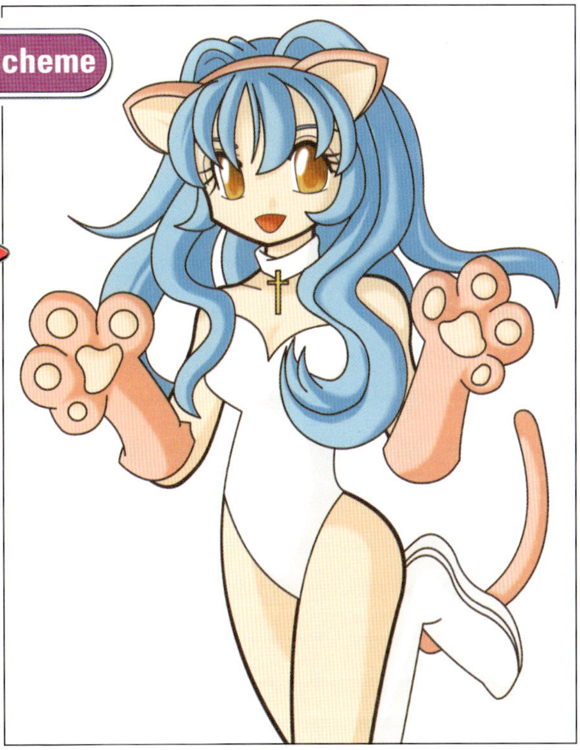

Solution:

On a whim, I made the leotard white. Then I used one of those dull colors from the original for shading. As much as possible, reserving dull colors for use only in narrow places is effectual and pleasing to the eye. Also, since dull shading on the clothing will make the other colors seem lighter, balancing them out by lowering their hue a bit would be a good idea.

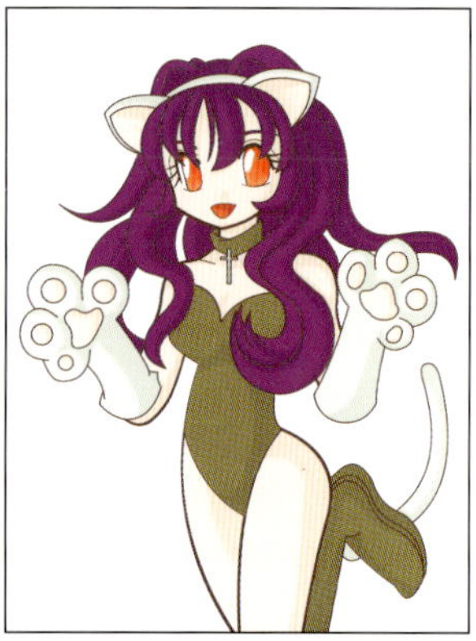

Similar Color Scheme

Problem:

The dull, skewed coloring here has poor balance and the brightness is off. Even a picture of a girl drawn cute as this one can leave a sour impression with this kind of discordant coloring.

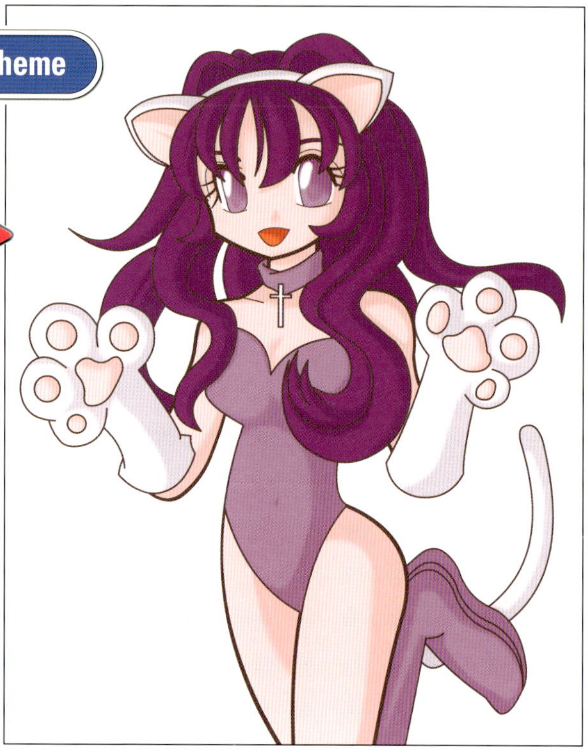

Solution:

When you want to use a color scheme with skewed brightness or dull shades, unify your colors for the best results. Here, I've tried unifying everything with purple. The hair, clothes, gloves and ears are all split into three levels of color, all with adjusted darkness. An orange-tinted skin tone should look beautiful with this scheme. Unfortunately, it didn't go well with the purple at all-it looked too dark-so I changed it to a shade of pink, and tried to make her brighter.

Point

You should think about balance when you decide the color of a character's skin, clothing, hair, etc. Colors that normally go beautifully together can look dirty, too light, or too dark when mixed with a third color, and completely alter the impression of your piece.

When you apply multiple colors, there is something between colors called "color affinity." For example, if you apply nothing but the darkest of color tones to your piece, it will be difficult to appreciate. On the other hand, apply only the lightest, dullest colors and you'll leave only a faint impression on the eye. So basically, if you mix dark and light, dull color tones, you'll end up with a tasteless piece of junk.

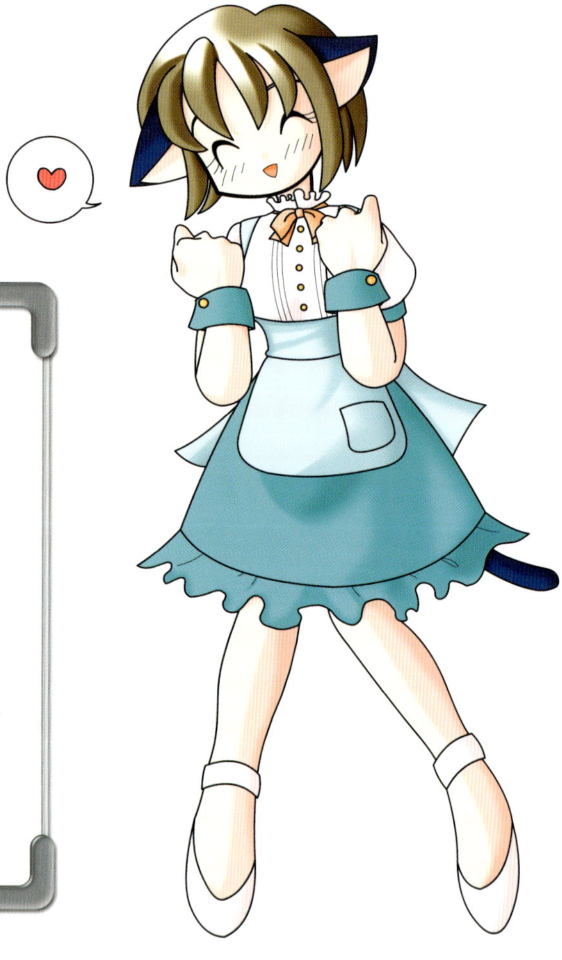

A Skin, Hair, and Eye Color Chart

With a single color scheme, you can express a variety of moods.

On the far right, I've set up "Fair," "Medium," and "Tanned" rows, and in each one I've tried to choose a hair and eye color to match them. I think you can probably come up with many other variations yourself. Try out different variations in your own work. The numbers indicate the RGB value of the brightest color used.

Fair Skin Color

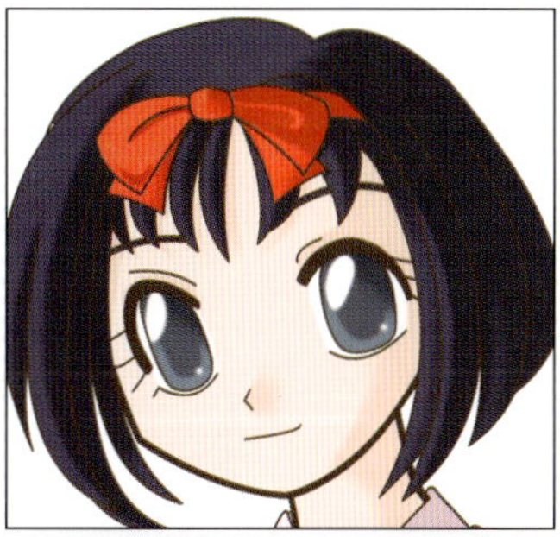

Skin (249, 221, 213)/ Hair (48, 44, 79)/ Eyes (86, 109, 142)

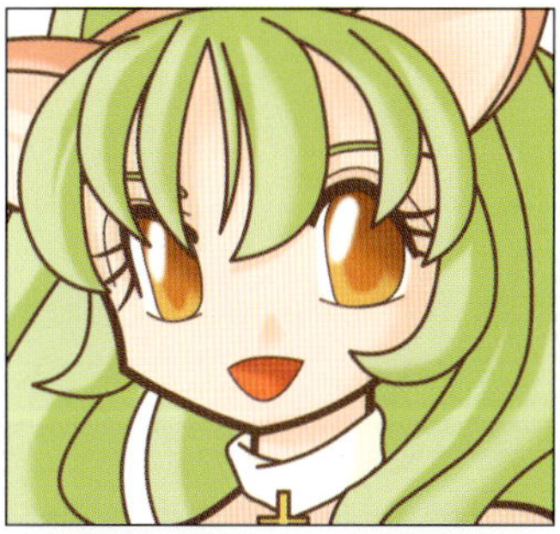

Skin (252, 224, 208)/ Hair (206, 216, 145)/ Eyes (227, 165, 33)

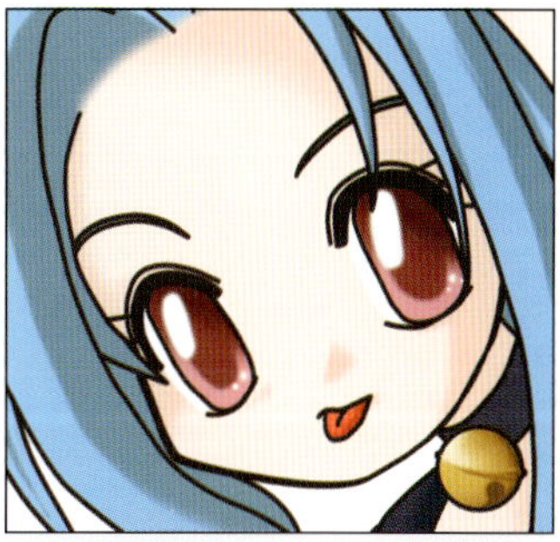

Skin (252, 230, 221)/ Hair (110, 182, 233)/ Eyes (222, 118, 141)

Medium Skin Color

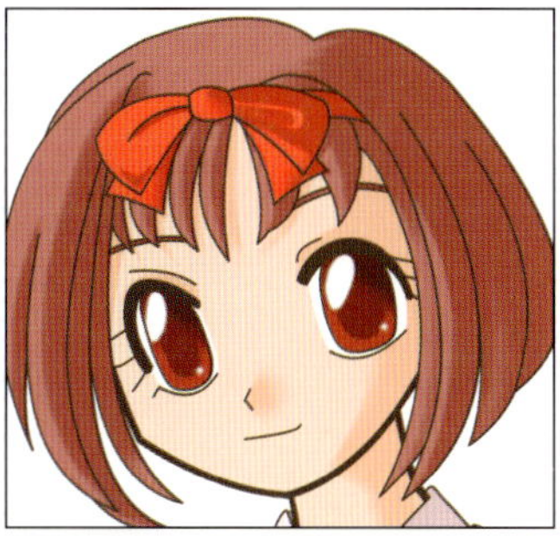

Skin (244, 208, 185)/ Hair (181, 86, 93)/ Eyes (160, 26, 20)

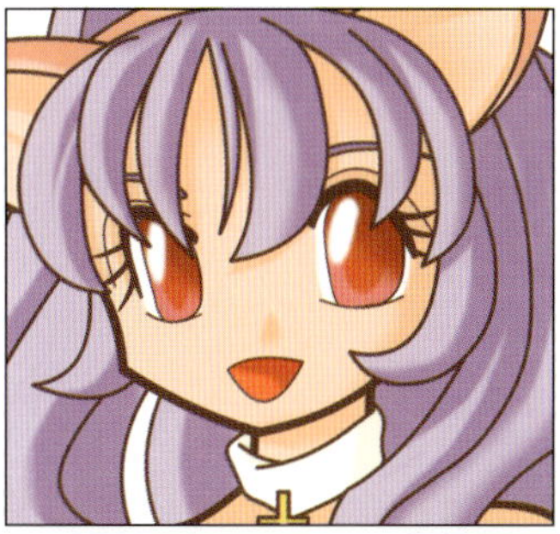

Skin (251, 207, 175)/ Hair (195, 168, 207)/ Eyes (210, 84, 96)

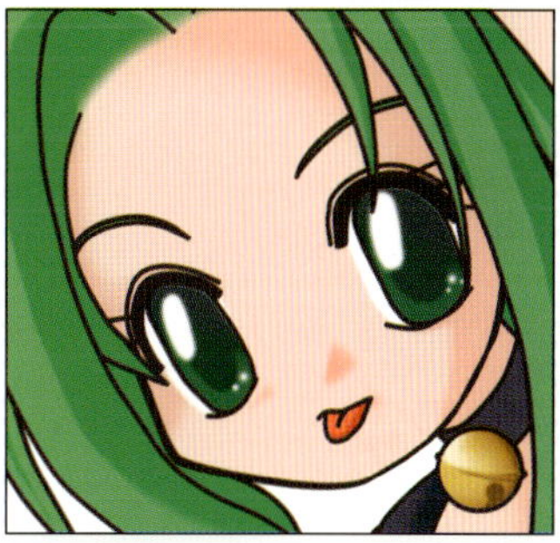

Skin (248, 201, 187)/ Hair (61, 153, 87)/ Eyes (0, 80, 46)

Tanned Skin Color

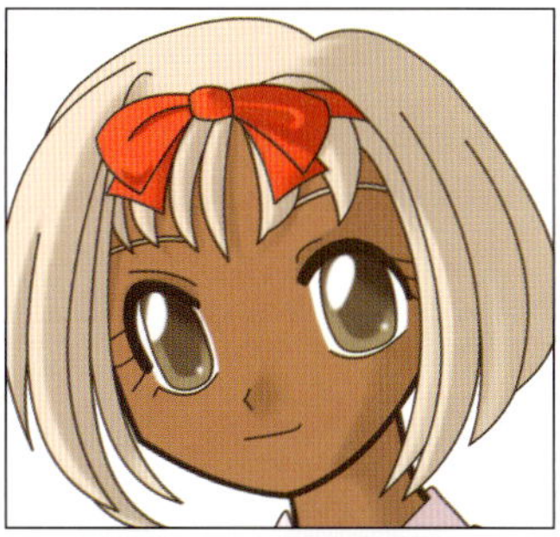

Skin (178, 105, 66)/ Hair (240, 211, 188)/ Eyes (156, 124, 90)

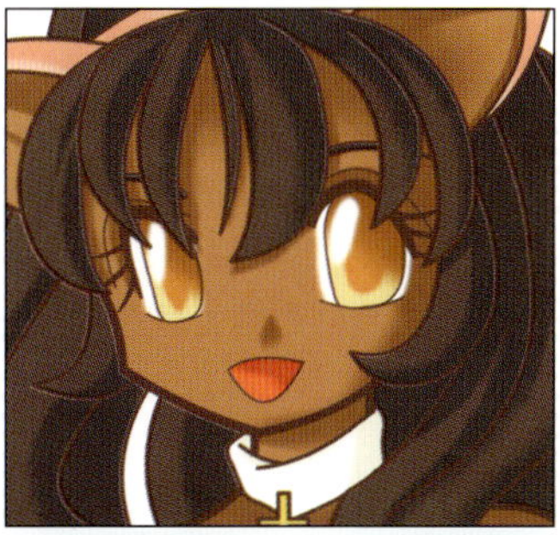

Skin (180, 105, 51)/ Hair (64, 43, 33)/ Eyes (238, 214, 120)

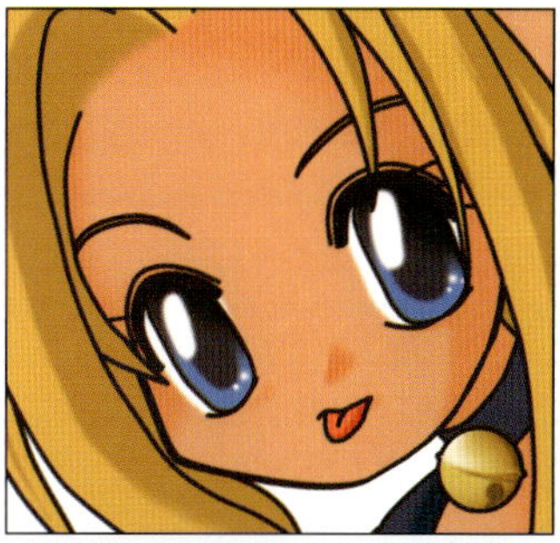

Skin (219, 124, 74)/ Hair (218, 150, 0)/ Eyes (64, 101, 182)

あとがき的座談会

Afterword:
A Round-Table Discussion

● On the Various Ways the Brush Tool is Used.

Aki Ito (hereafter "A"): Nice work, everyone. When it comes to using the Brush Tool in Flash, it seems like individuality always comes up.

Teru (hereafter "T"): The Brush is for the nose and eyes, I think. Recently I've been drawing mouths with it, too.

Gaten Boya (hereafter "G"): If we're talking manga, I do my main lines with it, too. Normally I'd just use it for facial features-eyes, nose, mouth, etc. Maybe the irises, too.

Tamotsu Nobayashi (hereafter "N"): I don't really use the Brush. I pretty much only use it when I need to edit something, like adding a dollop of paint somewhere. After I fill my outline I delete it, even if it's done in brushstrokes. By the rough sketch stage in Photoshop, I'm already drawing with the Graphic Pen filter anyway, so my outlining strategy is already taken care of.

T: I can't draw neatly with the brush, so I just draw with really fat lines, change the lines to fills, and then use the Arrow Tool to accentuate them. It's just neater than using the Brush.

G: Use the Brush on an A4 size Stage at 200-300% display ratio, and when you export your file you'll get just the right line thickness.

N: I've never exported anything to Photoshop from Flash before.

G: I'm talking about using the Brush for drawing manga. You can do it by exporting your file as a 600 dpi GIF file and importing that file to work on it in Photoshop. You could do just with the draw data, but I'd take a pass. It takes time to import that way.

T: I haven't really used the Paint Brush because it's so hard to draw with, but you use it all the time? Gaten, wow.

N: Without pressure sensitivity, the Brush is basically useless.

T: Yeah. No brush pressure = no point, right?

N: And do most people use tablets?

G: Exactly. I recommend them to everyone, but they don't catch on. I just don't get it.

N: [The Brush Tool] does make your file bigger.

Mimori Yusa (hereafter "M"): I don't get why everyone's so worked up about "accentuation."

N: I guess a lot of people would be uncomfortable without brushstrokes.

T: I wonder why. Maybe they're cutting corners with their lines.

M: Flash doesn't need brush stroking!

N: Whether they're because of its effect or force of habit, I think brushstrokes are a major factor.

G: Brushstrokes look cool. If you're good with them, that is.

T: They're really a big factor?

N: Flat lines are probably seen as cold and mechanical. I think that's a good thing, though.

G: Heh. I guess a lot of it depends on your taste, right?

● Fussing Over Lines

Sanbaisoku (hereafter "S"): I always forget to change the color of my lines when I'm done.

A: You change them to match their surrounding colors?

S: It's a method used a lot in "gal games." But in Flash you can't really change the order lines stack on each other, and setting bright lines on top of black ones looks bad.

A: Seems like a pain.

S: You could always separate your lines into Groups, but that's a pain, too.

T: Yeah, that's really difficult. That's why I just draw all my lines in the same color. I get asked about my lines a lot, because I can't draw them so well. I guess I'm not used to using Smooth.

A: You can't draw lines well in Flash? That's odd. For me, there's no tool out there that lets me draw exactly what I imagine better than Flash. Plus you can make as many changes as you like.

M: Yeah, really. On top of that, you can even move everything around after you're done drawing.

T: I think leaving the Snap to Objects button pressed is the problem.

G: I use it all the time these days. It's useful, I think. But your lines act weird if they get close to each other.

M: What? "Useful?" Dude, you're acting weird.

G: Oh. Really? But I've only just noticed the utility of letting it close off your lines for you.

The Artists

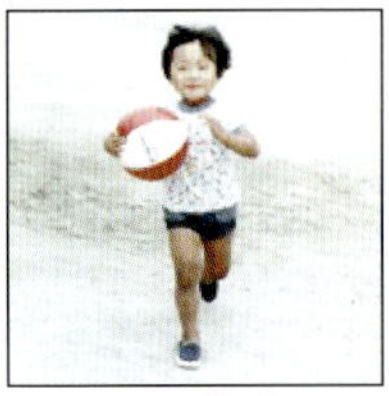

Tamotsu Nobayashi
I didn't have a really compelling reason to get into Flash. I just thought it looked interesting and started using it one day. Becoming friends with Teru probably had something to do with it, too.

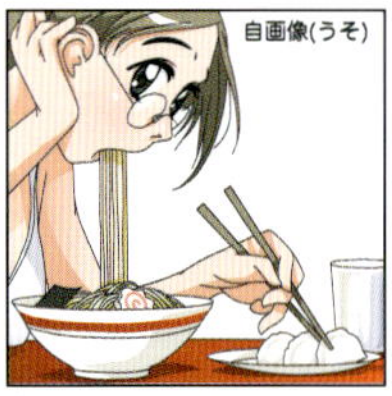

Sanbaisoku
I'm not so good at coloring. But with Flash you can paint and repaint freely, and I love the way the colors turn out so beautifully.

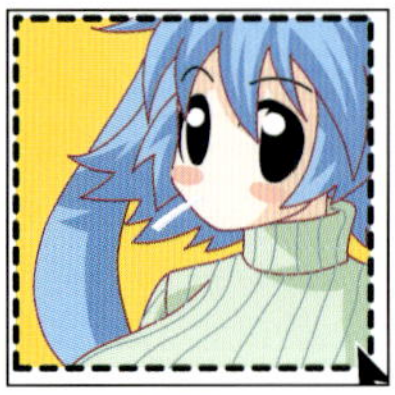

Mimori Yusa
I first met my love, Flash, by meeting Teru, I suppose. Until then I was struggling in Photoshop.

T: Snap to Objects isn't really suited to line drawing. It's better not to use it at the rough draft stage.

N: Having to readjust line thickness every time I start up Flash bugs the heck outta me.

G: I just use 'em at the default thickness.

N: I use the hairline setting.

M: I change the line thickness according to the situation.

G: Bah. Real men use 1 point lines.

N: Lines close themselves in Flash. An unclosed line might mean not being able to use fills. If you don't use a really thin line, then it's hard to see exactly where they stack up, isn't it? But, I do occasionally go back and change the line thickness afterward.

G: That's why I use Snap to Objects.

T: I only use it to finish off a line drawing.

N: I've never used it at all!

M: Doesn't it annoy you guys when your lines aren't closed off all the way? You can go hunting and searching for gaps, but when I try to apply a fill and nothing happens, I just go AAAARGH!

G: When that happens you just got to increase the magnification.

T: When I'm working I always want to hurry up to the coloring, so I just approximate my line drawings.

S: I like to feel as if my line drawing complete when I stop working on it. Everything else is rough-and-ready work. It's amazing to me that you stop in the middle of your coloring to redraw your lines.

T: But, haven't you ever wanted to change your work after you started coloring?

S: Yes, I have, but once you start tweaking stuff you could go on forever, couldn't you?

T: Well, yeah, but that's the fun part. If it's really rough, I usually leave the face and start from there. That's why when I start drawing an angel I end up with a kogyaru.

S: Whoa. Well, actually, I do end up making a few changes as I go, too.

● Drawing must be fun!

A: I use the Frankenstein method, because it takes forever for me to finish off a drawing.

S: Franken...what?

A: Drawing the body in separate parts and then putting them together.

S: Ah! I do that in Flash quite a bit as well.

T: I draw on a PC the same way I draw on paper.

S: It's been my experience that using the Rotate and Scale functions in programs like Photoshop takes an inordinate amount of time.

A: I agree. That's one of the great things about Flash. With my Frankensketches, I first fade them out, print them, and then take a pen and redraw them in place. Then I take that and load it as my rough sketch, repeating the process each time I draw something. That's how I compose my designs.

T: Wow. Seems tough.

S: That's what it's like for me when I use the Brush to draw rough sketches, especially if it doesn't turn out right. Sometimes, before I know it, I've got 20 layers stacked up, and the top one might not look anything at all like the bottom one.

A: Line drawings aren't that big of a deal. You can use your own judgment: this looks good, this looks bad. You only have to persevere until you're happy with the results. That's the best way to go about things. Coloring is a whole other ballgame, though.

S: Studying anime magazines is a great way to learn about cell animation coloring. How to highlight skin and hair, for example.

A: Ah, of course. I'd probably get faster if I drew more. Probably get better at coloring, too, right? But I don't enjoy it while I'm drawing it.

S: I think it's more fun to just start drawing randomly, and from those scratches and doodles, refine what you want to draw. It's almost like you're unearthing an image buried the screen. That's pretty much the way I draw for a bulletin board. But at first, I usually start by drawing a face without deciding anything about what I want to draw. Then, I really challenge myself by trying to come up with a pose and a matching outfit. If I can't quite get it right, then I just change the pose and costume. I have a lot of fun that way.

A: You may be on to something there.

S: You should definitely give it a try.

● It's Too Early to Say Goodbye...

A: Our little chat here isn't over yet, but...sorry! We're out of room on the page. To all our readers out there, this is goodbye! See ya 'round!

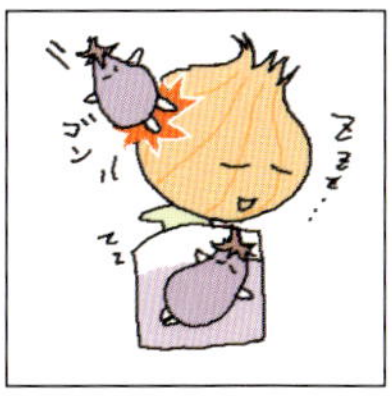

Teru

I first started with Flash 2. I had a low grade PC back then, and I was trudging along, searching for a lighter application that could still draw attractively.

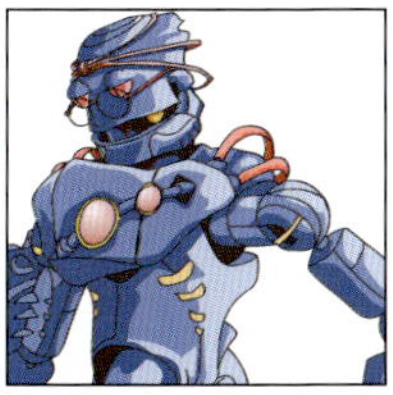

Gaten Boya

I used to use Flash's predecessor, SmartSketch. It was a drawing application, so file sizes were small, and it was really easy to work with. Those two qualities got me hooked in the first place.

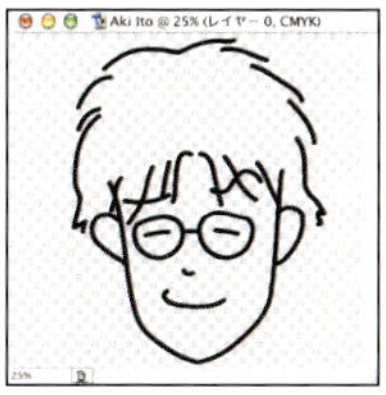

Aki Ito

Though it may take me some time, I can create what I wish by drawing in Flash. Watching you guys in action has taught me a lot of technique, too.

Afterword

After a three year hiatus, "This series" is back.

And this time around, it's all about Flash.

I have spent triple the time I usually do slicing-and-dicing our contributor's manuscripts for this volume. My goal has been to put together an easy-to-understand book that even CG novices can sink their teeth into.

Seemingly unaware they are even using them, I have extracted from our contributing artists' manuscripts the vital essences of graphic design, and added to them myself. I have also worked over the design and layout of this book in all its detail.

Whether you are just starting out in computer graphics, someone who always thought Flash could be used to draw quality art, or simply frustrated with other graphic applications, I am proud to present to you the world's premier Flash art manual.

Aki Ito

Editor: Aki Ito

http://www.quickcaman.com/banacolle/

Design & Layout
Toyonori Motoyoshi

Special Thanks to:
Masahiko Satake
(Graphic-sha Publishing Co., Ltd.)

Special Hangout:
Jonathan's (in Sakuragicho)

Special Drink:
Hoppy (from Hoppy Beverages)

Special Medication:
Estaronmoka 12

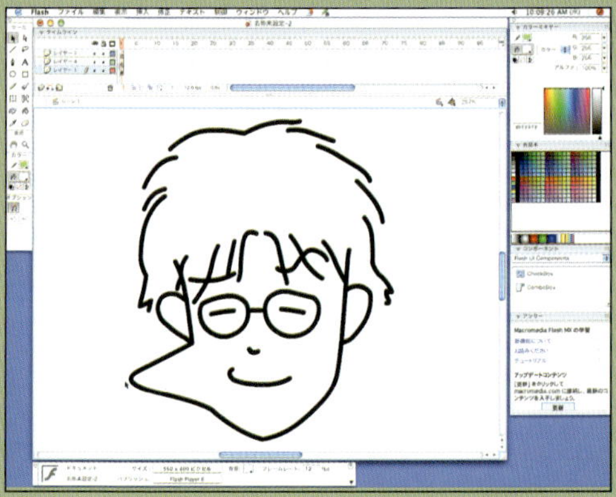